Dangerous Deterrent

Studies in Asian Security

A SERIES SPONSORED BY THE EAST–WEST CENTER

Muthiah Alagappa, Chief Editor
Director, East-West Center Washington

The aim of the Asian Security series is to promote analysis, understanding, and explanation of the dynamics of domestic, transnational, and international security challenges in Asia. Books in the series will analyze contemporary security issues and problems to clarify debates in the scholarly and policy communities, provide new insights and perspectives, and identify new research and policy directions related to conflict management and security in Asia. Security is defined broadly to include the traditional political and military dimensions as well as the nontraditional dimensions that affect the survival and well-being of political communities. Asia, too, is defined broadly, to include Northeast, Southeast, South, and Central Asia.

Designed to encourage original and rigorous scholarship, books in the Asian Security series seek to engage scholars, educators, and practitioners. Wide-ranging in scope and method, the series welcomes an extensive array of paradigms, programs, traditions, and methodologies now employed in the social sciences.

★　　★　　★

The East-West Center is an education and research organization established by the U.S. Congress in 1960 to strengthen relations and understanding among the peoples and nations of Asia, the Pacific, and the United States. The Center contributes to a peaceful, prosperous, and just Asia Pacific community by serving as a vigorous hub for cooperative research, education, and dialogue on critical issues of common concern to the Asia Pacific region and the United States. Funding for the Center comes from the U.S. government, with additional support provided by private agencies, individuals, foundations, and corporations and the governments of the region.

Dangerous Deterrent

NUCLEAR WEAPONS PROLIFERATION AND CONFLICT IN SOUTH ASIA

S. Paul Kapur

SPONSORED BY THE EAST–WEST CENTER

Stanford University Press • Stanford, California 2007

Published with the partial support of the
Sasakawa Peace Foundation (USA)

Stanford University Press
Stanford, California

Printed in the United States of America on acid-free, archival-quality paper

Library of Congress Cataloging-in-Publication Data
Kapur, S. Paul.
  Dangerous deterrent: nuclear weapons proliferation and conflict in South Asia / S. Paul Kapur.
    p. cm.
  Includes bibliographical references and index.
  ISBN-13: 978-0-8047-5549-8 (cloth : alk. paper)
  ISBN-13: 978-0-8047-5550-4 (pbk : alk. paper)
    1. Arms race—South Asia. 2. South Asia.—Military policy. 3. Nuclear weapons—South
Asia. 4. Nuclear nonproliferation—South Asia. 5. Balance of power. 6. Deterrence (Strategy)
I. Title.
UA832.7.K37 2007
355.02'170954—dc22

                                                                                    2006014676

Typeset by Newgen in 10/13 Bembo

For My Parents
Inder Lal Kapur and Mary Breton Kapur

Acknowledgments

I could not have written this book without the generous support of numerous individuals and institutions.

Muthiah Alagappa originally encouraged me to undertake the project and was a crucial source of assistance throughout the process.

The project benefited from advice, comments, and criticism at various stages from a number of individuals, including Samina Ahmed, Y. M. Bammi, Dara Cohen, J. N. Dixit, Alexander Downes, Lynn Eden, C. Christine Fair, James Fearon, Andrea Gabbitas, Šumit Ganguly, Charles Glaser, Ejaz Haider, David Holloway, David Kang, Cari Costanzo Kapur, Kirun Kapur, John Mearsheimer, T. V. Paul, Scott Sagan, K. Santhanam, Karthika Sasikumar, Kenneth Schultz, Jacob Shapiro, Devinder Singh, Jessica Stanton, Dean Wilkening, Matin Zuberi, and participants in seminars at the United Service Institution, New Delhi; Institute for Defence Studies and Analysis, New Delhi; Center for International Security and Cooperation, Stanford University; Program on International Security Policy, University of Chicago; and the Irving B. Harris School of Public Policy Studies, University of Chicago. Any shortcomings, of course, are wholly my responsibility.

Many former and current officials in India and Pakistan, some of whom I have named in the manuscript and some of whom remain anonymous, afforded me important insights into the issues discussed in this book. I thank them for their willingness to speak with me.

The East-West Center Washington provided me with an initial grant to begin research on the book. I received additional financial assistance from the

Keck Center for Strategic and International Studies. Claremont McKenna College also afforded me generous financial support and allowed me time off from classroom and other responsibilities to work on the manuscript. I completed most of the book while I was a visiting scholar at Stanford University's Center for International Security and Cooperation (CISAC). CISAC's combination of expertise on nuclear weapons and proliferation, interest in South Asia, rigorous intellectual standards, and genuine collegiality made it an ideal home for me. I owe the Center and its director, Scott Sagan, a deep debt of gratitude.

The United Service Institution in New Delhi was an especially helpful ally during my visits to South Asia.

Two sets of able research assistants greatly facilitated my work: Joslyn Barnhardt and Richard Helke at Claremont, and Madhavi Devasher and Raghav Thapar at Stanford. I thank them for all of their efforts.

Part of Chapter 6 appeared in slightly different form as an article in the autumn 2003 issue of *Security Studies*. A portion of Chapter 5 appeared in the April 2005 issue of *Asian Security*. And parts of Chapters 3, 6, and 7 appeared in an article in the fall 2005 issue of *International Security*. I thank the three journals, as well as the MIT Press and Taylor and Francis, for permission to utilize those materials here.

My greatest debts are to my family. Cari kept our world on track while serving as a tireless sounding board and editor and finishing her own dissertation project. Eleni reminded me every day of what was truly important. Kirun provided sage editorial and strategic advice. B. C. was a source of camaraderie and refreshment. And Nani supplied comic relief. Inder L. Kapur and Mary B. Kapur were deeply involved in the book from the beginning, serving alternately as teachers, advisors, cheerleaders, agents, logisticians, and benign critics. As with my other undertakings, their support for this project made all the difference. I dedicate the book to them.

Contents

Dangerous Deterrent

1

The Problem of Proliferation

In the hard-fought and often divisive United States presidential campaign of 2004, rivals George W. Bush and John F. Kerry found precious little common ground, particularly in the arena of foreign policy. However, in the midst of a televised debate, the two candidates nonetheless discovered a point upon which they agreed; both men argued forcefully that the global proliferation of nuclear weapons currently poses the gravest of all threats to U.S. security.[1] Bush and Kerry were not alone in their views regarding proliferation's dangers. They echoed a chorus of other leading voices in the world community, which have characterized the spread of nuclear weapons as one of the foremost global security challenges of our time. As International Atomic Energy Agency Director General Mohamed ElBaradei put it, "If the world does not change course" to prevent continued nuclear weapons proliferation, "we risk self-destruction."[2]

Despite such widespread concern, our understanding of nuclear proliferation's impact on the international security environment is limited. Predictions regarding nuclear proliferation's effects are based largely upon analyses of American and Soviet behavior during the Cold War, which may not apply to future nuclear rivalries elsewhere in the world. The spread of nuclear weapons to South Asia, where India and Pakistan tested nuclear weapons in 1998, therefore offers us an important opportunity for study. The Indo-Pakistani security competition has been bitter and enduring, with the two sides fighting four wars since independence in 1947 and waging a low-intensity conflict in the disputed territory of Kashmir since the late 1980s. The introduction of nuclear weapons into this antagonistic relationship enables us to investigate a number of important questions in a political and historical context different from that of the Cold War: Does nuclear proliferation cause ongoing security competitions to diminish or to intensify? Why does proliferation have these effects? And do these findings support or contradict the theories of nuclear deterrence that we derived from the U.S.-Soviet rivalry?

This book addresses these issues. Its findings are sobering, both as we assess the South Asian security environment and as we contemplate the possibility of future cases of nuclear proliferation. The study finds that nuclear weapons have significantly destabilized the subcontinent, due primarily to India's and Pakistan's territorial preferences and relative military capabilities. Specifically, proliferation has created strong incentives for conventional aggression by Pakistan because Pakistan is conventionally weak relative to India and is dissatisfied with the territorial status quo in Kashmir, the key issue of Indo-Pakistani contention. Aggressive Pakistani behavior has in turn triggered forceful Indian responses, which have further destabilized the subcontinent. Thus, this study finds that nuclear weapons have not only failed to prevent subnuclear conflict in South Asia, but they have actually made such conflict more likely.

Nuclear Proliferation: Background

Although nuclear weapons proliferation is a major subject of current international concern, the problem is by no means novel. Almost as soon as the United States acquired a nuclear capability, the U.S. government began to fear that its primary rival in the emerging Cold War would develop the weapons as well. The U.S. nuclear monopoly was the key to its military and diplomatic policy in the late 1940s. Militarily, atomic weapons enabled the United States to deter the Soviet Union from launching a conventional military attack on Western Europe. Diplomatically, the weapons gave the United States the confidence to pursue an assertive foreign policy without fear of a diplomatic crisis escalating to an armed confrontation with the Soviets.[3] Although U.S. officials knew for some time before its 1949 atomic test that the Soviet Union would soon possess the bomb, the Soviets' eventual acquisition of a nuclear capability was jarring and called into question the fundamental assumptions underpinning American foreign policy. Dean Rusk believed that, "U.S. strategic plans now had to be reexamined. Indeed, the nation's entire foreign policy posture required a reappraisal."[4]

The Soviets' acquisition of nuclear weapons did reduce American military and diplomatic leverage over the Soviet Union, but it did not ultimately result in a Soviet invasion of Western Europe or in the escalation of U.S.-Soviet diplomatic crises to the level of military confrontation. Nor did the subsequent nuclearization of Great Britain, France, and China during the 1950s and 1960s end in military or diplomatic disaster. Nonetheless, the United States and the other nuclear states were deeply concerned regarding the dangers of proliferation beyond their small group. They therefore sought to create an international nonproliferation regime to prevent any further spread of nuclear weapons. The bedrock of this regime was the 1968 Treaty on the Non-Proliferation of Nuclear Weapons (NPT). Predicated on the belief that "the proliferation of nuclear weapons would seriously enhance the danger of nuclear war," the treaty required nonnuclear states not to receive, manufacture, or seek assistance in the manufacture of nuclear weapons or nuclear explosive devices.[5]

Over the coming decades, some countries that had seriously considered pursuing a nuclear capability ultimately decided not to do so.[6] Other states that had actually succeeded in acquiring nuclear weapons capacities subsequently decided to dismantle them and accede to the nonproliferation regime.[7] By 2000, a total of 187 states had signed the Nuclear Non-Proliferation Treaty.

A handful of other states, however, had steadfastly refused to foreclose the option of acquiring nuclear weapons. India and Pakistan were among this group reserving the right to develop a nuclear capacity, and by the 1980s, they had become the subject of intense international concern.[8] The international community found the possibility of Indo-Pakistani proliferation particularly worrisome because of the two countries' violent history. Independent India and Pakistan had been born out of a bloody partition of British India in 1947, which saw the deaths of between 500,000 and 1 million people and the resettlement of 10 to 12 million.[9] Since then, the countries had fought three wars, two of them over the disputed territory of Kashmir. Although the Kashmir issue had appeared to subside during the 1970s and the early 1980s, by 1989 it was once again a major source of tension, with a Pakistan-backed insurgency wracking Indian Kashmir, and India flooding the territory with hundreds of thousands of security forces in an attempt to crush the uprising. Thus, many feared that if India and Pakistan in fact acquired a nuclear weapons capability, the likelihood of a nuclear conflict in South Asia would be considerable. CIA Director James Woolsey, for example, argued in 1993 that "mutual Indian and Pakistani suspicions have fueled a nuclear arms race, increased the risk of conflict, and gravely increased the cost of war, if it should occur . . . The arms race between India and Pakistan poses perhaps the most probable prospect for future use of weapons of mass destruction, including nuclear weapons."[10]

India's and Pakistan's nuclear programs dated back to their first decade of independence. Although the Indian government had established a Department of Atomic Research in 1954, Prime Minister Jawaharlal Nehru had publicly opposed the development of nuclear weapons. However, in the wake of their devastating loss in the 1962 Sino-Indian War and of China's 1964 nuclear test, the Indians began to reconsider their position. After Chinese threats to open a second front during the 1965 Indo-Pakistani War, unsuccessful attempts to secure a nuclear guarantee from the existing nuclear powers, and much internal debate, India abandoned its earlier antinuclear position. Choosing explicitly to keep its options open, it refused to accede to the Nuclear Non-Proliferation Treaty in 1970. Prime Minister Indira Gandhi, anxious to augment India's enhanced regional position in the wake of the Bangladesh War and to improve her domestic political fortunes, subsequently authorized India's first nuclear test, which took the form of a fifteen-kiloton "peaceful nuclear explosion" (PNE) on May 18, 1974.[11]

Pakistan's nuclear research program began in 1957 with the establishment of the Pakistan Atomic Energy Commission. Pakistan's nuclear efforts remained peacefully oriented through the mid-1960s with the country's leaders convinced that its conventional capabilities were sufficient to handle the Indian threat. This attitude began to change with Pakistan's failure to prevail in its 1965 war with India, the American decision to cut off the flow of U.S. arms to Pakistan in retaliation for that conflict, and growing evidence of India's conventional superiority. Pakistan refused to accede to the Nuclear Non-Proliferation Treaty in 1970. Then in 1972, after its crushing loss to India in the Bangladesh War, Pakistan began a full-fledged quest to develop a nuclear weapons capacity.[12]

India and Pakistan rejected the nuclear nonproliferation regime on both philosophical and strategic grounds. First, they believed that the regime created a world of inequality in which the existing nuclear powers enjoyed the political and military benefits that came with possession of the ultimate weapon, while other states had to reconcile themselves to second-class status. This double standard was particularly repugnant given India's and Pakistan's colonial history. Second, the nonproliferation regime failed to recognize the legitimate security concerns of nonnuclear states. Many nonnuclear countries were located in extremely dangerous regions and sorely needed nuclear weapons' deterrent effects to ensure their survival. Thus, in the Indian and Pakistani view, the nuclear nonproliferation regime was morally bankrupt and strategically unsound. As Indian Senior Advisor on Defense and Foreign Affairs Jaswant Singh argued,

> The first 50 years of Indian independence reveal that the country's moralistic nuclear policy and restraint paid no measurable dividends, except resentment that India was being discriminated against . . . If the permanent five continue to employy

nuclear weapons as an international currency of force and power, why should India voluntarily devalue its own state power and national security? Why admonish India . . . for not falling in line behind a new international agenda of discriminatory nonproliferation . . . Nuclear weapons powers continue to have, but preach to the have-nots to have even less.[13]

The Pakistani government maintained that "peace and security in South Asia cannot be promoted and sustained on the basis of discrimination and double standards. Those who advocate non-proliferation and disarmament must themselves be seen to practice this."[14] "We will not accept commitments which would permanently jeopardise the ability of Pakistan to deter the nuclear and conventional threats which India poses to our security."[15]

As their nuclear programs progressed, and particularly as India and Pakistan approached a de facto nuclear weapons capability during the 1980s,[16] there was much speculation as to whether the two countries would actually exercise their nuclear options and achieve an overt capacity.[17] Analysts worried that continuing Indo-Pakistani tensions were in fact likely to lead to such an outcome. As Leonard Spector argued, "If current trends persist . . . there is reasonable cause for concern that momentum will build for integrating nuclear armaments into the armed forces of both nations and for conducting tests."[18] Speculation on the subject continued during the 1990s after India and Pakistan had crossed the de facto nuclear threshold. Leading scholarly analysis during this period was extremely sanguine regarding the unlikelihood of overt Indo-Pakistani nuclearization. Devin Hagerty, for example, confidently predicted that India and Pakistan would almost certainly not seek to develop an overt nuclear capacity but rather would continue to maintain an "opaque" capability.[19]

The events of spring 1998 put this discussion to rest. On May 11 and 13, 1998, India carried out a total of five nuclear explosions at Pokhran in the Rajasthan Desert. Despite intense international pressure not to respond, Pakistan followed on May 28 and 30 with a total of six nuclear detonations of its own in the Chegai Hills. There was some controversy as to the magnitude of the explosions. The Indian government claimed to have detonated a thermonuclear device of 43 kilotons, a fission device of 12 kilotons, a 0.2 kiloton device on May 11, and devices of 0.2 and 0.6 kilotons on May 13. However, Western analysts were skeptical as to the size of the May 11 explosions and doubted whether the May 13 tests had even occurred. One leading American seismologist put the size of the May 11 detonations at a total of ten to fifteen kilotons.[20] The Pakistanis, for their part, claimed that their five devices tested on May 28 totaled forty to forty-five kilotons and put the largest of these devices at thirty to thirty-five kilotons. American analysts estimated the total yield of the Pakistani tests to be in the range of nine to twelve kilotons.[21] Despite this controversy, however, the incontrovertible fact was that India and Pakistan were now both nuclear weapons–capable states and possessed the ability to inflict enormous levels of destruction upon one another.[22]

The Question

This study seeks to determine the effects that India's and Pakistan's acquisition of nuclear weapons has had on the South Asian security environment. It focuses specifically on proliferation's impact on conventional military stability in the region.[23] Clearly, nuclear proliferation has not led to nuclear war in South Asia. Less obvious, however, are nuclear proliferation's conventional effects. The issue of conventional stability is important both because conventional conflict can itself be extremely costly and because conventional conflict between nuclear powers can potentially escalate to the nuclear level.[24] Thus, if nuclear proliferation has undermined South Asian conventional stability, it has rendered the region considerably less safe.[25] If, by contrast, proliferation has enhanced South Asian conventional stability, the nuclearization of South Asia has substantially increased regional security. Nuclear weapons' impact on South Asian security in turn will have implications for broader academic debates over the effects of nuclear proliferation and for American security policy, which assumes that the spread of nuclear weapons anywhere in the world is extremely destabilizing and dangerous.[26] This study therefore asks the following question: What impact has nuclear proliferation had on conventional military stability in South Asia?[27]

Unfortunately, despite intense debate, neither the policy nor the scholarly communities have been able to shed much light on this question. As I demonstrate, South Asian proliferation has left both policymakers and scholars mired in a seemingly intractable debate over nuclear weapons' effects on the region.

The Debate over Proliferation's Effects on South Asian Security

The Policy Community

Indian and Pakistani policymakers have argued that the spread of nuclear weapons to South Asia would stabilize regional security. "If deterrence works in the West . . . by what reasoning will it not work in India?" asked Jaswant Singh. "If the permanent five's possession of nuclear weapons increases security, why would India's possession of nuclear weapons be dangerous?"[28] Pakistani Foreign Secretary Shamshad Ahmad argued, "In South Asia, nuclear deterrence may . . . usher in an era of durable peace between Pakistan and India, providing the requisite incentives for resolving all outstanding issues, especially Jammu and Kashmir."[29]

The international community, by contrast, has long believed that proliferation would make South Asia less secure, and it reacted with considerable alarm to the 1998 Indo-Pakistani nuclear tests. For example, the United Nations Security Council, stating that "the proliferation of all weapons of mass destruction constitutes a threat to international peace and security," demanded that "India and Pakistan refrain from further nuclear tests." In addition, it called on them "immediately to stop their nuclear weapon development programs, to refrain from weaponization or from the deployment of nuclear weapons, to cease development of ballistic missiles capable of delivering nuclear weapons and any further production of fissile material for nuclear weapons" and urged the two countries "to become parties to the Treaty on the Non-Proliferation of Nuclear Weapons and to the Comprehensive Nuclear Test Ban Treaty without delay and without conditions."[30]

Western governments have echoed these concerns, arguing that nuclear weapons made South Asia more dangerous and slapping economic sanctions on both India and Pakistan in retaliation for the 1998 tests.[31] "The path that [India and Pakistan] have started down does not add to their security but diminishes it," said Bill Richardson, U.S. representative to the United Nations in June 1998. "We call upon them to turn back now."[32] U.S. President Bill Clinton argued that nuclear weapons "can only serve to increase tensions in an already volatile region. With their recent tests, Pakistan and India are contributing to a self-defeating cycle of escalation that does not add to the security of either country."[33] Clinton later famously remarked that nuclear proliferation had made South Asia "the most dangerous place in the world."[34]

The International Relations Literature

The scholarly community has been similarly divided on the issue of South Asian proliferation. Just prior to the 1998 tests, scholars such as Devin Hagerty argued that India's and Pakistan's undeclared nuclear capability had created robust deterrence between the two countries, stabilized their relationship, and defused Indo-Pakistani militarized crises that otherwise might have ended in outright conflict.[35] Hagerty made extremely powerful claims as to nuclear weapons' salutary effects, arguing that "Indo-Pakistani nuclear dynamics lend further support to our cumulative evidence that the chief impact of nuclear weapons is to deter war between their possessors. There is no more ironclad law in international relations theory than this: nuclear weapon states do not fight wars with each other."[36] Indeed, according to Hagerty, nuclear weapons' stabilizing effects were so powerful that even an undeclared nuclear capacity would continue to deter Indo-Pakistani conflict into the future, rendering open testing and proliferation unnecessary. As Hagerty argued, "nuclear weapons seem to deter war by virtue of their very existence." Therefore, given the substantial economic and political costs of open proliferation, India and Pakistan, along with "all future proliferants," will "nuclearize in an opaque manner."[37]

The 1998 Indo-Pakistani nuclear tests belied the prediction that all future proliferants would have such faith in nuclear weapons' deterrent effects as to forgo overt proliferation. Nonetheless, in the wake of the tests, many scholars continued to maintain that proliferation would have a highly stabilizing impact on the subcontinent. Indeed, with an overt capability now clearly threatening to make any war catastrophically costly, they argued, nuclear weapons rendered conflict in South Asia especially unlikely. As Kenneth Waltz claimed, both India and Pakistan "will be deterred [from aggression] by the knowledge that aggressive actions may lead to [their] own destruction."[38] According to K. Subrahmanyam, "India's nuclear capability is a stabilizing and balancing factor in a dangerous situation created by the fallout of cold war and proliferation permissiveness of major nuclear weapons powers."[39] Shireen Mazari argued that "nuclear deterrence [is] making an all-out war between India and Pakistan a receding reality."[40]

Other scholars rejected these rosy predictions, arguing that nuclear weapons in fact were likely to have destabilizing effects on the South Asian security environment due to a range of political, technological, and organizational factors. Scott Sagan, for example, maintained that "India and Pakistan face a dangerous nuclear future . . . [I]mperfect humans inside imperfect organizations . . . will someday fail to produce secure nuclear deterrence."[41] P. R. Chari argued that South Asian proliferation undermines a "widely held, *a priori* belief . . . that nuclear weapons states do not go to war against each other."[42] And Samina Ahmed maintained that it is "increasingly evident that a belief in the deterrent value of nuclear weapons has little basis in reality."[43] Thus, like the policymakers, the scholarly community has been divided over the issue of nuclear proliferation's impact on the South Asian security environment.

The Argument

In this study, I argue that although these competing analyses of nuclear proliferation's impact on South Asia capture important truths, they do not fully explain proliferation's effects on the regional security environment. It is certainly the case that nuclear weapons can promote stability-inducing caution on the subcontinent. For example, during the 1999 Kargil War, the fear of nuclear escalation prevented India from considering all-out conventional escalation against Pakistan.[44] However, as I will demonstrate, an examination of Indo-Pakistani military behavior during the proliferation process shows that as proliferation has progressed, the region has become increasingly volatile. Indeed, close analysis reveals that nuclear proliferation encouraged the outbreak of the very crises upon which nuclear weapons later had some stabilizing effect.

It is also true that, as pessimistic scholars claim, political, technological, and organizational pathologies have contributed to volatility on the subcontinent. For example, as noted earlier, repeated Pakistani aggression against India can be attributed at least in part to miscalculation stemming from dysfunctional political institutions.[45] The organizational biases of the Pakistan Army also underlay key mistakes that drove the decision to launch the Kargil conflict and could increase the likelihood of similar confrontations in the future.[46] Other factors such as close geographical proximity,[47] violent history and intense mutual distrust,[48] misunderstanding of nuclear strategy,[49] small nuclear arsenals,[50] technological shortcomings,[51] and personnel problems[52] could augment these dangers.[53]

However, while these problems are significant, they essentially exacerbate an already unstable situation; the fundamental incentives for risky behavior in a nuclearizing South Asia do not result from such shortcomings. Rather, they are a function of India's and Pakistan's territorial preferences and relative military capabilities. Pakistan is militarily weaker than India and is revisionist[54] regarding the territorial status quo in Kashmir, the source of the two countries' fundamental dispute. The acquisition of nuclear weapons by weak, revisionist Pakistan creates strong incentives for limited conventional Pakistani aggression.[55] This is the case for two reasons. First, Pakistani leaders believe that nuclear weapons, by deterring full-scale Indian conventional retaliation, will enable Pakistan to alter territorial boundaries in Kashmir through limited conventional military action. Second, Pakistani leaders believe that the danger of conventional hostilities escalating to the nuclear level can draw international attention, enabling Pakistan to secure outside mediation of the Kashmir dispute and to achieve a more favorable territorial settlement in Kashmir than it could have gotten by itself.

India, by contrast, is militarily strong relative to Pakistan and wishes to preserve the territorial status quo in Kashmir. The acquisition of nuclear weapons has not in itself created incentives for India to become more conventionally aggressive or to alter its military behavior in any significant manner. This is the case because India is largely satisfied with the status of Kashmir and does not seek to alter territorial boundaries. Therefore, it has little motivation to behave aggressively, with or without nuclear weapons. In addition, because India is conventionally stronger than Pakistan, the acquisition of nuclear weapons does not enable India to undertake any subnuclear aggression that it could not have launched prior to proliferation with purely conventional forces. Thus, progressing proliferation has encouraged increasingly aggressive Pakistani behavior, but nuclear weapons have not directly encouraged Indian aggression.

However, with progressing proliferation, the Indian government has engaged in more forceful anti-Pakistani behavior, both as a direct response to Pakistani provocations and in a broader effort to demonstrate that it is not intimidated by Pakistan's nuclear brinksmanship. These Indian actions have contributed to regional tension and played a significant role in further destabilizing the subcontinent. By creating incentives for aggressive Pakistani policies, then, nuclear weapons have increased militarized behavior on the Indian as well as the Pakistani side.[56]

A full understanding of proliferation's impact on South Asian security thus requires an appreciation not only of the structural, political, technological, and organizational pressures on states in general but also of the specific territorial preferences and military capabilities of India and Pakistan. And it leads to the broader conclusion that nuclear weapons' potential to make war catastrophically costly can also make conflict between new nuclear states more likely; the inverse relationship between nuclear danger and the probability of conventional violence, which nuclear deterrence theory has taken as an article of faith since the Cold War, does not apply to all nuclear rivalries. Thus, nuclear weapons proliferation, by introducing nuclear danger into what previously were purely conventional conflicts, may make the world a more violent place.[57]

Structure and Method

In this book, I seek to demonstrate that (1) South Asia has become more volatile since acquiring nuclear weapons than it was prior to proliferation and that (2) this increasing violence resulted largely from the incentives for aggression that proliferation can create for weak, revisionist states, not from some other unidentified factor. I therefore test my argument using both quantitative analysis and the comparative case study method. This two-tiered approach enables me to identify any correlation between progressing nuclearization and conventional violence and to engage in detailed process tracing, getting "inside" the South Asian case to determine whether my causal logic actually underlies the behavior that I observe.[58]

First, I employ quantitative analysis to determine the nature of the relationship between nuclearization and conventional stability in South Asia during three critical time periods from 1972 through 2002: the period from the end of India's and Pakistan's Bangladesh War through 1989; 1990 through May 1998; and June 1998 through 2002. I divide the three periods from one another according to their level of militarily relevant Indo-Pakistani nuclearization. Although by the early 1970s both countries possessed ongoing nuclear development programs, the first time period was nonnuclear. Pakistan had no nuclear capability, and although India did manage a "peaceful nuclear explosion" (PNE) in 1974, it did not achieve nuclear status in any substantive military sense. The PNE was not explicitly for military purposes and was planned and engineered in such a way as to have few military implications. Despite its test, then, India did not achieve nuclear weapons status in 1974, and both India and Pakistan remained nonnuclear weapons states from 1972 through 1989.[59] During the second time period, from 1990 through May 1998, India and Pakistan were de facto nuclear powers, not openly possessing a nuclear weapons capacity but probably able to assemble a nuclear device in short order. Then, after the May 1998 tests, both states openly possessed a military nuclear capability. The difference between the time periods that the project will cover should thus be clear: no militarily relevant nuclearization from 1972 through 1989, de facto military nuclearization from 1990 through May 1998, and open military nuclearization from June 1998 through 2002.[60] My quantitative analysis shows that a positive correlation exists between progressing nuclear proliferation across these time periods and conventional instability in South Asia.

I then seek to explain this correlation between proliferation and conventional instability through detailed case studies, which closely examine Indo-Pakistani military behavior during the three time periods just discussed. In the case studies, I process-trace, drawing on books, official documents, scholarly articles, memoirs, and press reports, as well as a series of in-depth interviews that I conducted with senior Indian and Pakistani diplomats, military officers, and political leaders.[61] This approach enables me to determine Indian and Pakistani leaders' beliefs and preferences regarding the territorial division of Kashmir; the two countries' relative conventional military capabilities; the ways in which these preferences and capabilities interacted with the two countries' growing nuclear capabilities; and the extent to which this interaction was actually responsible for changes in Indo-Pakistani military behavior as proliferation progressed.

The periodized nature of my study offers a number of methodological advantages. Dividing a single case into multiple time periods increases the number of observations within a study, in effect creating several cases out of one.[62] In addition, by looking at how behavior within one conflict dyad has changed over time, I am able to hold other variables more or less constant and focus on the effects of nuclear proliferation on Indo-Pakistani military behavior.[63] Dividing the Indo-Pakistani nuclear relationship temporally, then, enables me to compare the effects of three distinct levels of nuclearization on Indo-Pakistani behavior, derive three observations from a single "case," and control for potentially confounding variables other than nuclear proliferation.

As noted earlier, the implications of this book's findings extend well beyond the South Asian region. Territorial preferences and relative conventional capabilities should affect the strategic calculations of new nuclear states regardless of their geographical location. Therefore, I also include in the book brief studies of the behavior of new nuclear powers in regions beyond South Asia. First, I examine Chinese behavior during the Sino-Soviet Ussuri River conflict of 1969 to determine what role, if any, China's acquisition of nuclear weapons played in its decision to commence hostilities against the Soviet Union. The Sino-Soviet case adds variance to the study, allowing me to test my argument in a region other than South Asia and to show that my findings do not result from factors peculiar to India and Pakistan. I argue that while it is difficult to draw definitive conclusions regarding Chinese decision making during the Ussuri River conflict, available information indicates that the case is compatible with my argument. The Chinese were conventionally weaker than the Soviet Union and began seeking to alter territorial boundaries in the Ussuri River region just prior to their 1964 nuclear test. The Chinese subsequently launched a premeditated attack against Soviet forces in the area in 1969, triggering the Ussuri River conflict. The evidence shows that it is possible, though not certain, that the acquisition of nuclear weapons emboldened Chinese leaders to take such aggressive action.

Next, I examine a prospective case of proliferation using the book's theoretical framework to predict the likely behavior of a nuclear North Korea (Democratic People's Republic of Korea; DPRK). I argue that given its relative conventional weakness, the DPRK's likely behavior turns upon its territorial preferences. If North Korea is a status quo state, the acquisition of nuclear weapons is unlikely to result in conventional aggression. If, by contrast, North Korea harbors revisionist ambitions, then nuclear weapons are likely to encourage limited DPRK aggression. Finally, I briefly explore the applicability of my framework to the case of a nuclear Iran. Although these prospective discussions do not provide a test of my argument, they illustrate its utility in anticipating the actions of future proliferators in regions beyond South Asia.

The plan of the book is as follows: In Chapter 2, I present aggregate Indo-Pakistani militarized dispute data from 1972 through 2002 and employ quantitative tests to determine the nature and strength of the relationship between conventional conflict and progressing nuclear proliferation. In Chapter 3, I account for these quantitative findings. I explain how territorial preferences and relative military capabilities can create incentives for aggressive conventional behavior on the part of proliferating states. I then perform a detailed examination of the Indo-Pakistani military balance and discuss the two countries' territorial preferences regarding Kashmir. I show that Pakistan occupies the weak, dissatisfied position within the Indo-Pakistani conflict dyad, whereas India is strong vis-à-vis Pakistan and status quo on the issue of Kashmir. I argue that Pakistan's politico-military position within the Indo-Pakistani conflict relationship created significant incentives for aggressive Pakistani behavior. And while India's position did not create incentives for similar Indian behavior, Pakistani provocations led India to adopt increasingly forceful policies of its own. Chapter 3 concludes with a brief look at the international relations literature beyond South Asian proliferation scholarship, assessing the literature's discussion of war initiation by weak, dissatisfied states.

Chapters 4 through 6 offer detailed case studies showing how territorial preferences and relative military capabilities affected Indo-Pakistani behavior during the three proliferation time periods discussed earlier. In Chapter 4, I examine the nonnuclear period from 1972 through 1989 and explain why the absence of nuclear weapons helped to ensure that this time period remained largely peaceful. In Chapter 5, I examine the period from 1990 through May 1998, during which India and Pakistan were de facto nuclear powers, and explain how the two countries' growing nuclear capacity encouraged increasing regional instability. And in Chapter 6, I examine the period from June 1998 through 2002, during which both India and Pakistan openly possessed nuclear weapons, and explain how this overt nuclear capacity made the Indo-Pakistani security relationship even more conflictual than it had been in a de facto nuclear environment.

Chapter 7 summarizes the behavioral incentives that various combinations of the relevant political and military variables should create for new nuclear powers. It then applies this framework to cases of nuclear weapons acquisition beyond South Asia. First, I discuss the Sino-Soviet border war of 1969 to determine whether my findings are compatible with the only other case of protracted combat between nuclear weapons states. I then explore my argument's implications for the future behavior of a nuclear North Korea and briefly discuss the applicability of my framework to the case of Iran. Finally, Chapter 8 offers an assessment of the theoretical and policy significance of my findings.

2

Militarized Behavior During the South Asian Proliferation Process

In Chapter 1, we saw that the impact of nuclear proliferation on South Asian security is the subject of an intense debate in the international relations literature, with some scholars arguing that nuclear weapons are likely to stabilize the regional security environment and others maintaining that proliferation actually makes the subcontinent more dangerous. In this chapter, I examine the competing arguments more closely. I show that, despite their differences, scholars on opposing sides of the debate employ similar approaches to analyzing South Asian proliferation. First, many leading scholars privilege deductive arguments that downplay the importance of political and historical variables specific to the region. Second, most scholars evaluate empirical evidence in a piecemeal manner, citing specific incidents to support their claims rather than analyzing aggregate data on the South Asian security environment, identifying broad trends within it, and assessing the relationship between these trends and progressing regional proliferation. As a result, the South Asian proliferation debate is logically and empirically inconclusive, with both camps making equally plausible claims as to nuclear weapons' impact on Indo-Pakistani conventional behavior. I argue that, to gain a realistic understanding of nuclear proliferation's effects on the region, we first must systematically examine the empirical evidence on South Asian conventional conflict and identify trends in Indo-Pakistani behavior as proliferation has progressed over time. Therefore, in this chapter, I undertake a quantitative analysis of South Asian militarized dispute data. Doing so reveals that Indo-Pakistani militarized disputes have grown more frequent and more severe as proliferation has progressed.[1]

Assessing Competing Arguments

As noted, optimistic and pessimistic scholars offer widely divergent assessments of nuclear weapons' impact on the South Asian security environment. Nonetheless, scholarship on both sides of the South Asian proliferation debate shares two important characteristics. First, leading analyses tend to remain deductive in nature, discounting the theoretical importance of the region's history and politics.[2] Waltz and Sagan, for example, argue that factors specific to South Asia are not the primary determinants of proliferation's impact on the subcontinent. They maintain the same logic that drove the superpowers during the Cold War drives the actions of all nuclear states and will in turn determine Indian and Pakistani nuclear behavior. As Waltz writes, "With nuclear weapons, any state will be deterred by another's second-strike forces; one need not be preoccupied with the qualities of the state to be deterred . . ."[3] According to Sagan, "there are differences between the nuclear relationship emerging between India and Pakistan and the cold war system that developed . . . between the United States and Soviet Union. While the differences are clear, however, the significance of these differences is not."[4] Thus, despite their divergent views of proliferation's impact on South Asia, these scholars share a fundamental assumption: Knowledge of nuclear proliferation's impact on a regional security environment requires little specific historical or political knowledge of the region itself.

Second, the South Asian nuclear proliferation literature employs evidence in a piecemeal fashion.[5] Scholars assessing proliferation's regional impact argue that particular events support their position in the debate, without contextualizing the events as part of larger trends in the South Asian security environment and assessing the relationship between these trends and progressing nuclear proliferation. Even scholars whose work explicitly emphasizes the importance of regional variables tend to discuss empirical evidence from South Asia as a series of discrete cases rather than as part of a broader pattern.[6] As a result, for every incident that scholars on one side of the debate cite in favor of their position, opposing scholars are able to cite other events that appear to cut the opposite way. Indeed, scholars on opposing sides of the debate are often able to claim that the same empirical evidence supports their position in the controversy.

For example, optimistic scholars point out that, despite its supposed dangers, nuclear proliferation has not led to major war on the subcontinent. Moreover, they argue, nuclear weapons' deterrent effects prevented incidents such as the 1990 crisis, the 1999 Kargil conflict, and the 2001–2002 crisis from erupting into all-out war. Pessimistic scholars, by contrast, argue that organizational, technological, and political pathologies have contributed to substantial instability on the subcontinent since nuclear proliferation, including a Pakistan-supported guerrilla war in Kashmir, nuclear crises such as the 1990 standoff, and outright conventional conflict between India and Pakistan at Kargil. In response, optimistic scholars acknowledge ongoing Indo-Pakistani conventional violence but maintain that without nuclear weapons' pacifying effects, violent incidents would have been even more frequent, destabilizing, and dangerous.[7] Pessimists in turn reply that while low-level confrontations have not yet escalated to the threshold of all-out conventional conflict or nuclear war in South Asia,[8] nuclear weapons have not made such escalation impossible. Rather, the region has simply been fortunate that more conflicts have not erupted and that those that did erupt did not escalate further.[9]

Because of these logical and empirical factors, the debate between competing analyses of South Asian proliferation is largely inconclusive. To the extent that opposing arguments remain deductive in nature, it is impossible to adjudicate definitively between them. Both the South Asian proliferation "optimist" and "pessimist" arguments are equally plausible from a purely logical standpoint. For example, there is no deductive reason to believe that deterrence logic is more powerful than that of organization theory, or vice versa.[10] And because of its piecemeal nature, scholars' use of empirical evidence is unhelpful in resolving this logical indeterminacy.

I argue that this problem requires us to depart from the literature's deductive causal models and its piecemeal use of empirical evidence. Instead, we must assess the empirical evidence systematically, identifying any correlation between nuclear proliferation and trends in South Asian conventional behavior. Hence, I analyze the frequency and severity of militarized disputes on the subcontinent from 1972 through 2002. I demonstrate that a positive correlation exists between progressing nuclear proliferation and conventional instability in South Asia.

Analyzing the Data: Conventional Stability in South Asia over Time

As noted, it is unclear from the South Asian security literature whether, on balance, South Asian proliferation has been associated with increased or decreased conventional stability. Therefore, in this section, I examine the data on Indo-Pakistani conventional conflict from 1972 through 2002 to identify possible correlation between nuclear proliferation and conventional militarized disputes.

I draw my data from the Correlates of War (COW) project's Militarized Interstate Dispute data set. The COW data set includes all Indo-Pakistani militarized disputes from mere threats to use force to outright war from 1947 through 2001.[11] I limit my analysis to the years from 1972 forward. Although including the entire period from 1947 would have the advantage of increasing my sample size, careful consideration of the politico-military environment on the subcontinent shows that this is not the optimal approach. The Indo-Pakistani conventional military relationship underwent significant changes after 1971. As a result, the incentives for conventional aggression on the subcontinent were substantially different between 1947 and 1971 than they were from 1972 forward.

The 1971 Bangladesh War greatly strengthened India's conventional military position relative to Pakistan. India had always enjoyed conventional military superiority on the subcontinent. However, while it was significant, Indian military superiority had not been perceived as overwhelming. Prior to the Bangladesh War, despite its conventional inferiority, Pakistan had twice managed to fight India to a stalemate. Thus, in November 1971, senior Pakistani officers could boast that Pakistan had never lost a war to India, and they contemplated the possibility of a third conflict without undue trepidation. As Sisson and Rose explain, the Pakistani leadership believed that

> It was impossible for Pakistan to lose a war to India. Such an outcome was inconceivable . . . The belief was also commonly held that "Muslims had never been defeated by the Hindus." Muslims had created Pakistan against great odds and Hindu opposition; Kashmir had not been lost to India, but was an unresolved and continuing conflict; the 1965 war, though imprudently waged, had not been a defeat, even though victories on the battlefield had been sacrificed at Tashkent. As one senior general officer forcefully observed: "Never before had a Muslim sword been handed over to a Hindu . . ."[12]

By January 1972, however, India had utterly defeated Pakistan. Pakistan did not simply lose the 1971 war; it was dismembered, with India creating Bangladesh out of Pakistan's former eastern wing. In the wake of such a catastrophic Pakistani defeat, India's military superiority was plain for all to see, and Pakistani leaders could no longer rest assured that war with India would at worst result in a stalemate. Rather, it was now clear that fighting a war with India could put Pakistan in mortal peril. As Shahid Amin argues,

> So far the Pakistan psyche had been that in spite of being smaller than India in size, it could defeat or at least hold its own grounds against India in the battlefield, just as the Muslims in the past centuries had been able to defeat much larger Indian Hindu armies . . . But the illusions were to be wrecked in 1971 when the battle was lost within ten days in East Pakistan, whereas on the Western front also, no military offensive against India materialized.[13]

Thus, unlike the prior twenty-five years, from 1972 forward Pakistani leaders understood that going to war with India meant facing the possibility of catastrophic defeat. The Pakistan government therefore focused its efforts on rebuilding shattered domestic political institutions, revitalizing its military, and improving relations with other states in the Islamic world. It was far less interested in seeking conflict with India than it had been. As a result, during the time period immediately after 1971, South Asia was more peaceful than it had been earlier.[14] Pakistan launched nineteen militarized disputes, one of which reached the level of war, against India in the eighteen years prior to 1971. By contrast, it started only five militarized disputes, none of which reached the level of war, in the eighteen years from 1972 through the end of the nonnuclear period in 1989. In fact, the years 1973 through 1980 were completely dispute-free. Thus, the Bangladesh War fundamentally changed Pakistani calculations and the stability of the regional security environment from 1972 forward.

These facts are important to our analysis because they indicate that the introduction of nuclear weapons to the subcontinent occurred during a time in which the region was already less conflict prone than it had been prior to 1971. Since we are attempting to measure nuclear weapons' independent impact on South Asian stability, we should therefore test nuclearization's impact on the frequency of conventional conflict, drawing on data not from the entire period after 1947 but rather from the period from 1971 forward. Doing so would better enable us to isolate nuclear proliferation's effects on South Asia by holding the conventional Indo-Pakistani military relationship roughly constant; unlike a test including the entire 1947–2001 time period, we would now be testing a pre- and postproliferation South Asia in which the conventional military environment and nonnuclear incentives for conventional aggression were essentially the same.

I therefore analyze the nature of the relationship between nuclearization and conventional instability drawing on the COW project's militarized interstate dispute data from 1972 forward.[15] I make three modifications to the data set. First, I add a dispute to account for the 1986–1987 Brasstacks crisis.[16] Only one militarized interstate dispute (MID), 2644, appears in the COW data set from 1986 to 1987. Dispute 2644 begins in October 1986 and ends in November 1986. However, the Brasstacks crisis began in December 1986 and continued through early March 1987. I therefore add a case, which I label 1111, spanning from 1986 to 1987.[17]

Second, I separate the Kargil War from MID 4007. MID 4007 stretches from September 1993 into July 1999 in the COW data set and includes the Kargil War. In my view, Kargil was certainly not divorced from earlier Indo-Pakistani militarized conflicts over Kashmir, but to code it as part of an earlier dispute is misleading. The decision to cross the Line of Control (LoC) into Indian territory with Pakistan Army forces was qualitatively different from previous Pakistani policy in Kashmir, as was the intense, protracted Indo-Pakistani conflict that resulted from this decision. I therefore code Kargil as dispute 1112, separate from MID 4007.[18]

The final modification that I make to the COW data is to separate MID 4277 from the Indo-Pakistani military standoff following the December 2001 terrorist attack on the Indian Parliament. In the data set, MID 4277 begins with low-level violence along the LoC in July 2001, includes the buildup of forces following the Parliament attack, and ends on December 31, 2001. As in the Kargil case, the Parliament attack and the resulting militarized standoff were in important ways connected to earlier Kashmir-related Indo-Pakistani conflict. Nonetheless, to characterize the post-Parliament attack crisis as part of the same low-level violence that preceded it is misleading. The military standoff following the Parliament attack dwarfed activity along the LoC and international border just prior to it and involved the largest deployment in Indian history. I therefore count MID 4277 separately from the post-Parliament crisis, which I designate as dispute 1113, beginning in December 2001. I also continue dispute 1113 into 2002. Although the COW data extend only through the end of 2001, the post-Parliament standoff in fact continued until October 2002. Thus, I have modified the data to show dispute 1113 occurring in both 2001 and 2002.[19]

For the purposes of my analysis, I count each month in which a militarized dispute was occurring between India and Pakistan as a dispute month.[20] When a dispute extends beyond the month in which it began, I include all of the months in which it occurred.[21] I include in my analysis all Indo-Pakistani militarized disputes that occurred from 1972 through 2002, not only disputes that reached the level of "war." I do so for two reasons. First, if deterrence theorists are correct and nuclear weapons lead states to behave more cautiously, proliferation should discourage a wide range of disputes, from low-level conventional confrontations to outright war. This is not to argue that nuclear proliferation should completely rule out subnuclear conflict. However, if nuclear weapons have truly had a pacifying effect on the subcontinent, we should expect to see a decline across the spectrum of disputes as proliferation progressed. At the very least, we should not expect to find a positive correlation between progressing proliferation and conventional confrontation.[22]

Second, conventional confrontation below the level of war is an important phenomenon. It kills large numbers of people, it is economically costly, and it could escalate to the level of full-scale war.[23] Therefore, if we wish to

determine nuclear weapons' impact on regional stability, we should not focus exclusively on wars. Rather, our analysis should encompass all militarized
international disputes, including wars. I thus include in my data militarized
disputes that fall into the categories of "display of force" and "use of force" as
well as those that reach the level of "war."[24]

A potential problem in my effort to assess the impact of nuclear proliferation
on conventional stability is that a confounding variable other than proliferation
could be captured by my analysis and significantly affect my results. The most
obvious danger in this regard is that changes in the Indo-Pakistani conventional
relationship between 1972 and 2002 could have facilitated Pakistani aggression
and led to increased conflict on the subcontinent during the proliferation process
for reasons that have nothing to do with nuclear weapons. How could changes
in the conventional balance have affected Indo-Pakistani conflict behavior?

The most likely scenario would be that, over time, as Pakistan recovered
from its crushing defeat in the Bangladesh War, Pakistan became more conventionally powerful vis-à-vis India. As Pakistan's relative conventional power
grew, Pakistani leaders felt increasingly confident in challenging India at the
conventional level, quite apart from Pakistan's nuclear weapons capacity.[25]

Alternatively, it is possible that continued Pakistani conventional decline
even after the Bangladesh War encouraged aggressive Pakistani behavior toward India. According to this logic, Pakistani decision makers, recognizing
their country's downward trajectory, would have undertaken aggressive action
against India before the window of opportunity for doing so closed completely. Although this scenario of relative conventional decline encouraging
Pakistani aggression is logically possible, it is in reality unlikely to have caused
aggressive Pakistani behavior. Since Pakistan was already considerably weaker
than India in 1972, Pakistani leaders probably would not have felt sufficiently
confident to attack India as Pakistan declined further. Nor, given the outcome
of the Bangladesh War, would they view the 1972 conventional baseline as a
window of opportunity; the Pakistanis would probably have required a significant increase in relative conventional capabilities to make them feel sufficiently
confident to attack the Indians. Despite the unlikelihood of conventional decline encouraging aggressive Pakistani behavior, however, the operation of
such preventive-war or "window logic" is a possibility.[26] We therefore must
keep this scenario in mind as we look for trends in the Indo-Pakistani conventional data and consider how any changes might have affected the two
countries' conflict behavior independent of nuclear proliferation.

The book's case studies address the possibility that unidentified variables
other than nuclear proliferation could be affecting my findings of increased

subnuclear conflict as the Indo-Pakistani proliferation process progressed. By looking closely at the course of events and at decision-making processes within each nuclear period, the case studies can help us discern whether nuclear proliferation was actually causing the outcomes that I identify or whether some other variable was driving my results. As we will see, the case studies indicate that a number of nonnuclear factors, such as the Afghan War, the increasing Islamization of Pakistan, and the emergence of an indigenous Kashmiri independence movement, encouraged greater Pakistani adventurism in Kashmir. Shifts in the Indo-Pakistani conventional balance were not among these factors.

Nonetheless, it is useful to consider the Indo-Pakistani conventional balance from a quantitative standpoint at the outset of the study. Doing so will enable us to determine quickly the degree to which the balance has changed over time and whether such change could plausibly have affected the frequency and severity of Indo-Pakistani conventional conflict. As suggested, if conventional factors were driving increased Indo-Pakistani conflict, we would most likely see significantly increasing Pakistani conventional capabilities relative to India over time, though declining Pakistani capabilities could potentially also have led Pakistan to challenge India at the conventional level. By contrast, if the conventional balance between India and Pakistan remained relatively flat, without significant changes in the power differential between the two countries during the time period in question, conventional factors could not be causing increased frequency or severity of Indo-Pakistani conventional conflict.

I therefore include with my analysis of the South Asian militarized dispute data an assessment of the Indo-Pakistani conventional balance between 1972 and 2002. I compare Indian and Pakistani conventional capabilities in the following manner. First, I calculate the ratios of Indian to Pakistani assets and expenditures for each year along four axes: size of active-duty military forces, number of tanks, number of combat aircraft, and amount of defense spending.[27] I then average the four ratios to arrive at one aggregate ratio of Indo-Pakistani conventional capability for each year. These variables are by no means exhaustive and weighing them against each other does not provide a highly nuanced analysis of the Indo-Pakistani balance. Nonetheless, they constitute key determinants of raw conventional military power.[28] Thus, comparing Indian and Pakistani capabilities in these categories over time should enable us to determine whether or not significant shifts in the South Asian conventional balance have occurred and help us decide whether conventional rather than nuclear factors could in fact be driving Indo-Pakistani conventional conflict behavior. I provide the details of my analysis of the Indo-Pakistani conventional balance in the Appendix. I list the aggregate Indo-Pakistani conventional capabilities ratios, along with the rest of my Indo-Pakistani militarized dispute data, in Table 1.

An initial look at the data shows two things. First, the data indicate that military instability increased as the proliferation process progressed. For example, the period from 1972 through 1989 included 30 dispute months and 186 months that were free of militarized confrontation. The frequency of conflict during this period was approximately 0.14 conflicts per month. At this rate of conflict, the 156-month period from 1990 through 2002 should have included approximately 21.67 dispute months. In fact, the period from 1990 through 2002 included 118 dispute months. Thus, Indo-Pakistani militarized disputes were over five times more frequent from 1990 through 2002, at approximately 0.76 disputes per month, than they were from 1972 through 1989.

Dividing the 1990 through 2002 time frame further into de facto nuclear (1990 through May 1998) and overt nuclear (June 1998 through 2002) periods, we find that the 101-month de facto period included 73 dispute months, for a rate of approximately 0.72 disputes per month. This was over five times the rate at which disputes occurred during the nonnuclear period. During the 55-month overt nuclear period, 45 dispute months occurred, for a rate of approximately 0.82 disputes per month. This was an increase of nearly 14 percent over the dispute rate during the de facto nuclear period. If militarized disputes had occurred at the same rate during the de facto period as they had during the nonnuclear years, the de facto period would have experienced just over 14 dispute months. And if MIDs had occurred at the same rate during the overt nuclear period as they had during the de facto years, the overt period would have experienced just under 40 dispute months. Thus, the dispute rate during the de facto nuclear period increased markedly over what it had been during the nonnuclear period. And the dispute rate during the overt nuclear period increased somewhat further. Additionally, the data indicate that the nature of militarized disputes became more serious as the proliferation process progressed from the de facto to the overt level. Although no Indo-Pakistani wars occurred during the nonnuclear and de facto nuclear periods, the subcontinent's first war since 1971 erupted during the overt nuclear period, just after India's and Pakistan's 1998 tests.

The data indicate that shifts in relative Indo-Pakistani conventional military power are unlikely to have caused these results. The balance of conventional Indo-Pakistani military capabilities was fairly stable over the time period in question. In the immediate aftermath of the Bangladesh War, India's advantage was especially high, with the Indo-Pakistani conventional ratio standing at greater than 3:1. Although the Indian advantage began to decline somewhat after 1973, the balance averaged 2.79:1 for the decade of the 1970s. The 1980s saw the ratio of Indo-Pakistani conventional capabilities continue on this rough trajectory, with the Indian advantage ranging between 2.77:1 and 2.4:1 and averaging 2.53:1 for the decade. During the 1990s, India's conventional advantage declined further, ranging from a high of 2.43:1 to a low of 2:1, for an average ratio of 2.17:1. Finally, from 2000 to 2002, the Indian advantage increased over what it had been during the 1990s, ranging from a high of 2.88:1 to a low of 2.5:1, for an average ratio of 2.7:1. If we look at the trajectory of Indo-Pakistani conventional capabilities over nuclear periods rather than calendar decades, roughly the same picture emerges. The balance of conventional capabilities ranged between 3.33:1 and 2.21:1 and averaged 2.65:1 during the nonnuclear period; declined during the de facto nuclear period, ranging between 2.34:1 and 2:1 and averaging 2.1:1; and rose to range between 2.88:1 and 2.2:1 and average 2.51:1 during the overt nuclear period.

What is the significance of these conventional data for the purposes of our study? The data indicate that, other than several years of unusually high Indian advantage, at times exceeding 3:1 in the immediate aftermath of the Bangladesh War, and a brief dip to the vicinity of 2:1 in the early to mid-1990s, the balance of Indo-Pakistani conventional capabilities remained fairly static. It is true that despite general stability in the conventional balance, India's advantage over Pakistan did decrease with time. However, it is unlikely that this trend encouraged aggressive Pakistani behavior and increased the frequency of Indo-Pakistani militarized disputes. As noted, the change in Indo-Pakistani relative capabilities, while steady, was also modest. The Pakistani military was prostrate in the immediate aftermath of the Bangladesh War, and it is not surprising that Pakistan's relative capabilities improved somewhat as the country recovered from the crushing effects of that loss. However, Pakistan's recovery, though real, was insufficient to change its fundamentally inferior status vis-à-vis India; despite relative Pakistani improvements, Indian conventional capabilities remained roughly 2 to 2.5 times greater than those of the Pakistanis throughout the time period in question.[29]

A useful way to measure the import of this Indian advantage is to weigh it against the balance of conventional capabilities in South Asia just prior to the Bangladesh War. In 1971–1972, the ratio of Indo-Pakistani conventional capabilities stood at 2.21:1.[30] Thus, a subsequent Indo-Pakistani balance in this vicinity should indicate a potentially disastrous level of conventional inferiority

TABLE I

Year	MID	Dispute Months	Initiator	Revisionist	Hostility Level	Nuclear Level	India-Pakistan Conventional Ratio
1972	2638	1	Pakistan	Pakistan	Use of force	No nuclear capability	3.17 : 1
1973					No militarized action	No nuclear capability	3.33 : 1
1974					No militarized action	No nuclear capability	2.77 : 1
1975					No militarized action	No nuclear capability	2.66 : 1
1976					No militarized action	No nuclear capability	3.11 : 1
1977					No militarized action	No nuclear capability	2.96 : 1
1978					No militarized action	No nuclear capability	2.61 : 1
1979					No militarized action	No nuclear capability	2.31 : 1
1980					No militarized action	No nuclear capability	2.52 : 1
1981	2639	5	Pakistan	Pakistan	Use of force	No nuclear capability	2.43 : 1
1982	2640	1	India	Pakistan	Display of force	No nuclear capability	2.51 : 1
1983	2641	3	Pakistan	Pakistan	Use of force	No nuclear capability	2.47 : 1
1984	2641	1	Pakistan	Pakistan	Use of force	No nuclear capability	2.73 : 1
1984	2642	3	Pakistan	Pakistan	Use of force	No nuclear capability	2.73 : 1
1985	2643	10	Pakistan	Pakistan	Use of force	No nuclear capability	2.44 : 1
1986	2644	2	India	Pakistan	Use of force	No nuclear capability	2.47 : 1
1986	1111	1	India	Neither	Display of force	No nuclear capability	2.47 : 1

1987	1111	3			Display of force	No nuclear capability	2.51 : 1
1988					No militarized action	No nuclear capability	2.77 : 1
1989					No militarized action	No nuclear capability	2.4 : 1
1990	3959	11	India	Pakistan	Use of force	De facto nuclear capability	2.34 : 1
1991	3985	5	India	Both	Use of force	De facto nuclear capability	2.1 : 1
1992					No militarized action	De facto nuclear capability	2.01 : 1
1993	4007	4	Pakistan	Pakistan	Use of force	De facto nuclear capability	2.04 : 1
1994	4007	12	Pakistan	Pakistan	Use of force	De facto nuclear capability	2.01 : 1
1995	4007	12	Pakistan	Pakistan	Use of force	De facto nuclear capability	2 : 1
1996	4007	12	Pakistan	Pakistan	Use of force	De facto nuclear capability	2.22 : 1
1997	4007	12	Pakistan	Pakistan	Use of force	De facto nuclear capability	2.2 : 1
1998	4007	12	Pakistan	Pakistan	Use of force	Overt nuclear capability	2.3 : 1
1999	4007	4	Pakistan	Pakistan	Use of force	Overt nuclear capability	2.43 : 1
1999	1112	3	Pakistan	Pakistan	War	Overt nuclear capability	2.43 : 1
1999	4223	5	India	Neither	Use of force	Overt nuclear capability	2.43 : 1
2000	4223	10	India	Neither	Use of force	Overt nuclear capability	2.5 : 1
2001	4277	5	Pakistan	Pakistan	Use of force	Overt nuclear capability	2.88 : 1
2001	1113	1	India	Pakistan	Use of force	Overt nuclear capability	2.88 : 1
2002	1113	10	India	Pakistan	Use of force	Overt nuclear capability	2.72 : 1

for Pakistan; in 1971, it had allowed India sufficient military advantage to vivi-sect the country. It is therefore highly unlikely that Pakistani leaders would be emboldened to behave aggressively toward India in a conventional environment even remotely resembling this pre-Bangladesh scenario. Rather, the Pakistanis would require significant sustained improvement in their relative conventional status over the pre-Bangladesh balance before challenging the Indians.

Even at its lowest ebb during the early to mid-1990s, the balance of Indian to Pakistani capabilities, at roughly 2:1, was essentially on par with this pre-Bangladesh ratio. Thus, it is very unlikely that the observed changes in the balance of Indo-Pakistani conventional capabilities could have emboldened the Pakistanis to behave more aggressively toward the Indians during the time period in question. Regardless of whether the Indian advantage was 2.5:1 or 2:1, the Pakistanis were thoroughly outmatched at the conventional level throughout the period from 1972 to 2002. Indeed, even during the years most favorable to Pakistan, the Pakistanis' disadvantage against the Indians was simi-lar to what it had been just before the Bangladesh defeat.[31]

It is worth noting that when we look at the balance of relative Indo-Pakistani conventional capabilities across nuclear time periods rather than across calendar decades, we find not only that shifts in the balance of capabilities were mod-est but also that these shifts did not correlate with the increasing conventional instability that occurred as the nuclearization process progressed. The Indian conventional advantage over Pakistan declined between the nonnuclear and the de facto nuclear time periods and increased between the de facto and overt nuclear phases. However, as noted, conventional instability increased from the nonnuclear through the overt nuclear time periods. Thus, during the overt nu-clear period, Pakistan's relative conventional capabilities declined from the level that they had attained during the de facto nuclear period, but Indo-Pakistani disputes nonetheless became more frequent than they had been during the de facto years. This lends further support to our claim that shifts in the balance of conventional capabilities did not lead to increased conventional disputes during the time period in question.

Statistical Tests

An initial look at the data thus would seem to confirm the pessimistic argu-ment that nuclear weapons have not succeeded in stabilizing South Asia and in fact have encouraged greater instability in the region. However, to assess the accuracy of this initial impression, we need to subject the data to statistical analysis. Doing so will enable us to determine the likelihood that the find-ings just noted were simply the result of chance rather than of some under-

TABLE 2

Cross Tabulations

			NUCLEAR		
			Nonnuclear	Nuclear	Total
HOSTILITY	Peace	Months	186	38	224
		% of Peace Months	83.0%	17.0%	100.0%
	Dispute	Months	30	118	148
		% of Dispute Months	20.3%	79.7%	100.0%
Total		Months	216	156	372
		% of Total Months	58.1%	41.9%	100.0%

Chi-square p < .001

lying, causal mechanism. It will also precisely quantify the nature and strength of any correlation between conventional instability and nuclear proliferation on the subcontinent. I therefore perform two simple statistical tests to determine the nature and strength of the relationship between nuclear proliferation and conventional military stability in South Asia. The results support our earlier impression regarding increasing conflict during the nonnuclear, de facto, and overt nuclear time periods; statistical analysis shows that a positive correlation exists between nuclear proliferation and militarized disputes in South Asia and that this correlation is very unlikely to result from chance.

In my first test, I cross tabulate nuclear proliferation against conventional disputes. My cross tabulation seeks simply to determine whether any type of militarized action was associated with any presence of nuclear weapons, de facto or overt, on the subcontinent. I use a dummy variable for disputes, coding it 0 if no militarized dispute occurred during a dyad month and 1 if any militarized dispute occurred. Similarly, for nuclear weapons, I code the absence of nuclear weapons as 0 and the presence of nuclear weapons as 1, regardless of whether the nuclear weapons were de facto or overt. I count the months from 1972 through 1989 as nonnuclear and the months from 1990 through 2002 as nuclear. My results, shown in Table 2, indicate that a relationship between nuclear weapons and militarized disputes indeed exists in South Asia (chi-square p < .001) Specifically, I find that peace was nearly five times more common in a nonnuclear South Asia (83 percent of months) than it was after the region became nuclearized (17 percent of months). Militarized disputes were nearly four times more common in a nuclear environment (79.7 percent of months) than they were when the subcontinent was nonnuclear (20.3 percent of months). The odds that this outcome resulted from chance are less than 1 in 1,000.[32]

TABLE 3

Correlations

(N = 372)

	Nuclear Level	Hostility Level
Nuclear Level		
Correlation coefficient	1.000	.606
Sig. (1-tailed)	.	<.001
Hostility Level		
Correlation Coefficient	.606	1.000
Sig. (1-tailed)	<.001	.

Having shown that nuclear weapons and conventional militarized disputes are in fact related, I next perform a bivariate correlative test to determine the nature and strength of the relationship between nuclear weapons and Indo-Pakistani hostility. Specifically, I seek to determine whether increasing levels of nuclearization are correlated with increased hostility levels. In this test, I specify three nuclear levels: no nuclear weapons, coded 0; de facto nuclear weapons, coded 1; and overt nuclear weapons, coded 2. I also specify five hostility levels: no conflict, coded 0; threat to use force, coded 1; display of force, coded 2; use of force, coded 3; and war, coded 4. As Table 3 demonstrates, this test reveals a strong positive correlation (.606) between nuclearization and hostility.[33] The significance of this result is < .001, meaning that the likelihood of the outcome resulting from chance is less than 1 in 1,000.[34]

The data thus show a significant positive correlation between progressing nuclear proliferation and conventional military instability in South Asia. We should also note that the data reveal that Pakistan was responsible for most of the instability observed during the period in question, initiating the militarized disputes that accounted for 99 of 148 dispute months from 1972 through 2002. All of these dispute months resulted from confrontations in which Pakistan sought to alter the territorial status quo. One such confrontation was the 1999 Kargil conflict, the subcontinent's only war during the time period in question. India, by contrast, initiated militarized disputes that accounted for 49 of 148 dispute months from 1972 through 2002. Just 5 of these dispute months resulted from a MID in which India attempted to alter the territorial status quo. India initiated disputes accounting for 44 other conflict months in efforts to counter Pakistani threats to the status quo.[35]

One potential concern with my findings is that the second half of the non-nuclear period, from 1981 through 1987, saw an upswing in Indo-Pakistani disputes. The trend essentially continued, with a break in 1988 and 1989, into the de facto nuclear period. This could indicate that the catalyst driving increased conflict on the subcontinent was not nuclear proliferation but rather some other factor that emerged during the 1980s, before the spread of nuclear weapons to the region.

As I explain in subsequent chapters, nuclear weapons were one key variable facilitating increased conflict in South Asia; they were not the sole cause of this phenomenon. The nonnuclear 1980s did see the emergence of other destabilizing factors, such as increased Islamization within Pakistan and Pakistani support for a Sikh insurgency in the Indian Punjab. However, despite these factors, the frequency of militarized disputes remained much lower during the 1980s than it became later, once India and Pakistan had acquired a nuclear weapons capacity. Let us compare the frequency of disputes during the 1980s with dispute frequency during the de facto and overt nuclear periods. The years 1980 through 1989 saw 29 dispute months out of 120 calendar months, for a frequency of approximately 0.24 disputes per month. The dispute rate during the de facto nuclear period, by contrast, was approximately 0.72 disputes per month. And the dispute rate during the overt nuclear period was 0.82 disputes per month. Thus, even if we assess just the 1980s, excluding the peaceful period of the 1970s, we find that the frequency of Indo-Pakistani disputes was far lower in the absence of nuclear weapons than it was during the de facto and overt nuclear periods.

Statistical tests yield similar results. Dropping from our analysis the peaceful 1970s and cross tabulating data only from 1980 forward yields the following result: 91 months of peace (70.5 percent of months) in a nonnuclear South Asia versus 38 months of peace (29.5 percent of months) in a nuclear environment; 29 months of dispute when the subcontinent was nonnuclear (19.7 percent of months) versus 118 months of dispute after nuclearization (80.3 percent of months); and a chi-square p-value of < .001. A bivariate correlative test yields a correlation of .500 between hostility and nuclearization, with a significance of < .001. Thus, my statistical results remain quite robust despite the exclusion of the 1970s from the nonnuclear period; conflict was over four times more common in a nuclear than in a nonnuclear environment, while peace was over twice as common in a nonnuclear than in a nuclear environment. And a strong posi-tive correlation existed between nuclear proliferation and Indo-Pakistani militarized disputes.

My quantitative findings provide us with a more comprehensive view of the relationship between nuclear proliferation and conventional stability in South Asia than exists elsewhere in the literature. Of course, they do not demonstrate that nuclear proliferation accounted for increased conflict in South Asia. That is not their purpose; my argument in this chapter has been purely correlative, not causal. I offer a causal explanation for increased Indo-Pakistani conflict in Chapter 3 and in the book's case studies.

What these quantitative findings do show is that the South Asian region became less stable as the nuclear proliferation process progressed. This challenges the claims of scholars sanguine as to nuclear weapons' effects on the subcontinent. Despite deterrence theorists' argument that nuclear danger induces conventional caution, a clear positive correlation exists between nuclear proliferation and conventional instability in the region. Not only did militarized disputes occur more frequently as proliferation progressed, but militarized disputes also became more serious. Indeed, India and Pakistan fought an outright war just after the 1998 tests, thereby belying the optimist claim that nuclear weapons states do not fight wars. By contrast, these findings appear to support scholars maintaining that nuclear weapons in fact have had destabilizing effects on the subcontinent; their arguments would expect conventional instability to increase as nuclear proliferation progressed. However, as we will see in the next chapter, whether or not these scholars can actually account for this increased instability, and for Pakistan's role in instigating much of it, depends on why the instability actually occurred.

Conclusion

This chapter argued that the international relations literature is both logically and empirically inconclusive regarding nuclear weapons' effects on South Asian security. Strong deductive arguments on both sides of the proliferation debate and piecemeal use of empirical evidence from the region render the literature unable to offer a clear answer to a fundamental question: Has the South Asian security environment become more stable or less so since India and Pakistan acquired a nuclear weapons capability? By systematically analyzing militarized dispute data from the region, this chapter has shown that South Asia has become significantly less stable as the nuclear proliferation process progressed from 1972 through 2002.

This empirical finding challenges the arguments of optimistic scholars claiming that nuclear weapons make South Asia less conflict prone. However, whether or not it supports the arguments of proliferation pessimists depends on *why* South Asia became less stable as proliferation progressed. Our finding of increased Indo-Pakistani disputes would support the pessimist literature if it were the case that organizational, political, or technological pathologies underlie the relationship between progressing nuclear proliferation and growing regional instability. But if the correlation between nuclear proliferation and regional instability did not result from these factors, then our empirical analysis does not support the arguments of the pessimist literature. If this is the case, we must venture beyond the pessimists and devise a new explanation for nuclear proliferation's destabilizing effects on South Asia.

In Chapter 3, I attempt to offer such an explanation. I show that political, technological, and organizational pathologies, while important, do not fully explain the relationship between nuclear proliferation and South Asian conventional instability. Rather, these problems exacerbate a situation in which the incentives for conflict against a nuclear backdrop are already high as a result of India's and Pakistan's territorial preferences and their relative conventional military capabilities. Specifically, its weak, revisionist position within the Indo-Pakistani conflict relationship has encouraged a newly nuclear Pakistan aggressively to challenge the South Asian territorial status quo. Pakistani aggression in turn has provoked forceful Indian action to defeat Pakistani adventurism and to defend existing territorial boundaries. As Chapter 3 demonstrates, this dynamic drove the spiral of conflict that destabilized South Asia during the nuclear proliferation process.

3

Territorial Preferences and Military Capabilities

In Chapter 2, I showed that the South Asian security environment became considerably less stable during the region's nuclear proliferation process. In this chapter, I explain this correlation between nuclear proliferation and militarized disputes. I argue that the acquisition of nuclear weapons can encourage a conventionally weak, revisionist state to challenge the territorial status quo through aggressive conventional behavior. Nuclear weapons create this emboldening effect by insulating a weak aggressor against conventional retaliation by its stronger adversary and by attracting international attention to ongoing territorial disputes. In the South Asian context, I show that because Pakistan was conventionally weaker than India and dissatisfied with territorial boundaries in Kashmir, nuclear weapons encouraged Pakistani leaders to behave aggressively in the region; Pakistan could violently challenge regional boundaries, safe from the danger of full-scale Indian conventional attack, while attracting third-party mediation of the Kashmir conflict. Nuclear danger thus created incentives for conventional aggression in South Asia and drove growing instability during the regional proliferation process. My argument contradicts proliferation optimists' claims that the danger of nuclear conflict will deter lower level disputes among new proliferants. It also differs significantly from the position of proliferation pessimists, who typically attribute proliferation's dangers to organizational, political, and technological pathologies rather than to rational calculations based on states' politico-military environments.

Explaining the Data: Politico–Military Incentives for Conflict

The data that we examined in Chapter 2 indicate that since the acquisition of nuclear weapons, India and Pakistan have behaved more aggressively than they did in a purely conventional military environment; militarized disputes were nearly four times more common after India's and Pakistan's achievement of a nuclear capability than they were when South Asia was nonnuclear, and progressing proliferation was positively correlated with increasing levels of conflict from 1972 through 2002. How could the acquisition of nuclear weapons encourage states to behave more aggressively than they had prior to nuclear proliferation?

As noted earlier, the South Asian security literature is divided on the question of whether nuclear proliferation is, on balance, harmful or beneficial to the regional security environment. Nonetheless, both sides in the debate recognize that conventional conflict has continued in a nuclear South Asia. Scholars are virtually unanimous as to the source of this ongoing violence, attributing it to a phenomenon known as the stability/instability paradox. According to the paradox, strategic stability, meaning a low likelihood that conventional conflict between nuclear powers will escalate to the nuclear level, reduces the danger of launching a conventional war.[1] But in lowering the potential costs of conventional conflict, strategic stability also makes the outbreak of lower level violence between nuclear-armed adversaries more likely.[2]

Is the literature correct in attributing ongoing violence on the subcontinent to the stability/instability paradox? If so, we need look no further than the Cold War deterrence literature for an explanation of increased Indo–Pakistani conventional conflict in a nuclear South Asia. Such a conclusion would have important implications for the regional security environment. Given the dangers of confrontation between nuclear-armed adversaries, policymakers have sought to stabilize the Indo–Pakistani security relationship both at the strategic and at the tactical level, minimizing the danger of nuclear war, while simultaneously reducing the likelihood of conventional violence. For example, the 1999 Lahore Declaration, signed by Indian Prime Minister Atal Behari Vajpayee and Pakistani Prime Minister Nawaz Sharif, stated that India and Pakistan would adopt policies "aimed at the prevention of conflict" in both "the nuclear and conventional fields."[3] And as Indian and Pakistani officials prepared for high-level peace talks in early 2004, they considered the negotiation of "a joint agreement to lower the threat of a nuclear or conventional war" between the two countries.[4] Senior Indian Ministry of External Affairs officials view the promotion of such dual stability as a "major goal" of the peace process, while the Pakistan Foreign Ministry's Director General for South Asian Affairs, Jalil

Jilani, argues that the "[achievement] of stability at both the conventional and strategic levels" is "the ultimate aim" of Indo-Pakistani negotiations.[5]

If the stability/instability paradox is responsible for ongoing South Asian conventional conflict, these attempts to stabilize Indo-Pakistani relations at both the nuclear and the subnuclear level could be futile, or even dangerous, as increased strategic stability allows more low-level violence. By contrast, if ongoing violence in South Asia has not resulted from the stability/instability paradox, then recent conflict would not demonstrate any necessary incompatibility between tactical and strategic stability in the region or suggest that conventional danger inheres in current attempts to minimize the likelihood of nuclear war.

A conclusion that the stability/instability paradox explains ongoing South Asian violence will also have theoretical implications well beyond the region, suggesting that the inverse relationship between strategic and conventional stability that held for the United States and Soviet Union during the Cold War also applies to emerging nuclear conflict dyads.[6] But if we conclude that continuing Indo-Pakistani conflict runs counter to the expectations of the stability/instability paradox, then the relationship between strategic and tactical stability may be quite different for future proliferants than it was for the United States and Soviet Union.

As I demonstrate, the stability/instability paradox does not explain Indo-Pakistani militarized behavior in a nuclear South Asia. Contrary to the expectations of the paradox, a very small probability of lower level conflict escalating to the nuclear threshold has not encouraged aggressive conventional behavior in the region. Rather, ongoing violence has resulted from a significant possibility of subnuclear conflict escalating to the nuclear threshold. Thus, a substantial degree of *instability* at the strategic level has encouraged lower level South Asian violence. I refer to this phenomenon as an "instability/instability paradox."

Why the Stability/Instability Paradox Does Not
Explain Increased South Asian Violence

As noted, scholars are virtually unanimous in their belief that, through the stability/instability paradox, nuclear weapons have created new incentives for low-level violence and thereby driven continued conflict in South Asia. Šumit Ganguly, for example, argues that the 1999 Indo-Pakistani border war at Kargil

> conformed closely to the expectations of the "stability/instability paradox." This
> proposition holds that nuclear weapons do contribute to stability at one level, for fear
> of nuclear escalation. Simultaneously, however, they create incentives for conven-
> tional conflicts in peripheral areas as long as either side does not breach certain shared
> thresholds.[7]

Kenneth Waltz accounts for ongoing South Asian conventional violence by explaining that

> because nuclear weapons limit escalation, they may tempt countries to fight small wars. Glenn Snyder long ago identified the strategic stability/tactical instability paradox . . . The possibility of fighting at low levels is not a bad price to pay for the impossibility of fighting at high levels. This impossibility becomes obvious, since in the presence of nuclear weapons no one can score major gains, and all can lose catastrophically.[8]

According to David J. Karl, through the stability/instability paradox, "the spread of nuclear weapons may actually promote the outbreak of crisis situations;" "the shield of nuclear deterrence is thought to lead states . . . to calculate that it is safe to challenge the status quo through low-level military action." Karl maintains that India's and Pakistan's Kargil border war "is arguably the latest and most virulent expression of the stability–instability paradox in the Indo-Pakistani security rivalry."[9] Feroz Hasan Khan argues that, through the stability/instability paradox, "nuclear weapons may create instability by encouraging one or both sides to engage in 'limited' military adventures against the other, as long as they do not put at risk the vital interests of the target country." Khan maintains that the stability/instability paradox drives continued Indo-Pakistani conventional violence by creating a stable nuclear threshold below which "there is room to continue ongoing hostilities without regard to the new reality of nuclearization."[10] Jeffrey W. Knopf claims that "flare-ups in South Asia since the Indian and Pakistani nuclear tests of 1998 indicate the continued relevance of Glenn Snyder's 'stability–instability paradox,' in which the belief that nuclear deterrence prevents large-scale conventional conflict creates confidence in the safety of engaging in lower intensity conflict."[11] And Lowell Dittmer claims that due to stability/instability logic, "nuclearization of a dyadic, adversarial relationship may . . . create conditions permitting conflict at lower levels." According to Dittmer, "the outbreak of hostilities in the Kargil region of Kashmir barely a year after the conduct of the [Indo-Pakistani nuclear] tests" in fact resulted from the "'stability–instability paradox': i.e., precisely *because* nuclearization is assumed to provide a 'cap' on escalation, . . . [preventing] large-scale war for fear of escalation to the nuclear level, . . . this facilitates the resort to violence."[12]

Despite scholars' agreement as to the stability/instability paradox's destabilizing effects, the literature is unclear as to how the paradox actually causes instability in South Asia. Some scholars suggest that the possibility of lower level conflict spiraling to the nuclear threshold facilitates regional violence under the paradox. For example, Ganguly broadly attributes the stability/instability paradox's effects to a "fear of nuclear escalation."[13] Similarly, Dittmer states that "fear of escalation to the nuclear level . . . facilitates the resort to violence" under the stability/instability paradox.[14] Other scholars, by contrast, claim that the paradox allows lower level violence in South Asia through a *lack* of escalatory potential. Waltz, for example, maintains that under the stability/instability paradox, "The impossibility of fighting at high levels" creates "the possibility of fighting at low levels."[15] Khan claims that, through the stability/instability paradox, nuclear weapons create a stable nuclear threshold below which "there is room to continue ongoing hostilities without regard to the new reality of nuclearization."[16] And Scott Sagan argues that conventionally aggressive behavior turns on the belief that "a stable nuclear balance . . . [permits] more offensive actions to take place with impunity."[17] Still other scholars do not specifically discuss the probability of strategic escalation but instead refer generally to "nuclear deterrence" in explaining the stability/instability paradox's impact on South Asia. For example, Karl argues that "the shield of nuclear deterrence" encourages states to undertake conventional aggressive behavior. Knopf claims that under the stability/instability paradox, "the belief that nuclear deterrence prevents large-scale conventional conflict creates confidence in the safety of engaging in lower intensity conflict."[18] And according to P. R. Chari, "The availability of the nuclear deterrent to Pakistan encouraged its undertaking the Kargil intrusions, while increasing its cross-border terrorism and proxy war in Kashmir."[19]

Despite their agreement as to the stability/instability paradox's effects, then, scholars do not offer a clear explanation of how the paradox has actually destabilized South Asia. This lack of clarity is a problem because to determine whether the stability/instability paradox explains regional violence, we need first to understand how the paradox works. In the following section, I therefore briefly revisit the stability/instability paradox's emergence during the Cold War.[20] I show that the paradox's destabilizing impact arises from a very small probability of subnuclear conflict escalating to the nuclear level, which erodes nuclear weapons' ability to deter conventional violence and thus makes lower level conflict more likely.

Stability/Instability Logic During the Cold War

The problem of nuclear stability potentially facilitating conventional aggression first emerged during the mid-1950s, as America sought to extend nuclear deterrence to its European allies. The United States realized that growing U.S. and Soviet arsenals would make a nuclear conflict between the two states catastrophically destructive. This posed a problem for the conventionally weaker

United States, which sought to deter Soviet conventional aggression against Western Europe with the threat of American nuclear retaliation.[21] As Richard Smoke explains, according to the logic of U.S. policy, "Although the Soviets could not be physically stopped from seizing Europe," they would be prevented from doing so by the knowledge that "their own homeland would be destroyed behind them if they did."[22] The difficulty was that this threat was becoming less credible due to increasing Soviet strategic power. While the United States might resort to nuclear war in defense of its homeland, it was unlikely that the United States would launch a full-fledged nuclear conflict and invite catastrophic destruction on its home territory to protect France or Germany from a Soviet invasion.[23]

Despite American threats, then, a conventional war in Europe was unlikely to escalate to the nuclear level. And therefore, it was possible that the Soviet Union, as the conventionally stronger power,[24] would initiate a conventional conflict in Europe, encouraged by the belief that it could prevail over NATO without triggering a nuclear war.[25] "Were the United States in a position to do little other than resort to all-out war," Robert Jervis explains, "the most obvious danger is that the Soviets would invade Western Europe."[26] Stability/instability logic thus undermined American nuclear deterrence and threatened the United States' ability to defend its West European allies.[27]

The United States dealt with this stability/instability problem by adopting policies at both the tactical and the strategic levels designed to increase the probability that a Soviet conventional attack on Western Europe would result in nuclear war. In the tactical realm, the United States sought to make the uncontrolled escalation of a conventional conflict in Europe to the nuclear level more likely. Because the threat to respond deliberately to Soviet conventional aggression by launching an all-out nuclear war was not believable, the United States threatened to initiate a process of escalation that would begin locally but that could end at the strategic level.[28] Thus, a Soviet attack on Western Europe would automatically trigger an escalatory process and create the risk of a strategic nuclear response from NATO, even without a deliberate American decision to launch a nuclear war.[29]

To this end, the United States introduced conventional ground forces as well as tactical (TNF) and eventually intermediate-range (INF) nuclear weapons to the Continent. These assets would, of course, enhance NATO's ability to defend Europe in the event of a Soviet attack.[30] However, the purpose of stationing American forces in Europe was not simply to defend against the Soviet military but also to ensure that the Soviet Union understood that the United States would be automatically involved in the event of any aggression against

Western Europe. The logic, as Thomas Schelling put it, was that "whether we wished to be or not, we could not fail to be involved if we had more troops being run over by the Soviet Army than we could afford to see defeated." The mission of American ground forces in this regard was to "die heroically, dramatically, in a manner that guarantees that the action cannot stop there."[31] American conventional ground forces thus would act primarily as a trip wire to trigger nuclear escalation rather than simply as a means of defending Western Europe.[32]

Like conventional ground forces, the deployment of American nuclear weapons to Europe could improve NATO's ability to thwart a Soviet conventional attack.[33] Beyond such a denial role, however, tactical nuclear weapons were intended to demonstrate an American commitment to Europe by automatically involving U.S. nuclear forces in any conflict that took place. In case of war with the Warsaw Pact, American nuclear weapons in Europe would either get attacked by invading forces or be used.[34] As Jervis explains, "In either event the American strategic force would be triggered; the Russians, understanding this, would have to choose between starting World War III or leaving Europe alone."[35]

At the strategic level, the United States built into its force structure and doctrine measures to make the deliberate American use of nuclear weapons more likely. For example, the United States adopted limited nuclear options (LNOs), under which the United States would attack restricted Soviet target sets, leaving other targets that the Soviets valued unscathed and hostage to future American strikes. The threat to employ LNOs was deemed more credible than threats to launch all-out nuclear attacks against the Soviet Union because LNOs, by sparing a range of enemy targets, created Soviet incentives not to respond to a U.S. attack with a full-scale retaliatory strike. The United States could therefore expect a relatively restrained Soviet response to limited American nuclear attacks, and Soviet decision makers would be likely to believe U.S. threats to launch such limited strikes in the event of a conventional European war.[36]

In addition to LNOs, the United States sought to make its nuclear threats more credible through counterforce, which would destroy enemy nuclear assets rather than civilian targets. Counterforce could be used to enhance the U.S. limited nuclear options just discussed. Since counterforce would strike Soviet nuclear weapons while sparing civilian targets, it could provide the United States with a means of attacking a restricted target set and thereby avoiding all-out Soviet retaliation.[37] Additionally, counterforce could increase the likelihood of American use of nuclear weapons by creating incentives for a U.S. preemptive attack during a crisis. By striking first with counterforce and destroying a significant number of Soviet nuclear weapons, the United States could in theory limit damage to itself by reducing the Soviets' retaliatory capability.[38] Thus, as Schelling put it, while limited nuclear options sought to provide the enemy with an "incentive not to shoot us even if he has the weapons to do it," counterforce involved "the destruction of enemy weapons so that [the enemy] cannot shoot us even if he wants to."[39] Despite this difference, both LNOs and counterforce served the same strategic purpose: making the deliberate American use of nuclear weapons more likely by reducing the probability of an all-out Soviet counterattack.

The United States thus responded to the dangers of strategic stability during the Cold War at both the tactical and the strategic levels. In the tactical realm, the United States took steps to ensure that a conventional war would create the danger of conflict spiraling out of control to the nuclear level. In the strategic realm, the United States adopted policies under which it would remain fully in control of its actions and employ nuclear weapons in a limited fashion in response to Soviet conventional aggression.[40] Both approaches increased the likelihood that the United States would use nuclear weapons in the event of a conventional war in Europe. And this increased likelihood of nuclear use enhanced America's ability to extend deterrence to its European allies; the greater the likelihood of an American nuclear response to a Warsaw Pact attack, the less confident the Pact could be in its ability to prevail over NATO in a purely conventional contest. Now any conflict in Europe was more likely to trigger the use of strategic nuclear weapons. And this fact in turn reduced the likelihood that the Soviet Union would engage in conventional aggression against Western Europe.

This brief examination of the Cold War case helps to clarify how the stability/instability paradox actually operates: A very small probability of subnuclear conflict spiraling to the nuclear threshold facilitates conventional violence under the stability/instability paradox. The unlikelihood of nuclear escalation reduces nuclear weapons' ability to deter conventional conflict, thereby making low-level aggression more likely. This is why the United States adopted tactical and strategic measures designed to increase the likelihood of nuclear escalation during the Cold War. A high probability of conventional conflict reaching the nuclear level would make conventional conflict more dangerous, thereby reducing the likelihood of Soviet aggression.

This fact has a crucial implication for our assessment of the stability/instability paradox's impact on the South Asian security environment: The stability/instability paradox cannot logically explain the region's increase in conventional violence since India and Pakistan acquired nuclear weapons. As we have seen, under the stability/instability paradox, a *decrease* in the likelihood of nuclear conflict would result in an increased probability of low-level violence. However, the proliferation of nuclear weapons to South Asia could not have made nuclear conflict in the region *less* likely. On the contrary, India's and Pakistan's acquisition of nuclear weapons necessarily *increased* the likelihood of Indo-Pakistani nuclear war.[41] Thus, South Asia has experienced an increase in conventional violence even as the probability of nuclear conflict in the region has risen. This runs directly counter to the logic of the stability/instability paradox.

Indo-Pakistani military behavior in a nuclear South Asia thus appears to contradict an important aspect of our experience in the Cold War and the nuclear logic that we derived from it. How could such an outcome be possible? I argue that Indo-Pakistani behavior diverges from Cold War deterrence logic because the South Asian security environment is fundamentally different from that of Cold War Europe. During the Cold War, a low likelihood of nuclear escalation threatened to facilitate Soviet aggression because the Soviets, the potentially revisionist power in Cold War Europe, were conventionally stronger than NATO.[42] Since American nuclear escalation was very unlikely, the conventionally strong Soviet Union could potentially have defeated NATO and seized West European territory with little fear of triggering a nuclear conflict. If the Soviet Union had been conventionally weak relative to NATO, it would have been unlikely to prevail over the alliance in a strictly conventional conflict, and a low likelihood of nuclear escalation would not have encouraged aggressive Soviet behavior.[43]

These conditions, through which the stability/instability paradox facilitated conventional violence during the Cold War, do not apply to contemporary South Asia. Pakistan, the revisionist state in the Indo-Pakistani conflict dyad, is conventionally weak relative to India. Therefore, a high degree of strategic stability, by undermining Pakistani nuclear weapons' conventionally deterrent effects, would reduce Pakistan's insulation from Indian conventional strength. This would make aggression extremely dangerous for Pakistan; India could crush any Pakistani adventurism with a full-scale conventional response, confident that the ensuing conflict was unlikely to escalate to the nuclear level.

Strategic conditions very different from those that threatened to destabilize the Cold War in fact allow ongoing violence in a nuclear South Asia. Specifically, instability in the strategic realm encourages conflict at the conventional level. It does so in the following manner: In the South Asian security environment, limited Indo-Pakistani conventional conflict is unlikely to provoke an immediate nuclear confrontation. However, in the event that a limited conventional confrontation subsequently spirals into a full-scale conventional conflict, escalation to the nuclear level becomes a serious possibility. This danger of nuclear escalation allows weak, revisionist Pakistan to undertake limited conventional aggression against India in hopes of altering regional boundaries without provoking a full-scale Indian conventional response. In addition, nuclear danger draws international attention, potentially securing for weaker Pakistan third-party mediation of its territorial dispute with India and a diplomatic settlement superior to any that Pakistan could achieve on its own.

Thus, contrary to Cold War stability/instability logic, the outbreak of lower level violence in South Asia has required the existence of a substantial degree of strategic *instability*.[44] The phenomenon facilitating conventional conflict in the region thus might better be characterized as an "instability/instability paradox." Ironically, the characteristic of the regional strategic environment that Cold War logic predicts should impede subnuclear conflict has actually facilitated ongoing violence.[45] To understand better how this phenomenon actually works in South Asia, let us now closely examine the impact that territorial preferences and relative conventional capabilities have on a new nuclear state's incentives for conventional aggression.

Territorial Preferences and Military Capabilities

Under what conditions would a new nuclear state be encouraged to undertake aggressive conventional behavior? First, a state would need to have a reason to behave aggressively. Its leaders would have to be dissatisfied with the territorial status quo and anxious to change it. If a state's leadership were satisfied with the status quo, they would have little reason to behave aggressively, with or without nuclear weapons.[46] Second, a state's leaders would need to believe that the acquisition of nuclear weapons had altered the state's military relationship with its primary adversary, enabling the state potentially to change the status quo where it previously could not. Such a state would be conventionally weak relative to its adversary. If it were conventionally strong, the state would not need nuclear weapons to enable it to alter the status quo; it could have used its superior conventional forces to change the status quo even without nuclear weapons. Nuclear proliferation would likely create incentives for aggression, then, in the case of conventionally weak proliferants anxious to revise existing territorial boundaries. Let us now more closely examine the behavioral incentives for weak, revisionist proliferants to better understand why this is the case.

Military Incentives

In a purely conventional world, a weak, revisionist state would be unlikely to engage in aggressive behavior. Despite its desire to change the status quo, any attempt to do so would likely result in failure at best and risk all-out defeat at worst. Nuclear weapons, however, change the military relationship between a weak state and its stronger adversary, altering the weak state's behavioral incentives. Nuclear weapons do this not by increasing the weak state's military capabilities relative to its adversary but rather by potentially reducing the stronger state's willingness to employ its full military might against its weaker enemy. This circumspection on the part of the stronger state results from the dangers of attacking a nuclear-armed adversary. The weaker state might respond to a conventional attack with escalation to the nuclear level, particularly if it starts to lose badly and believes that its territorial integrity is at stake.

Even if it is unlikely that either side would wish to use nuclear weapons, the dangers of a conventional conflict spiraling to the nuclear threshold are significant due to the possibility of inadvertent escalation. War between nuclear powers can escalate from the conventional to the nuclear level even if neither side desires such an outcome. As Barry Posen argues, "large-scale conventional operations may come into direct contact with the nuclear forces of an adversary and substantially affect the victim's confidence in his future ability to operate these forces in ways that he had counted upon." The victim could view such operations as a major threat and respond with policies ranging from "heightened preparations for nuclear operations, including loosening of central civilian control . . . and dissemination of launch authority to military commanders" to "responses that actually employed nuclear weapons, ranging from limited demonstrative or tactical employment, through large-scale theater attacks, to full-scale counterforce exchanges." Significantly, this problem will be especially acute for small and medium-sized powers because they will face the greatest challenges in building survivable nuclear forces.[47]

In the Indo-Pakistani context, Pakistan's "fear of having [its] small nuclear arsenal destroyed" by an Indian first strike could lead it to "delegate launch authority to military leaders in the field" during a crisis. A subsequent "conventional Indian attack that severed Pakistani command and control might lead a Pakistani military officer to launch a nuclear attack on his own."[48] According to India's former director general of military operations, this danger is especially acute given "inadequate warning capabilities, first-generation command and control arrangements, [and] exclusive military control over nuclear weapons in Pakistan," all of which "combine to raise the risks of inadvertent . . .

nuclear war" in South Asia.[49] Conventional war between nuclear powers such as India and Pakistan thus creates a significant risk of nuclear conflict even if neither side enters into a conventional conflict expecting to use nuclear weapons. This risk of nuclear confrontation can embolden a weak state to behave aggressively at the subnuclear level by reducing the likelihood of robust conventional retaliation by its stronger adversary.

This is not to argue that nuclear proliferation makes conventional aggression by a weak state cost-free. A strong state can retaliate conventionally against a weak aggressor despite the weak state's nuclear weapons. Indeed, as I will demonstrate later, powerful states will have considerable incentives to do just this to defeat weak states' attempts to alter the status quo and to demonstrate more broadly that the powerful states are unmoved by weak states' nuclear threats. The point is simply that nuclear weapons may prevent weak states from having to pay the full preproliferation price for aggression because strong states may be deterred from launching an all-out retaliation and will probably seek to avoid threatening weak states' existence. Thus, a weak state can engage in adventurism secure in the knowledge that, even if its operations go wrong, it will probably not face the danger of catastrophic defeat at the hands of its stronger adversary.

Pakistani behavior in Kashmir since the late 1980s illustrates this argument. Pakistan's emerging nuclear capacity was crucial to the Pakistani government's decision in about 1989 to undertake an extensive program of support for the anti-Indian insurgency that had erupted in Jammu and Kashmir. Pakistani leaders believed that their budding nuclear capability would prevent India from launching a full-scale conventional attack on Pakistan in retaliation for this policy. Extensive Pakistani involvement in the insurgency continued through the 1990s without any large-scale Indian response. Later, the 1999 Indo-Pakistani conflict at Kargil demonstrated Pakistani leaders' faith in nuclear weapons' insulating effects even more dramatically. After the 1998 Indo-Pakistani nuclear tests, Pakistani leaders believed that their overt nuclear capacity would provide them with more robust deterrence than their earlier undeclared capability had done. Encouraged by this belief, they deployed Pakistani forces across the Line of Control, seizing territory that enabled them to threaten vital Indian lines of communication to northern Kashmir. As we will see, India did fight back against the Pakistani intrusion at Kargil, and the international community condemned Pakistan, which was ultimately forced to vacate the region. Nonetheless, the Indian government ruled out the possibility of all-out conventional retaliation during the Kargil conflict, abandoning its longstanding policy of responding to Pakistani aggression in Kashmir with full-scale horizontal escalation. Such escalation could have resulted in catastrophic defeat for the Pakistanis. Indian refusal to consider all-out conventional escalation was due largely to the potential dangers of provoking a nuclear-armed Pakistan. Thus, while nuclear weapons did not make Pakistani action successful or cost-free, it did significantly reduce the price of aggression; Pakistan almost certainly paid less dearly for its adventure than it would have prior to acquiring nuclear weapons.

Diplomatic Incentives

Nuclear proliferation also creates diplomatic incentives for weak, revisionist states to engage in conventionally aggressive behavior. In purely bilateral negotiations with their stronger adversaries, weak states are unlikely to achieve their territorial aims. However, by bringing outside parties into the negotiating process, weak states can mitigate the bilateral power imbalance and reduce their stronger adversary's diplomatic advantage. This can help weak states to achieve a more favorable settlement of key territorial disputes than they could have secured on their own. Weak proliferants can bring third parties into the diplomatic process by starting a conventional conflict with their nuclear-armed adversary, thereby creating the possibility of a nuclear crisis. Anxious to resolve a dispute between nuclear powers that could ultimately result in catastrophe, outside states are likely to help negotiate an end to the conflict— something that they might not do if the belligerents did not possess nuclear weapons.

Evidence from several South Asian militarized disputes illustrates this point. When conflict on the subcontinent has been purely conventional, outside powers have shown relatively little interest in its outcome. During the 1965 Indo-Pakistani War, for example, the United States pressured India to stop the fighting, but it displayed little interest in the nature of the war's settlement or in its relations with India or Pakistan after the conflict. During the 1971 Bangladesh War, the United States made only a minimal effort to signal support for its Pakistani ally by sending a carrier group into the Bay of Bengal and largely ignored the subcontinent in the conflict's aftermath.[50]

However, third parties have been deeply interested in preventing a nuclear exchange in South Asia and have been willing to mediate to avoid one. In 1990, for example, a militarized Indo-Pakistani crisis over Kashmir resulted in high-level diplomatic intervention by the Bush administration, despite the fact that neither India nor Pakistan yet openly possessed nuclear weapons and that no shots were actually fired during the standoff. In the view of three former Pakistani officials, "So grave was the concern that the United States

President sent Robert Gates as his personal emissary to Pakistan and India on a successful mission of preventive diplomacy."[51] And during the Kargil conflict, the Clinton administration became directly involved in negotiations to end the crisis. The administration ultimately brokered a cease-fire agreement whereby Pakistani forces withdrew from the Line of Control, and Clinton promised to take a personal interest in promoting ongoing efforts to resolve the Kashmir conflict. Drawing international attention to the Kashmir dispute was a key goal in Pakistani leaders' original decision to undertake the Kargil incursions. Thus, by launching a conventional conflict, Pakistan has been able to increase the likelihood of outside diplomatic intervention in the Kashmir dispute, which could result in a territorial settlement superior to anything that Pakistan could achieve on its own.[52]

The acquisition of nuclear weapons, then, could encourage a weak, revisionist state to engage in conventional aggression for two distinct reasons. First, conventional military action could forcefully change existing borders while the weak state's nuclear capacity deters full-scale conventional retaliation by its stronger adversary. Second, conventional military action could create a high-visibility international crisis, in which the danger of nuclear escalation draws outside diplomatic intervention and results in a territorial settlement more favorable to the weak state than the weak state could otherwise have secured.

Conventional Aggression and Nuclear Brinksmanship

For a state to further its territorial goals by deliberately creating the danger of nuclear conflict is risky behavior. Nonetheless, the international relations literature has long recognized that such nuclear brinksmanship can serve as an effective means of coercion. A coercing state generates and shares nuclear risk, giving its adversary the choice as to whether to comply with its demands and avoid further escalation of the danger or whether to ignore its threats, increase the danger, and court disaster. The coercing state does not actually threaten to take catastrophically costly action if its adversary fails to comply. Rather, the coercing state threatens to begin, continue, or escalate behavior that creates the possibility that catastrophe could occur for reasons beyond its control. As Thomas Schelling explains, "One can incur a moderate probability of disaster, sharing it with his adversary, as a deterrent or compellent device, where one could not take, or persuasively threaten to take, a deliberate last step into disaster."[53]

A state employing such a coercive strategy can generate nuclear risk by behaving in a manner that creates the possibility of large-scale conventional war. Such war would not automatically result in nuclear conflict, but rather would initiate a process of confrontation that could escalate to the nuclear level, "through a compounding of actions and reactions, of calculations and miscalculations, of alarms and false alarms, of commitments and challenges."[54] The coercing state would threaten to engage in such risky behavior unless its adversary acceded to its demands. Thus, the coercer would leave its adversary with the choice as to whether to comply and defuse the situation or ignore the threat, thereby launching both parties down a road that begins with conventional war and potentially could end in disaster. By giving the adversary the "last clear chance" to avoid an unpredictable and possibly catastrophic conflict, the state may be able to convince its adversary to meet its demands. As Schelling argues, "It is our sheer inability to predict the consequences of our actions and to keep things under control, and the enemy's similar inability, that can intimidate the enemy" and achieve the desired result.[55]

This logic can encourage a weak, revisionist state to undertake conventional aggression in the wake of nuclear proliferation. Conventionally aggressive behavior generates risk, creating the danger of a full-fledged conventional war, which could escalate to the nuclear level. A weak, revisionist state can use this danger for both deterrent and compellent purposes.[56] In either case, whether or not a full-fledged war actually erupts depends not on the weak, revisionist state but rather on the parties that the weak state is attempting to coerce. In a deterrent scenario, if its adversary acquiesces in the weak state's aggression, conventional war will not occur, and nuclear danger will recede. If, however, the adversary retaliates and tries to undo the weak state's aggression, war will likely occur, setting in motion a train of events that are impossible to predict and that could well end in nuclear confrontation. Thus, the weak, revisionist state, through its aggressive behavior, gives its adversary the last clear chance to avoid conventional war, along with such a conflict's unpredictable, potentially disastrous consequences, and thereby deters the adversary from launching a full-scale retaliation in response to the weak state's aggression.

In a compellent scenario, a weak, revisionist power would behave aggressively and then use the danger of conventional conflict escalating to nuclear war to force its adversary, along with other, third-party states, to alter their behavior in ways that further the weak state's territorial ambitions. For example, the weak state can use the threat of full-scale conventional war erupting against a nuclear backdrop to convince its adversary to quit a particular territory that the weak state desires. The weak state can use the same danger to convince third parties to intervene diplomatically in a crisis, thereby offsetting the strong state's diplomatic leverage and enabling the weak state to achieve a more favorable territorial settlement than it otherwise could have. As with deterrence, in a compellent scenario, the weak state gives other parties the last clear chance to avoid disaster by doing the weak state's bidding and putting a stop to its risky behavior.

Nuclear proliferation thus can create powerful military and diplomatic incentives for weak, revisionist states to engage in conventionally aggressive behavior from behind a nuclear shield. What impact would such behavior likely have on a weak state's stronger adversaries? As noted, the acquisition of nuclear weapons itself would not create incentives for strong-state aggression; a nuclear capacity would not enable a conventionally strong state to take military action against its weaker adversary that it could not have taken prior to proliferation if it had so desired. However, weak-state brinksmanship is likely to encourage strong states to respond with forceful policies of their own. This is the case for two reasons. First, strong states will seek to reverse any actual conventional aggression that weak states have undertaken and to increase the conventional costs of the weak states' aggressive behavior. Second, strong states will seek to demonstrate that they are not cowed by weak states' nuclear threats, both to prevail in the current confrontation and to inoculate themselves against further nuclear coercion in the future. To accomplish these goals, strong states will likely seek to respond as forcefully as possible to weak states' provocations without actually crossing the weak states' nuclear thresholds. This will require strong states to engage in brinksmanship of their own, retaliating against weak states up to the edge of nuclear confrontation to make the actual and potential costs of conventional aggression too high for their weaker adversaries. Although such forceful behavior promises to enable strong states to counter weak states' brinksmanship strategies, it also feeds the ongoing cycle of violence and pushes both sides closer to potential disaster.

What are the implications of this logic for the security environment in South Asia? To answer this question, we must determine India's and Pakistan's territorial preferences and relative military capabilities. As I explain in the following section, in the Indo-Pakistani conflict relationship, Pakistan is both weak and revisionist; Pakistan is conventionally outmatched by India and is dissatisfied regarding the current division of Kashmir, the two countries' key territorial dispute. India, by contrast, is strong and status quo, far outstripping Pakistan's conventional military capabilities and wishing to maintain current territorial boundaries in Kashmir. Let us now carefully examine the two countries' territorial preferences and conventional military capabilities to see how this is so.

Territorial Preferences and Military Capabilities in South Asia

Pakistan, India, and the Status Quo

For much of the period since independence, "Indo-Pakistani relations . . . have been dominated by the dispute over Kashmir."[57] The two countries fought a war for control of the territory in 1947–1948, which left approximately one-third of the region under Pakistani rule (Azad Kashmir and the Northern Areas) and two-thirds under the control of India (Jammu and Kashmir). Since then, the region has been the site of one full-fledged Indo-Pakistani War (1965) and, beginning in the late 1980s, an ongoing Pakistan-supported insurgency against Indian Kashmir.[58] Thus, Kashmir has been a "dominant force in shaping the foreign policies of both India and Pakistan; and there can be no doubt that it has infected every aspect of the internal political life of the two nations . . ."[59]

In the Indian view, the territory has been an integral part of the Indian Union since the maharajah of Kashmir signed an instrument of accession and joined India in 1947. The Indian government believes that Pakistani support for the Kashmir insurgency and Pakistan's cross-border incursions at Kargil are simply the latest in a long list of Pakistani attempts to take this vital territory by force. The Pakistan government, for its part, believes that Kashmir's accession to India was illegal and undemocratic. Further, the Pakistanis argue that India's refusal to hold a plebiscite on the question of accession denies the Kashmiri people their right to self-determination.[60] Support for the insurgency, and the ultimate goal of "liberating" Indian Kashmir, is a central national project,[61] and the Kashmir dispute, in the Pakistan government's view, constitutes the "core issue" in Indo-Pakistani relations.[62]

Why is Kashmir so important to India and Pakistan? The fate of the region matters deeply to both countries for strategic and symbolic reasons. At the strategic level, Kashmir contains the headwaters of several rivers important to both sides, including the Indus and the five rivers of the Punjab. Beyond this, the Indians believe that foreign control of Kashmir's mountains would open the plains of Punjab, Haryana, and potentially, Delhi to attack. The Pakistanis, for their part, fear that Islamabad's proximity to Kashmir would leave the capital vulnerable to assault by a hostile power in the region. Pakistani leaders also believe that the incorporation of Kashmir's territory would give their country badly needed strategic depth. Finally, Kashmir borders directly on China and Afghanistan, two states of considerable strategic importance to both India and Pakistan.[63]

At the symbolic level, the Kashmir dispute directly engages India's and Pakistan's fundamental conceptions of statehood. Pakistan was created out of the perceived need for a religiously based home for South Asian Muslims. India, by contrast, was conceived as a heterogeneous democracy, capable of serving as a homeland to the full spectrum of South Asia's religious and ethnic groups. The disposition of Muslim-majority Kashmir thus has profound implications for both India and Pakistan.[64] If Pakistan were to cede the region to India, it would suggest that South Asian Muslims do not need a religiously based homeland and could in fact live in a secular, polyglot state—and thereby call into question Pakistan's very reason for existence. If, on the other hand, India were to cede Kashmir to Pakistan, it would suggest that a religious or ethnic minority cannot live within a heterogeneous South Asian democracy and that statehood should in fact be a function of religion or ethnicity—a dangerous suggestion for a state as diverse as India.[65] Thus, at both the strategic and symbolic levels, India and Pakistan view possession of Kashmir as essential to their very survival, and neither side can relinquish the territory.

Despite these similarities of motivation regarding Kashmir, there is an important difference between Indian and Pakistani goals in the region. India is essentially a status quo power vis-à-vis Kashmir. Following the 1972 Simla Agreement, the Indian government began to view the LoC as a permanent international border. The Indians thus seek to maintain and legitimize the Line of Control.[66] Although India has large numbers of security forces in Kashmir and is waging a low-intensity conflict in the region, it is fighting an essentially defensive, counterinsurgency battle to solidify the LoC and maintain the territory in its possession. Its leaders are largely satisfied with territorial boundaries as they currently stand and have made clear that they would be willing to convert the LoC into a permanent international border.[67]

Pakistan, by contrast, is highly revisionist with regard to Kashmir. The Pakistanis do not believe that the Simla Agreement's creation of the Line of Control produced a permanent international border. Pakistani leaders thus do not accept the Line of Control and seek to delegitimize and alter it by wresting territory from Indian Kashmir. They fear that India will be able to use its military superiority to force Pakistan to accept conversion of the LoC into an international boundary. Pakistani leaders are determined to avoid such an outcome, even if doing so requires them to resort to violence.[68]

This is in no way to argue that India's position on Kashmir is more just than that of Pakistan or that India has not behaved aggressively in the region. Indeed, the Kashmir insurgency erupted during the late 1980s in reaction to decades of

Indian misrule in the region, which included the arrest of popularly elected officials, the rigging of elections, and a steady erosion of Kashmir's autonomous status within the Indian Union. India has been widely condemned for systematic human rights abuses against the Kashmiri population in its efforts to quell the rebellion.[69] India has also proven willing to seize contested territory in Kashmir, such as Siachen Glacier, long after the Simla Agreement and establishment of the Line of Control—though the capture of Siachen did not technically violate the LoC.[70] My point here is only that, right or wrong, Indian policy in the region has been motivated primarily by a desire to retain the Kashmiri territory on the Indian side of the Line of Control rather than to take territory in Pakistani Kashmir. The Indians therefore seek to maintain, rather than to undermine, the LoC and the current territorial division of the region. Pakistani policy, by contrast, has been motivated by a desire to undo the existing division of Kashmir. Right or wrong, Pakistani leaders believe that the LoC is unjust and view its existence as the problem that continues to drive the Kashmir dispute rather than as a potential solution to the conflict. Thus, my labeling of India as a status quo power and Pakistan as revisionist regarding the current territorial division of Kashmir is not based on any normative judgment regarding Indian or Pakistani policy. Rather, these labels are empirical in nature and reflect the clear preferences of the Indian and Pakistani governments.

Pakistan and the Conventional Balance

Pakistan is conventionally weaker than India. Prior to acquiring a nuclear weapons capacity, it had fought three wars with India, in 1948, 1965, and 1971. It achieved a stalemate in two of them (1948 and 1965) and lost one (1971).[71] Pakistan's 1971 defeat was devastating and demonstrative of India's overwhelming conventional superiority; India cut its adversary in two, creating Bangladesh out of the former East Pakistan, taking 93,000 prisoners of war, and capturing approximately 5,000 square kilometers of Pakistani territory in southern Punjab and Sindh before declaring a unilateral cease-fire.[72]

Since then, the conventional balance has continued to favor India. In 2001, India's $15.6 billion defense budget was nearly five times that of Pakistan.[73] In 2002, the Indian armed forces consisted of 1,173,000 active-duty service members and 840,000 reservists compared to Pakistan's 550,000 active and 513,000 reservists.[74] The Indian Air Force possessed thirty squadrons of ground-attack aircraft and nine fighter squadrons for a total of over 700 combat aircraft, against Pakistan's six ground-attack and twelve fighter squadrons totaling approximately 360 combat aircraft. In addition, the Indian Army fielded approximately 3,900 main battle tanks and 1,660 armored infantry fighting vehicles and armored personnel carriers versus Pakistan's 2,300 main battle tanks and 1,200 armored personnel carriers.[75] Economic and demographic indicators favor India as well. Indian GDP in 2001 was $471 billion, as opposed to $62.8 billion for Pakistan, and India's population was more than 1 billion, against Pakistan's approximately 160 million.[76] Finally, Pakistan suffers from a serious geographical handicap. The country lacks strategic depth, and several important cities such as Lahore are located within 100 miles of the Indo-Pakistani border. Thus, "Pakistan is very vulnerable to a major Indian attack using conventional forces."[77]

This conventional weakness, though significant, would not allow an easy Indian victory in the event of conflict. Despite overall Indian numerical superiority, rough military parity prevails in the vicinity of the Indo–Pakistan border, with dispersed peacetime deployment patterns limiting India's ability to bring its forces to bear on Pakistan.[78] In fact, in the short term, Pakistan may be able to field a slightly larger force in the border region than the Indians.[79] Pakistani defenses are thus sufficiently robust to ensure that any Indian offensive, even if ultimately successful, would be slow and costly. Additionally, conventional deterrence is a major component of Pakistan's strategic doctrine and a "dominant theme of [its] defense planners."[80] Under their strategy of "offensive defense," Pakistani forces would seek to "hold and defeat Indian offensives and to go on the offensive as soon as possible in selected corridors," thereby ensuring that "the war would be fought on the Indian soil."[81] The goal, former Chief of Army Staff Mirza Aslam Beg writes, is that "even in an environment where they may be outnumbered, these perceived capabilities of our armed forces, serve as a deterrence, and strikes fear into the hearts and minds of our enemies . . . "[82] As President Pervez Musharraf puts it, "However many of us they kill," this policy of "strategic defense through tactical offense" will enable Pakistan to "kill enough [Indians] to make their losses unacceptable."[83] Pakistani attacks on Indian territory would likely be directed at the area between Poonch and Pathankot in an attempt to sever India's road links with Kashmir. In addition, Pakistan could launch diversionary offensives to the south in Rajasthan and the Punjab.[84] Given these factors, Indian victory in a full-scale conventional war against Pakistan would require a period of months rather than weeks. And as one analyst has argued, because a long war "threatens to be incredibly costly and could result in a painful campaign of attrition, India is unlikely to pursue one so long as it represents the only feasible avenue of pursuing objectives of unlimited aims."[85]

Pakistan's ability to deny India a quick victory significantly reduces the likelihood of an Indian attack, but it does not completely insulate Pakistan from such a possibility. Where a potential attacker's offensive motivations are very strong, conventional deterrence may fail despite the prospect of a protracted conflict.[86] Indian decision makers could well be so motivated in the event of significant Pakistani aggression in Kashmir. Indian strategy has traditionally been to escalate horizontally, and thereby to threaten Pakistan with all-out conflict, in the event of hostilities in the region. As Indian Prime Minister Jawaharlal Nehru said in 1952, if Pakistan "by mistake invades Kashmir, we will not only meet them in Kashmir, but it will be a full-scale war between India and Pakistan."[87] In 1965, India made good on this threat, attacking across the international border in Punjab in response to Pakistani aggression in Kashmir. Although the advance ultimately bogged down in a stalemate, Indian forces drove deep into Pakistani territory, moving simultaneously toward Lahore and Sialkot and forcing Pakistan to withdraw from Akhnur.[88]

If India were to repeat this escalatory policy, the results could be devastating despite Pakistani defensive capabilities. By roughly six weeks into a crisis, India would be able to deploy approximately twenty-eight divisions plus further independent brigades to the theater versus Pakistan's twenty-one divisions plus considerably fewer additional independent brigades.[89] Although these ratios are not overwhelming, they would be sufficient for India to begin driving armor and mechanized infantry into southern Pakistani Punjab, while simultaneously fighting holding actions to fix Pakistani forces in northern Punjab and Kashmir. The Indians could also launch deep penetration attacks from Rajasthan toward Rahimyar Khan and the Indus River, Suleimanki or Bahawalpur, and Sukkur or Hyderabad. Over a period of months, such offensives would not simply enable India to inflict serious losses on Pakistan; they could well lead to decisive victory in which India destroyed vital Pakistani military assets (including electric power grids, petroleum, oil, and lubricant facilities, communications networks, transportation systems, air bases, marshaling yards, and staging areas), cut crucial lines of communication between Karachi and Rawalpindi, Gujrat, Lahore, and Kasur, and captured key territory in Kashmir and within Pakistan itself, including the area of West Punjab in which Lahore is located.[90] According to one detailed analysis, India's advantage in such a scenario would be sufficiently great that, even if Pakistan attempted to blunt the Indian attack with tactical *nuclear* weapons, "At the very least, India could simply prolong the war, mobilize to amass the requisite force superiority over time, and destroy the flower of Pakistan's military capabilities, perhaps irrevocably."[91] Thus, despite its extensive military capabilities, Pakistan suffers from a significant degree of conventional insecurity in relation to India.

Pakistan, then, has been conventionally weak and revisionist regarding the territorial division of Kashmir since independence. India, by contrast, has been militarily strong and territorially status quo. If our earlier analysis is correct, Pakistan may therefore have become emboldened by nuclear weapons, engaging in more belligerent behavior as its nuclear capacity increased in the hope of altering key territorial boundaries and attracting third-party mediation of its dispute with India.[92] India, by contrast, should not have been directly encouraged by nuclear weapons substantially to alter its behavior—though India may have adopted increasingly forceful policies in response to Pakistani provocations.

As noted earlier, the South Asian militarized international dispute data support this analysis. Indo-Pakistani conflict became more frequent and increased in severity as the nuclear proliferation process progressed through the non-nuclear, de facto, and overt nuclear time periods. And in the vast majority of the cases, Pakistan was responsible for instigating the violence. In the case studies that follow, I show that Indo-Pakistani territorial preferences and relative military capabilities were in fact responsible for this outcome. In the wake of its 1971 defeat, Pakistani leaders did not accept the territorial status quo in Kashmir as enunciated by the Simla Agreement[93] but at the time could do nothing to change it; the Pakistanis' attempts to wrest Kashmir from India had failed in 1948 and 1965, and they had suffered a crushing loss in the Bangladesh War. Thus, from 1972 through the late 1980s, Pakistan largely refrained from confrontation with India, with its government focusing instead on relations with the Arab world and domestic political concerns in the wake of the country's vivisection and regime change.[94] Indian leaders, for their part, were satisfied with the territorial status quo as enunciated in the Simla Agreement and wished to maintain it. Thus, the first period of time covered in this study was relatively peaceful.

By the late 1980s, India and Pakistan had become de facto nuclear powers. Although neither country possessed an open nuclear capability, both could probably have assembled a nuclear weapon in short order. This growing nuclear capacity, by insulating Pakistan from the danger of Indian retaliation, encouraged the Pakistan government to begin providing extensive support to the anti-Indian insurgency erupting in Jammu and Kashmir. Pakistani support for the Kashmir insurgency in turn led to a spiral of Indo-Pakistani troop deployments and belligerent rhetoric, culminating in a major militarized standoff in 1990. Thus, thanks in large part to progressing nuclear proliferation on the subcontinent, the second time period covered in this study was considerably less stable than the first.

The Indo-Pakistani relationship became still more conflictual after India and Pakistan acquired an overt nuclear capability in 1998. Overt nuclearization convinced Pakistani leaders that they enjoyed even greater insulation against a conventional Indian attack than their earlier de facto nuclear capability had afforded them. As a result, they were encouraged to adopt policies bolder than they had hitherto pursued in Kashmir. Pakistani leaders acted on these beliefs at Kargil, ordering Pakistan Army forces across the Line of Control and launching the first Indo-Pakistani war in twenty-eight years—secure in the belief that, as Nawaz Sharif put it, Pakistan's overt acquisition of nuclear weapons made the country "militarily impregnable"[95] and that conventional conflict against a nuclear backdrop "would draw the attention of the international community towards the Kashmir issue"[96] by "practically [proving] our stand that the Kashmir issue is a nuclear flashpoint."[97]

The argument that I have formulated in this chapter has important implications. First, it explains our finding of increased violence in a nuclear South Asia without relying on assumptions of irrationality or other pathologies in Indo-Pakistani decision making. Given the nature of the South Asian strategic environment, the acquisition of nuclear weapons creates incentives even for wholly rational decision makers to adopt conventionally aggressive policies. Second and more generally, my argument questions our fundamental assumptions regarding nuclear weapons' effects on states' militarized behavior. It does so by showing that the inverse relationship between nuclear and conventional danger, which nuclear deterrence theory had taken as an article of faith since the Cold War and which was embodied in the stability/instability paradox, may not apply to new nuclear conflict relationships.

Cold War deterrence logic tells us that, all things being equal, nuclear danger deters lower level violence. This does not mean that the possibility of nuclear war makes subnuclear conflict impossible. However, it does mean that if we hold other factors constant, increasing the risk of nuclear conflict should reduce the likelihood of lower level violence. This assumption has underlain the proliferation optimist claim that more nuclear weapons may be better; because the presence of nuclear weapons automatically creates a degree of nuclear danger, selectively spreading nuclear weapons around the globe should help to pacify the international security environment. Significantly, even proliferation pessimists have not challenged this fundamental deterrence logic. Pessimists have argued that a range of suboptimal political, technological, and organizational conditions could lead to deterrence failures among nuclear states. But their analysis does not challenge the validity of nuclear deterrence theory's bedrock premise that nuclear weapons' ability to make any conventional war extremely costly should make the outbreak of conventional war less likely. The pessimists simply show that certain suboptimal conditions can make conflict against a nuclear backdrop possible *despite* such conflict's potentially high costs and these costs' deterrent effects.[98]

My argument, by contrast, directly challenges the Cold War deterrence logic, showing that nuclear proliferation may fail to prevent conventional conflict, not *despite* the potentially high cost of war in a nuclear environment but *precisely because of* the potentially high cost of war in a nuclear environment. I argue that the potentially high costs of conventional war against a nuclear backdrop may tempt weak, revisionist states to behave aggressively because such high costs can deter opponents from retaliating against weak-state aggression and can attract international attention to the weak states' cause. This argument does not depend on the existence of suboptimal political, technological, or organizational conditions or on the operation of any related pathologies within the belligerent states' decision-making processes.[99] To the contrary, my argument turns on weak, revisionist states' rational responses to the incentives for conventional aggression that the acquisition of nuclear weapons creates for them—incentives for conventional aggression that result directly from the potentially high costs of war that Cold War deterrence theory predicts will help to prevent conflict. This means that the negative relationship between nuclear and subnuclear danger, a fundamental principle of our Cold War experience and of nuclear deterrence logic, does not necessarily apply to new instances of nuclear proliferation. In cases of weak, revisionist nuclear powers, nuclear danger may be a catalyst for conflict rather than an impediment to it.

Alternative Explanations

We have seen that the nuclear proliferation and nuclear deterrence literatures offer two alternative explanations for increasing South Asian violence during the nuclear proliferation process. Proliferation pessimists argue that organizational, political, and technological pathologies can result in conflict between new nuclear powers. And a range of scholars, with widely differing views as to nuclear weapons' effects on South Asian security, argue that the stability/instability paradox accounts for conventional violence in the wake of nuclear proliferation. I have argued that the factors stressed by pessimists are important but exacerbate a situation already prone to violence due to India's and Pakistan's territorial preferences and military capabilities. And I showed that the stability/instability paradox logically cannot account for increased conventional instability in the wake of India's and Pakistan's acquisition of nuclear weapons. In this section, I turn briefly to the broader international relations literature, which does not directly address the issues of nuclear proliferation or South Asian security. I seek to determine whether this scholarship provides any other plausible explanations for the correlation between nuclear proliferation and conventional conflict that we have discovered in the region.

The broader international relations literature does offer a number of theories examining the conditions under which relatively weak, dissatisfied states may instigate wars with stronger powers. Despite their lack of specific focus on nuclear weapons or South Asia, these theories could potentially shed light on rising conventional instability on the subcontinent by explaining Pakistan's willingness to confront India despite Pakistani conventional weakness. As I demonstrate, however, they do not do so. Although these theories illuminate important ways in which weak states could be emboldened to attack stronger adversaries, their arguments and assumptions do not fit the conditions of the current South Asian security environment and thus cannot explain growing conventional violence in the region.

Two of the most prominent theories addressing the issue of war initiation by weaker states focus on the destabilizing effects of power shifts in the international system. A. F. K. Organski and Jacek Kugler's power transition theory argues that aggressor states are most likely to "come from a small group of dissatisfied strong countries; and it is the weaker, rather than the stronger power, that is most likely to be the aggressor." [100] According to this model, war is likely to erupt as relative power within the international system shifts, and a weaker but rising challenger begins to overtake the system's leading state. Because it did not play a role in shaping the existing international order, the challenger does not benefit from the status quo to the same extent as the dominant state, which established the system according to its own interests. The rising state is therefore dissatisfied with the international system and wishes to change it. This desire grows stronger as the challenger becomes increasingly powerful and believes itself to be entitled to a greater role in shaping international politics. Conflict erupts when the challenger eventually draws abreast of the leader and threatens to surpass it. According to Organski and Kugler, "it is an attempt to hasten this passage that leads the faster-growing nation to attack. At the same time it is a desperate attempt on the part of the still-dominant nation to intercept the challenger's progress that leads to war." [101] This process is especially likely to occur where power shifts are rapid, leaving both the leader and the challenger state unprepared to deal with their new relationship and increasing the likelihood of miscalculation. Thus, according to power transition theory, "an even distribution of political, economic, and military capabilities is likely to increase the probability of war; peace is best preserved when there is an imbalance of national capabilities between disadvantaged and advantaged nations." [102]

Robert Gilpin's hegemonic war theory also focuses on the destabilizing effects of power shifts within the international system. Gilpin argues that, over time, states' differential rates of development and growth alter the global distribution of power. As a result, leading states find it increasingly difficult to maintain the existing international order. Simultaneously, rising states, which can realize significant benefits by changing the current system's rules of behavior, spheres of influence, and territorial divisions, find it relatively less costly to challenge the status quo. In this situation, a leading power attempts to thwart a rising state's efforts to change the system either by increasing the resources it expends on maintaining the status quo or by decreasing its international commitments in a manner that enables it to preserve its leading position—a strategy under which the leading state may launch a preventive war to stop the rising challenger while it still can. If the leading state is unsuccessful in these efforts, its competition with the rising state will be resolved through a hegemonic war, "the ultimate test of change in the relative standings of powers in the existing system."[103] According to Gilpin, such conflicts are "total," drawing in most other states in the system, employing unlimited means, and usually resulting in a fundamental transformation of the defeated society. Part of an unending cycle of ascendance, maturation, and decline, these conflicts "have reordered the international system and propelled history in new and uncharted directions. They resolve the questions of which state will govern the system, as well as what ideas and values will predominate, thereby determining the ethos of succeeding ages."[104]

T. V. Paul's theory of asymmetric conflict focuses not on the destabilizing effects of power transitions but rather on the ability of a particular type of military strategy to embolden weak belligerents. Paul argues that weak, dissatisfied states may initiate wars against stronger powers if weak states believe they can achieve their politico-military goals through a rapid, limited offensive, which presents the stronger power with a fait accompli.[105] A limited aims strategy is attractive to weak states because it may not provoke an all-out military response by strong adversaries. For example, the strong state may be deterred by the weaker power's ability to mount robust defenses to protect the fruits of a quick territorial grab. The strong state may also not believe that large-scale mobilization is necessary to deal with a weaker opponent employing such a strategy or may be unprepared to deal with a relatively modest threat to its security. Additionally, a limited aims approach may enable the weak state to achieve a political victory without having to defeat its stronger adversary militarily.[106] Paul concludes that "deterrence and war prevention may not be achieved merely by the possession of gross military and economic power" because "a motivated

weaker adversary can employ military force if its key decision-makers perceive
that they can achieve their limited objectives in a short war." [107]

Although none of these theories is primarily about nuclear proliferation,
all three works discuss nuclear weapons' implications for their arguments.
Organski and Kugler maintain that nuclear weapons do not change the fundamental principles of international relations or the mechanisms by which wars
occur. Thus, while power transition theory was derived from the analysis of
nonnuclear data, its arguments and predictions apply to nuclear environments
as well. Indeed, the behavior of nuclear states confirms the theory's claims that
war is most likely to occur when a rising challenger rapidly overtakes a leading
state. "If nuclear weapons have influenced the rules of international politics
inherited from prenuclear times," they argue, "the influence has not operated
in the expected direction: the weapons have not modified these rules, they
have instead *reinforced* them." [108]

Unlike Organski and Kugler, Gilpin believes that nuclear weapons have in
fact fundamentally modified the rules of international politics. According to
Gilpin, "it would be foolish to argue that the advent of nuclear weapons and
other weapons of mass destruction have not altered the role and the use of
force in the contemporary world. Indeed, these weapons have had a profound
effect on the conduct of statecraft." [109] Nonetheless, Gilpin is uncertain as
to the precise nature of nuclear weapons' effect on world politics and of the
implications of this effect for international stability. He argues that by guar-
anteeing the physical integrity of nuclear states and threatening to raise the
cost of any war between them to catastrophic levels, nuclear weapons tend to
deter conflict and preserve the status quo. Despite these pacifying tendencies,
however, Gilpin points out that nuclear weapons could also have destabilizing
effects on the international system. For example, rising states could use nuclear
weapons for blackmail, launching limited conventional wars to change territorial boundaries, while employing nuclear threats to prevent leading states
from taking action to preserve the status quo. Ironically, a stable system of
mutual nuclear deterrence could exacerbate nuclear weapons' destabilizing effects, making nuclear deterrent threats incredible and enabling a rising state to
use its local conventional superiority to alter territorial boundaries. Thus, in
Gilpin's view, nuclear weapons have both deterrent and potentially destabilizing effects, and on balance, their impact on international stability is indeter-
minate. As Gilpin argues, although

> an effort to translate nuclear weapons into political gains might very well turn
> out to be irrational, can one with assurance deny that a future statesman might be

daring enough or desperate enough to exploit mankind's fear of nuclear war in order to advance his political goals . . . ? Unfortunately, the history of international politics provides no reassurance that nuclear weapons will forever serve only a deterrent function.[110]

Therefore, Gilpin maintains, "The thesis that nuclear weapons have made hegemonic war or a system-changing series of limited wars an impossibility must remain inconclusive."[111]

Like Organski and Kugler, Paul argues that nuclear weapons do not alter the predictions of his theory. According to Paul, just as in a conventional world, weak states in a nuclear environment are likely to attack strong powers when they believe they can achieve their goals through a limited aims strategy. Indeed, weak states may be willing to start wars with strong nuclear powers even if weak states lack nuclear weapons. As Paul argues, nuclear weapons "tend to have a limited role in averting a conflict between a 'nuclear have' and a 'nuclear have not' . . . [T]he mere possession of nuclear capability and an ambiguous threat of use does not provide sufficient deterrent against a challenger without nuclear weapons."[112]

Do any of these theories shed light on the correlation between progressing nuclear proliferation and increased conventional violence in South Asia? The answer is no. The causal mechanism driving the outbreak of war in Organski and Kugler and in Gilpin is a fundamental shift in the balance of power. Despite their differences, both theories hold that conflict erupts when a rising challenger's growing power threatens to surpass that of the international system's leading state. Nuclear weapons proliferation in South Asia, by contrast, has not involved any such systemic shift in the global balance of power. Nor has it involved a fundamental change in the balance of power even between India and Pakistan. The proliferation of nuclear weapons does alter the military relationship between weak and strong adversaries, insulating the weak state from the danger of destruction at the hands of its conventionally superior adversary. However, nuclear weapons do not result in any real power shift beyond this insulating effect; even after acquiring nuclear weapons, the weak state still occupies the inferior position in the conflict relationship, and the strong state retains its dominant status.[113] Thus, although Pakistan's nuclear weapons shield it from the danger of catastrophic defeat in a conflict with India, Pakistan continues to trail India in virtually every measure of national capability and retains its position as the weaker party in the Indo-Pakistani relationship. With India's economy in the throes of a major expansion, the disparity between the two countries is unlikely to diminish during the coming years.[114] Therefore, even after nuclear proliferation, the fundamental hierarchy of the dyadic relationship, as well as of the international order, remains intact.

Conventional conflict in the wake of nuclear proliferation therefore does not occur because nuclear weapons transform a weak state into a potential leading power, threatening to overtake and surpass its stronger adversary. Rather, as discussed, the weapons' insulating effects afford the weak state opportunities to engage in nuclear brinksmanship, which may in turn enable it to alter the territorial status quo—not by militarily overmatching its adversary but rather by running risks that its enemy is unwilling to tolerate. In contrast to power transition theories, then, conventional instability in South Asia has not resulted from a process by which a previously weak state becomes strong and able to utilize this newfound strength to alter the international status quo. Rather, instability has resulted from a weak state's acquisition of weapons that enable it to challenge territorial boundaries *despite* its relative weakness.

As noted, T. V. Paul's theory focuses not on the destabilizing effects of power transitions in the international system but rather on a particular conventional military strategy's ability to embolden weak states to attack stronger adversaries. Nonetheless, Paul's theory, like those of Organski and Kugler and Gilpin, fails to capture the causal factors actually driving conventional instability in a nuclear South Asia. As we have seen, Paul argues that weak, dissatisfied states may launch wars against stronger adversaries when weak states are able to employ conventional limited aims strategies. Paul claims that limited aims strategies are attractive to weak states largely because they reduce the likelihood that stronger powers will respond to weak-state aggression with all-out retaliation.

Paul's theory offers a powerful explanation of a number of important asymmetric conflicts, including the Indo-Pakistani War of 1965. However, the theory, with its focus on conventional military strategy, does not account for the correlation observed earlier between rising conventional violence and progressing nuclear proliferation on the subcontinent. The theory itself offers us no reason to believe that limited aims strategies, or any other conventional military strategy, became more available to Pakistan as the nuclear proliferation process progressed and thereby drove an increase in militarized Indo-Pakistani disputes. As I have argued, this correlation is explained largely by the emboldening effect that a burgeoning nuclear capacity had on Pakistani conventional behavior; nuclear weapons promised to deter stronger India from launching all-out retaliation against Pakistan as well as to compel third parties to intervene diplomatically in emergent crises.[115] By insulating weaker Pakistan from the possibility of catastrophic defeat and attracting international attention toward the Kashmir dispute, nuclear weapons thus encouraged aggressive Pakistani behavior quite apart from Pakistani conventional military strategies.

This is not to argue that Paul's and my logics are incompatible. I do not deny that the ability to employ a conventional limited aims/fait accompli strategy can encourage a weak state to attack a strong opponent. My argument simply shows how nuclear weapons can increase the incentives for weak-state conventional aggression by making such behavior safer and potentially more effective. Since its causal logic does not incorporate the effects of nuclear weapons on weak states' military calculations, Paul's theory does not explain growing conventional violence in an increasingly nuclearized South Asia.[116]

Organski and Kugler, Gilpin, and Paul's arguments regarding nuclear weapons' effects on international stability also differ from actual events in South Asia. As we have seen, Organski and Kugler maintain that nuclear weapons do not significantly transform the fundamental principles of statecraft and do not have implications for international stability beyond those of conventional weapons. Rather, nuclear states behave according to precisely the same logic as states operating in a purely conventional military environment, with rising challengers launching wars as they match and surpass the capabilities of leading powers. Gilpin, for his part, argues that nuclear weapons do significantly alter international behavior. However, he is uncertain as to their overall impact on the likelihood of conflict; because he believes that nuclear weapons are at once pacifying and emboldening, Gilpin maintains that the evidence as to their effects on international stability is inconclusive. Paul, like Organski and Kugler, argues that nuclear weapons do not alter the fundamental behavior of states. Regardless of the presence of nuclear weapons, weak, dissatisfied powers are likely to attack stronger opponents when weak states can employ a limited aims strategy. Evidence from South Asia, however, indicates that, in contrast to Organski and Kugler and Paul, under certain conditions nuclear weapons do fundamentally alter international behavior, leading states to behave differently from how they would in a purely conventional environment. Moreover, in contrast to Gilpin, the evidence indicates that they do so in a clearly destabilizing manner; by insulating weak, revisionist states from all-out retaliation by their adversaries and by attracting international attention, nuclear weapons create strong military and diplomatic incentives for such states to alter the territorial status quo through conventional aggression. These powerful theories thus point to important ways in which weak challengers can be emboldened to attack stronger adversaries conventionally. However, they do not explain increased conventional violence in South Asia since India's and Pakistan's acquisition of a nuclear weapons capacity.

Conclusion

In Chapter 2, I showed that despite their differences, South Asia proliferation optimists and pessimists share important similarities, downplaying the importance of regional variables and employing evidence in a piecemeal fashion in their efforts to explain nuclear weapons' impact on the subcontinent. As a result, the debate over nuclear weapons' effects on the South Asian security environment has been inconclusive, with each side making equally plausible logical arguments and supporting their claims with limited empirical data. Chapter 2 addressed this problem by performing a quantitative analysis, which demonstrated that a positive correlation in fact exists between nuclear proliferation and conventional conflict in South Asia. In this chapter, I developed an argument to explain these empirical findings. I explained how new nuclear powers' territorial preferences and relative conventional military capabilities can combine with ongoing proliferation to create strong incentives for conventionally aggressive behavior. This logic, which I labeled an "instability/instability" paradox, differs fundamentally from that of the stability/instability paradox, which many scholars mistakenly argue explains ongoing conventional violence in a nuclear South Asia. Indeed, my instability/instability logic indicates that the inverse relationship between nuclear danger and conventional conflict, encapsulated in the stability/instability paradox and taken as an article of faith by Cold War nuclear deterrence theory, may not apply to new nuclear conflict dyads. Finally, this chapter explained that, despite apparent similarities, my argument fundamentally differs from theories of weak-power conflict initiation in the broader international relations literature.

The chapters that follow offer detailed case studies showing that my causal argument largely explains Indo-Pakistani military behavior since the two countries acquired nuclear weapons and accounts for much of the correlation between progressing proliferation and conventional instability that my quantitative analysis revealed. In the next chapter, I examine the period from 1972 through 1989. I show that while the Pakistan government was highly dissatisfied with the Simla Agreement's territorial division of Kashmir, it was simply too weak to challenge India in the region in the wake of the Bangladesh War. It therefore turned its attention during this period primarily to the task of rebuilding domestic institutions, developing its relationship with other Islamic states, and supporting a guerrilla war against the Soviet presence in Afghanistan. And the Pakistanis launched a nuclear weapons program, which they hoped would serve as an antidote to their conventional inferiority vis-à-vis India and eventually enable them to pursue their territorial agenda in Kashmir once again.

The Indian government, by contrast, was satisfied with the Simla Agreement and hoped to transform the agreement's division of Kashmir into a permanent international border. It therefore did not undertake significant anti-Pakistani aggression during this period and instead waited for Prime Minister Zulfikar Ali Bhutto to formalize the LoC.

4

The Nonnuclear Period

In Chapter 2, I showed that despite the optimistic predictions of many scholars and policymakers, the Indo-Pakistani military relationship has not become more stable since the proliferation of nuclear weapons to the subcontinent. Rather, militarized disputes between the two countries became more frequent and serious as proliferation progressed. In Chapter 3, I argued that this was the case because the acquisition of nuclear weapons created strong incentives for weak, revisionist Pakistan to engage in limited conventional aggression in pursuit of its territorial and diplomatic goals in Kashmir and for strong, status quo India to respond forcefully to Pakistani provocations.

In this chapter, I examine Indo-Pakistani security relations during the nonnuclear period from 1972 through 1989. I show that this period was largely peaceful; 186 of the 216 months during this period were completely free of militarized conflict. Militarized conflicts that did occur from 1972 through 1989 remained below the level of outright war. I argue that the nonnuclear period was stable for two main reasons. First, India was satisfied with the territorial division of the subcontinent after its victory in the Bangladesh War and had no reason to undertake any aggression against Pakistan. Second, Pakistan was dissatisfied with the territorial division of the subcontinent following the Bangladesh War, particularly in Kashmir. However, in its weakened state, Pakistan could not risk any action to alter Kashmiri territorial boundaries and thus avoided confrontation with India.

Despite the relative peace of the nonnuclear years, I show that several developments occurred during this period that would encourage renewed Indo-

Pakistani conflict in the future. First, a process of Islamization within Pakistan made the Kashmir dispute an even more important Pakistani national goal than it had been. Second, the Afghan War's anti-Soviet guerrilla campaign offered Pakistan a model of low-intensity conflict (LIC) to employ against Indian Kashmir. Finally, Pakistan's burgeoning nuclear weapons capability made pur suit of a LIC strategy in Kashmir less risky, protecting Pakistan against the possibility of all-out Indian retaliation. These factors would combine to make militarized disputes on the subcontinent more frequent and severe during the coming de facto and overt nuclear periods.

Frequency and Level of Conflict

As shown in Table 1, the nonnuclear period from 1972 through 1989 was relatively stable both in qualitative and in quantitative terms. This span included 30 dispute months and 186 months that were free of militarized confrontation. By contrast, the period from 1990 through 2002 included 118 dispute months. Thus, the rate of militarized Indo-Pakistani disputes during the nonnuclear period was less than one-fifth the rate of disputes after de facto nuclearization in 1990. Additionally, unlike during the post-1990 period, disputes that did occur during the nonnuclear period never reached the threshold of interstate war.

The most significant Indo-Pakistani militarized dispute to occur during the nonnuclear period was the 1986–1987 Brasstacks crisis, named after a large-scale Indian military exercise. The Brasstacks exercise triggered a cycle of Pakistani and Indian force deployments that resulted in a large-scale militarized standoff in early 1987. Despite the seriousness of the crisis, it in retrospect appears to have resulted largely from misperception and lack of communication between the two sides rather than from any deliberate attempts at aggression by either party. India did not inform Pakistan of Brasstacks' scope prior to commencing the exercise, and during the crisis, there was little communication between the parties despite the existence of a "hotline" for just such a purpose. Pakistani leaders therefore feared that a large-scale war game in fact was the precursor to imminent Indian aggression. Unsure of Pakistani intentions, India then made similar worst-case assumptions regarding Pakistan's defensive response. Thus, while an important event, Brasstacks is compatible with our earlier finding that the period in Indo-Pakistani relations from 1972 to 1989 was relatively stable; the crisis did not result in any direct confrontation between the two sides and seems to have been driven primarily by misperception rather than by aggressive designs. I address these points in detail later during my discussion of the Brasstacks crisis.

Explaining Stability During the Nonnuclear Period

Why was the nonnuclear period from 1972 through 1989 relatively peaceful? As many scholars have pointed out, from the late 1960s through the late 1980s, the Kashmir dispute was not a major issue for India and Pakistan.[1] Thus, the principal territorial disagreement driving Indo-Pakistani conflict lay dormant during this period. This de-escalation of the Kashmir dispute undoubtedly played a major role in the lack of militarized conflict between India and Pakistan during the nonnuclear years.

But why did the Kashmir dispute de-escalate in the first place? Did the two sides' territorial preferences converge during this period, removing any reason for conflict over Kashmir? The answer is no. Indian and Pakistani territorial preferences regarding Kashmir during the nonnuclear period were as incompatible as before and became more so as the years progressed. Lack of conflict resulted from the fact that India, the victor in the 1971 Bangladesh War, was satisfied with the division of Kashmir in the wake of that conflict and wished to maintain the territorial status quo. The Indian government therefore spent the years from 1972 through 1989 attempting to consolidate its hold over its own portion of Kashmir rather than seeking to acquire further territory in the region.[2]

Pakistani leaders, by contrast, were deeply dissatisfied with the division of Kashmir following the Bangladesh conflict and did not believe that its postwar settlement with India constituted a final adjudication of the Kashmir issue. However, given their devastating loss in 1971, the Pakistanis could do little in the war's aftermath to change the existing territorial settlement. The Pakistan government therefore did not immediately attempt to alter territorial boundaries in Kashmir. Instead, it implemented social policies that made Kashmir even more important to Pakistan and sought military capabilities that would eventually enable Pakistan to alter the division of Kashmiri territory despite its conventional weakness relative to India. These developments would help to make Indo-Pakistani relations in the years following the nonnuclear period far more volatile than they had previously been. In the sections that follow, I explain these developments in greater detail.

Pakistani Policy During the Nonnuclear Period

Pakistan held its first national election in October 1970. The Bengali Awami League, under the leadership of Mujibur Rehman, won a majority of seats in the National Assembly. However, Pakistani President Yahya Khan, under pressure from Pakistan People's Party (PPP) leader Zulfikar Ali Bhutto and concerned by the Awami League's demands for increased Bengali autonomy, hesitated to allow Rehman to form a government. Bhutto, for his part, refused to countenance any power-sharing arrangement between the PPP and the Awami League, calling instead for new elections. The result was widespread rioting in East Pakistan, which spiraled out of control with the desertion of Bengali police personnel and government officials protesting against the Pakistani government's behavior. The central government dispatched West Pakistani troops to quell the uprising. However, these forces succeeded only in increasing the level of violence, launching large-scale attacks on East Pakistan's civilian population in March 1971. Students, intellectuals, Awami League members, and Hindus were massacred, and Pakistan plunged into civil war.[3]

Millions of refugees fleeing the violence in East Pakistan soon began flooding across the border into India. Unable to absorb such a large population influx, the Indian government decided forcibly to separate East Pakistan from the country's western wing and end the civil war. Therefore, in October and November 1971, India began supporting Mukhti Bahini insurgents operating against government forces in East Pakistan. In response, on December 3, Pakistan launched air strikes against air bases in India. India replied with air, sea, and land operations, ultimately attacking East Pakistan with six army divisions and quickly pushing through East Pakistani territory toward Dhaka. The Pakistanis hoped that Chinese or American intervention in the crisis would rescue them from impending disaster. However, no outside intervention was forthcoming,[4] and India defeated Pakistani forces holding Dhaka by December 16. India declared a unilateral cease-fire the next day.[5]

Pakistan's defeat in the Bangladesh conflict was crushing at a military, diplomatic, and psychological level. Militarily, Pakistan had been cut in two in a matter of days. India had captured roughly 5,000 square kilometers of Pakistani territory, along with more than 90,000 prisoners, and facilitated the creation of an independent state out of Pakistan's former east wing. As the Pakistan government's official Hamoodur Rehman Commission Report on the Bangladesh War put it, "This was a war in which everything went wrong for the Pakistan Armed Forces. They were not only outnumbered but also out-weaponed and out-Generaled. Our planning was unrealistic, strategy unsuited, decisions untimely and execution faulty. Even our troops were ill-equipped and ill-trained."[6] Clearly, Indian military superiority was such that Pakistan risked catastrophic defeat in any future conflict against India.

Diplomatically, the war demonstrated that Pakistan could not rely on other states to rescue it in times of crisis. The Pakistanis had traditionally sought allies to equalize the disparity between Indian and Pakistani military capabilities.[7] Despite the Pakistan government's high hopes for outside assistance during the Bangladesh conflict, Pakistan's erstwhile friends had left it to face superior Indian forces alone. Now it was clear that Pakistan would have to devise some other means of compensating for its relative military weakness.

Psychologically, the Bangladesh War belied Pakistan's myth of martial superiority. Many Pakistanis had previously believed that a Muslim army could not lose a war to a Hindu force, but Bangladesh proved that Hindus could in fact prevail over Muslim Pakistan in combat.[8] Even more significantly, Pakistan's defeat dealt a heavy blow to the two-nation theory upon which Pakistan had been founded. The civil war in East Pakistan showed that Islam was an insufficient basis for state building in the region. Ethnic factors such as language were at least as important as religion to state cohesion.[9]

The Bangladesh War thus fundamentally transformed the South Asian geopolitical and security environment. The implications of this transformation differed substantially for India and for Pakistan. Many Indians, until the Bangladesh War, feared that smaller Pakistan might be able to defeat India militarily, much as small Muslim armies had done to Hindu forces over the centuries. India's overwhelming victory in 1971 allayed these fears, however, and significantly bolstered Indian confidence with regard to Pakistan. For Pakistan, by contrast, the effects of the 1971 conflict were devastating. As Shahid Amin argues, in the wake of the Bangladesh War, "the hard reality was that Pakistan's prestige had suffered greatly . . . The repression of Bengali separatists had aroused severe criticism of Pakistan . . . The quick surrender of the Pakistani army in Dhaka shattered its reputation and led to a reappraisal of Pakistan's military prowess. East Pakistan's separation raised questions about the very viability of Pakistan."[10]

Despite the enormity of politico-military transformations wrought by the Bangladesh conflict, both India and Pakistan maintained their prewar designs on the disputed territory of Kashmir. The difference now was that India was in a much stronger position than before to force a settlement on Pakistan in accordance with Indian preferences. The Pakistan government therefore had to devise a means of protecting its interests in Kashmir in a manner that was acceptable to India. Pakistan was largely able to achieve this dual goal through the Simla Agreement.

The Simla Agreement

In late June 1972, Prime Minister Indira Gandhi and President Zulfikar Ali Bhutto met at the Indian hill station of Simla to settle outstanding issues in the wake of the Bangladesh War. The Indian government's major objectives at Simla were to ensure that all future disagreements between India and Pakistan would be resolved strictly through bilateral negotiations; to normalize Indo-Pakistani diplomatic relations; to repatriate prisoners of war; and to establish the legitimacy of current territorial divisions between India and Pakistan. The Pakistan government's major objectives were to recover its 93,000 prisoners and 5,000 square kilometers of West Pakistani territory captured during the Bangladesh conflict, to ensure that Bangladesh would not subject Pakistani soldiers to war crimes trials, and to maintain its position on the Kashmir dispute.[11]

The final agreement, reached as the summit was drawing to a close, achieved many of these goals. It reestablished Indo-Pakistani diplomatic relations and provided for the repatriation of all prisoners of war, enabling Pakistan to avoid the problem of war crimes trials. Especially relevant for the purposes of this study were the agreement's provisions regarding bilateral dispute resolution and the territorial division of Kashmir. Article 1 (ii) stated that "the two countries are resolved to settle their differences by peaceful means through bilateral negotiations or by other means mutually agreed upon by them." Article 4 (ii) stated, "In Jammu and Kashmir, the Line of Control resulting from the cease-fire of December 17, 1971 shall be respected by both sides without prejudice to the recognized position of either side. Neither side shall seek to alter it unilaterally . . . Both sides further undertake to refrain from the threat or use of force in violation of this Line."[12]

Given this language, the Simla Agreement would appear to have committed India and Pakistan (1) to resolving their disputes between themselves, free of outside involvement, and (2) to maintaining the sanctity of the Line of Control as the legitimate dividing line between Indian and Pakistani Kashmir. That was certainly the Indian view of the matter. As P. R. Chari argues, "India secured Pakistan's acceptance in Simla to the principle of bilateralism in Indo-Pak relations. The old cease-fire line was also imbued with a new identity as the line of control in Jammu and Kashmir," thereby acquiring "the attributes of permanence. The Simla Agreement heralded, in brief, a new beginning . . . "[13]

The Pakistani view of Simla, however, was quite different. On the issue of bilateralism, Pakistani analysts argue that Article 1 (ii) must not be read in isolation. Rather, one must consider it in conjunction with Clause (i) of Article 1, which states "the principles and purposes of the Charter of the United Nations shall govern relations between the two countries."[14] As Pervaiz Iqbal Cheema argues,

> The existence of Clause (i) of Article 1 clearly indicates that both parties had agreed to the principles and purposes of the UN Charter, and, hence, one can neither attribute preference to Clause (ii) over the UN Charter, nor exclude recourse to the UN. Besides, Articles 34 and 35 of the UN Charter specifically empower the UN

Security Council to investigate any dispute independently or at the request of a member state. In addition, Article 103 of the UN Charter . . . categorically states that the obligations of the member states take precedence over the obligations under any other international agreement.[15]

In Zulfikar Ali Bhutto's words, "There is nothing in the Simla Agreement to prevent Pakistan from taking the dispute to the United Nations. The Kashmir dispute has been before the United Nations for the past thirty years. Still the problem has remained unsolved. The PPP Government therefore wanted to exhaust the bilateral avenues fully before returning to the United Nations."[16] Bhutto's daughter, former Pakistani Prime Minister Benazir Bhutto, characterizes her father's position as follows: "[T]here was a desire on the part of my father's government . . . to pursue peaceful bilateral means to resolve the [Kashmir] issue. Nonetheless, Pakistan felt strongly that it could not bargain away the rights that the Kashmiri people had gained under the United Nations." Thus, "while we hoped that we could succeed in bilateral negotiations for the resolution of this dispute peacefully, we left to future generations of Kashmiris the right to exercise the right of the UN if they so chose."[17] In the Pakistani view, then, the presence of Article 1 (i) means that the Simla Agreement did not in fact commit India and Pakistan to strictly bilateral dispute resolution.

What was the Pakistani interpretation of the Simla Agreement's strictures regarding the Line of Control? According to Zulfikar Ali Bhutto, by agreeing to change the boundary's name to the Line of Control, Pakistan did not renounce its claim to Kashmir or abandon its position that Kashmir was a disputed territory. In addition, Bhutto pointed out that although the agreement required the line to be "respected by both sides," it also stipulated that this respect for the LoC would not "prejudice . . . the recognized position of either side." Thus, by agreeing to honor the LoC, Pakistan in no way weakened its earlier stance on Kashmir. Moreover, Bhutto argued that Article 6 of the agreement made clear that Simla was not a final settlement of the Kashmir issue. Article 6 states that "Both Governments agree that their respective Heads will meet at a mutually convenient time in the future" to discuss, among other things, "a final settlement of Jammu and Kashmir."[18] Therefore, Bhutto maintained that the Simla Agreement should not be understood as freezing the current territorial division of Kashmir indefinitely.[19] According to Benazir Bhutto, in her father's government's view, the LoC "was not set in stone in Simla. What was set in Simla was that we would not try to upset the Line of Control through non-political and non-peaceful means . . . But at the same time we did not take away the right of future generations to seek recourse under the United Nations Charter . . . [T]he insistence on having the Line of Control set in stone creates the conditions for the next war, or creates the conditions for the next threat of war."[20]

In the Pakistani view, then, Simla was a temporary solution to the Kashmir dispute, which in no way compromised Pakistan's long-standing position on the issue and which would enable the two sides to coexist peacefully pending a final arrangement on Kashmir at some point in the future. As Cheema argues, "Despite being in a very difficult and complex situation at Simla, Pakistan's gains included implicit recognition of Kashmir's disputed nature publicly and a promise for future negotiation in order to find a final settlement."[21]

Pakistani preferences regarding its key territorial dispute with India thus did not fundamentally change with the Bangladesh War and the Simla Agreement. Indeed, in the wake of the Bangladesh conflict, Pakistan's commitment to Kashmir became even stronger. The Bengalis of East Pakistan had been relatively uninterested in Kashmir's fate; Kashmir had always been much more salient for the people of West Pakistan. Now, with the east wing severed, the West Pakistanis constructed a new country, in which Kashmir became a central unifying theme. As Lawrence Ziring argues, the Pakistani civil war

> transformed the long-standing Kashmir dispute into a fetish of national identity. If the Kashmir issue were important in the original Pakistan, the Muslim state that emerged from the civil war and the nation's dismemberment would be even more tied to the Kashmir territory . . . Kashmir became sacred land and Pakistan's *raison d'être* was intertwined with the jihad to liberate it from Indian non-believers.[22]

Pakistan's goals in Kashmir could not be pursued at present, given the country's weakened state. It was for this reason that Pakistan had made a prudential decision to seek a *modus vivendi* with India, until such time as it was in a stronger position to pursue its interests in Kashmir. Bhutto believed that, at Simla, he had stood fast on the issue of Pakistani support for Kashmiri self-determination so that Pakistan could further pursue this goal in the future, when the country was in a stronger position to do so.[23] Presently, he said, "I cannot go to war. Not in the next 5, 10 or 15 years." But this did not mean that Pakistan renounced its territorial goals, or its right to fight for them, indefinitely. "[I]f tomorrow the people of Kashmir start a freedom movement," Bhutto continued, ". . . we will be with them. We have not compromised anything . . . We will fight if we want to fight . . . This is an eternal position."[24]

In the meantime, Pakistan pursued a foreign policy not immediately related to its territorial dispute with India. Severed from its Bengali ties to the subcontinent and seeking to emphasize its Muslim identity, the government turned its attention to forging closer relations with the Islamic states of the Middle East. Bhutto went on two tours of Muslim countries in early 1972, shoring up diplomatic and material support for Pakistan. Then, in 1974, Pakistan hosted the Islamic Summit Conference at Lahore. The summit was convened to discuss the environment in the Middle East following the 1973 Arab-Israeli War and the Arab oil embargo. Attendees included Saudi Arabia's King Faisal, Libya's Muammar Qaddafi, Egypt's Anwar Sadat, Syria's Hafez al-Assad, and the Palestine Liberation Organization's Yasser Arafat. At the meeting, Bhutto announced Pakistan's official recognition of Bangladesh, criticized Israeli sei- zure of Arab lands, and strengthened his ties with important Middle Eastern leaders. The Islamic Summit proved to be a considerable success for Pakistan. It demonstrated to the world that Pakistan was not isolated but in fact enjoyed the friendship of many wealthy and powerful countries. This had strategic implications for Pakistan's relationship with India and also significantly en- hanced Pakistan's prestige.[25]

As it drew closer to the Middle East, the Pakistan government began to re- duce its ties to the United States and the West. Bhutto believed that Pakistan's alliances with the United States had increased Pakistani dependence on Western countries and in the end proved to be largely fruitless; the United States had embargoed arms shipments to Pakistan and failed to come to the country's aid in time of war. Given this lack of American support, and with Bangladeshi indepen- dence reducing Pakistan's interest in Southeast Asia, Pakistan withdrew from the South East Asian Treaty Organization (SEATO). In an effort to shed its colonial past and assert greater independence, Pakistan also withdrew from the British Commonwealth of Nations. Pakistan remained in the Central Treaty Organi- zation (CENTO), however, because members of that alliance included Islamic states to which Pakistan was trying to move closer, such as Turkey and Iran.[26]

Yet even as it was pursuing foreign policy initiatives not directly linked to its territorial dispute with India, in the years following the Bangladesh War, the Pakistan government also undertook policies that would bear directly on the Kashmir issue, increasing Pakistan's ability and desire to pursue its goals in the region. The first such policy was Pakistan's effort to rebuild its military. At the conventional level, Bhutto took a number of steps to enhance the ef- fectiveness of the army, such as diversifying the sources of its arms purchases to make Pakistan less dependent on its unreliable American ally; critiquing the army's performance during the Bangladesh conflict; and making the military more tractable to civilian authority.[27]

Even more important than these conventional efforts, however, was Pakistan's commencement of a nuclear weapons program. Bhutto had been committed to the goal of acquiring a nuclear weapons capacity since before the Bangladesh

War. As he had famously remarked in 1966, to counter any potential nuclear threat from India, "even if Pakistanis have to eat grass, we will make the bomb." [28] Now, after the debacle of 1971, the need for a nuclear weapons capacity was painfully evident. In the absence of such an equalizer, Pakistan would have no hope of protecting itself from Indian predations or of prevailing in its territorial dispute with India. The Pakistan government thus began the dedicated pursuit of a nuclear weapons capacity in 1972 in direct reaction to its overwhelming loss to India in the Bangladesh War. [29]

The Indian nuclear explosion of 1974 heightened Pakistan's sense of urgency in pursuing a nuclear capability. The Indian "peaceful nuclear explosion" was not explicitly for military purposes and was engineered in such a way as to have had few military implications. [30] As Ashley Tellis argues, "the first Indian test in 1974 was a 'nuclear explosion,' but was emphatically not a 'nuclear weapon test explosion.' " The test

> was of greater interest to physicists than to weaponeers in that the former could declare any device that successfully generated fission energy through a controlled detonation to be an effective "nuclear bomb," whereas the latter would reserve such an appellation only for a device that conformed to certain shape, weight, and stability parameters and that would detonate successfully on command in the face of all the stresses associated with the operation of its carrier system. In point of fact, India certainly did not possess a nuclear bomb of this sort in 1974, and the test conducted that year was not designed to validate any nuclear weapon design. [31]

As George Perkovich puts it, "The PNE program was too unlike a nuclear weapon program to signify a meaningful militarily strategic" policy. [32] In fact, the peaceful nuclear explosion was designed primarily to capitalize on India's improved regional status following the Bangladesh conflict as well as to boost Mrs. Gandhi's domestic political fortunes. [33]

Thus, the PNE did not afford India a nuclear weapons capacity in any substantive sense, and Pakistan did not launch its nuclear weapons program in reaction to the blast. Nonetheless, the PNE increased Pakistan's determination to continue forward with its ongoing nuclear program [34] and amplified public demands within Pakistan for the achievement of a nuclear capability. In the wake of the PNE, Bhutto called for the creation of an "Islamic bomb," since the Communists, Christian states, and now the Hindus had bombs of their own. Bhutto's proposal immediately met with strong popular support. [35]

What would an "Islamic bomb" do for Pakistan? First, it would help to increase Pakistan's prestige and enhance its leadership among Muslim states. [36] It would also bolster the Pakistani government at home, given the overwhelming domestic support for Pakistan's nuclear program. [37] More important, a nuclear weapons capacity would protect Pakistan from Indian aggression, threatening to inflict punishment upon India so severe as to outweigh any benefits of an Indian attack. This would ensure Pakistan's ability to defend itself against either nuclear or conventional aggression by its stronger adversary. Additionally, however, a Pakistani nuclear capability could enable Pakistan to pursue territorial goals that had been out of reach since its crushing 1971 defeat. With nuclear weapons insulating it from large-scale retaliation by its stronger adversary, Pakistan could begin actively supporting Kashmiri independence from Indian rule and potentially seize some or all of the territory outright. In launching its nuclear weapons program, Pakistan thus took a crucial step not only toward enhancing its prestige and ensuring its security but also toward being able to resume its "eternal position" on Kashmir and forcefully pursue territorial objectives that the debacle of 1971 had temporarily sidelined.

Pakistan's second post-Bangladesh policy that bore directly on its territorial dispute with India was that of Islamization. As noted earlier, Pakistan's Islamic identity had become more important after 1971 than it had been previously. The war had shown that the country could not be built solely on a foundation of religious identity; ethnic and regional factors had ripped Pakistan apart during the civil war, driving both East Pakistani separatism and the bloody crackdown by West Pakistani forces that followed. Nonetheless, religious identity would now have to serve as the glue that enabled the country to reconstitute itself in the wake of that conflict. Thus, as Stephen Cohen argues, "If the Pakistan movement and the first twenty-five years of the history of Pakistan can be characterized as a struggle to turn Indian Muslims into Pakistanis," the years after 1972 saw "an extension of the process: a struggle to turn Pakistanis into good Muslims."[38]

Central to this Islamist trend was General Mohammed Zia ul-Haq, who made the Islamization of Pakistan an official policy and a centerpiece of his regime. Zulfikar Ali Bhutto had appointed Zia Chief of Army Staff (COAS) in 1976. Bhutto believed that the pious Zia would be a pliant COAS, loyal to the president and to the Pakistani Constitution, and unlikely to involve the army in politics. In fact, however, in the chaos following Bhutto's controversial victory in the March 1977 national elections,[39] Zia removed the president from power, took control of the country, and put the military at Pakistan's helm once more. Although he initially promised new elections and a return to civilian rule within ninety days, Zia ultimately refused to relinquish power and ruled Pakistan for the next eleven years.[40]

Zia had originally launched the coup against Bhutto not out of religious conviction but rather in an effort to save the Pakistani nation and army from the breakdown in law and order that had resulted from civilian misrule. Once in power, however, Zia's religious beliefs began to play a major role in his vision for the nation and in the formulation of his policy.[41] Zia believed that just as with the initial formation of Pakistan in 1947, Islam was the primary rationale for the re-formation and continuation of Pakistan after the Bangladesh War. Reconstructing Pakistan on the basis of the country's Islamic identity made Pakistani state building more than simply a technocratic exercise. Rather, the re-creation of the Pakistani state became a genuine moral and spiritual project. Past neglect of ethical and religious imperatives, in an effort to imitate Western political models, had stunted the emergence of a national culture in keeping with Pakistan's purpose and heritage. Indeed, Western-style democracy and political parties were antithetical to the Islamic character of the Pakistani nation and had led to opportunism, corruption, lawlessness, and a lack of social cohesion. If Pakistan were to survive the effects of its civil war and avoid a catastrophic fragmentation of its social order in the future, it would have to return to the religious and ethical roots that had underlain the founding of the Pakistani nation in the first place.[42]

Zia therefore called for the creation of a Nizam-i-Mustapha, a political system modeled after the rule of the Prophet. To this end, Zia banned political parties, extended martial law, and began a process of Islamization, which "became the most identifiable feature of the Zia regime and increasingly its main *raison d'être*."[43] The Islamization program included the creation of Shariat courts to operate an Islamic legal system in tandem with Pakistan's existing system of secular law; the appointment of a Majlis-i-Shura, or Muslim consultative assembly, to advise the government; the implementation of zakat and ushr charity taxes; the elimination of interest (riba) on domestic transactions; the introduction of punishments based on the Koran and Sunnah, such as public floggings; and the expansion of the madrassah system to train scholars for positions within the new Islamic legal system.[44]

The army, the primary source of political power in Pakistan, was a major target of Zia's Islamization efforts. In its early years, the Pakistan Army had not been particularly religious in outlook. Its officer corps, which had grown up in the British Indian Army, was generally well educated, Westernized, and fairly secular. They served a Muslim country, but they were not necessarily devout in their private lives. Their professional goal was to defend the Pakistani state, not to transform Pakistan into a bastion of Islam. In the years following independence, while the army changed in certain relatively minor, symbolic ways, its basic institutional orientation did not. The army's main focus, the creation of an effective military organization and formulation of strategic doctrine, remained practical rather than religious.[45]

The Pakistan Army's close association with the American military during the 1950s and 1960s reaffirmed this outlook. During this period, many Pakistani officers completed some training in the United States or with Americans, and the Pakistani military began large-scale utilization of American equipment, adoption of American educational techniques, and employment of American tactics and doctrines. Through this process, Pakistani officers also were exposed to American professional and popular culture.[46]

The army's relatively secular orientation began to change due to two main factors. The first was a shift in officer recruitment patterns. Previously, army service had been an elite profession, with officers hailing from Westernized, educated, and secular backgrounds. Increasingly, however, military service became a middle-class occupation, with the officer corps being drawn from less cosmopolitan, more traditional, and more religious sectors of society. In addition, Pakistan's military setbacks prompted introspection among army officers and the search for a new approach to military organization better suited to Pakistan's social and strategic needs than secular British or American models.[47]

Zia seized upon these trends, seeking to create soldiers who were not simply professionally competent but who also were religiously observant. Indeed, an officer's professional competence was to be grounded in and shaped by his religious belief. To this end, Islamic teaching assumed an important role in military education. At institutions such as the Command and Staff College, for example, officers were taught that while they might explore non-Muslim sources in their study of strategy, ultimately the Koran would provide them with the means of determining truth and falsehood. The Pakistani officer thereby became not "merely 'a professional soldier . . . '" Rather, officers became "'Muslim soldiers . . . Muslim officers and Muslim *men.*'"[48] Thus, under Zia, the most powerful institution in Pakistan became increasingly Islamized and in turn accelerated the Islamization process in other sectors of Pakistani society.

Geopolitical events in the region furthered this Islamization trend. Most important, the Soviet Union's 1980 invasion of Afghanistan drove millions of Afghan refugees into Pakistan and put Soviet forces dangerously close to the Pakistani border. Together with the Indians to the East, this threatened to confront Pakistan with a two-front conflict. Such multidimensional danger further convinced Zia that Islam was the only solution to Pakistan's internal and external security problems. He responded by redoubling his domestic Islamization efforts and by transforming Pakistan into a conduit for Islamic anti-Soviet resistance.[49]

The combination of Zia's Islamization policies and the Afghan War ensured that the Indo-Pakistani dispute over Kashmir not only retained its position as Pakistan's central national concern but in fact increased in importance. This was the case for two reasons. First, as Islam continued to become a conceptually more important force in Pakistani society, the battle over Muslim-majority territory between India and Pakistan assumed even greater national salience. Second, the Afghan War empowered a variety of mujahideen groups as well as elements within the Pakistani military and Inter-Services Intelligence (ISI). These actors, with extensive covert assistance from the U.S. Central Intelligence Agency, played a key role in the jihad that ultimately forced the Soviet Union to abandon Afghanistan. After honing their skills against the Soviets, the mujahideen and their Pakistani supporters began to turn their attention toward Kashmir. If jihad could defeat the mighty Soviet Union in Afghanistan, surely it could force India to quit Kashmir, finally bringing to a successful conclusion the unfinished business of partition.[50] Thus, the Afghan War gave Pakistan a new tactic of low-intensity warfare to employ in its attempts to wrest Kashmiri territory from India physically.

The war in Afghanistan not only provided Pakistan with a new means of waging low-intensity conflict against Indian Kashmir, but it also enabled Pakistan to acquire a nuclear capability, which would help to make the adoption of a Kashmiri LIC strategy possible. As noted, Pakistan launched its nuclear weapons program in the wake of the Bangladesh War, hoping to acquire an equalizer to compensate for its conventional inferiority relative to India. This would not only guarantee Pakistani security against Indian aggression but also would eventually enable Pakistan to attempt to alter the status quo in Kashmir militarily, while insulated from all-out Indian retaliation. Nuclear weapons would thus free Pakistani territorial ambitions from the constraints imposed by the debacle of the Bangladesh War.

Despite its promise, however, the Pakistani nuclear program soon ran afoul of American antiproliferation efforts. In 1977, the United States convinced France to renege on an agreement to sell Pakistan a nuclear reprocessing plant. Zulfikar Ali Bhutto later claimed that this move thwarted the Pakistani program just as it was on the verge of a full nuclear capability.[51] Tough new American domestic legislation created further difficulties for Pakistan. The 1976 Symington Amendment to the International Security Assistance and Arms Export Control Act prevented U.S. military or economic aid to states that imported unsafeguarded uranium enrichment or plutonium reprocessing technology. The Carter administration in 1977 and 1979 imposed military and economic sanctions against Pakistan under the Symington Amendment to slow advances in the Pakistani nuclear program.

The Soviet invasion of Afghanistan largely ended American efforts to prevent Pakistani acquisition of a nuclear weapons capacity. The Reagan administration waived economic and military sanctions against Pakistan and launched large-scale aid programs to buttress its newfound ally in the anti-Soviet struggle. While ignoring Pakistan's growing nuclear capabilities, the administration argued that increased conventional military assistance would assuage Pakistan's security concerns and thereby eliminate Pakistani incentives to acquire nuclear weapons. The 1984 Pressler Amendment subsequently attempted to slow Pakistani advances by requiring the United States to impose military and economic sanctions against Pakistan unless the president could annually certify that Pakistan did not possess a nuclear device and that American assistance would significantly reduce the likelihood that Pakistan would acquire one. However, the administration responded by certifying that Pakistan did not possess a nuclear weapons program even after Pakistan had acquired the capacity to enrich uranium beyond 5 percent U235. This enabled further American military assistance to Pakistan, including the sale of F-16 aircraft that could potentially serve as nuclear weapons delivery platforms in the future.[52]

As we have seen, a nuclear weapons capacity was crucial to Pakistan's Kashmir strategy because it would enable Pakistan to wage a low-intensity conflict in the region while insulated from all-out Indian retaliation. Given Pakistan's conventional military inferiority, such an Indian response could result in catastrophic Pakistani defeat. By protecting Pakistan against such a possibility, then, a nuclear capacity would once again make possible Pakistani attempts to change the territorial status quo in Kashmir militarily. And therefore, by convincing the Americans to ignore Pakistani nuclear advances, the war in Afghanistan set the stage for an aggressive Pakistani Kashmir policy. As a result of the Afghan War, a favorable settlement on Kashmir became more than simply the far-off, conceptual goal that it had been since Pakistan's 1971 defeat. Now Pakistan had a means of striking directly at India and undermining India's position in Kashmir in a dramatic and immediate fashion. Pakistan would capitalize on this opportunity in the years to come, making low-intensity conflict in Kashmir a major aspect of its security policy.

We should note that although Pakistan's weakened condition forced it to minimize confrontation with India from 1972 through 1989, Pakistan did not completely avoid anti-Indian activity during this period. During the 1980s, the Pakistanis provided substantial support, including money, weapons, and advice, to a bloody Sikh separatist movement that had erupted in the Indian

Punjab.[53] The Pakistanis' policy contributed to increased Indo-Pakistani tensions. For example, the Indian military exercises that provoked the 1986–1987 Brasstacks crisis were intended in part to discourage further Pakistani support for the Sikhs.[54]

Nonetheless, Pakistani backing of the Sikh uprising was less extensive than Pakistan's later support for the Kashmir insurgency. Violence associated with the Sikh rebellion became particularly virulent in the mid-1980s. From 1981 through 1983, a total of 135 civilians, police, and militants were killed in the Indian Punjab. By contrast, 1986 saw a total of 598 people killed, and in 1987, 1,238 people died.[55] Pakistani involvement became most prevalent after 1984's Operation Bluestar, in which Indian government forces stormed the Golden Temple in Amritsar, resulting in deep anger within the Sikh community.[56] Yet as Stephen Cohen points out, Pakistan's post-1984 support for the Sikh insurgency was "limited," and it declined during the ensuing years, as the Indian government regained its grip on the Punjab.[57] By 1987, a year that saw more than twice as many deaths as any previous year of the uprising, even Indian officials were admitting that Pakistani support for the Sikh militancy had begun to wane.[58] At no point did Pakistani backing of the Sikhs involve such measures as Pakistan Army personnel crossing de facto borders to confront Indian forces, as the Pakistanis did during the 1998–1999 Kargil operation in Kashmir.[59] And according to C. Christine Fair, hard evidence that the Pakistanis provided direct training to Sikh militants remains elusive.[60] As I explain in Chapter 5, such evidence is not lacking in Kashmir. Pakistan's support for the Sikh rebellion, then, was less extensive than its later backing of the anti-Indian uprising in Kashmir, where Pakistan became involved "even more directly than it had been in Punjab."[61]

The effects of Pakistan's support for the Sikh insurgency were also far less damaging to the Indo-Pakistani relationship than was the impact of its later involvement in Kashmir. As my quantitative analysis shows, the frequency and severity of Indo-Pakistani disputes during the 1980s remained considerably below the levels that they would reach between 1990 and 2002. Thus, Pakistan's support for the Sikh insurgency, although important, does not undercut my earlier characterization of Pakistani behavior during the nonnuclear period; prior to the acquisition of nuclear weapons, the Pakistanis were relatively nonconfrontational toward India, and the overall Indo-Pakistani relationship was relatively stable.

To summarize our discussion of the nonnuclear period thus far: In the wake of the Bangladesh War, the Pakistan government was deeply dissatisfied regarding the settlement of its key territorial dispute with India but, given the country's weakened state, could do nothing to alter the division of Kashmir. In the years that followed, Pakistani domestic and security policy was characterized by three important factors that impacted both Pakistan's territorial preferences and its ability to alter the status quo in Kashmir. First, General Zia's Islamization policies made the Indo-Pakistani territorial dispute over Kashmir even more important to Pakistan than it had been. Second, the Afghan War both reinforced Islamization trends within Pakistan and empowered mujahideen and Pakistani military and intelligence elements eager to transform the anti-Soviet jihad into a struggle against Indian rule in Kashmir. This new strategy of low-intensity conflict gave Pakistan a means of directly undermining India's position in Kashmir and altering the existing division of the territory. The Afghan War also led the U.S. government to curtail its efforts to prevent Pakistani acquisition of a nuclear weapons capability. Third, Pakistan's growing nuclear weapons capacity would make Pakistani pursuit of a LIC strategy in Kashmir safer and facilitate Pakistani efforts to alter the Kashmiri status quo. Thus, although aggressive Pakistani behavior was relatively infrequent from 1972 through the late 1980s, Pakistan was not satisfied with the resolution of its key territorial dispute with India. Rather, it remained dissatisfied with the Kashmir settlement but was preparing for the day that Bhutto had promised in the wake of Simla, when Pakistan would again be able to take up its eternal fight to oust India from Kashmir.

In the following section, I discuss Indian policy during the nonnuclear weapons period. I explain that, in the wake of the Bangladesh War, India was largely satisfied with the settlement of its key territorial dispute with Pakistan and saw little cause for dispute. Thus, even as it acquired a nuclear weapons capacity, India refrained from anti-Pakistan aggression, and the subcontinent remained largely peaceful from the early 1970s until the late 1980s.

Indian Policy During the Nonnuclear Period

The Indian government hoped that the territorial division of Kashmir had been settled in the aftermath of the Bangladesh War. As noted, Indian leaders believed that the Simla Agreement had committed Pakistan to bilateral dispute resolution with India and to an acceptance of the newly named Line of Control as the legitimate boundary between Indian and Pakistani Kashmir.

This belief was based partially upon Indian leaders' textual analysis of the Simla document itself. Article 4 (ii) of the agreement stated, "In Jammu and Kashmir, the Line of Control resulting from the ceasefire of December 17, 1971 shall be respected by both sides without prejudice to the recognized position of either side. Neither side shall seek to alter it unilaterally . . . Both sides further undertake to refrain from the threat or use of force in violation of this Line."[62] Thus, in the Indian view, the plain language of the agreement made abundantly clear that the LoC would now serve as the official dividing line separating Pakistani from Indian Kashmir.

Indian leaders' belief that the Pakistan government had accepted the legitimacy of the Line of Control was also based on their understanding of Prime Minister Bhutto's unofficial statements to Mrs. Gandhi during the Simla meetings. Most Indian accounts of the meetings contend that Bhutto told Gandhi that he was amenable to finalizing the territorial division of Kashmir along the Line of Control and that he would seek to do so in the future. Bhutto said that he could not settle Kashmir along the LoC at present, according to these accounts, because of his current domestic political weakness.[63]

Although no record of such statements exists, Indian analysts believe that the circumstantial evidence points strongly in the direction of Bhutto having made them and of the existence of a secret Bhutto-Gandhi understanding on the issue of the LoC. For example, Chari cites testimony to this effect from P. N. Dhar, former secretary to Indira Gandhi. Dhar claims that Gandhi told him of her agreement with Bhutto permanently to divide Kashmir along the Line of Control. According to Dhar, Bhutto and Gandhi agreed not to make their understanding part of the official agreement to avoid domestic political opposition in both of their countries but ensured that the agreement was worded in such a way as to make implementation of their understanding possible.[64] Chari also points out that just after the Simla meetings, Indian Defense Minister Jagjivan Ram asked the army whether it would be amenable to the conversion of the Line of Control into a permanent international border in Kashmir. Chari acknowledges that neither Gandhi nor Bhutto admitted to the existence of a secret understanding regarding the LoC but points out that their denials were circumspect, evasive, and not surprising given domestic opposition in both India and Pakistan to any compromise on the Kashmir issue. Thus, Chari maintains, one can reasonably conclude that Bhutto did agree at Simla to divide Kashmir permanently along the Line of Control. Such "Surmises, admittedly, cannot substitute for facts," he argues, "but these surmises are not illogical."[65]

Bhutto vigorously denied the existence of any secret understanding with Gandhi at Simla, calling reports to that effect a "canard," part of a "barrage of fantastic yarns" that his opponents had concocted in the wake of the agreement.[66] Pakistani officials present with Bhutto at Simla similarly reject the notion of a covert Bhutto-Gandhi agreement.[67] Pakistani analysts agree. Cheema, for example, points out the lack of documentary evidence of any clandestine agreement as well as Bhutto's and Gandhi's denial that they had struck such a deal. He also suggests that revelations such as those of P. N. Dhar were designed to boost India's position in Kashmir at a time when Indian rule had become highly unpopular. Finally, he argues that for Mrs. Gandhi to reach an agreement regarding the disposition of Kashmiri territory in the absence of the chief minister of Kashmir would have violated the Indian Constitution.[68] Thus, Cheema concludes, "the Pakistani set of arguments undoubtedly appear to be more credible than those of the Indians," and "it is indeed extremely difficult to accept the contention that there ever was any secret deal."[69]

Despite this controversy, the fact remains that in the wake of Simla, Indian leaders believed that Pakistan had agreed to settle the Kashmir dispute along the Line of Control. In their view, both the plain language of the agreement and the unofficial Bhutto-Gandhi understanding committed Pakistan to accept the territorial status quo in the region. Thus, after 1972, India was essentially satisfied with the disposition of the key Indo-Pakistani territorial dispute. Indian leaders had gotten what they wanted at Simla, and India therefore had few incentives to undertake any anti-Pakistani aggression in the years that followed.

India's basic satisfaction with the territorial status quo in Kashmir did not entirely prevent Indian adventurism against Pakistan during the nonnuclear period. From the late 1970s until 1990, India sought to convey an image of firmness, freely using force to demonstrate its ability to play a leading regional role.[70] In Kashmir during this period, India pursued small territorial gains over Pakistan in parts of the region that had not been clearly demarcated by the Simla Agreement. The Indian capture of Siachen Glacier, in far northwestern Kashmir, is the best example of such behavior.

The Line of Control is clearly marked for approximately 800 kilometers, from a point just west of the Chenab River in Jammu, north and northeast to grid coordinate NJ 9842, about 19 kilometers north of the Shyok River in the Karakoram Mountains. The 1949 Karachi Agreement, which established the cease-fire line (CFL) upon which the 1972 LoC was based, stated that from NJ 9842, the CFL ran "north to the glaciers."[71] India and Pakistan subsequently disagreed as to the meaning of this language. India maintained that the LoC ran directly north from NJ 9842 to the Chinese border, an interpretation that would put most of Siachen under Indian control. Pakistan disagreed with the Indian claim. When Pakistan began licensing mountaineering expeditions to Siachen, accompanied by Pakistani personnel, and acquiring materiel that could enable Pakistan to take the region, India preemptively seized it in April 1984. It has since been a festering point of contention and the locus of a low-grade conflict.[72]

It is important to note that this action was certainly forceful, but it was not *revisionist* regarding the Line of Control because the status of the LoC was ambiguous in the vicinity of Siachen. Indeed, for all intents and purposes, there was no LoC in the region. As Robert Wirsing writes,

> The CFL/LOC ends at NJ 9842, and there does not exist today any known international agreement that would warrant delineating any sort of boundary between the Karakoram Pass and map coordinate NJ 9842 . . . [N]othing is said in either [the Karachi or the Simla Agreements] about any extension beyond this coordinate . . . The truth is that the inner boundary between Indian and Pakistani-held parts of Kashmir is today unquestionably incomplete. Its northernmost sector awaits delineation.[73]

Thus, in taking Siachen, India seized previously unoccupied territory but was not trying to alter the existing division of Kashmir as delineated by the Line of Control. Rather, it was attempting to establish a de facto territorial division in a small area where the Line of Control was at least ambiguous and perhaps nonexistent. In the majority of Kashmir, where the line was clearly marked, India was satisfied with the existing territorial division and did not attempt to alter it forcefully during the nonnuclear period.[74]

Nuclear Weapons

Like Pakistan, India actively pursued a nuclear weapons program during the 1970s and 1980s. Several competing explanations of India's pursuit of nuclear weapons exist. However, none suggest that the Indians viewed their burgeoning nuclear capacity as a potential means of undoing the status quo on the subcontinent. Rather, the explanations indicate that India's nuclear weapons program was driven by some combination of traditional defensive security concerns, ideology, domestic political calculations, and a desire for prestige or great-power status.

Perkovich argues that domestic political factors were more important than external security concerns in driving India's nuclear weapons program. Perkovich focuses particularly on the symbolic importance of nuclear weapons acquisition for a developing, postcolonial state; on domestic political actors' promotion of an Indian nuclear capability for partisan gain; and on the role of the Indian nuclear and missile establishment, or "strategic enclave," in driving Indian nuclear aspirations.[75] Ganguly, by contrast, argues that India's nuclear program was driven primarily by the perception of external security threats, particularly from China and Pakistan. China possessed nuclear weapons and had badly defeated India in a 1962 border war. And Pakistan had benefited significantly from Chinese arms transfers, particularly in the area of ballistic missiles. As Ganguly argues, "ample evidence suggests that India's security misgivings did play an important role in the evolution of the program . . ."[76]

Sagan departs from both Perkovich and Ganguly in arguing for a multicausal explanation of nuclear weapons proliferation that incorporates security factors, domestic political variables, and issues concerning norms and state identity. In the Indian case, Sagan believes that a domestic politics approach is especially useful, accounting for aspects of Indian behavior that security-based arguments cannot explain.[77] Baldev Raj Nayar and T. V. Paul also offer a multicausal explanation of India's nuclear weapons program. According to Nayar and Paul, India's acquisition of a nuclear weapons capability had its "immediate origins in [India's] long-standing concerns over national security in relation to China and Pakistan and their military relationship." An important additional factor, however, was the "enduring and deep-rooted aspiration of India for the role of a major power, and the related belief that the possession of an independent nuclear capability [was] an essential prerequisite for achieving that status." Significantly, this quest for great-power status was not driven simply by a desire for prestige. Rather, it had a critical geostrategic element, as "major powers by definition are those states that are least vulnerable to direct military coercion or attacks, and are most capable of deterring any potential attacks and of defending their security from other major and minor powers."[78] Thus, although multilayered, Nayar and Paul's explanation of the Indian nuclear weapons program is based primarily on a form of national-security logic.

If Sagan and Perkovich are correct, India's nuclear weapons program was largely inward directed, driven by domestic political calculations rather than by the need to protect against external threats or by a desire to alter the international status quo. However, even if Ganguly's and Nayar and Paul's emphasis on national security concerns is warranted, it does not mean that Indian leaders hoped that the acquisition of nuclear weapons would enable them to pursue revisionist ambitions. Rather, Indian security motives were to minimize the risk of catastrophic defeat at the hands of China, blunt the threat posed by burgeoning Pakistani nuclear and missile capabilities, and prevent coercion or attack from any other quarter. In short, the Indians hoped that nuclear weapons would enable them to preserve the status quo rather than to undo existing territorial boundaries.

In summary, then, from the early 1970s forward, India sought stable relations with Pakistan, in which both sides accepted the existing territorial division of Kashmir and Pakistan acquiesced in Indian primacy on the subcontinent. The Indian government anticipated, in the wake of the Bangladesh War, "a less aggressive and more submissive country on India's northwestern border," whose "relationship with India was not expected to be different from those of Bangladesh, Nepal, and Bhutan."[79] Despite overwhelming conventional superiority and pursuit of a nuclear program, it did not wish to alter boundaries and, despite some limited adventurism, did not launch serious aggression against Pakistan.

Brasstacks: A Potential Counterexample?

The Brasstacks crisis offers a possible counterexample to my argument that Indian leaders sought stable, nonconfrontational relations with Pakistan from 1972 through 1989. Brasstacks was India's biggest-ever military exercise, on par in scale with major NATO operations. Brasstacks began in 1986 with paper and sand-table exercises, and it culminated in early 1987 with actual maneuvers in the Rajasthan Desert. During the maneuvers, Indian mechanized infantry and armor massed near the Pakistan border in the vicinity of Sindh, where the Pakistan government was fighting an ongoing battle against separatist elements and felt particularly vulnerable to any potential military strike. Pakistan responded by massing forces on its side of the border in such a way as potentially to have undertaken a pincer movement against Punjab or possibly to have launched offensives against Kashmir and Punjab simultaneously. India followed with further deployments to defend against any offensive moves by these Pakistani forces. Despite tough public statements and much mutual consternation, the two sides eventually held talks to ratchet down tensions, and within a few weeks, the crisis had passed without any direct Indo-Pakistani confrontation.[80]

Did the Brasstacks crisis result from a serious attempt at Indian aggression? Or was it instead largely the result of misperception and lack of communication between the two parties and not driven by any aggressive Indian designs? The answer to this question has important implications for our assessment of the nonnuclear time period. If Brasstacks was in fact driven by serious aggressive intentions, then it calls into question our characterization of the nonnuclear period as being largely nonconfrontational. If, by contrast, the Brasstacks crisis actually was caused by a spiral of misperception rather than any aggressive Indian intentions, then the episode does not pose any difficulty for our characterization of the nonnuclear time period; while an important crisis did occur during the nonnuclear years, it resulted primarily from mistake and accident, and not from either India or Pakistan actually wanting war.

The South Asian security literature is divided on the question of the Indian government's motivation in undertaking Brasstacks. Some scholars believe that Brasstacks was far more than a mere military exercise. Scott Sagan, for example, maintains that Brasstacks was in fact a thinly veiled attempt by Indian Army Chief of Staff Krishnaswamy Sundarji to provoke a preventive war with Pakistan. According to this argument, by the mid-1980s, the Indians realized that Pakistan was on the brink of achieving a nuclear capability, which would threaten India and impose severe constraints on the Indians' ability to use force against Pakistan in the future. The Indian Army, at Sundarji's direction, thus designed and executed an operation that would directly threaten the Pakistanis and lead them preemptively to attack India. This Pakistani action in turn would provide the Indians with a justification for launching a large-scale assault on Pakistan and destroying its incipient nuclear capability in a preventive attack. Sagan argues that this logic not only explains India's decision to launch Brasstacks but also accounts for Indian conduct just prior to and during the crisis, including failure to notify the Pakistanis fully of the impending exercise and failure to utilize a hotline connecting Indian and Pakistan Army operations directorates during the crisis. Thus, as Sagan writes, "the key [to understanding Brasstacks] is to understand the preventive-war thinking of . . . General Krishnaswamy Sundarji."[81]

In support of this argument, Sagan cites a passage from the memoirs of Lieutenant General P. N. Hoon, commander of India's Western Army during Brasstacks, claiming that "Brasstacks was no military exercise. It was a plan to build up a situation for a fourth war with Pakistan."[82] Sagan also points out that General Sundarji encouraged the senior Indian political leadership preventively to attack Pakistan during Brasstacks. According to Sagan, "Sundarji advocated a preventive strike against Pakistan during the crisis. Considerations of an attack on Pakistani nuclear facilities went all the way up to the most senior decision makers in New Delhi in January 1987."[83]

Other scholars disagree with this preventive-war assessment, arguing that insufficient evidence exists to conclude that Brasstacks was anything more than a large-scale military exercise that inadvertently evolved into a crisis through a spiral of misperception and miscommunication. Devin Hagerty, for example, points out that former Indian officials, including General Sundarji, have consistently denied the existence of any ulterior motives in designing and executing the Brasstacks exercise. Rather, they have maintained that Brasstacks was intended primarily to test the effectiveness of new Indian mechanized infantry forces as well as the Indian military's ability to execute its new offensive–defensive doctrine, which would defend Indian territory against a Pakistani attack and then launch an Indian assault into Pakistan.[84]

Hagerty acknowledges Indian officials' hope that, beyond its purely military purposes, Brasstacks would send the Pakistanis a message regarding the danger of continuing their aid to the Sikh insurgency in Indian Punjab. However, Hagerty notes that in this regard, Brasstacks was similar to most other military exercises, which are intended at least in part to serve as a warning to potential adversaries. And while he acknowledges the Indians' failure to communicate with the Pakistanis through the army hotline, Hagerty argues that such lack of communication was consistent with the Indian desire to send the Pakistanis a warning. If part of the Indian intent in launching Brasstacks was to highlight Pakistani vulnerabilities, the Indians may not have wished to reassure the Pakistanis as to their safety during the exercise. Indian failure to communicate during Brasstacks therefore does not necessarily indicate that the exercise was designed as a precursor to an attack on Pakistan. Thus, on balance, Hagerty finds no solid evidence of Indian ulterior motives in designing and executing Brasstacks. As Hagerty concludes, "Convincing support for that thesis is still lacking."[85]

Other scholars take a similar position. Ganguly, for example, recognizes the undeniably coercive nature of Brasstacks but does not go so far as to claim that the exercise was explicitly designed to provoke Pakistan into launching a war. According to Ganguly, the Indian Army's purposes in undertaking the Brasstacks exercise included the testing of new mechanized units; determining the effectiveness of a new, indigenously designed command, control, communications, and intelligence network; and assessing a new conventional deterrence strategy.[86] Ganguly notes that, in addition to these purely military purposes, Brasstacks was designed to convey a political message to the Pakistan government. Indian officials, in designing and executing a large-scale exercise such as Brasstacks, sought to demonstrate to the Pakistanis that regardless of the costs of the ongoing Sikh insurgency, the Indians could still seriously damage Pakistan. Therefore, "embedded in the Brasstacks military exercise" was the "element of coercive diplomacy."[87] Significantly, however, Ganguly does not include the provocation of a preventive war with Pakistan as one of Brasstacks' purposes. While Ganguly notes the coercive aspect of the exercise, he does not claim that General Sundarji, or any other Indian official, devised and launched Brasstacks in a veiled attempt to instigate an Indo-Pakistani war.

Kanti Bajpai, P. R. Chari, Pervaiz Iqbal Cheema, Stephen Cohen, and Šumit Ganguly offer by far the most detailed study of the Brasstacks crisis. Bajpai et al. provide little evidence to support the preventive-war thesis. Indeed, the 1995 study, which drew upon in-depth testimony from most of the major living participants in the crisis, largely undermines the preventive-war argument. It shows instead that most of the evidence supposedly indicating ulterior motives in India's design and execution of Brasstacks in fact had far less sinister explanations. For example, the authors argue that:

- The Indian government's primary motive in designing an exercise on the immense scale of Brasstacks was Rajiv Gandhi's personal fascination with military operations of enormous size.

- The military logic for conducting an exercise such as Brasstacks in the area east of the Indira Gandhi Canal in Rajasthan was "impeccable," and the exercise's primary shortcoming was the failure to keep open Indo-Pakistani lines of communication rather than selection of a needlessly provocative area of operations.

- The Indians undoubtedly hoped that Brasstacks would warn the Pakistanis as to Indian military capabilities. However, military exercises, beyond their narrow tactical purposes, typically serve such a broader warning function.

- Because Brasstacks was viewed within the Indian military establishment as a continuation of the earlier exercise Digvijay, senior officers did not anticipate that Brasstacks would seriously concern the Pakistanis and escalate into a crisis.

- The Indians delayed shifting troops into forward defensive positions in reaction to the potentially threatening movement of Pakistan's Army Reserve South across the Sutlej River in late January 1987. The only plausible explanation for this delay was an Indian effort to forestall a crisis with the Pakistanis.

- Indian officials probably avoided using a hotline connecting Indian and Pakistan Army operations directorates because the Indians did not trust information coming from Pakistan; mutual suspicion was sufficiently severe to erode the utility of confidence-building measures such as the hotline.

- The view of Brasstacks "at the highest level of the [United States] Department of State was that a war with Pakistan would be costly and risky [for India], and could uncork the nuclear genie in an unpredictable way. A war in 1987 would not, as might a war in 1984, stop a Pakistani nuclear weapon from being developed—and this was probably India's estimate also."[88]

The book concludes that the Brasstacks crisis was largely the result of misperception and miscommunication pushing two countries to the brink of conflict. The problem in this case, then, was not that an Indian military officer launched the Brasstacks exercise in a deliberate attempt to instigate a preventive war with Pakistan. Rather, the problem was that in the absence of open communication between the Indians and the Pakistanis, a large-scale military exercise led to a spiral of mutual suspicion and fear that threatened to result in outright hostilities despite the fact that neither side desired such an outcome. As the authors put it, Brasstacks showed that the ordinary dangers of a large-scale military exercise in the Indo-Pakistani context "are exacerbated by the concomitant reality that the absence of communications between the military leaderships provides a fertile opportunity . . . to construct worst-case scenarios that add to the tensions and could indeed become self-fulfilling prophesies." Thus, in the authors' view, a major lesson emerging from the Brasstacks crisis is "the imperative need to maintain military communications, especially in moments of high tensions."[89]

What are we to make of these various arguments? Was the Brasstacks crisis the inadvertent result of a large-scale military exercise in which poor communication and misperception led to worst-case assumptions on the part of the antagonists? Or was the Brasstacks exercise in fact a veiled attempt by the Indian Army's Chief of Staff to provoke a preventive war with Pakistan? The weight of the analyses favors a conclusion that the Indians did not have ulterior motives in designing and launching Brasstacks and that they did not hope that the exercise would enable them to launch a preventive war against the Pakistanis. The majority of the evidence suggests instead that Brasstacks was essentially what the Indians claimed it to be—a large-scale military exercise designed to test the operation of new units, technologies, and strategies. The Indians no doubt hoped that the Brasstacks exercise would convey a political message to Pakistan as well, warning the Pakistanis that Indian conventional capabilities remained potent despite the drain of the Sikh insurgency. However, as noted, such a broad warning function, beyond the achievement of immediate tactical objectives, is a standard goal of military exercises. And sending such a political message to a potential adversary is far different from launching a preventive war.

We should also note that, in addition to the considerable data supporting a misperception interpretation of the Brasstacks crisis, the evidence that does exist in favor of the preventive-war argument is quite limited. The preventive-war argument rests primarily upon two key pieces of evidence: a quote in P. N. Hoon's memoirs and General Sundarji's advocacy of a preventive strike on Pakistan during the Brasstacks crisis. Close examination reveals the latter of these two evidentiary sources to be problematic. Although preventive-war proponents characterize Sundarji as having advocated a preventive strike on Pakistan during the Brasstacks crisis, the type of attack that Sundarji was promoting would be better described as preemptive in nature. Sundarji advocated a strike on Pakistan during Brasstacks because the Indians had begun to fear that the Pakistanis were preparing to launch an attack on India. Sundarji sought to respond to this emerging threat from Pakistani forces and attack them before they could hit India. An Indian strike on Pakistani nuclear

facilities would have been an essential element of this preemptive attack, elimi-
nating the Pakistanis' ability to retaliate against Indian conventional preemption with nuclear weapons.

Significantly, Perkovich, upon whose work the preventive-war argument
draws, also characterizes the contemplated Indian strike on Pakistan during
Brasstacks as being preemptive rather than preventive in nature. As Perkovich
puts it, in January 1987, Indian Prime Minister Rajiv Gandhi

> considered the possibility that Pakistan might initiate war with India. In a meeting
> with a handful of senior bureaucrats and General Sundarji, he contemplated beating
> Pakistan to the draw by launching a preemptive attack on the Army Reserve South.
> This would have included automatically an attack on Pakistan's nuclear facilities to
> remove the potential for a Pakistani nuclear riposte to India's attack.[90]

The contemplated Indian strike on Pakistan in January 1987 thus fit the
classic definition of a preemptive attack, in which a state responds to an impending enemy offensive by striking the enemy first. The potential Indian offensive does not fit the definition of a preventive war, in which a state responds
to emerging enemy capabilities by attacking the enemy before those capabilities can evolve into a serious threat. The Indian government's January 1987
contemplation of an attack on Pakistan therefore does not provide strong
evidence in favor of the preventive-war argument.[91] This leaves us just with
General Hoon's quote in favor of the preventive-war thesis against the weight
of analysis and evidence that has been discussed. In the absence of further
information to the contrary, we must conclude that the Brasstacks crisis most
likely resulted not from an Indian general's plan to provoke a preventive war
but rather from a large-scale military exercise that evolved into a crisis through
a spiral of misperception and miscommunication.

Conclusion

During the nonnuclear period from 1972 through 1989, Indo-Pakistani relations were relatively stable; conflict occurred in only 30 of the 216 months
during this period, making militarized disputes less than one-fifth as common
as they would be from 1990 through 2002. Militarized disputes during the
nonnuclear period also tended to be relatively minor, with none reaching the
threshold of interstate war. The one major crisis that occurred during this period was largely the result of misperception and miscommunication rather than
deliberate aggressive intent on the part of either party. This quantitative and
qualitative stability did not result from any commonality of interest between
India and Pakistan during the nonnuclear period. Indeed, Indian and Pakistani
territorial preferences during this time frame were diametrically opposed. The

Indian government was satisfied with the territorial boundaries that arose out of the Bangladesh War and used its superior diplomatic and military position in the wake of the conflict to preserve them. The Pakistan government, by contrast, was deeply dissatisfied with post-Bangladesh territorial boundaries but, following the war, was too weak to make any effort to change them. As a result, India and Pakistan were able largely to avoid conflict with one another despite their divergent territorial interests.

Significantly, however, Pakistani leaders did not believe Pakistan to be committed to the post-Bangladesh territorial settlement and looked forward to the day when their country would once again be able to press its claims on Kashmir. Several developments during the nonnuclear time period made the arrival of that day more likely. First, the Islamization of Pakistani society made Pakistan's central territorial dispute with India an even more important national issue than it had been. Second, the Afghan War offered Pakistan a potentially winning strategy to employ against India in Kashmir, along with a seasoned cadre of military, intelligence, and mujahideen elements prepared to pursue it. Finally, Pakistan's nuclear weapons program would make a more aggressive approach to Kashmir safer, shielding Pakistan against all-out Indian conventional retaliation and preventing catastrophic defeat despite Pakistani conventional military weakness.

As I show in Chapter 5, this confluence of developments would begin to bear fruit as Pakistan achieved an opaque nuclear weapons capacity. A burgeoning nuclear capability emboldened Pakistani leaders to begin a deep involvement with the anti-Indian Kashmir insurgency, funding, arming, and training militants fighting against Indian rule. This policy soon became nothing short of a Pakistani low-intensity conflict against India. It resulted in strong Indian military counterresponses, which in turn led to further Indo-Pakistani crises. As a result, militarized disputes between India and Pakistan during the de facto nuclear period became more frequent and intense than they were during the nonnuclear period.

5

The De Facto Nuclear Period

In the previous chapter, we saw that the nonnuclear period from 1972 through 1989 was relatively peaceful both in quantitative and qualitative terms; 186 of the 216 months during this period were completely free of militarized disputes, and the disputes that did occur remained at fairly low hostility levels.[1] I argued that this was the case because the Indian government was satisfied with existing territorial divisions on the subcontinent and had no reason to behave aggressively against Pakistan. The Pakistan government, for its part, was dissatisfied with the division of the subcontinent during this period and wished to alter territorial boundaries in Kashmir. However, following its defeat in the Bangladesh War, Pakistan was too weak to force a change in Kashmiri territorial boundaries and therefore generally avoided conflict with India. I also showed that, during the nonnuclear period, a process of Islamization within Pakistan, the war in Afghanistan, and Pakistan's growing nuclear capacity increased the importance of Kashmir as a Pakistani national issue and began to improve Pakistan's ability to change the territorial division of Kashmir by force.

In this chapter, I discuss the Indo-Pakistani security relationship from 1990 through May 1998, a period during which the two countries possessed an undeclared nuclear capability. I show that this period was considerably less peaceful than the nonnuclear period, with militarized disputes occurring at a much higher rate that they did from 1972 through 1989. One of these disputes, a militarized Indo-Pakistani standoff in 1990, reached an extremely high level of tension and had the potential to trigger a large-scale conventional conflict against a de facto nuclear backdrop. I argue that this decreased stability resulted largely from Pakistan's support for the anti-Indian insurgency in Kashmir and from Indian attempts to coerce Pakistan into ceasing its involvement in the conflict. I show that Pakistani support for the insurgency was in turn facilitated by Pakistan's de facto nuclear weapons capacity, which enabled Pakistan to pursue a low-intensity conflict strategy in Kashmir while insulated from all-out Indian conventional retaliation.[2] Thus, the de facto nuclearization of the subcontinent played a key role in destabilizing the Indo-Pakistani security relationship during this period.

Frequency and Level of Conflict

Table 1 shows that militarized disputes were far more common during the de facto nuclear period than they had been during the nonnuclear years. While 186 of the 216 months from 1972 through 1989 had been dispute-free, the 101-month period from 1990 through May 1998 included 73 dispute months. Thus, during the de facto nuclear period, militarized disputes were over five times more frequent than they were during the period from 1972 through 1989. The de facto nuclear period also saw the eruption of a major militarized Indo-Pakistani dispute in 1990, in which hundreds of thousands of troops massed along the Indo-Pakistani border, dire warnings emanated from New Delhi and Islamabad, and large-scale war seemed imminent. Because India and Pakistan were by this time de facto nuclear powers, any conventional war between the two countries threatened to escalate to the nuclear level. This danger resulted in high-level diplomatic intervention by the United States in hopes of defusing what had become a dangerous standoff.

Explaining Increased Conflict During the De Facto Nuclear Period

Why was the de facto nuclear period more conflict prone than the nonnuclear years discussed in Chapter 3? In this chapter, I show that the de facto nuclear period saw the South Asian territorial dispute over Kashmir once again take center stage in Indo-Pakistani relations, significantly increasing tension between the two countries. As I explain, the reemergence of the Kashmir issue resulted from a combination of social, political, and economic developments within the territory itself as well as from Pakistan's burgeoning nuclear capability. Developments within Kashmir led to widespread popular discontent with Indian rule, sparking a violent anti-Indian insurgency in the territory. Pakistan's nuclear capacity increasingly enabled it to take advantage of the uprising; its de facto nuclear arsenal encouraged Pakistan to arm, fund, and train anti-Indian forces in Kashmir while insulated from full-scale Indian retaliation. As a result, what began as an indigenous insurgency became an outright proxy war between Pakistan-supported guerrillas and Indian security forces. And this low-intensity conflict in turn drove a spiral of militarized tension between the two countries, which led to a large-scale confrontation between Indian and Pakistani armed forces in early 1990. In the sections that follow, I explain the outbreak of the Kashmir insurgency, trace Pakistan's growing involvement in the anti-Indian struggle, and discuss nuclear weapons' impact on Pakistani decision making. I show how Pakistani policy once again made Kashmir the locus of Indo-Pakistani militarized conflict, fueling an ongoing conflict within the territory and triggering the 1990 crisis, which arose out of Indian attempts to force Pakistan to cease its support for the insurgency.

The Kashmir Insurgency

As noted, the Kashmir dispute had lain relatively dormant from 1972 to 1989. During the late 1980s, however, Kashmir once again emerged as a major issue plaguing Indo-Pakistani relations. This was the case because in 1989 an armed insurgency against Indian rule erupted in the territory of Jammu and Kashmir, killing large numbers of civilians and security personnel and threatening to undermine Indian control of the region. The reasons for popular discontent with Indian rule were complex, but basically they were driven by a break between the region's Kashmiri-speaking Muslim population and the Indian central government. This break resulted from a combination of political mobilization and institutional decay within Kashmir. The Indian government's regional development efforts had politically energized younger Kashmiris, making them increasingly aware of their political rights. Simultaneously, however, the Indian government had deinstitutionalized Kashmiri politics, severely limiting the outlets available for legitimate political expression. As a result, Kashmiri resentment increased over time, until it finally exploded into violence.[3]

India took control of the territory of Jammu and Kashmir in 1947. Kashmir's Hindu ruler, Maharajah Hari Singh, had been undecided whether to join India or Pakistan when British India was partitioned between the two states. However, in early October 1947, a tribal rebellion erupted in the Poonch region of Kashmir. Soon a force of Pathan tribesmen and Pakistan Army personnel disguised as locals had captured Muzaffarabad and was marching on the Kashmiri capital of Srinagar. Hari Singh turned to the British Viceroy, Lord Louis Mountbatten, in search of Indian help in fending off the raiders. Mountbatten, along with Prime Minister Nehru, agreed to provide Hari Singh with Indian troops, but only if the maharajah would agree that Kashmir would accede to India and would sign an instrument of accession to this effect.

The instrument of accession was to be ratified by a vote of the Kashmiri people at a later date, after the ongoing hostilities had ceased and peaceful conditions prevailed. Hari Singh agreed and signed the instrument of accession on October 26. Indian troops were then quickly deployed to Srinagar.[4]

The Indians pursued both diplomatic and military tracks in battling Pakistan over Kashmir, lodging a complaint against Pakistani aggression with the UN Security Council on January 1, 1948, while simultaneously engaging the Pakistanis in periods of intense ground combat. Attacking forces had already managed to capture roughly one-third of Kashmir's territory by the time the Indians arrived in the region. The Indians successfully defended Srinagar and fought Pakistan-backed forces, as well as regular Pakistan Army elements, in a series of battles over the coming months. Nonetheless, the territorial balance changed little, and the conflict ground to a stalemate, with India controlling approximately two-thirds of Kashmir and Pakistan holding roughly one-third of the region. With both sides spent and unable to make further territorial inroads, the war ended with a United Nations–sponsored cease-fire on January 1, 1949.[5]

The propriety of Kashmir's accession to India has been the subject of an extensive and acrimonious debate, the details of which are beyond the scope of this study. The important points, for our purposes, are that the Pakistan government believes that Kashmir's accession to India was illegal and undemocratic. Pakistani critiques focus especially on India's failure to hold a plebiscite on the question of accession. Such a vote was promised by Nehru and demanded by the United Nations Security Council, which in 1948 called on India to "undertake that there will be . . . in Jammu and Kashmir . . . a plebiscite as soon as possible on the question of the accession of the State to India or Pakistan."[6] In the Pakistani view, India's refusal to put the issue of accession to the ballot denies the Kashmiri people their right to self-determination and clearly demonstrates India's malign intentions in the region.[7]

In the Indian government's view, by contrast, Kashmir has legally been part of the Indian state since Hari Singh signed the instrument of accession. The Indians point out that although Nehru did promise that the Kashmiri people would be able to vote on the question of accession, this vote was to occur once Pakistani aggression had ceased and the region had returned to normalcy, neither of which have happened. Similarly, the United Nations Security Council did call on India to hold a plebiscite on the question of accession but only after peace and order had been restored in the territory. Specifically, paragraph 1 (a) of Security Council Resolution 726 required Pakistan "To secure the withdrawal from the State of Jammu and Kashmir of tribesmen and Pakistani nationals not normally resident therein who have entered the state for the purpose of fighting, and to prevent any intrusion into the State of such elements and any furnishing of material aid to those fighting in the state."[8] Only after Pakistan had complied with paragraph 1 (a) did Resolution 726 require India to draw down its forces in Kashmir and subsequently hold a plebiscite in the territory. Since these conditions have not been met, India maintains that Resolution 726 does not in fact obligate it to hold a vote on the question of accession. The Indian government believes that continuing Pakistani support for Kashmiri separatism is an attempt to take by force what Pakistan was unable to acquire lawfully.[9]

Significantly, the Kashmiri population was, until fairly recently, unwilling to oppose Indian rule violently, despite India's failure to conduct a plebiscite on the question of accession. Since joining India, Kashmir had enjoyed a unique, autonomous status within the Indian Union. The instrument of accession had limited the Indian government's jurisdiction over Kashmir to the areas of defense, foreign affairs, and communications. When the Indian Constitution was ratified in 1950, Article 370 gave the federal government the authority to legislate for Kashmir in these areas but only "in consultation with the Government of [Jammu and Kashmir] State." The Constitution also gave the federal government legislative authority on other specific subjects contained in India's Union and Concurrent Lists but only with the final consent of the Jammu and Kashmir Assembly.[10] The Indian Constitution thus codified Jammu and Kashmir's special, autonomous status within the Indian Union.[11]

This unique relationship with New Delhi did not lead to widespread Kashmiri satisfaction with Indian rule, but it did somewhat limit India's direct interference in the region's domestic politics and thus reduced local resentment. In addition, low education and literacy levels, along with the absence of mass media, made the majority of Kashmiris politically inactive. Therefore, most Kashmiris, though not entirely content with Indian control, possessed neither the political awareness nor the skills necessary to resist the prevailing governmental arrangements.[12]

Kashmiris proved unwilling to oppose Indian control of the territory violently even when outsiders presented them with ample opportunity to do so. In 1965, for example, Pakistan sought to wrest Kashmir from India by fomenting a domestic uprising in the territory. Pakistan's military government was convinced by anti-Indian rioting that the time was right to capitalize on Kashmiri discontent with Indian rule.[13] The Pakistanis therefore planned to infiltrate soldiers disguised as tribesmen into the Kashmir Valley. The infiltrators were to spark a popular rebellion, which would be followed by an invasion of the territory by the Pakistan Army. In August 1965, Pakistan launched the first phase of the plan, Operation Gibraltar, secreting roughly 5,000 lightly armed guerrillas into Kashmir. However, the infiltrators did not receive the anticipated welcome from local residents. Instead, Kashmiris turned the intruders over to Indian authorities. Thus, despite extensive Pakistani efforts to raise a guerrilla force and infiltrate it into Indian Kashmir at a seemingly opportune moment, the mission failed completely. The Kashmiri people simply did not desire violent secession from India and chose to cooperate with Indian security forces rather than to support the intruders' efforts.[14]

In spite of considerable discontent with Indian rule, then, Kashmiris in 1965 were unwilling to attempt to overthrow it violently—even when Pakistan went to great lengths to present them with the opportunity to do so. Over time, however, Kashmiris' attitudes toward Indian rule changed. This was the result of two important developments. First, thanks to the efforts of both the Kashmiri National Conference[15] and the Indian central government, educational institutions proliferated, literacy rates increased, and access to mass media grew significantly in Kashmir. As a result, the Kashmiri population became more politically informed, active, and aware of its rights than earlier generations of Kashmiris had been.[16]

However, even as Kashmiris were becoming more politically active and aware, political institutions in Kashmir steadily decayed, again as the result of the policies of both the local and central governments. Within Kashmir, Sheikh Abdullah and his National Conference retained a monopolistic hold on power, preventing the emergence of any legitimate political opposition in the territory. At the federal level, the Indian government turned a blind eye to the National Conference's undemocratic behavior. In addition, the central government dealt with Kashmir in an increasingly authoritarian manner. The 1975 Kashmir Accord, for example, reaffirmed Kashmir's special status under Article 370 of the Indian Constitution but made the state a "constituent unit of the Union of India." This enabled the central government to pass legislation for Kashmir designed to prevent "activities directed toward disclaiming, questioning or disrupting the sovereignty and territorial integrity of India or bringing about cession of a part of the territory of India from the Union or causing insult to the Indian national flag . . . national anthem and the Constitution."[17] The accord thus gave India crucial control over the Kashmiri government and regional political activity and led many observers to believe that the issues of plebiscite and self-determination were now moot.[18] Over the next decade, the Indian government continued its high-handed approach, dismissing legitimately elected Kashmiri leaders, passing draconian antiterrorism legislation, and refusing to brook any suggestion of political opposition in the territory. The result was to centralize power in New Delhi, thereby eroding Kashmir's unique, autonomous status within the Indian union and alienating an increasingly resentful Kashmiri population.[19]

This combination of factors created an environment ripe for revolt in Kashmir. The tipping point came when National Conference leader Farooq Abdullah conspired with New Delhi to rig the outcome of the 1987 Kashmiri state assembly elections. This malfeasance led to widespread outrage and closed off the last remaining avenue for legitimate political activity in Kashmir. Violent, extra-institutional opposition now remained the only option open to Kashmiris dissatisfied with the political status quo. In 1988, a series of demonstrations and strikes as well as limited attacks against government targets occurred in the Kashmir Valley. These attacks increased in frequency during 1989, and militants kidnapped the daughter of Indian Home Affairs Minister Mufti Mohammad Sayeed.[20] By 1990, violent clashes between insurgents and security forces had become daily occurrences, leading the Indian government to dissolve the Kashmiri state assembly and place the territory under Governor's Rule. A full-blown insurgency dedicated to overturning Indian rule in the territory had erupted.[21] Thus, as Ganguly argues, "The early decay of political institutions in Kashmir, which the government in New Delhi did little to stem (and in some cases encouraged), and the dramatic pace of political mobilization proved to be a combustible mix,"[22] driving Kashmiris to the armed rebellion that they had previously rejected.

Pakistani Involvement in the Insurgency

As we have seen, the insurgency against Indian rule in Jammu and Kashmir had deep indigenous roots, resulting from Kashmiri resentment at malfeasance and mismanagement by both the Kashmiri and central Indian governments. Therefore, the separatist movement was not primarily the creation of any outside power. Despite its Kashmiri origins, however, the uprising was not a purely indigenous phenomenon; from the outset, Pakistan was intimately involved in the insurgency. As Wirsing argues, "Pakistani intelligence organs took advantage of discontents developing among Kashmiri Muslims in Indian Kashmir *prior* to the onset of the uprising and, in so doing, exerted some influence on its scale, timing, tactics, and objectives."[23] Specifically, Pakistan's Inter-Services Intelligence (ISI), fresh from its success against the Soviet Union in Afghanistan, discovered in the late 1980s that, unlike in decades past, Kashmiris had become sufficiently disaffected with Indian rule to rebel violently against it. The ISI thus sensed genuine Indian vulnerability and, at last, an opportunity for effective Pakistani action in Kashmir. Between 1988 and 1990, the ISI capitalized on the situation, assisting the Jammu and Kashmir Liberation Front (JKLF), which viewed Pakistan as a key strategic ally, in starting the anti-Indian rebellion. The revolt touched a chord with the local population and spread rapidly through the valley. Soon large numbers of young men from the valley were crossing into Pakistani Kashmir, receiving weapons and training and returning to fight the Indians.[24]

Supporting the anti-Indian uprising in Kashmir was attractive to Pakistani policymakers on multiple levels. First, the insurgency presented Pakistan with the chance to help liberate Kashmir from Indian control. As we have seen, Pakistani leaders had never abandoned their goal of wresting Kashmiri territory from the Indians. However, they lacked the means to pursue their objective, given the enormous military disparity between the two countries that emerged in the wake of the Bangladesh War. Thus, until the late 1980s, the idea of taking action designed to promote Kashmiri liberation was not popular among Pakistani decision makers. Given the gulf between Indian and Pakistani military capabilities, India's ability to maintain its hold on Kashmir and eventually force Pakistan to accept the LoC as a permanent border seemed beyond challenge. This perception changed significantly with the outbreak of a large-scale Kashmiri Muslim separatist movement, which led to the view among Pakistani policymakers that historical forces had turned against multiethnic states like India and the belief that now Pakistan's territorial goals in Kashmir might ultimately come within its grasp.[25]

Additionally, Pakistani leaders believed that the Kashmir insurgency offered them an opportunity to begin redressing the enormous material discrepancies that existed between India and Pakistan. Specifically, a protracted, low-intensity conflict could "bleed" India and its much larger military, depleting Indian resources and thereby reducing Indian material advantages over time as well as demoralizing its army and sullying India's international reputation.[26] Thus, in addition to possibly wresting Kashmiri territory from the Indians, Pakistani pursuit of a LIC strategy in Kashmir could yield important military and diplomatic dividends in Pakistan's broader security competition with India.

To this end, the Pakistanis began a policy of active support for violent separatism in Kashmir. Although the Pakistani government has always maintained that it offers only moral and political backing to the insurgents,[27] in fact it has provided them with extensive material support, including indoctrination, training, arming, and infiltration and exfiltration of fighters across the Line of Control, under the auspices of the Pakistan Army and the ISI. Indeed, the forbidding nature of the terrain in which the insurgents operate virtually requires them to rely on Pakistani assistance.[28] Pakistani support for the rebellion became so extensive as to make it a key aspect of Pakistani foreign policy, which in turn fundamentally shaped the nature of the Kashmir insurgency.[29] As Wirsing argues,

> Pakistan's support (or withholding of it) has unquestionably been a key organizational variable in Kashmir; and its patronage has no doubt exerted a powerful influence on the rise and fall in fortunes of practically every militant group active there. Some of the militant organizations may be largely or even entirely the creatures of the ISI, and all of the principal groups . . . are dependent to some extent for their financing and supplies on the resources of that intelligence unit.[30]

The insurgency, and the nature and degree of Pakistani involvement in it, has gone through several phases. Initially, the Kashmiri rebellion was spearheaded by the Jammu and Kashmir Liberation Front, which sought the territory's freedom from both India and Pakistan. Although the Pakistanis at first supported the JKLF, they soon became disenchanted with the group's dedication to the goal of Kashmiri independence. The ISI therefore began to undermine the JKLF, cutting off aid to the Front, encouraging factionalism within it, and supporting the creation of new insurgent groups such as the Hizbul Mujahideen (HM), which sought not just to break away from Indian rule but also to join Kashmir with Pakistan.[31]

By 1993, this Pakistan-supported factionalism, the rise of the Pakistani-backed HM, and aggressive tactics by Indian security forces had largely marginalized the JKLF. However, the HM, despite its ascendancy, faced problems of its own. Although outside support had made possible its predominance, HM's pro-Pakistan orientation also alienated many Kashmiris, who sought independence for the territory rather than merger with Pakistan. Thus, by 1994, the insurgency was plagued by a fundamental contradiction, with pro-Pakistani militants fighting on behalf of a Kashmiri population that favored independence.[32] As a result, by the mid-1990s, the momentum of the Kashmir conflict had shifted away from the insurgents and toward the Indian government. Not only had the Kashmiri population become resentful of Pakistan's deep involvement in the independence movement, but many former guerrillas had renounced their allegiance to the rebellion, becoming "renegades" and joining the Indian counterinsurgency forces. The Indians thus began to gain the upper hand in Kashmir militarily. With the JKLF defeated, the HM facing resentment from the population and serious pressure from Indian and "renegade" security forces, and most other insurgent groups disbanded or ineffective, the Kashmiri rebellion from 1996 to 1998 entered a state of "demoralization and atrophy."[33]

The Indian government hoped that the insurgency's downturn would afford it an opportunity simultaneously to crush remaining armed resistance
and to restart Kashmir's political process through legislative assembly elections, thereby ending Kashmiri separatism once and for all. In fact, however,
the 1996–1998 lull in the insurgency did not have these effects. Rather, by
1999, it had led to the adoption of new techniques by the militants as well
as increased efforts by their Pakistani supporters to reenergize the rebellion.
I discuss these issues in the next chapter. Here, I briefly examine the effects
that the insurgency had on Kashmir and on India from the late 1980s through
the mid-1990s.

Effects of the Insurgency

The nuclear proliferation literature pays relatively little attention to the issue
of low-intensity conflict. Both sides in the debate focus primarily on the question of whether proliferation is likely to lead to the use of nuclear weapons,
or at least to large-scale conventional war. When the literature does mention
low-intensity conflict, it treats such fighting as a minor irritant rather than
as a serious real-world and theoretical problem. This is especially true of the
proliferation optimist literature, which tends to be dismissive of any conflict
occurring in a nuclear environment that does not reach the level of a major
war. Hagerty, for example, claims that nuclear weapons states do not fight
wars, while simultaneously admitting that nuclear weapons cannot prevent
the occurrence of guerrilla warfare between nuclear powers.[34] This implies
that guerrilla conflict is not sufficiently significant to count as warfare or to
undermine Hagerty's claims as to nuclear weapons' powerful stabilizing effects.
Similarly, Waltz argues that although low-level conflict can occur in a nuclear
environment, "The possibility of fighting at low levels is not a bad price to
pay for the impossibility of fighting at high levels."[35] Here, low-level warfare
is characterized not just as a minor problem; such conflict is portrayed as a
bargain.

It is certainly true that the consequences of low-intensity conflict are not
nearly as horrific as those of a nuclear exchange or even of a large-scale conventional war. Nonetheless, low-intensity conflict can be exceedingly costly in
political, economic, and human terms. The Kashmir insurgency is no exception. The conflict has been extremely damaging to Kashmiris and to India at
all three of these levels. These costs led the Indians to take the Kashmir insurgency very seriously during the de facto nuclear period and to view Pakistan's
support for the rebellion as a major provocation. Let us now briefly examine the costs of the Kashmir insurgency from the outbreak of the rebellion

through the mid-1990s in the following areas: deaths among Indian government security forces, civilian deaths, violent insurgent actions, security force commitment, the flight of non-Muslim minorities from the Kashmir Valley, and India's international image.[36]

Deaths among security forces and government officials: The Kashmir insurgency took a significant toll on Indian security forces and on federal and state government officials, such as politicians, judges, and other functionaries, between 1989 and the mid-1990s. According to Indian Home Ministry figures, the death toll totaled more than 1,000 per year from 1990 to 1993, with nearly 2,000 dying in 1992. By 1994, a total of nearly 5,700 security personnel and officials had died at the hands of the insurgents.[37]

Civilian deaths: According to the Indian Home Ministry, from 1990 through 1993, 2,224 civilians died as a result of violence associated with the insurgency.[38] Indian Army statistics put the number at 2,233 civilian deaths. This figure jumps to 4,041 if one includes the number of civilians killed in the "crossfire" of confrontations between militants and security forces.[39] By this count, more than 1,000 civilians were killed per year during this period.

Violent insurgent actions: Acts of violence, including attacks on security forces and others, explosion and arson, and other miscellaneous violent incidents perpetrated by separatist forces totaled 390 in 1988.[40] In 1990, 4,158 violent incidents occurred, and in 1993, a total of 5,247—an average of more than ten violent incidents per day.[41]

Security force commitment: The spiral of violence in Kashmir led India to deploy large numbers of security forces to the region. These forces were divided between the state police, paramilitary units, and the regular army. State police, which in 1993 totaled approximately 34,000, was roughly equally divided among "armed police," civil police, and criminal investigation and security. Paramilitary forces, which included the Border Security Force (BSF), Central Reserve Police Force (CRPF), the Indo-Tibetan Border Police (ITBP), and Rashtriya Rifles (RR), numbered between 100,000 and 150,000. The Indian Army headquartered one of its five regional commands, two of its ten corps (the 15th and 16th Corps), and seven of its thirty infantry divisions in Jammu and Kashmir, for a total of approximately 150,000 troops. All told, then, Indian security forces in Jammu and Kashmir in 1993 totaled roughly 300,000 to 400,000.[42]

Flight of non-Muslim minorities: When the Kashmir insurgency began, roughly 130,000 to 140,000 Kashmiri Pandits, who are Hindus, lived in Kashmir Valley. By early 1990, in the face of some targeted anti-Pandit attacks and rising overall violence in the region, approximately 100,000 Pandits had fled the valley, many of them ending up in refugee camps in southern Kashmir. Although there is some controversy over whether this exodus occurred primarily because of a deliberate anti-Pandit terror campaign or as a result of Indian government instigation, the fact remains that, due to the insurgency, the valley has been largely cleansed of its Hindu population.[43]

India's international image: India's international image suffered severely as a result of the insurgency. By fighting to suppress an indigenous autonomy movement and by refusing to hold a plebiscite after promising the Kashmiri people a vote on the question of accession, Indian policy in Kashmir appeared undemocratic and hypocritical. More significantly, Indian efforts to combat the Kashmiri insurgents and restore law and order led to large-scale human rights violations in the region. These abuses received widespread coverage in the press and by human rights groups. Human Rights Watch, for example, reported in 1996 that Indian security forces in Kashmir, and their local allies, employed such counterinsurgency tactics as extrajudicial killing, kidnapping, rape, and torture, including "severe beatings, electric shock, crushing the leg muscles with a wooden roller, and burning with heated objects." The report argued that such behavior was not limited to occasional isolated incidents but rather was systematic in nature and charged that the "Indian government's failure to account for these abuses and take rigorous action against those members of its forces responsible for murder, rape, and torture amounts to a policy of condoning human rights violations."[44] These reports threatened to tarnish India's reputation as a law-abiding, liberal, democratic state and greatly concerned the Indian government.[45]

This brief overview of the Kashmir insurgency's effects shows that, by the mid-1990s, the conflict had become a major politico-military crisis for India. The rebellion was killing significant numbers of Indian security personnel and government officials, visiting carnage and chaos upon Indian territory, diverting vast military resources from other uses, and severely damaging India's international reputation. Thus, although international relations theorists may characterize low-intensity violence such as that occurring in Kashmir as relatively cheap, from the Indian perspective, the insurgency was no bargain. In fact, by 1994, the 5,700 Indian security and government personnel that had been killed in the Kashmir insurgency had exceeded the number of Indian combat deaths in the 1948 and 1965 Indo-Pakistani wars combined and was only about 30 percent fewer than the number of Indian combat deaths in the Bangladesh conflict.[46]

Therefore, by funding, arming, and training the militants, Pakistan was, in a very real sense, waging war on India. And this enabled Pakistani leaders, sensing Indian weakness, to begin to press their advantage on the Kashmir issue. For example, during 1990 talks between Indian foreign minister Inder Gujral and Pakistani foreign minister Sahibzada Yaqub Khan, Khan reportedly took a position "almost challenging the Indian state's authority on Kashmir, saying nothing in the past was binding them and the Simla Agreement was not relevant."[47] It is important to keep these facts in mind when assessing the impact of Pakistan's support for the Kashmir insurgency on Indo-Pakistani relations. They clarify the extent of the challenge that Pakistani actions posed to India and highlight the boldness of Pakistani policy in Kashmir. They also explain the vigor with which India has attempted to crush the insurgency and coerce the Pakistanis into ceasing their support for the rebellion.

The question now arises: Why was Pakistan, from the late 1980s through the mid-1990s, willing to adopt such a bold and aggressive policy? As noted, despite its continued commitment to the Kashmir cause, Pakistan had largely avoided the issue since 1972, fearful of confronting a conventionally stronger India. Now, however, Pakistan was prosecuting a violent proxy war in Indian Kashmir. What had changed by the late 1980s to alter Pakistani strategic calculations and encourage it to take such provocative actions?

First, regional and world events created an opportunity for Pakistan in Kashmir. As we have seen, the Kashmir insurgency exploded in 1989 largely from indigenous causes and was not primarily a Pakistani creation. And the Afghan War offered a model that Pakistan could employ to defeat a stronger, occupying power in Kashmir over time, as well as seasoned military and intelligence services capable of executing such a strategy. The end of the war in Afghanistan also freed large numbers of mujahideen from their battle with the Soviets, creating the possibility that these fighters could be redirected to wage *jihad* in Kashmir. Benazir Bhutto, whose first term as Pakistani prime minister spanned from December 1988 to August 1990, recalls, "There was a proposal to send 100,000 battle-hardened . . . mujahideen to Kashmir." "There was a belief in some quarters that [they] could be redirected to the assistance of the Kashmiri people."[48] Bhutto claims that she vetoed this proposal and ensured that "all foreigners [were] kept out of the dispute." Nonetheless, she and most analysts believe that the Afghan mujahideen later became widely involved in the Kashmir insurgency.[49]

Beyond Afghanistan, international developments led Pakistani leaders to believe that the world community might now be more willing to address the Kashmir issue than previously. As Bhutto explains, in 1989, "the fall of the Berlin Wall and the expectations of freedom, the collapse of the Soviet Union, the emergence of newly independent states in central Asia and in Europe gave rise to a sense of expectation that the winds of freedom were blowing, that the borders conceived at the end of the Second World War at Yalta were now being reviewed and revised." Therefore, Pakistani decision makers hoped that an anti-Indian uprising in Kashmir would lead India and the international community to revisit the Kashmir dispute.[50] Together, these regional and international developments, which themselves had little or no connection to Pakistani policy in Kashmir, gave Pakistan its first chance in decades to inflict serious costs on Indian J&K and potentially to wrest the territory from India.

But if the Kashmir revolt, the Afghan War, and the Cold War's end created an opportunity for Pakistan, pursuing that opportunity could potentially be extremely costly. As noted, India was deeply committed to maintaining its grasp on Indian Kashmir and had explicitly threatened horizontal escalation against Pakistan in the event of Pakistani aggression in the region—a threat on which India had made good in the past. The Bangladesh War had demonstrated to Pakistani leaders the dangers of a full-scale conflict with India. If Pakistan once again adopted an aggressive policy in Kashmir, India might retaliate with an all-out conventional attack, coercing the Pakistan government into abandoning its support for the Kashmir militancy, seizing further Kashmiri territory, or even subjecting Pakistan to catastrophic defeat. Despite these risks, the Pakistanis nonetheless pursued an aggressive policy in Kashmir, capitalizing on the opportunities that regional and world developments created for them by launching a proxy war against Indian Kashmir. What emboldened the Pakistanis to adopt such a risky strategy?

To some extent, the semicovert nature of the Pakistanis' policy could insulate them from the dangers of Indian retaliation. In supporting the Kashmir insurgency, Pakistan was not launching a direct attack on India or on the Indian armed forces. Rather, it was enabling others to do so. This reduced the likelihood that India would respond to the growing unrest with an attack on Pakistan. However, such a strategy afforded Pakistan only limited deniability; it was difficult to conceal the origin of the large amounts of equipment and personnel flowing into the Kashmir Valley. The Indians were thus aware of Pakistani involvement in the Kashmir insurgency from the beginning, and as early as 1989 Indian analysts were already attributing spiraling violence in the region to Pakistan's "foreign hand."[51]

Despite its semicovert nature, then, Pakistan's adoption of a low-intensity conflict strategy in Kashmir was well known to the Indians, and pursuit of the policy therefore posed a potential danger of large-scale Indian retaliation. Pakistani confidence that this danger would not materialize, and that India would not in fact respond in this manner, turned on yet another development that in itself was unrelated to Kashmir—Pakistan's budding nuclear capability. As noted, by the late 1980s, Pakistan was a de facto nuclear state. Although Pakistan did not actually possess nuclear weapons, it probably could have assembled them in short order if the need had arisen. Pakistani policymakers thought that this de facto capability could be useful to Pakistan at multiple levels.

Benazir Bhutto explains the Pakistani leadership's thinking on the nuclear issue. According to Bhutto, Pakistani leaders believed that "having nuclear capacity would ensure that India could not launch a conventional war, knowing that if it did, it would turn nuclear, and that hundreds of millions would die . . . [I]t would have meant suicide not just for one, but for both nations." [52] Such a deterrent capacity would be valuable to Pakistan for two main reasons. First, it would enable Pakistan to ensure its physical security against the threat of Indian predations. Pakistani leaders were acutely aware of the danger of Indian conventional military strength as well as Pakistan's inherent vulnerability to ethnic separatism. Both of these dangers had figured prominently in the loss of East Pakistan, which continued to weigh heavily upon Pakistani decision makers in the late 1980s.

According to Bhutto, prior to acquiring a de facto nuclear capability, the Pakistanis believed that they "could sustain a war [against India] for two or three weeks" but that it would be "very difficult for us to continue fighting . . . beyond a limited period of time . . . Ultimately, the Indians had greater military resources than we did, they are five times larger than we are, and they can fight for five times longer than we can." Thus, in the absence of international intervention, "the only way to stop an Indian advance" and avoid the possibility of catastrophic defeat would be "to threaten a retaliation." Pakistan's acquisition of a de facto nuclear capacity made such a threat possible. Once the Pakistanis achieved this capability, "we thought our nuclear deterrent would prevent India from doing a war against us." [53]

Pakistani leaders were worried not only about India's ability to launch a traditional military assault against Pakistan. They also feared that India might exploit Pakistan's ethnic divisions in an effort to stoke domestic unrest and perhaps even split the country with the aid of separatists. As Bhutto explains, "We have suffered the division of Pakistan with the separation of East Pakistan. We are a federation with many difficulties among some of our federating units. It was a concern that a neighbor might take advantage of these ethnic sentiments within our own country and try to create a situation." Nuclear weapons could help the Pakistanis guard against this threat as well, deterring the Indians from pushing too hard at Pakistan's ethnic fissures. [54]

In the first instance, then, Pakistani leaders viewed their nuclear capability as defensive in nature, "conceived as part of a policy of parity with India, to protect and promote the territorial integrity of Pakistan."[55] Additionally, however, Pakistani leaders came to believe that a nuclear deterrent capacity would enable Pakistan to attain strategic objectives beyond mere self-defense—objectives that previously, in a purely conventional environment, would have been too dangerous to pursue. According to Bhutto, "somewhere down the line" the Pakistani leadership began to view its nuclear capacity not merely as a defensive capability but also as a means of effecting change in Kashmir while insulated from Indian retaliation. Around 1989, the de facto Pakistani nuclear capability's "ability to ward off a conventional [Indian] act may have led to the conclusion that a low-scale insurgency in the disputed area of Jammu and Kashmir could focus international attention" on the Kashmir conflict. "Perhaps a low-scale uprising could convince India and the rest of the world community, including the United Nations, to address this very important issue."[56] Pakistani leaders' subsequent decision to begin providing political, material, and military support for the anti-Indian insurgency in Kashmir was thus taken in the belief that Pakistan's nuclear weapons would protect it against any full-scale Indian response. According to Bhutto, the Pakistanis were convinced that India "[could] not wage a conventional war against Pakistan" in retaliation for provocations in Kashmir because of the risk that "a conventional war could turn nuclear."[57] For Pakistani leaders, then, the country's growing nuclear capacity began to acquire an important new offensive purpose in addition to its original defensive role, enabling Pakistan to challenge the territorial status quo in Kashmir once again.[58]

Pakistan's emerging nuclear capacity did not completely insulate it from the possibility of Indian retaliation. Indeed, Pakistan's willingness to adopt an aggressive policy in Kashmir from behind its nuclear shield ran the risk of sparking a crisis that could escalate to the level of a direct military confrontation with India. The best example of this danger during the de facto nuclear period was the Indo-Pakistani militarized crisis of 1990. As noted, Brasstacks, the most serious Indo-Pakistani crisis of the nonnuclear period, probably resulted largely from misperception and not from a deliberate attempt by either country to coerce or attack the other. This was not the case with the crisis of 1990. The 1990 dispute arose out of a direct Indian attempt to intimidate Pakistan and coerce it into ceasing its support for the Kashmir insurgency.

This is not to argue that India wanted war in 1990 or that misperception did not play a significant role in the crisis. As I will explain, the evidence indicates that neither India nor Pakistan wished the dispute to escalate to the level of outright conflict and that spiraling tension during the crisis resulted largely from a series of mutual misperceptions. We should also note that the 1990 crisis did not result solely from Indo-Pakistani tensions over Kashmir. Despite the enormous importance of the insurgency, the causes of the 1990 crisis were complex and multilayered. A confluence of variables, including weak domestic leadership in India and Pakistan, a shifting international environment in the wake of the Cold War, and the aftereffects of previous Indo-Pakistani crises such as Brasstacks, helped to drive the outbreak and escalation of the 1990 dispute.[59] Nonetheless, the Indians did spark the 1990 crisis with an attempt to apply coercive leverage against Pakistan in response to spiraling violence in Kashmir. Thus, the Kashmir insurgency was the key factor behind the outbreak of the 1990 dispute. As a recent study argues, the "underlying cause of the crisis" was "the explosion of dissidence and separatist feelings in Kashmir," which "necessitated major Indian military movement" and "raised the possibility of Indian forces crossing the LoC to attack training camps located in Pakistan-administered Kashmir or Pakistan itself. The events in Kashmir became a backdrop to subsequent calculations and recalculations of larger military and strategic moves by both sides."[60]

The 1990 Crisis

When the Kashmir insurgency erupted, India began augmenting its security forces in Kashmir and Punjab with regular army infantry units in hopes of stemming militant infiltrations from Pakistan and Azad Kashmir onto Indian territory. In response, Pakistan deployed armored units into Bahawalpur and Bhawalnagar, facing Indian Punjab and Rajasthan, and into the Shakargarh salient across from the road connecting Jammu to Punjab. In addition, forces from Pakistan's December 1989 Zarb-i-Momim military exercise, the largest in Pakistan's history, did not return to their peacetime stations and lingered in their exercise area near the international border and the LoC in Kashmir. The Indians feared that these movements were designed to support and possibly capitalize on terrorist operations within Indian territory. Meanwhile, in February, two Indian armored units deployed to a firing range in Rajasthan. The Pakistanis feared that these forces could form the nucleus of another Brasstacks-like military exercise or even launch an attack on Pakistan directly from range.[61]

This cycle of military action and reaction touched off a series of heated exchanges in the press between Indian and Pakistani leaders. In mid-March, Prime Minister Benazir Bhutto, during a visit to Pakistani Kashmir, announced that Pakistan was prepared for "one thousand years of war with Hindu India" in pursuit of Kashmiri freedom from Indian rule. Indian Prime Minister V. P. Singh, in an early April speech to the Lok Sabha, responded, "I warn them [that] those who talk about a thousand years of war should examine whether they will last a thousand hours of war." Singh also encouraged Indians to prepare "psychologically" for conflict.[62]

By mid-April, roughly 200,000 army and paramilitary forces were deployed in Indian Kashmir, where they faced off against approximately 100,000 troops across the LoC in Pakistani Kashmir. In places, a mere 200 meters separated Indian and Pakistani forces. In the Punjab, both sides had deployed infantry close to the border, while keeping armor and artillery at their peacetime bases. And in Rajasthan, three Indian divisions, including an armored division, faced a Pakistani corps, minus its armored division, which did not leave its peacetime station. Indian policymakers worried that Pakistan could use its forces to sever vital lines of communication between Punjab and Kashmir and to aid the Kashmiri insurgency. The Pakistanis, for their part, feared a major Indian armored thrust in Sindh as well as Indian raids on insurgent camps in Azad Kashmir.[63]

India and Pakistan were not the only parties concerned by the events unfolding in early 1990. By April, Indo-Pakistani force deployments and bellicose rhetoric had attracted the attention of the U.S. government, which decided to intervene diplomatically in hopes of defusing the crisis. In mid-May, deputy National Security Advisor Robert Gates traveled to Islamabad and New Delhi, where he urged restraint on Pakistani and Indian leaders. Gates informed both sides that the United States had thoroughly assessed the prevailing military situation and that while India would win any full-scale Indo-Pakistani war, the costs of doing so would exceed the benefits of victory. He secured a promise from Pakistani President Ghulam Ishaq Khan and Army Chief of Staff Mirza Aslam Beg to shut down Pakistani training camps for the Kashmiri insurgents and relayed this assurance to the Indians. Gates also offered to provide both sides with satellite reconnaissance data as an assurance to each party that the other was in fact withdrawing from its forward positions. Soon after Gates's visit, the situation began to de-escalate. India announced the return of its forward-deployed armor to peacetime stations and proposed a number of confidence-building measures to Pakistan. Within two weeks of the Gates mission, the 1990 crisis was over.[64]

Why did the crisis end without escalating to the level of outright conflict? Several factors likely contributed to this outcome. Outside intervention, particularly in the form of the Gates visits to Islamabad and New Delhi, probably helped. Even if outside intervention was not solely responsible for ending the crisis, it certainly did not harm the situation and enabled both sides to climb down from the aggressive positions that they had taken during the stand-off, while avoiding the appearance of weakness.[65] Additionally, discussions between the Indian and Pakistani foreign ministers in the United States in late April may have had a pacifying effect on the standoff. Despite the talks' lack of substantive results, the two parties agreed on the need for greater mutual restraint in the future.[66]

Proliferation optimists have attributed the defusion of the 1990 crisis to the stabilizing effects of nuclear weapons. Hagerty, for example, believes that India was deterred from aggression by the knowledge that Pakistan probably possessed a nuclear weapons capacity. Had the Pakistanis lacked such a capability, he claims, the crisis would almost surely have escalated to the level of outright war. According to Hagerty,

> In a nonnuclear South Asia, India would most likely have chosen to punish Pakistan for its transgressions in Kashmir, as it did in 1965. However, in the context of opaque nuclear capabilities and the existential deterrent effect they create, India was forced to limit its military operations to Indian-held Kashmir. In short, existential nuclear deterrence inhibited escalation from unconventional conflict to conventional or nuclear war.[67]

Despite considerable logical and intuitive appeal, this argument suffers from an important shortcoming: As Richard Smoke and Alexander George explain, in a possible deterrence scenario, "the absence of attack could mean . . . that no attack was ever intended." Deterrence requires a potential aggressor to "perceive an interest in attacking or encroaching upon" another state.[68] In this case, for Pakistan's opaque nuclear capacity to have deterred India from war, Indian leaders must have been intending to launch a conflict and subsequently decided not to do so out of concern that such a confrontation could escalate to the nuclear level.[69]

Did the defusion of the 1990 crisis meet these criteria? Although it is difficult to answer this question definitively, the preponderance of available evidence indicates that the answer is no. Four main factors support the argument that Pakistani nuclear weapons deterred India from attacking in 1990. First, India and Pakistan believed each other to be nuclear weapon–capable states by 1990. Second, an extremely tense militarized crisis, which resulted from a major Indo-Pakistani political dispute over Kashmir, did not escalate to the level of outright war. Third, India had in 1965 attacked Pakistan in retaliation for Pakistani provocations in Kashmir. Finally, even if India had been deterred from attacking Pakistan in 1990, Indian officials would be loath to admit it because doing so would acknowledge both Indian recklessness and weakness.[70]

These are important points, but they do not make a wholly convincing case for a "prodeterrence" interpretation of the 1990 crisis. First, the extent to which the Indian and Pakistani governments actually believed each other to be nuclear capable in 1990 is unclear. Neither country had a reliable delivery platform or a nuclear doctrine, and each side harbored doubts as to the other's possession of an operational nuclear weapon.[71] According to S. K. Singh, Indian foreign secretary during the 1990 crisis, the Indian government "failed to see Pakistan's 'burgeoning' nuclear capability as a major . . . threat to ourselves."[72] Second, as noted earlier, the absence of an attack does not necessarily indicate the operation of deterrence. To conclude that India was deterred from attacking Pakistan, we would need evidence beyond the fact that India and Pakistan were involved in a bitter political battle over Kashmir. Specifically, we would require information that India was actually planning to attack Pakistan but was convinced not to do so by the expected costs of such a policy. Third, Indian behavior in 1965 says little about Indian intentions in 1990. The fact that twenty-five years earlier India had attacked Pakistan in retaliation for aggression in Kashmir does not mean that in 1990 Indian leaders were planning to do so. Finally, Indian leaders have proven willing to admit that Pakistani nuclear weapons led them to reject options for aggressive retaliation against Pakistani provocations in Kashmir. For example, former senior Indian officials have confessed that they ruled out cross-border attacks on Pakistan during the 1999 Kargil crisis because of Pakistan's nuclear weapons capacity.[73]

Thus, the evidence supporting a prodeterrence interpretation of the 1990 crisis is limited. What evidence exists to suggest that India was *not* in fact deterred from attacking Pakistan in 1990? Quite simply, it does not appear that India was undertaking any military action to prepare for an imminent strike. Hagerty's own description of Indian and Pakistani force deployments suggests a lack of any serious hostile intent on the part of either party. As he points out, in Kashmir, Punjab, and Rajasthan, India and Pakistan together possessed a total of four armored divisions. Only one of these, the Indian division at the firing range in Rajasthan, was deployed outside its peacetime station, and none of these units was moving toward the Indo-Pakistani border during the crisis.[74]

Testimony from senior Indian military officers also suggests that the Indian Army was not preparing for hostile activity in early 1990. For example, a retired Indian general, who commanded an infantry division in the Punjab plains during the standoff, was ordered to continue his division's normal training regimen throughout the crisis. The general notes that during this period he observed none of the usual indicators preceding imminent conflict. He recalls, "There was no stoppage of leave. I myself took one month leave. No stoppage of courses. No vacation of forward-area hospitals. No hiring of vehicles. And no indications [of plans for hostilities] from superiors. We were never on the brink of conflict, and there was no indication whatsoever of preparation for it."[75] Based on his conversations with fellow division commanders at the time, the general is confident that their experiences were similar to his.

Satish Nambiar, India's Deputy Director General of Military Operations in 1990, monitored developments in the crisis on an "hourly" basis. According to Nambiar, the Indians did closely follow Pakistan's Zarb-i-Momim military exercise, though they were not unduly concerned by the Pakistani operation; the Indians had received plans of the exercise in advance, and Pakistani forces were "by and large following details as given." Nambiar states that he "never got the sense that the Indian political leadership wanted to escalate" the 1990 standoff. "The usual indicators of impending conflict, such as the dumping of ammunition and the laying of mines, were not seen." And any attempts at aggressive "low-level moves at the command level were stopped by higher authority," as the Indian government did not want to appear to be taking threatening actions "even in a cautionary manner." Thus, in Nambiar's view, India was not seriously contemplating an attack against Pakistan, and nuclear deterrence was not a factor in the crisis. "The nuclear element never entered into our calculations," Nambiar concludes.[76] American military attachés in India and Pakistan, granted wide access to both sides' forces, support these claims, concluding that Indian and Pakistani deployments during the crisis did not constitute unusual activity or indicate unduly hostile intentions.[77]

Senior Indian civilian officials hold similar opinions regarding the 1990 crisis. For example, according to S. K. Singh, the claim that India and Pakistan were on the brink of war in 1990 "was a fairy tale then and remains one now." "The so-called Crisis of 1990," Singh continues, "was an elephantine Non-Crisis. That India had any need to attack Pakistan did not cross anyone's mind in the Indian policy making community anytime during those weeks. And the 'Crisis' itself evaporated as rapidly as it had built up—leaving not a trace."[78]

Significantly, Pakistani leaders appear to have shared these views regarding Indian intentions. According to Benazir Bhutto, the Pakistan government never believed that the Indians were planning to attack. Bhutto explains, "I believe the 1990 crisis was just overblown . . . we never looked upon the threat as a serious threat from India, and we saw it more as a domestic Indian issue . . . it never was any danger point." Additionally, Bhutto continues,

> In 1990 we had not put together the bomb. We had the bomb, but the bomb components had to be put together to be used. If we had considered this a real threat . . . if we expected India to attack us we would put together the nuclear de-

vice to signal to the rest of the world community that this war can go nuclear so you better intervene. So if we had considered it a serious threat, we would have had a meeting of the nuclear command committee, and put together a device. We never did that.[79]

Considerable evidence therefore suggests that India was not in fact preparing for a possible strike against Pakistan in 1990. Of course, this does not *prove* that Pakistani nuclear weapons did not deter India from attacking Pakistan during the standoff. It is possible that Indian leaders harbored hidden intentions to attack Pakistan despite their lack of statements to that effect, despite their apparent dearth of military preparations, and despite Pakistani leaders' failure to perceive an imminent Indian threat. However, the foregoing discussion gives us reason to be skeptical of such an interpretation. Rather, the preponderance of the evidence points in the opposite direction: The defusion of the 1990 crisis appears to have occurred primarily because "neither India nor Pakistan *wanted* to go to war in early 1990, despite the fact that the tension level between them had risen to an alarmingly high level."[80] Thus, strictly speaking, India seems not to have been deterred from war in 1990 by Pakistani nuclear weapons or by any other factor.

Moreover, the argument that Pakistan's de facto nuclear capacity deterred war in 1990 overlooks the role that Pakistani nuclear weapons played in causing the crisis in the first place. As we have seen, the 1990 standoff began when India deployed forces to Kashmir and Punjab in hopes of reducing the infiltration of insurgents from Pakistan and Azad Kashmir into Indian J&K. Support for the militants was part of Pakistan's low-intensity conflict strategy in Kashmir, which sought to capitalize on the Kashmir insurgency in an attempt to attrit Indian resources and wrest Kashmiri territory from Indian rule. Pakistan's willingness to adopt such a strategy resulted in large part from its burgeoning nuclear capacity, which Pakistani leaders believed insulated Pakistan from the possibility of large-scale Indian retaliation. Had Pakistan not possessed this nuclear capability, it probably would not have been willing to adopt such an aggressive policy in Kashmir. Nuclear weapons thus encouraged the Pakistani actions that provoked the outbreak of the 1990 standoff. Not only did nuclear weapons probably not deter the outbreak of war during the Indo-Pakistani crisis of 1990, but in an important sense, nuclear weapons underlay the crisis' emergence and thus were responsible for the largest militarized dispute of the de facto nuclear period.

Conclusion

In this chapter, I showed that Indo-Pakistani relations during the de facto nuclear period from 1990 through 1998 were considerably more volatile than they had been during the nonnuclear period. Militarized disputes occurred more frequently than they did before India and Pakistan acquired an opaque nuclear capacity. I argued that while factors such as the Islamization of Pakistani society, the Afghan War, and Kashmiri disaffection with Indian rule contributed to this outcome, increased militarized conflict during the de facto nuclear period was directly facilitated by Pakistan's emerging nuclear capability. Nuclear weapons emboldened Pakistani leaders to pursue a low-intensity conflict strategy against Indian Kashmir, extensively funding, arming, and training militants fighting Indian rule in the region in hopes of bleeding Indian resources, attracting international attention, and wresting Kashmiri territory from India. Pakistani leaders pursued such an aggressive strategy in the belief that Pakistan's de facto nuclear status would deter India from launching an all-out conventional retaliation. Although India did not react with a large-scale attack during the de facto nuclear period, it did respond assertively to Pakistani machinations, substantially increasing force deployments and antiterrorist operations in Kashmir and Punjab. As the Indo-Pakistani crisis of 1990 showed, these actions further increased militarized tension in the region and threatened to trigger a full-scale conventional war.

In Chapter 6, I examine the impact of the transition from opaque to overt nuclearization on Indo-Pakistani security relations. I show that the nuclear tests of 1998 did not reduce Indo-Pakistani conflict levels below those of the nonnuclear or de facto nuclear periods. Rather, within less than one year after the nuclear tests, conflict had escalated to a level unseen in nearly three decades. I argue that this occurred because the acquisition of an overt nuclear capacity further emboldened Pakistan to alter the territorial status quo in Kashmir through conventional military adventurism. Pakistani leaders believed that Pakistan's open nuclearization would deter India even more effectively than its opaque nuclear capability had previously done. In addition, they hoped that the danger of Indo-Pakistani conventional conflict escalating to the nuclear level would attract third-party diplomatic intervention to resolve the Kashmir dispute. The result was two major Indo-Pakistani militarized confrontations in the wake of the 1998 nuclear tests: the Kargil conflict, India's and Pakistan's first war in twenty-eight years, and a major Indo-Pakistani militarized standoff that nearly led to large-scale war on the subcontinent in 2002.

6

The Overt Nuclear Period

In Chapter 5, I discussed the de facto nuclear period from 1990 through May 1998 and showed that this period was less stable than the previous non-nuclear period. I argued that this instability resulted largely from Pakistani political, financial, and military support for the anti-Indian insurgency in Kashmir. I maintained that this support was encouraged by Pakistan's burgeoning nuclear capacity, which allowed Pakistan to pursue a strategy of low-intensity conflict in Kashmir while insulated from the danger of all-out Indian conventional retaliation.

In this chapter, I assess the effect of the transition from de facto to overt nuclear status on the subcontinent's security environment. I show that open nuclearization did not reduce the level of militarized Indo-Pakistani conflict below what it had been during the nonnuclear and de facto nuclear periods. In fact, within one year of the 1998 nuclear tests, conflict between the two rivals escalated to the point of outright war, its highest level in twenty-eight years. I argue that this occurred because the overt acquisition of nuclear weapons increased Pakistani leaders' confidence in their ability to alter the territorial status quo in Kashmir through conventional adventurism without fear of large-scale Indian retaliation. Additionally, Pakistani leaders hoped that conflict between two openly nuclear powers would attract international attention to the Kashmir dispute and possibly lead to third-party mediation of the conflict, resulting in a settlement superior to any that Pakistan could have secured on its own. In the sections that follow, I compare the militarized interstate dispute data during the overt nuclear period from June 1998 through 2002 with MID data from the de facto nuclear period from 1990 through May 1998. I then explain how Pakistan's overt acquisition of nuclear weapons encouraged Pakistani conventional adventurism, resulting in forceful Indian responses, which together led to increased instability during the overt nuclear period. Finally, I illustrate my argument with discussions of the two major militarized crises during this period: the 1999 Kargil War and the 2001–2002 militarized Indo-Pakistani standoff following the terrorist attack on the Indian Parliament.

Frequency and Level of Conflict

The frequency of Indo-Pakistani disputes following the 1998 nuclear tests was higher than it had been during the de facto nuclear period. As noted in Chapter 2, the 101 calendar months from 1990 through May 1998 included 73 dispute months, for a rate of approximately 0.72 disputes per month. The 55 calendar months from June 1998 through 2002, by contrast, included 45 Indo-Pakistani dispute months, for a rate of approximately 0.82 disputes per month. Thus militarized disputes during the overt nuclear period became nearly 14 percent more frequent than they had been during the de facto period, when disputes were over five times more frequent than they had been during the nonnuclear period. Additionally, the hostility level reached during the overt period exceeded that of any Indo-Pakistani militarized dispute since the Bangladesh War in 1971. The Kargil conflict, which occurred between May and July 1999, involved protracted combat between the Indian and Pakistani Armies and resulted in approximately 1,300 battle deaths, qualifying the conflict as an interstate war. The overt nuclear time period's other major dispute, the 2001–2002 crisis, escalated only to the level of "use of force" and did not reach the threshold of outright war. Nonetheless, the 2001–2002 standoff was a very serious crisis. In the wake of a terrorist attack on its Parliament, India mobilized approximately 500,000 troops along the Line of Control and international border, hoping to force Pakistan to check cross-border infiltration in Kashmir and to turn over to India a list of twenty suspected criminals. This was the largest mobilization in Indian history, and it brought the two countries to the brink of a large-scale war. Thus, while this MID remained at the level of "use of force," it probably deserves to be viewed as more serious than any of the other Indo-Pakistani militarized disputes that had occurred during the nonnuclear or de facto nuclear time periods. In terms of severity of conflict, then, the overt nuclear period was even less stable than the de facto nuclear years in South Asia.

Why did the frequency and severity of militarized Indo-Pakistani disputes increase with the subcontinent's transition from de facto to overt nuclear status?

As noted in Chapter 5, the achievement of de facto nuclear status emboldened Pakistani leaders to adopt a strategy of low-intensity conflict in Kashmir. They supported the anti-Indian insurgency in the region in hopes of draining Indian resources and altering territorial boundaries, confident that Pakistan's opaque nuclear capacity would insulate it from the danger of full-scale Indian conventional retaliation. Despite its provocative nature, however, there were clear limits to this policy. The Pakistanis materially supported foreign and Kashmiri militants in the struggle against Indian rule in Jammu and Kashmir but did not employ Pakistani forces in the conflict; as we have seen, the Pakistani strategy was, in essence, war by proxy. This was the case because although the Pakistanis believed that an opaque nuclear capacity afforded them a shield against Indian aggression, they realized that there was still room for doubt among the Indians and the international community as to actual Pakistani nuclear capabilities. But now, in the wake of the 1998 tests, India and the world knew beyond question that Pakistan possessed a nuclear weapons capacity.

The overt acquisition of nuclear weapons therefore emboldened the Pakistanis to consider operations in Kashmir more audacious than those that they had previously adopted. Now, instead of using only proxy forces in their attempt to alter the status quo in Kashmir, the Pakistanis were prepared to employ Pakistan Army forces against the Indians. Specifically, the Pakistanis implemented a plan to attack across the Kargil sector of the Line of Control, seizing a swath of territory that would enable them to threaten Indian lines of communication in Kashmir. It was a plan that had originally been conceived during the 1980s in retaliation for India's seizure of Siachen Glacier in northern Kashmir. However, the operation had been rejected as too dangerous and impractical by a succession of Pakistani leaders. But now in 1998, as an overt nuclear power, the idea of seizing a piece of Indian territory at Kargil began to look attractive and feasible to the Pakistanis. And Pakistani leaders therefore decided to revisit the idea of attacking across the Line of Control not just with foreign and Kashmiri insurgents but with forces of the Pakistan Army.

The Genesis of the Kargil Plan

It appears that the Pakistan Army originally devised plans for incursions in the Kargil region during the late 1980s[1] in reaction to India's 1984 capture of Siachen Glacier. Since then, army officers had floated the idea with a number of Pakistani military and civilian leaders who had rejected it, fearing a negative international reaction and a direct confrontation with Indian forces. Benazir Bhutto claims that she was presented with a Kargil-like plan on two occasions—once by Chief of Army Staff Mirza Aslam Beg in 1989 and again by Director General of Military Operations Pervez Musharraf in the mid-1990s. According to Bhutto, the army "bitterly resented" Pakistan's loss of Siachen Glacier to India in 1984 and since then had devoted considerable resources to devising a means of regaining the territory.[2] The army formulated a scheme by which Pakistani and Kashmiri forces would occupy the mountain peaks overlooking the Kargil region as soon as the winter snows began to melt. The logic behind the plan was that "if we scrambled up high enough . . . we could force India to withdraw" by severing their supply lines to Siachen. Bhutto continues, "[T]he idea was to be up there early enough . . . that they secured the peaks, and therefore the Indians would be stuck, and to dislodge us or to dislodge the Kashmiris they would have to resort to conventional war. However, they could not resort to conventional war because we had nuclear deterrence. They knew that if they resorted to a conventional war and we suffered a setback, we could use the nuclear response."[3] Bhutto claims that she rejected the plan because even if it succeeded tactically, Pakistan lacked the political and diplomatic resources to translate that tactical victory into a broader strategic success. "I said even if you take Srinagar, the world community will force us out, and we will be humiliated, and I don't want that to happen."[4]

According to a retired Pakistani general's detailed account, the Kargil operation was finally approved in November 1998, when a small group of senior officers proposed it to Chief of Army Staff General Pervez Musharraf.[5] Musharraf reportedly instructed the group to begin preparations for the incursions but to keep their activities secret. The Kargil plan was then discussed briefly with Pakistani Prime Minister Nawaz Sharif in December 1998 and with the rest of the army leadership in March 1999. The prime minister and the other service chiefs received their first formal briefing on the operation in April 1999.[6] The Indian government maintains that Musharraf played a direct conceptual role in the Kargil operation, refining the existing plan during his tenure as Director General of Military Operations from 1993 to 1995. According to the Indian account, the Kargil operation was finally approved after Musharraf presented it to Sharif in October 1998 and again in January 1999.[7] According to Pakistan Army sources, Sharif was first briefed on the Kargil operation in February 1999, and the prime minister formally approved the plan during the second week of March.[8] Despite their differences, these and most other accounts of the Kargil operation's genesis agree on several fundamental points: Plans for incursions in the Kargil area were originally devised by the Pakistan Army in response to India's seizure of territory elsewhere in Kashmir; such plans had been in existence for a number of years prior to the actual launch of the Kargil operation in late 1998 [9]; and Pakistan's civilian leadership was aware of the Kargil plan before the army carried it out.

Sharif later claimed to have been completely excluded from the Kargil planning process, maintaining that Pakistan Army leaders did not even inform him of the Kargil operation until it was already under way.[10] Taped intercepts of telephone conversations between Musharraf and Chief of General Staff Lieutenant General Mohammed Aziz, released by the Indians, do suggest that the army's desire to maintain "total secrecy" around the Kargil operation had left Sharif largely in the dark as to the incursions.[11] And there is evidence to indicate that Sharif was not fully apprised of the disposition of Pakistani nuclear forces during the crisis. According to Bruce Riedel, when Clinton asked the prime minister during a July 4 meeting "if he knew how advanced the threat of nuclear war really was" and whether he realized that "his military was preparing its nuclear-tipped missiles," Sharif "seemed taken aback" and "said only that India was probably doing the same."[12] Sharif later confirmed the Riedel account. "President Clinton mentioned are you aware of [Pakistani nuclear preparations]?" Sharif recalled. "And frankly I was taken aback. I had no idea about it."[13]

However, army officials and many Pakistani commentators reject Sharif's claim of total ignorance regarding the Kargil operation, arguing that the military had briefed the prime minister well in advance.[14] Benazir Bhutto also believes that Sharif knew of the Kargil plan, maintaining that if the army trusted her with knowledge of the operation, it certainly would have informed Sharif, who was far more popular with the military. In addition, Bhutto points out that, despite what she sees as its focus on tactical victory as opposed to strategic vision, the army leadership understands that Pakistani military success depends on competent political leadership. It is "appreciated by the military high brass that wars are not won just on military skills, but through diplomatic, political, and economic initiative." Therefore, Bhutto argues, "the stamp of approval from the Prime Minister . . . would need to be considered," and "I don't believe that the Army would start an operation like Kargil without political sanction."[15] As noted, the Indian government takes a similar view, maintaining that the army briefed Sharif on the Kargil plan in October 1998.[16]

According to Owen Bennett Jones, the weight of the evidence indicates that "most likely . . . the army did tell Sharif what was happening," though "a full discussion did not develop."[17] Sharif's comments during an interview with the author suggest a similar interpretation; he did not claim to have been completely ignorant of the army's Kargil plans, but rather to have been deceived as to their actual nature. "I was misled by Musharraf on Kargil," Sharif recalled. "He did not tell me a lot of things. He kept me in the dark by not really giving me the true picture. The true picture was shared only with the top three or four officers directly involved in the episode. Even corps commanders were not informed." [18]

In the end, it may be impossible to ascertain Sharif's exact level of involvement in, or knowledge of, the Kargil operation's planning process. However, as we will see, Sharif ultimately was able to travel to Washington, strike a deal with Clinton to defuse the crisis, and then call Pakistani forces back from the LoC. This indicates that he eventually succeeded in exerting a substantial degree of control over Pakistani policy during the Kargil conflict.

The Kargil Conflict

Pakistani leaders probably did not expect the Kargil operation to grow as large as it ultimately did.[19] Rather, the initial incursions expanded in scale as Pakistani forces began moving forward across the Line of Control in late 1998 and continued to discover unoccupied positions.[20] By the first week of May 1999, troops from the Pakistan Army's Northern Light Infantry (NLI), supported by civilian insurgents, had occupied a 150-kilometer segment of the LoC. Indian government estimates ultimately put the total number of intruders between 1,500 and 2,400, approximately 70 percent of which were Pakistan Army forces.[21]

The intruders penetrated Indian territory to depths of eight to twelve kilometers and secured a vantage point in the mountain peaks overlooking the strategic Srinagar-Leh Highway (NH 1A), enabling them to threaten Indian lines of communication to Ladakh and Siachen in northern Kashmir. The incursion caught India completely unawares. Given the difficulty of occupying such harsh terrain[22] and the improved Indo-Pakistani relations prevailing at the time,[23] Indian leaders did not foresee any large-scale Pakistani military operations in the vicinity.[24]

India initially attempted to dislodge the intruders with light ground forces. The Indian attacks required "an arduous climb over 70 to 80 degree steep, treeless slopes . . . at heights above 15,000 feet, under accurate artillery and machinegun fire"[25] and were easily repulsed by Pakistani forces. On May 26, India unleashed its air force (IAF) against the intruders in its first use of air power supporting military operations in Kashmir since 1971. Despite losing two aircraft early in the fighting, the IAF continued to attack Pakistani positions through the rest of the month.[26] By early June, the air campaign, in tandem with army operations employing heavy Bofors howitzers, had enabled Indian forces to begin recapturing key positions along the Tololing ridge line, which closely overlooked National Highway 1A. As the month wore on, a combination of air and artillery attacks and uphill infantry assaults continued to erode Pakistani positions. By June 20, Indian forces had taken the highest point on Tololing ridge, significantly reducing the Pakistani threat to Indian lines of communication in Kashmir.[27]

During the fighting, the Indians considered escalating their operations horizontally, crossing the Line of Control into Pakistani Kashmir and opening a second front in less difficult terrain. Doing so would have reduced India's reliance on uphill attacks into heavily fortified Pakistani positions. However, Indian forces ultimately did not cross the LoC and restricted their military operations to the Indian side of Kashmir. This restrained approach was difficult and costly from a military perspective, but it afforded the Indians important political benefits, enabling them to appear less aggressive than their adversaries.[28]

By the beginning of July, the Pakistan government found itself in a difficult military and diplomatic situation. Despite the Indian decision not to cross the LoC, Indian forces had managed to take key positions in Kargil and were inflicting mounting losses on the Pakistani intruders.[29] In addition, Pakistan was receiving little international support for its position on the Kargil crisis, particularly from the United States, which Pakistani leaders had hoped would be sympathetic to their cause.[30] Although the Pakistan government had publicly denied the involvement of its forces in the incursions, U.S. officials did not believe it.[31] In late June, the Americans had sent General Anthony Zinni, Commander in Chief of U.S. Central Command, to Islamabad to tell the Pakistan Army to withdraw its troops from Kargil. Zinni had also been uncooperative regarding Pakistani attempts to link resolution of the Kargil crisis with a solution to the larger Indo–Pakistani conflict over Kashmir. The Indians, meanwhile, had stated that while they were willing to talk to the Pakistanis to defuse the current situation, any diplomacy regarding the ongoing crisis would be limited solely to the issue of Kargil.[32]

Former Pakistani Prime Minister Nawaz Sharif characterizes the resulting environment as one of "extreme pressure." "The international community started blaming Pakistan for this episode, international pressure was mounting," he recalls. "The Indian prime minister called and asked 'why have you done this to us?' He said that Pakistan had stabbed India in the back. I felt the same way. I had the feeling that General Musharraf had stabbed *me* in the back." Additionally, Sharif feared the possibility of further conventional escalation, possibly culminating in an Indo-Pakistani nuclear confrontation. "This episode," he argues, "could have become a larger war between the two countries," which "absolutely could have become nuclear."[33]

Faced with this deteriorating military and diplomatic situation, Sharif decided that he had an "obligation" to seek a way out of the crisis.[34] On July 4, he therefore visited Washington and asked President Clinton for assistance in devising a face-saving means of enabling Pakistan to withdraw from Kargil. The president informed Sharif that the United States could be of no help until Pakistan agreed unconditionally to pull its forces back behind the Line of Control. Clinton then ratcheted up the pressure, informing Sharif that if he did not cooperate, the United States was prepared to blame Pakistan publicly for the ongoing crisis. Thus, "Sharif had a choice, withdraw behind the LoC and the moral compass would tilt back toward Pakistan or stay and fight a wider war with India without American sympathy."[35]

Sharif decided to cooperate. After intense deliberation, he signed an American-prepared statement committing him "to take concrete and immediate steps for the restoration of the LoC."[36] This would be followed by a cease-fire in Kargil and a return to the Lahore Process. On July 12, in a nationally televised speech, Sharif announced to the Pakistani people that he was calling for the withdrawal of the militants back across the Line of Control.[37] Intruding forces began to retreat two days later, and by July 26, the Kargil conflict was over. Losses were estimated at 499 Indians and 772 Pakistanis killed in action.[38]

Pakistani Calculations

In launching the Kargil operation, Pakistan behaved in a highly provocative manner, breaching the LoC and triggering a military confrontation with a nuclear-armed India. Why did Pakistani leaders adopt such an aggressive and dangerous policy?

The primary motives underlying the decision to launch the Kargil operation appear to have been the Pakistani leadership's wish to avenge India's seizure of Siachen and to draw international attention to Pakistan's dispute with India over Kashmir, thereby attracting third-party mediation of the conflict. Nawaz Sharif stated in a nationally televised speech on July 12, 1999, that "in my opinion, the basic objective of the mojahedin's capture of Kargil was to draw the attention of the international community towards the Kashmir issue."[39] According to President Pervez Musharraf, "Kargil was fundamentally about Kashmir." "You have to understand," Musharraf explains, "that emotions run very high here on Kashmir . . . And the Indians have been snapping up bits of Pakistani territory in Kashmir, for example at Siachen. Siachen is barren wasteland, but it belongs to us."[40] Admittedly, a relatively small number of intruders could not seize enough ground at Kargil to alter the territorial balance in Kashmir significantly. However, in Musharraf's view, by crossing the LoC and severing key lines of communication in Indian Kashmir, the intruders could make a point.[41]

According to Pakistani Ministry of Foreign Affairs Director General for South Asia Jalil Jilani, this point was one of principle—namely, that "Countries [like Pakistan] do not just give up their territory." If they do, "there will be no end to it," and "the high and mighty will continue to [take Pakistani territory] on a regular basis." The Kargil operation, according to Jilani, sought to make this point on two levels. Tactically, Kargil "would enable Pakistan to block the supply of [Indian] troops in Kashmir. And there would be limits as to what India could do in response." Diplomatically, the operation would say to the outside world that "India's adverse possessions" at Siachen and elsewhere in Kashmir "should be looked at."[42]

To achieve these goals, Pakistan needed to accomplish two major tasks. First, its armed forces needed to take and hold territory at Kargil. Second, the Pakistan government needed to ensure that Kargil became a high-visibility international crisis, leading to third-party diplomatic intervention in the conflict and possibly in the larger Indo-Pakistani dispute over Kashmir. Pakistani decision makers' confidence that they would be able to accomplish these tasks rested in part on their tactical and political assumptions regarding India and the international community. At the tactical level, Pakistani leaders believed that retaking the Kargil heights from entrenched defenders would prove to be an extremely difficult, if not impossible, task for India. As noted, Kargil's harsh topography heavily favored the Pakistanis, who were entrenched in the sector's mountain peaks and able to dominate the exposed approaches to their positions.[43] The Pakistanis thought that this problem would be exacerbated by India's large-scale military commitments elsewhere in Kashmir, which they believed had left the Indians overextended and unable to respond to new threats in the region. As the former head of Pakistan's Inter-Services Intelligence agency put it, "THE INDIAN ARMY IS INCAPABLE OF UNDERTAKING ANY CONVENTIONAL OPERATIONS AT PRESENT . . . [The Indian military] is so hopelessly imbalanced and has made it so tempting for Pakistan that should it decide to exploit—India within a few days would be brought to the brink of virtual defeat . . ."[44]

At the political level, Pakistani leaders thought that the international community would be supportive, or at least tolerant, of the Kargil operation, given Pakistan's perilous position vis-à-vis a conventionally powerful, newly nuclear India. Indeed, the Pakistanis believed that the international community's possible sympathy for Pakistan could result in international intervention to end the Kargil crisis.[45]

Even more fundamental to Pakistani confidence at Kargil than these tactical and political assumptions, however, were Pakistani decision makers' beliefs regarding the strategic and diplomatic leverage that their country had gained with the overt acquisition of nuclear weapons. At the strategic level, Pakistani leaders were encouraged to risk taking territory in Kargil by the belief that Pakistan's new status would prevent India from launching an all-out conventional war in retaliation. Their belief rested on the view that Pakistan's nascent nuclear capability had worked to prevent Indian escalation during crises in the 1980s and early 1990s. According to public statements by senior Pakistani foreign-policy and defense officials, "The [deterrent] value of nuclear capability was illustrated on at least three occasions" prior to overt proliferation in 1998.[46]

Pakistani policymakers believed that Pakistan's overt nuclear capacity would now have an even more powerful deterrent effect. According to Jilani, "since Pakistan's acquisition of [an overt] nuclear capacity, Pakistan has felt much less threatened" by Indian conventional capabilities. In the absence of a clear Pakistani nuclear capacity, "India wouldn't be restrained." But with such a capability, Pakistani leaders could be "more confident" relative to India and adopt policies that "put a check on Indian ambition" in South Asia.[47] Thus, in 1999, with an overt nuclear capacity providing what they perceived to be even more robust deterrence against Indian retaliation, Pakistani leaders were willing to take even bolder steps than they had previously, crossing the LoC with Pakistan Army forces.[48]

At the diplomatic level, the Pakistanis could be confident that a shooting war at Kargil between two overt nuclear powers would attract significant international attention and third-party efforts to defuse the conflict. As we have seen, in 1990, a militarized Indo-Pakistani crisis over Kashmir had resulted in high-level diplomatic intervention by the Bush administration, despite the fact that neither India nor Pakistan yet openly possessed nuclear weapons and that no shots were actually fired. The international reaction to a crisis in which both India and Pakistan were overt nuclear states and were engaged in intense combat surely would be even greater. Indeed, in the wake of the conflict, Nawaz Sharif stated that Kargil had "practically proved our stand that the Kashmir issue is a nuclear flashpoint."[49] As noted earlier, Sharif continues to maintain that Kargil "absolutely could have" become "a nuclear conflict" between Pakistan and India.[50]

Thus, not only did South Asian nuclearization fail to prevent conflict in Kargil, but it was a major factor underlying the Kargil War. Indeed, as Tellis et al. put it, "Pakistan's possession of nuclear weapons functioned as the critical *permissive* condition that made contemplating Kargil possible"[51]; Pakistani leaders' immediate political and tactical assumptions regarding India and the international community mattered, but within a larger nuclear context in which the incentives for Pakistani aggression were already high. Significantly, Pakistani decision makers' opinions of Kargil in the wake of the conflict suggest that nuclear weapons may continue to have such an emboldening effect on Pakistani behavior into the future. According to Jilani, for example, Kargil successfully "made the point that India's adverse possessions [in Kashmir] should be looked at." Therefore, he argues, the operation was "justified." Benazir Bhutto maintains that there are still "elements within the military who believe that the Kargil climb-down was an act of cowardice. According to their thinking, India was sabre-rattling," and "irrespective of the presence of troops and the threat of war, India could not have launched a conventional war" because of Pakistani nuclear weapons. Therefore, "they felt that Pakistan should not have blinked when India and President Clinton asked for climb-down." Pakistani President Pervez Musharraf, for his part, has refused to rule out the possibility of "another Kargil" in the future.[52]

Recognizing that the overt acquisition of nuclear weapons encouraged the outbreak of conflict at Kargil, however, raises the following questions: How do we know when this is likely to happen? Why did the overt acquisition of nuclear weapons have such an emboldening effect on Pakistan but not similarly embolden India? As I argue, the overt acquisition of nuclear weapons had little direct impact on India but encouraged aggressive Pakistani conventional behavior because of the same two variables that had determined the two countries' reaction to the achievement of a de facto nuclear capability: India's and Pakistan's level of satisfaction with the territorial status quo in Kashmir and their relative conventional capabilities.

In the aftermath of the 1998 nuclear tests, India's strong status quo position relative to Pakistan meant that the overt acquisition of nuclear weapons had little impact on its behavior. Just as before, Indian leaders were largely satisfied with the territorial division of Kashmir and did not seek to alter territorial boundaries. Therefore, they had little motivation to engage in cross-border aggression, with or without an open nuclear weapons capacity. Second, because India was conventionally stronger than Pakistan, the overt acquisition of nuclear weapons did not enable India to undertake any aggression that it could not have launched earlier with either a de facto nuclear capability or with purely conventional forces; anything India could do conventionally to Pakistan after the nuclear tests it probably could have done before. The open acquisition of nuclear weapons therefore did not create incentives for India to become more conventionally aggressive or to alter its military behavior in any significant manner.[53] Thus, as we have seen, not only was India the defender at Kargil, but Indian decision makers were caught completely unawares by the Pakistani incursions. With its forces withdrawn to their winter positions and its political leaders pursuing "bus diplomacy" and the Lahore Process, the Indian government simply did not see war with Pakistan as a serious possibility in early 1999.

The overt acquisition of nuclear weapons by weak, revisionist Pakistan, by contrast, significantly increased its incentives to engage in aggressive behavior. As we have seen, Pakistani leaders were highly dissatisfied regarding their key issue of contention with India and wanted to alter territorial boundaries in Kashmir. But because Pakistan was conventionally far weaker than India, the Pakistanis had been unable to launch a military operation to take territory in Kashmir without risking large-scale war and catastrophic defeat. Pakistan's prior de facto nuclear status had afforded it some measure of protection against Indian conventional capabilities, making "limited warfare in Kashmir a viable option" for the Pakistanis and encouraging them to support the insurgency by funding, arming, and training the militants fighting against Indian rule. As Shirin Mazari argues, "While this scenario was prevalent even when there was only a covert nuclear deterrence, the overt nuclear capabilities demonstrated by both [India and Pakistan] . . . further accentuated this situation."[54] Now that Pakistan clearly had a shield against total defeat, its leaders could adopt still riskier policies, including limited operations by the Pakistani military to take territory in Kashmir. Even if such operations went wrong, the Pakistanis now had less reason to fear dismemberment at the hands of the Indians, who would be deterred from launching an all-out war against it.[55] As Nawaz Sharif put it, Pakistan's 1998 nuclear tests had made the country "militarily impregnable."[56]

In addition, the open possession of nuclear weapons increased the likelihood that the Pakistanis would succeed in their quest to internationalize the Kashmir dispute by convincing outside states to intervene to end a spiraling Indo-Pakistani crisis. As noted, third parties were deeply interested in preventing a nuclear exchange in South Asia, even when India and Pakistan possessed only a de facto nuclear capability. Now, in the wake of the nuclear tests, outside powers would be even more likely to mediate to avoid such an outcome. This third-party diplomatic intervention would not only protect Pakistan from total defeat but might also result in a postwar settlement in Kashmir superior to anything that Pakistan could have achieved on its own.

Thus, as Jilani explains, nuclear weapons played a dual role in Pakistani strategy at Kargil. They "deterred India" from using its conventional military capabilities against Pakistan. In addition, Pakistani nuclear weapons sent a message to the outside world. "War between nuclear powers is not a picnic. It's a very serious business . . . [I]t is always possible for [conventional conflict] to get out of hand. So the international community has a stake in achieving peace in this region." "Otherwise," Jilani concludes, "one little incident in Kashmir could undermine everything."[57] Unlike the Indian government, then, which could hardly envision war in the wake of the 1998 nuclear tests, Pakistani leaders saw an opportunity to further their country's longstanding strategic goals in Kashmir through conventional military operations. They therefore deployed their forces across the Line of Control in early 1999, triggering the first Indo-Pakistani War in twenty-eight years at Kargil.

A Potential Counterargument

One might argue that, contrary to my claims, the Kargil case does not indicate that overt nuclear proliferation has destabilized the South Asian security environment. According to this counterargument, Kargil was a limited conflict, which did not escalate because the Indian government made a deliberate decision not to cross the Line of Control and provoke an openly nuclear-armed Pakistan. Thus, Kargil demonstrates that rather than destabilizing South Asia, nuclear weapons' deterrent effects have prevented conflict escalation and thereby made the region safer. Though this argument appears plausible on its face, it in fact substantially overstates the scope and significance of nuclear weapons' stabilizing impact on the Kargil crisis and ignores their role in starting the conflict.

It is true that the Indian government decided not to cross the Line of Control and escalate the Kargil conflict horizontally. However, the Indian decision against violating the LoC was not driven primarily by a fear of Pakistani nuclear weapons. According to V. P. Malik, Indian Army Chief of Staff during Kargil, the Indian desire to avoid crossing the Line of Control resulted mainly from a confluence of nonnuclear factors, including the military's slowness to recognize and respond to the Pakistani intrusion. Most important, the Indians were concerned with the impact that horizontal escalation could have on international opinion. "The political leaders felt that India needed to make its case and get international support" for its position in the conflict. "This was essential." To do so, India had to make clear to the international community that Pakistan was the aggressor at Kargil and India the injured party. The

Indian government calculated that by exercising restraint even in the face of clear Pakistani provocations at Kargil, it could further this aim.[58]

G. Parthasarathy, India's high commissioner to Pakistan during the Kargil conflict, offers a similar analysis. Indian leaders refrained from expanding their counteroffensives across the LoC, he explains, because they believed that a policy of restraint would result in "political gains with the world community." Staying on its side of the LoC enabled India to "keep the moral high ground," which in turn helped it bring international pressure on Pakistan. "There was no reason to become the bad guy" at Kargil, Parthasarathy maintains.[59]

Former Indian National Security Advisor Brajesh Mishra echoes these arguments. The fact was that "*Pakistan* had crossed the LoC," he explains. As a result, "everything was on our side—morality, international support." If India had crossed the LoC in response, "sympathy and respect for India would have diminished." By exercising restraint, "we retained international support and allowed for condemnation of Pakistan's actions by the international community. And ultimately that was important. When Nawaz Sharif appealed for help from President Clinton, what did Clinton say? Withdraw."[60]

Mishra points out that domestic political constraints also played an important role in preventing the Indians from crossing the Line of Control. As he explains, "The [Vajpayee] government had been defeated in Parliament in April and elections had been ordered." In this situation, crossing the LoC and commencing a large-scale war with Pakistan "politically would have been difficult." The government's "'caretaker' status was a problem."[61]

Despite the importance of these domestic and international political factors, however, Indian leaders would have been willing to cross the Line of Control if doing so had proved to be necessary. Malik emphasizes that the Indian government's "overriding political goal at Kargil was to eject the intruders." The civilian leadership therefore instructed its military chiefs that if they ever felt the need to cross the LoC, the cabinet would review its decision against horizontal escalation. This did not occur, according to Malik, because within a few weeks the Indians began winning at Kargil and were confident of victory by early June. However, he maintains that "if the tactical situation had not gone well, India would have crossed the LoC" and not been deterred by Pakistan's nuclear capacity.[62] After all, Malik explains, Pakistan had just demonstrated with the Kargil operation that attacks across the Line of Control were feasible and need not end in nuclear escalation. The Indian leadership was therefore confident that while it did not know the precise location of the "red lines" marking Pakistan's nuclear thresholds, these points lay well within Pakistani territory and not on the LoC. Thus, in the Indian government's view, if necessary, Kargil could now be "done the other way."[63]

Mishra concurs with Malik that despite its desire to limit the scope of the conflict, the Indian government did not rule out crossing the LoC at Kargil. "The army never pushed the government to cross," he explains. "If the army had wanted, the government would have considered crossing." Mishra maintains that, in this situation, Pakistan's nuclear capacity would not have deterred the government from granting the army permission to violate the LoC because Pakistan would be unlikely to use nuclear weapons even in a large-scale Indo-Pakistani War. "Just see the size of the two countries," Mishra argues. "Pakistan can be finished by a few bombs. But India is much too large." "[A]nyone with a small degree of sanity would know that [nuclear war] would have disastrous consequences for Pakistan."[64]

Parthasarathy agrees with Malik's and Mishra's assessment regarding the Indian government's willingness to violate the LoC. India "definitely would have crossed the LoC if the tactical situation had gone badly," he argues. As it happened, India had no reason to conduct cross-LoC operations because "before Nawaz went to D.C., the game was over militarily. The Pakistanis hadn't been totally pushed out" by this point, "but Tololing and Tiger Hill had been cleared, so they couldn't interdict [National Highway 1A], and their strategic purpose was lost." According to Parthasarathy, the Indian government estimated that if the Pakistanis decided to remain in position and fight, Indian forces would have required another two months of combat to evict the intruders completely from the Kargil heights and would have suffered hundreds of more casualties. However, he explains, the Indians believed that "such a Pakistani exercise would have been pointless, since the Pakistanis couldn't dominate the road," and the Indian counteroffensive was taking a steady toll on the intruders, with artillery barrages "blowing away entire hilltops." Thus, Indian leaders were willing to be patient and refrain from expanding the Kargil conflict horizontally. In the end, Parthasarathy argues, "India didn't cross the LoC because it didn't need to," not because of Pakistani nuclear weapons, which "were not an issue" in Indian decision making on this question.[65] Parthasarathy, like Malik, believes that Kargil helped convince Indian leaders that they could launch such limited offensives if necessary, without triggering a nuclear conflict. Indian decision makers came to the conclusion, as Parthasarathy puts it, "that there is strategic space [in the Indo-Pakistani security relationship] to fight limited conventional war below the strategic threshold."[66]

Former Defense Minister George Fernandes provides further support for these assessments. According to Fernandes, Indian leaders did not initially contemplate crossing the Line of Control because the Indian military was un-prepared to do so and seriously misunderstood the scope of the Pakistani intrusion. "The Kargil incursions caught India totally unawares," explains Fernandes. "Given the post–Lahore summit Indo-Pak relationship, no defense people anticipated that after all of this Pakistan would behave aggressively." The armed forces thus were not ready to mount a large-scale cross-LoC re-sponse in early May because "war requires preparation." Also, Fernandes con-tinues, "at first the incursions seemed small, and the army thought that they could easily handle it. And they told the government that it *was* small. The size of the problem emerged only two weeks later." However, by the time the true nature of the Pakistani intrusion became clear and India's counter-offensive began in earnest, there was no need to cross the LoC because the government was convinced that "India was in control" and "did not believe that the tactical situation was going to deteriorate." Simultaneously, the Pakistanis were suffering an international backlash, with "the United States . . . pressuring Pakistan" to undo the Kargil incursions. Thus, by Fernandes's ac-count, the tactical and diplomatic environment, rather than the existence of Pakistani nuclear weapons, was responsible for the Indian decision not to cross the LoC.[67]

Fernandes also believes that the Kargil conflict demonstrated that India could fight limited wars with Pakistan against a nuclear backdrop. As he argues,

> Pakistan did hold out a nuclear threat during the Kargil War . . . But it had not absorbed the real meaning of nuclearization; that it can deter only the use of nuclear weapons, but not all and any war . . . [S]o the issue was not that war had been made obsolete by nuclear weapons . . . but that conventional war remained feasible though with definite limitations.[68]

Former Indian Prime Minister Atal Bihari Vajpayee supports the claims of Malik, Parthasarathy, Fernandes, and Mishra. According to Vajpayee, India's Kargil operation had "a limited objective: to throw out the invaders from Indian territory. There was no need to cross the LoC because militarily India was successful. But nothing was ruled out. If ground realities required mili-tary operations beyond the LoC, we would have seriously considered it." Vaj-payee also believes that Kargil demonstrated India's ability to use substantial conventional force against Pakistan without triggering nuclear escalation.[69]

Pakistani leaders, for their part, took the possibility of Indian cross-LoC escalation seriously. Sharif, for example, publicly worried during the Kargil crisis that India might not merely undertake a limited cross-LoC attack but "was getting ready to launch a full-scale military operation against Pakistan."[70] As noted earlier, this fear of escalation was a key motivation for Sharif's trip to

Washington. And he continues to believe that if Kargil had not ended when it did, the crisis "could have become a larger war between the two countries. It could have taken the shape of an open, full-scale war."[71]

This is not to argue that Pakistan's nuclear capacity played no role in Indian decision making during the Kargil conflict. The existence of Pakistani nuclear weapons did have a significant impact on Indian leaders, making clear to them that full-scale conventional war with Pakistan was not an option.[72] However, as Malik puts it, while Pakistani nuclear weapons "mattered" in this sense and encouraged Indian caution, they were "not decisive" in India's refusal to violate the LoC because the Indians believed that cross-LoC offensives would not necessarily result in full-scale war.[73] Thus, although nuclear weapons did have a stabilizing effect on the Kargil conflict, we should not overstate the case. It is clear that the danger of a Pakistani nuclear response would have prevented India from deliberately launching a full-scale war against Pakistan. However, Pakistan's nuclear capacity was not primarily responsible for preventing India from crossing the LoC. The decision against such escalation turned mainly on nonnuclear considerations. And as we have already seen, nuclear weapons encouraged Pakistan to launch the Kargil conflict in the first place, regardless of the weapons' subsequent cautionary effects.

Contrary to the counterargument that has been offered, then, the Kargil case indicates that overt nuclear proliferation has had significant destabilizing effects on the South Asian security environment. The open acquisition of nuclear weapons encouraged Pakistani leaders to launch the Kargil conflict and left the Indian government convinced that it could cross the LoC and fight a limited conventional war in retaliation. Although nuclear weapons discouraged all-out conflict, and India and Pakistan managed to avoid a nuclear confrontation, such an outcome was hardly a foregone conclusion, given the dangers of inadvertent escalation. Nor is there any guarantee of similar outcomes in future Indo-Pakistani conflicts—conflicts that nuclear weapons' presence in South Asia may make more likely.

The 2001–2002 Crisis

The Kargil operation's failure was costly for Pakistan from both a political and a military standpoint. The adventure contributed to Pakistan's reputation as a revisionist, irresponsible state. In addition, Pakistan lost hundreds of soldiers, it was diplomatically isolated, and it experienced increased civil–military tension, which contributed to the October 1999 coup. And as we have seen, in the end, Pakistani forces withdrew from the area.[74] Despite these significant costs, provocative activity by Pakistan and its proxies continued unabated in the months following the war. Militants continued to flow across the Line of Control into Indian territory from Pakistani Kashmir and to launch attacks on targets both in J&K and within India proper. Some of the major terrorist incidents that occurred during this period included the hijacking of an Indian Airlines aircraft to Afghanistan by Pakistani militants, which forced India to release several individuals imprisoned for terrorist actions in Kashmir, and an attack outside the Jammu and Kashmir Assembly in October 2001. This wave of violence culminated in a terrorist assault on the Indian Parliament in New Delhi on December 13, 2001. Although the Parliament was in session at the time of the attack, no members were harmed. However, five Indian security personnel died in the ensuing gun battle before the terrorists themselves were killed.[75]

The Indian government immediately launched an investigation into the attack. The Indians concluded that the Parliament assault was the work of two Pakistan-backed militant groups: Lashkar-e-Toiba and Jaish-e-Mohammed.[76] This marked an important turning point in Indian policy. The Indian government had already decided in principle, following the Kargil conflict, to take a more aggressive stance in dealing with Pakistani or Pakistan-backed aggression. Up to that point, the perceived dangers of conflict escalating from the conventional to the nuclear level had encouraged considerable Indian caution in responding to Pakistani provocation. As a recent study explains,

> An impression has been created that Pakistan could use its nuclear weapons in a variety of ways: in a pre-emptive mode, early in a war, when the going gets tough, or when ultimately pushed to the wall by India's conventional forces. This has instilled uncertainty amongst Indian planners, and especially the political leadership which believes Pakistan's rash military leadership cannot be trusted with nuclear weapons.[77]

This sense of uncertainty had helped to dissuade India from launching large-scale responses to Pakistani or Pakistan-backed aggression. As we have seen, despite its conventional advantage, India refrained from retaliating against Pakistan's proxy war by attacking insurgent bases and infrastructure in Pakistani Kashmir. And during the Kargil conflict, India ruled out full-scale war even in response to incursions into Indian territory by Pakistan Army forces, thereby abandoning India's longstanding policy of retaliating against Pakistan attacks on Kashmir with all-out horizontal escalation. In both cases, Indian caution resulted at least in part from concern over the possibility of a Pakistani nuclear response.

After Kargil, however, the Indians began to take a more sanguine view of strategic stability on the subcontinent. Indian civilian and military leaders became increasingly convinced that Pakistan's aggressive behavior was based on "bluff and bluster," "exaggerating the likelihood of nuclear escalation" to "blackmail" India and the international community.[78] In truth, according to a senior serving Indian Army officer and strategic analyst, many Indian policymakers came to believe that "Pakistan will not use nuclear weapons until it is half gone."[79] Pakistan would be very unlikely to launch a nuclear strike on India, former Indian Defense Minister George Fernandes argues, because if it did so, India would retaliate in kind. Given the size disparity between the two countries, the effects of such an exchange would be grossly unequal; a nuclear confrontation would be extremely costly to India but would probably mortally damage Pakistan. As Fernandes puts it, after an initial Pakistani nuclear strike on India, "We may have lost a part of our population." But after India's retaliatory strike on Pakistan, "Pakistan may have been completely wiped out."[80]

This asymmetry, combined with Pakistan's diplomatic, economic, and conventional military weakness, led Indian policymakers to conclude that India could fight a limited conventional conflict against Pakistan without escalation to the level of full-scale conventional war or nuclear confrontation.[81] Ironically, Pakistan's own actions in Kashmir may have provided Indian leaders with the most compelling evidence of the feasibility of limited conventional war in a nuclear South Asia. As V. P. Malik explains, "Kargil showed the way. If Pakistan could do Kargil [without escalation to the strategic level], India could do something similar" in response to continued Pakistani provocations in Kashmir without fear of a nuclear confrontation. Thus, after Kargil, there was "increasing realization in India that stability exists in the strategic balance. How low or high stability is will always be a question mark. But it's there."[82]

As its confidence in the subcontinent's strategic stability grew, the Indian government threatened to become more conventionally aggressive in its response to continued Pakistani provocations. In contrast to its previous restraint, India adopted a policy of compellance, vowing to launch limited conventional war against Pakistan if it did not curb cross-border violence in Kashmir. Possible Indian action ranged from attacking terrorist camps and Pakistani military assets within Pakistani Kashmir to destroying military assets and seizing territory within Pakistan proper. "In effect, India threatened to lock Pakistan's military into a limited war of attrition in which India could exploit its numerical superiority."[83]

In the wake of the 2001 Parliament attack, the Indian government "deliberated and finally decided that written and verbal threats would not do anymore. Something concrete needed to be done to show people at home and in the international community that India meant business."[84] Indian leaders therefore decided to put their new compellent strategy into action. On December 18, India launched Operation Parakram, mobilizing 500,000 troops along the Line of Control and the international border. The Indians demanded that Pakistan turn over to New Delhi twenty criminals suspected to be residing in Pakistan, unequivocally renounce terrorism, shut down terrorist training camps in Pakistani territory, and check militant infiltration into Jammu and Kashmir.[85] Most important, the buildup was meant as a warning against any follow-on terrorist attacks, which the Indians feared were imminent. As Fernandes explains,

> there were intelligence reports that there could be more such attacks on different targets in the country. So the message that went by mobilizing our forces and keeping them there for a length of time was that if anything should happen from any quarter, then there will be no notice given to anyone; it will just be move in . . . In that situation we would have taken [Pakistan] on in a conventional war.[86]

In the event of Pakistani noncompliance, the Indians planned to launch rapid, multiple strikes across the Line of Control into Pakistan-administered Kashmir, destroying terrorist training camps and infrastructure and seizing territory that would enable Indian forces to staunch the flow of cross-border infiltration. In case Pakistan sought to relieve pressure on Kashmir by escalating the conflict horizontally, Indian Army forces deployed along the international border would be prepared to meet and repulse any Pakistani attacks. The logic of the Indian plan was "to inflict on Pakistan a hundred cuts rather than one amputation in the form of . . . cutting the country in two."[87]

Indian threats initially met with a degree of Pakistani cooperation. In January 2002, President Pervez Musharraf banned the militant organizations Lashkar-e-Toiba and Jaish-e-Mohammed and publicly promised not to allow Pakistani territory to be used as a launching ground for terrorism in Kashmir.[88] U.S. Secretary of State Colin Powell, in New Delhi after a stop in Islamabad, assured Indian officials that President Musharraf was in fact taking concrete steps to rein in terrorist activity and was seriously considering the extradition of non-Pakistani suspects on India's list of twenty fugitives.[89] This apparent success of Indian coercive diplomacy, combined with a loss of strategic surprise after the initial mobilization and a concomitant fear of high casualty rates in the event of war, led the Indians to decide against attacking Pakistan in January 2002.[90] Despite this decision, however, Indian forces remained deployed along the LoC and international border, prepared to increase military pressure on Pakistan if necessary.

The necessity arose on May 14, 2002, when terrorists launched another major attack that killed thirty-two people at an Indian Army camp at Kaluchak in Jammu. Most of the victims were family members of army personnel.[91] An

enraged Prime Minister Vajpayee, on a visit to the region following the incident, told Indian soldiers to prepare for a "decisive battle" against Pakistan.[92]
According to a detailed study of the 2001–2002 crisis, Indian military plans
following the Kaluchak attack were considerably more ambitious than they
had been in January. Now, rather than merely crossing the LoC and seizing
territory in Pakistani Kashmir, the Indians envisioned a major thrust into
Pakistan proper aimed at destroying the offensive capabilities of the Pakistan
Army. India reportedly planned to drive three strike corps (1, 2, and 21) from
Rajasthan into the Pakistani Thar Desert, engaging and destroying Pakistan's
two strike corps (1 and 2) and seizing territory in the Thar. These plans, which
were "so audacious that they had never been war-gamed before," "would have
given India two advantages: Pakistan's military centre of gravity, its two strike
corps, would have been destroyed in details, and land captured in the Thar
would have yielded some advantage on the negotiating table after the war."[93]

The May–June 2002 period was critical for Indian decision makers. If
Pakistani cooperation with Indian demands remained unsatisfactory and warranted an Indian attack, this time frame offered the Indians a tactical window
of opportunity; Indian forces were fully deployed along the LoC and international border and ready to strike, and the weather remained favorable for
offensive action. By early July, the monsoon would arrive, flooding the Punjab
and critical areas of Jammu and rendering armored strikes into Pakistan impossible. Additionally, a delay would enable Pakistan to move its Army Reserve
North farther south into Rajasthan, blocking an Indian offensive in the region.
Thus, V. K. Sood argues, "end May or early June was *the* time to hit if India
was going to do so."[94]

At this point, however, the United States once again intervened diplomatically in the crisis. In early June, U.S. Deputy Secretary of State Richard Armitage extracted a promise from President Musharraf not merely to staunch
the flow of terrorist infiltration into Indian Kashmir but to end infiltration
"permanently." Armitage then conveyed Musharraf's pledge to Indian officials. Musharraf's commitment, American assurances that he would honor it,
and a notable decrease in terrorist infiltration into Indian Kashmir[95] led Indian
leaders to conclude that, in Brajesh Mishra's words, "coercive pressure was
working"[96] and that conflict would probably not be necessary.[97]

India ultimately did not strike Pakistan, and Indian forces began withdrawing from the international border and LoC in October. According to
top officials, India did not attack during Operation Parakram because the
deployment had been a success; it had prevented further terrorism on the
scale of the Parliament attack and had secured a Pakistani pledge to prevent

any future infiltration, thereby obviating the need for an Indian offensive or for continued mobilization. As Fernandes argues, India had "no reason to attack" during Operation Parakram. Indian forces "stayed mobilized to make the point that another [terrorist] attack would result in an immediate response . . . Those that should have gotten the message got the message. No further attacks happened."[98] According to Mishra, Operation Parakram's "national goal was to curb terrorism emanating from Pakistan. And if you see down the road . . . that mobilization . . . helped to curb terrorism, although we know Pakistan can do more. So it achieved quite a lot. That national goal . . . was achieved."[99] Significantly, American diplomacy played a central role in convincing the Indians that their coercive efforts had been successful. As former Prime Minister Vajpayee explains, "All preparations were made for attacking Pakistan to punish it for the attack on Parliament. But America gave us the assurance that something will be done by Pakistan about cross-border terrorism, both in January and in May 2002. America gave us a clear assurance. That was an important factor" in persuading Indian leaders that coercion had succeeded and that military action was unnecessary.[100] Additional reasons for India's failure to attack Pakistan include loss of the element of surprise, concern with the conventional costs and nuclear risks of a large-scale Indo-Pakistani conflict, and a desire to avoid angering the United States by attacking America's key ally in the Afghan War.[101]

Yet despite official claims of success, Pakistani compliance with Indian demands in the wake of the Parliament attack was mixed. As we have seen, India was the victim of a major terrorist attack in May 2002. And despite a temporary lull in cross-border infiltration, the flow of militants into Jammu and Kashmir by mid-2002 had begun to increase once again.[102] Finally, Pakistan flatly refused to turn over to New Delhi the Indians' list of twenty wanted fugitives.

Thus, many independent analysts and senior military officers viewed Parakram not as a victory but rather as a costly exercise in futility, achieving none of its stated aims and taking a heavy toll on the Indian exchequer and military readiness. As Sood argues, "What did the Indians achieve" with Operation Parakram? "There was no let-up in terrorism. Pakistan remained belligerent. Coercive diplomacy didn't work. It was a knee-jerk reaction."[103] In the view of former Indian Army Chief of Staff Shankar Roychoudhry, Parakram's "build-up and back-down" was a "pointless gesture" that "compromised Indian credibility greatly."[104] And Praveen Swami calls Parakram "arguably the most ill-conceived manoeuvre in Indian military history," which "ended as an ignominious retreat after having failed to secure even its minimum objectives"—despite a total estimated price tag of roughly $400 million to $1 billion. This economic cost does not include injuries and deaths suffered by Indian personnel during the mobilization or lost and damaged equipment.[105] Regardless of the success or failure of Indian policy during the 2001–2002 crisis, however, India's October 2002 demobilization did not mark an abandonment of India's limited war strategy. Rather, the Indian government hoped that the "strategic relocation" of its forces would enable it to husband its resources and "fight another day" under more favorable circumstances.[106] India's posture remained, in the words of V. P. Malik, "All-out conventional war, no. Limited conventional war, yes."[107]

India's continuing adherence to this approach has coincided with the emergence of a more restrained Pakistani posture over time, with Pakistan gradually taking steps to reduce, though not eliminate, cross-border violence.[108] The ensuing thaw in Indo-Pakistani relations has seen the initiation of a cease-fire along the Line of Control; a resumption of air and rail links between India and Pakistan; a written commitment by Pakistan not to allow its territory to be used for terrorist activity; meetings between the Indian government and leaders of the Kashmiri separatist All Parties Hurriyat Conference; and peace talks between Indian and Pakistani foreign secretaries.

A range of factors has contributed to these developments, including growing international pressure to curb terrorism in Kashmir; India's renewed willingness to discuss the Kashmir issue; Pakistan's A. Q. Khan nuclear proliferation scandal; and attempts by Islamist militant groups to kill President Musharraf, which have triggered forceful government measures against them.[109] It is therefore difficult to determine precisely what effect New Delhi's compellent policy has had on Islamabad's behavior. Also, it remains to be seen whether or not the current trend of improving Indo-Pakistani relations will continue. What is clear, however, is that the post-Kargil perception of increased strategic stability on the subcontinent did not result in greater Indian restraint or in greater Pakistani aggression. Rather, the Indian belief that conventional conflict need not escalate to the nuclear level emboldened India seriously to contemplate more aggressive actions. This threat of aggression did not succeed in the immediate achievement of specific Indian security goals, but it has broadly coincided with the emergence of more moderate Pakistani behavior—an outcome that former Indian officials believe would have been unlikely in the absence of Indian coercive diplomacy. As Mishra argues, the

> attack on Parliament aroused the passions of the country and came from a country headed by a military dictator. India decided we must get Pakistan to stop this. And if you look at the situation from January 2002 onwards, a significant change has come.

[Coercive diplomacy] was a big factor. Musharraf knew that if something like this happened again, India was not going to tolerate it.[110]

Did nuclear weapons have a stabilizing or a destabilizing effect on the 2001–2002 crisis? Nuclear weapons played only a limited role in preventing Indian leaders from launching large-scale attacks against Pakistan during Operation Parakram. Indian officials believed that Parakram's planned offensives, while significant, would not have been sufficient to trigger a Pakistani nuclear response. As Prime Minister Vajpayee puts it, "We did not think that Pakistan would have responded with nuclear weapons even if we had attacked. Nuclear war was ruled out."[111] The Indians' restraint resulted mainly from the belief that their coercive diplomacy had succeeded and that the actual use of force was unnecessary.

However, nuclear weapons did prevent the Indians from contemplating an all-out attack against Pakistan. As former Indian Army Vice Chief of Staff V. K. Sood explains, "India could sever Punjab and Sindh with its conventional forces." However, "Pakistan *would* use nuclear weapons in that scenario. So the answer [during the 2001–2002 crisis] was not to do this, but rather to draw Pakistani forces into battle . . . and inflict damage from which Pakistan would take a long time to recover." The goal was "not to fight for real estate" but rather "to attrit the Pakistani Army."[112]

Thus, nuclear weapons' impact on the 2001–2002 crisis is mixed. Pakistani nuclear weapons did not prevent India from planning large-scale attacks against Pakistan, but they did ensure that the scope of the Indian attacks would be sufficiently limited so as not to threaten Pakistan with catastrophic defeat. In addition, nuclear weapons encouraged de-escalation of the dispute in June and the eventual demobilization of Indian forces, although they were one of several factors contributing to this outcome. By exercising restraint, the Indians also sought to avoid antagonizing the United States and incurring high costs in a conventional conflict. Most important, Indian officials believed that their coercive diplomacy had been successful and that large-scale military pressure on Pakistan was no longer needed.

In evaluating nuclear weapons' impact on the 2001–2002 crisis, however, we must not overlook their role in fomenting the standoff. As we have seen, the 2001–2002 crisis resulted from India's large-scale mobilization and associated coercive diplomacy, which in turn was a reaction to an attack on the Indian Parliament and an Indian Army installation by Pakistan-backed Kashmiri terrorist groups. The Parliament and Kaluchak attacks were part of a larger pattern of Pakistani low-intensity conflict, which was promoted by Pakistan's possession of a nuclear weapons capacity; Pakistan's acquisition of an opaque nuclear capability originally encouraged it to launch a proxy war against Indian Kashmir, and overt nuclearization emboldened Pakistan even further, facilitating the actual seizure of Indian territory with Pakistan Army troops at Kargil. Despite Kargil's failure, Pakistan continued with its strategy of supporting anti-Indian militancy after Kargil, confident that it was insulated from the possibility of large-scale Indian retaliation. This strategy resulted in the Parliament and Kaluchak attacks in December 2001 and May 2002. Apart from any later effects they may have had on the 2001–2002 dispute, then, nuclear weapons played an instrumental role in instigating the crisis in the first place.

Conclusion

In this chapter, I showed that India's and Pakistan's overt acquisition of a nuclear weapons capability in 1998 did not make the Indo-Pakistani security relationship more stable than it had been during the de facto nuclear period. Rather, militarized Indo-Pakistani disputes after the 1998 nuclear tests occurred even more frequently than they had from 1990 through May 1998. Additionally, these disputes became more serious than they had been in nearly thirty years, with the 1999 Kargil conflict crossing the threshold of outright war. And although the 2001–2002 standoff did not ultimately erupt into war, it was nonetheless a very serious crisis, resulting in the largest mobilization in Indian history.

I argued that this heightened frequency and intensity of militarized disputes resulted primarily from the increased confidence that Pakistani leaders gained with their acquisition of an overt nuclear capacity. An opaque nuclear capability afforded Pakistan a substantial measure of protection against Indian attack, but it still left open the possibility that Pakistan was not in fact an operational nuclear power and thus undermined Pakistani deterrence. Overt nuclearization, by contrast, left no room for doubt as to the existence of a Pakistani nuclear weapons capacity. It therefore afforded Pakistan an even more robust measure of protection against Indian conventional superiority than its de facto nuclear capability had previously done. In addition, Pakistan's acquisition of an overt nuclear capacity increased the likelihood that the international community would take an interest in any Indo-Pakistani conventional conflict and seek to mediate the two countries' ongoing dispute over Kashmir. Therefore, Pakistan's overt nuclear capacity emboldened Pakistan to take even more provocative steps than it had before. Now, rather than fighting an exclusively proxy war by supporting Kashmiri and foreign militants, the Pakistan government was willing to use its own army forces to seize territory in Indian

Kashmir, precipitating a direct confrontation between the Indian and Pakistani militaries. This was a risk that Pakistan had been unwilling to take since 1971. Even after the failure of the Kargil operation, Pakistani leaders remained sufficiently confident in their position to continue Pakistan's strategy of low-intensity conflict against Indian rule in Kashmir unabated. Their adherence to this strategy led to the 2001–2002 Indo-Pakistani crisis and nearly set off a large-scale conventional war.

In Chapter 7, I briefly expand the geographical scope of my study beyond the South Asian region. First, based on my preceding analysis, I recap the behavioral incentives that the proliferation of nuclear weapons should create for states with various combinations of territorial preferences and military capabilities. I then apply this framework to the cases of Chinese and North Korean acquisition of nuclear weapons. In the case of China, I attempt to determine whether Chinese behavior in the 1969 Sino-Soviet Ussuri River conflict is compatible with the logic of my argument. And in the case of North Korea, I speculate as to the behavioral incentives that nuclear proliferation is likely to create for the DPRK. I close the chapter with a brief discussion of the likely effects of nuclear weapons acquisition on Iran.

7

Beyond South Asia

Although this study has focused on the international security environment in South Asia, it has implications beyond the region. My findings not only help to explain nuclear proliferation's impact on Indo–Pakistani conventional military behavior but also shed light on proliferation's likely effects on new nuclear states generally. Through its examination of the South Asian case, the study clearly indicates that we cannot know what incentives proliferation is likely to create for new nuclear states, and thus what types of conventional behavior we should expect from them, without specific knowledge of the states in question. Abstract models, drawing on such analytic frameworks as deterrence and organization theory, can make powerful deductive cases for different sets of possible outcomes. However, the extent to which these or other models will be able to predict and explain states' behavior in a given case will depend on politico–military factors particular to that conflict relationship.

In this chapter, I briefly recap the behavioral incentives that should result for new nuclear powers from various combinations of the political and military variables that I have discussed in this book. I show that the acquisition of nuclear weapons is likely to encourage aggressive conventional behavior only on the part of weak, revisionist states. No other combinations of territorial preferences and military capabilities are likely to promote increased conventional aggression by new nuclear powers.

I then apply my politico–military framework to two instances of nuclear weapons proliferation outside South Asia: the cases of China and North Korea. In the China case, I seek to determine whether Chinese behavior during the

1969 Sino–Soviet Ussuri River conflict follows the logic of my argument regarding territorial preferences and military capabilities. I show that while a lack of evidence makes definitive conclusions regarding Chinese decision making during the Ussuri River conflict difficult, the available data indicate that the case is compatible with my argument. The Chinese were conventionally weak vis-à-vis the Soviet Union and began seeking to alter territorial boundaries in the Ussuri River region just before their 1964 nuclear test. The Chinese subsequently launched a premeditated attack against Soviet forces in the area in 1969, sparking the Ussuri River conflict. It is possible that the acquisition of nuclear weapons emboldened Chinese leaders to formulate this aggressive regional policy.

In the case of North Korea (Democratic People's Republic of Korea; DPRK), I use my framework to predict the likely effects of nuclear weapons proliferation on the DPRK's future conventional military behavior. I show that since North Korea is conventionally weaker than its South Korean and American adversaries, our prediction of DPRK behavior hinges on the territorial preferences of the North Korean regime. However, given the difficulty of discerning the North Korean leadership's territorial preferences, we cannot confidently categorize North Korea as either a status quo or as a revisionist state. I therefore specify the implications of different assumptions regarding the North Korean leadership's territorial goals. I show that if we believe that North Korea is a revisionist state dissatisfied with existing territorial boundaries, the acquisition of nuclear weapons is likely to encourage limited North Korean conventional aggression. If, by contrast, we conclude that North Korea is a status quo state satisfied with existing territorial boundaries, then nuclear weapons are unlikely to create strong incentives for North Korean conventional aggression. In this case, the greatest danger in North Korean proliferation is likely to be the possibility that a cash-strapped DPRK will spread nuclear weapons materials and technologies to other states and parties around the world. The chapter concludes with a brief discussion of my argument's applicability to Iran.

Politico–Military Variables and Behavioral Incentives

As we have seen, the behavioral incentives that proliferation creates for new nuclear states are largely a function of the states' territorial preferences and military capabilities. Are new nuclear states satisfied with the territorial status quo, or do they wish to change it? And how conventionally powerful are new nuclear states relative to their adversaries? Various combinations of territorial preferences and conventional capabilities will create incentives for different types of conventional military behavior for new nuclear powers.

Strong States

Let us look first at the incentives that the acquisition of nuclear weapons creates for conventionally strong states. Regardless of whether a conventionally strong state has status quo or revisionist territorial preferences, nuclear proliferation is unlikely to increase its incentives for conventional aggression. If it has status quo preferences, a strong newly nuclear state will be satisfied with existing territorial divisions and have no reason to attempt to change them. If a strong state has revisionist preferences, nuclear proliferation is still unlikely to increase its incentives for conventionally aggressive behavior; because the state is conventionally stronger than its adversary, it does not need nuclear weapons to alter territorial divisions in its favor. Anything that the conventionally strong state can do to change the status quo after acquiring nuclear weapons it probably could have done beforehand. Thus, proliferation is unlikely significantly to alter such a state's propensity for conventional aggression.[1]

Weak States

Let us now turn to the behavioral incentives that nuclear proliferation is likely to create for conventionally weak proliferants. If a conventionally weak state has status quo territorial preferences, the acquisition of nuclear weapons will be unlikely to encourage it to behave in a conventionally aggressive manner. Since it is satisfied with existing territorial divisions, the weak state will have little reason to engage in conventional aggression with or without nuclear weapons. However, if the weak state has revisionist territorial preferences, the acquisition of nuclear weapons could create significant incentives for conventional aggression, enabling it to challenge the territorial status quo in ways that previously would have been too dangerous. The weak state could engage in limited conventional aggression while remaining insulated from the danger of large-scale conventional retaliation by its adversary. Additionally, the weak state could attract diplomatic intervention in the conflict from outside states anxious to defuse a potential nuclear confrontation. As we have seen, this is the logic underlying Pakistani conventional behavior since its acquisition of a nuclear weapons capacity.

This framework summarizes the conventional military incentives that nuclear proliferation is likely to create for the full range of states and should allow us to expand our analysis to regions beyond South Asia. Specifically, based on my framework, we should be able to accomplish two tasks. First, we should be able to explain the past conventional military behavior of new nuclear states other than India and Pakistan. Second, my framework should help us to predict the conventional military behavior not just of South Asian proliferants but also of future nuclear powers and to determine the nature of any threat that such states may pose to international stability.

In the sections that follow, I attempt to accomplish these tasks with short case studies drawn from beyond the South Asian region. These sections are not as detailed as my analysis of Indo-Pakistani military behavior and do not purport to provide comprehensive discussions of the issues that they address. Their goal, rather, is to enable us briefly to test my argument against another set of historical facts and to offer a glimpse into how we might expect nuclear proliferation to affect conventional military stability in a future proliferation scenario. I look first at the only instance of direct combat between nuclear-armed powers outside of South Asia: the 1969 Ussuri River border conflict between the Soviet Union and China. I argue that although available information on this conflict is far from definitive, existing data indicate that the Ussuri River case is compatible with my claim that nuclear weapons are likely to embolden weak, revisionist powers to engage in conventionally aggressive behavior.

Next, I discuss the implications of my analysis for a new nuclear proliferant that is the subject of considerable international concern: North Korea. I argue that given North Korean relative military weakness, the likely behavior of a newly nuclear North Korea turns upon its territorial preferences. If the DPRK regime seeks to alter existing regional boundaries, then the acquisition of nuclear weapons is likely to encourage more conventionally aggressive North Korean behavior. If, by contrast, the North Koreans have status quo preferences, then nuclear weapons, while not without their dangers, should not have conventionally emboldening effects on the DPRK.

Finally, I briefly discuss the possible implications of nuclear weapons acquisition by Iran. I argue that, as with India, Pakistan, China, and North Korea, a nuclear Iran's behavior is not predictable in the abstract. Rather, the behavior of a nuclear Iran would be a function of its specific territorial preferences and military capabilities.

Beyond the Subcontinent: Nuclear Proliferation's Impact Elsewhere in Asia

The Sino-Soviet Case

The 1999 Indo-Pakistani Kargil War was not the first case of protracted conventional combat between nuclear-armed adversaries. Rather, a similar case occurred thirty years earlier, when Chinese and Soviet forces clashed along the Sino-Soviet border in the vicinity of Zhenbao Island on the Ussuri River in Siberia.[2]

Borders in the Ussuri region had been formalized by the 1860 Treaty of Peking, part of the system of "unequal treaties" by which foreign powers carved China into spheres of influence during the nineteenth century. In 1963, the year before it tested nuclear weapons, China began openly to challenge the legitimacy of the Sino-Russian border, arguing that it had been forced upon the Chinese people by imperialist powers.[3] In 1964, a joint boundary commission failed to resolve the dispute, and over the next several years, the Ussuri region was the site of numerous Sino-Soviet clashes that, while violent, did not involve gunfire and were rarely fatal.[4] On March 2, 1969, however, a shootout on the Ussuri's Zhenbao Island killed approximately thirty Soviet troops, marking a major escalation in the border dispute and setting off a series of violent clashes in the Ussuri region that continued over the next several months.[5]

There is some disagreement as to who precipitated the March 2 clashes. American policymakers and analysts immediately blamed China for provoking the incident.[6] However, some scholars subsequently challenged this view. Neville Maxwell, for example, argued that Soviet Frontier Guards, in an effort to enforce the Soviet Union's claims to the river's entire surface up to the Chinese shore, began harassing Chinese fishermen and peasants in the Zhenbao area in 1967. The Soviets extended this harassment to Chinese Frontier Guards patrolling on or near Zhenbao Island in the winter of 1967–1968, beating and seriously injuring Chinese soldiers on numerous occasions. According to Maxwell, the March 1969 clashes were a culmination of this ongoing Soviet aggression, which ultimately forced the Chinese to take defensive measures against their tormentors. On March 2, when a party of Soviet Frontier Guards opened fire on a Chinese patrol, the Chinese fired warning shots and then shot back in earnest, killing and wounding approximately seventy Soviet soldiers. This incident triggered the series of clashes that wracked the Sino-Soviet border region over the coming months.[7]

Most scholars and analysts, however, disagree with this characterization of events and blame the March 2 incident squarely on China. Abram Shulsky, for example, argues that the Chinese launched a premeditated ambush against Soviet forces "designed to ensure that casualties would be higher than in previous incidents."[8] As Lyle Goldstein notes, newly available evidence supports this interpretation; both Russian and Chinese sources agree that the Ussuri River clashes resulted from deliberate Chinese aggression. Thus, while one "might be tempted to attribute . . . uniformity of opinion among Russian contemporary narratives to a persistent nationalist viewpoint," in fact "a consensus among their PRC counterparts is apparently inclined to agree."[9] Chinese analysts argue that PRC forces had in fact begun preparations for a small border war in 1968, and attempted to provoke confrontations before March 1969, but that the Soviets had refused to engage. The March 1969 Chinese attack caught Soviet forces by surprise and thus was successful.[10]

Although fighting remained confined to the Ussuri region, there is considerable evidence that the Soviets contemplated the possibility of launching a preventive nuclear strike against China's burgeoning strategic capabilities during the crisis. For example, on August 18, 1969, a Soviet KGB officer approached a U.S. State Department official in Washington to inform him that the USSR was considering an attack against Chinese nuclear facilities and to ask what the likely American reaction to such a move would be.[11] During this time frame, the Soviets apparently also were discussing the possibility of a nuclear strike on China with East European officials. U.S. intelligence reported activity consistent with preparations for a nuclear attack at Soviet air bases in Siberia and the Far East. And an editorial in *Pravda* referred directly to the dangers that Chinese nuclear weapons posed to the Soviet Union.[12] The U.S. government subsequently informed the Soviets that it would be "deeply concerned" if the crisis escalated any further.[13]

Why was the Soviet government willing to consider taking so drastic a step against China as nuclear escalation? The Soviets, despite their vast conventional and nuclear capabilities, feared that if the Ussuri conflict continued, the Chinese could resort to massive human-wave attacks against Soviet border positions. Additionally, the Soviets worried that the Chinese might decide to expand the fighting beyond the Ussuri region, turning the length of the Sino-Soviet border into a "running sore." Soviet leaders understood that nuclear weapons would be of little use in defending against such Chinese offensives. And they believed that their conventional forces risked being overwhelmed by what they characterized as Chinese "hordes." The Soviets therefore considered the possibility of resorting to nuclear measures to deter or defeat such Chinese expansion of the Ussuri conflict.[14]

Soviet contemplation of a preemptive strike may have been further encouraged by the apparent lack of seriousness with which the Soviets regarded China's nuclear capacity in the late 1960s. Many Western analysts argue that China's lack of a viable delivery system for its nuclear weapons and its arsenal's vulnerability to preemption greatly reduced the Chinese weapons' effectiveness and hence their deterrent effects. Soviet decision makers appear to have held a similar view of Chinese nuclear capabilities during the Ussuri River crisis. The Soviets had been closely involved with the development of the Chinese nuclear weapons program and possessed detailed knowledge of its characteristics and capabilities. The Soviets believed that although China's nuclear capacity was growing, the Chinese arsenal during the Ussuri crisis was too small and vulnerable to constitute a major retaliatory threat.[15] Western scholars' interviews of Soviet military officers indicate that Soviet strategic rocket forces in the Far Eastern region did pull back from the border during the Ussuri conflict in the anticipation of possible Chinese conventional assaults. But Soviet rocket forces officers were not concerned with the possibility of a Chinese nuclear strike against Soviet strategic assets during the crisis.[16]

There is some evidence that Chinese leaders themselves may have been skeptical of China's nuclear capabilities during this time period. As Mao Zedong reportedly stated shortly before the Ussuri conflict, "Our country, in a sense, is still a non-nuclear power. With this little nuclear weaponry, we cannot be counted as a nuclear country. If we are to fight a war, we must use conventional weapons."[17] Chinese leaders also apparently harbored doubts as to nuclear weapons' overall strategic utility. Mao had famously argued that the horrors of nuclear conflict were exaggerated and claimed that nuclear weapons would not prove decisive in a war. In the wake of the bombings of Hiroshima and Nagasaki, Mao stated that "Some of our comrades . . . believe that the atom bomb is all-powerful; that is a big mistake."[18] He subsequently claimed, "The atom bomb is a paper tiger used by the US reactionaries to scare people. It looks terrible, but in fact it isn't. Of course, the atom bomb is a weapon of mass slaughter, but the outcome of a war is decided by the people, not by one or two new types of weapon."[19] Immediately after China's 1967 hydrogen bomb test, the *Liberation Army Daily* stated that although the achievement of a thermonuclear capability was a great achievement for China, in truth "atom bombs, guided missiles and hydrogen bombs, all in all, are nothing much to speak of."[20] "Man is the factor that decides victory or defeat in war," claimed a New China News Agency Press communiqué discussing the H-bomb detonation. China's nuclear tests had been conducted "entirely for the purpose of defense, with the ultimate aim of abolishing nuclear weapons."[21]

Yet Mao had also made very different statements regarding the political and military efficacy of nuclear weapons, suggesting that a nuclear weapons capacity might embolden China in dealing with its adversaries. For example, he argued that a Chinese nuclear capacity would "boost our courage and scare others."[22] And even as the Chinese were downplaying the effects of their thermonuclear capability in the wake of the 1967 hydrogen bomb test, they also stated that the H–bomb detonation had "dealt a heavy blow at US imperialism and Soviet Revisionism, the two nuclear overlords who have been carrying out nuclear blackmail through their monopoly of nuclear weapons."[23] With "the atom bomb, guided missile and hydrogen bomb," the Chinese claimed, "[o]ur great homeland had never been so powerful as it is today. We absolutely forbid the British imperialists to misbehave in Hong Kong."[24]

The Chinese government apparently took its nuclear capacity seriously enough to issue nuclear threats against the Soviet Union. In August 1969, Chinese Premier Zhou Enlai told Pakistani Air Marshal Nur Khan that if the Soviet Union attacked China, the "Chinese knew that they would be vastly outweighed in technology and materiel." However, he warned that the Chinese were prepared to respond to Soviet aggression in a war "that would 'know no boundaries.'"[25] Later, in a September 11 meeting with Soviet Premier A. N. Kosygin, Zhou argued for restraint in the Ussuri conflict, reminding Kosygin that the USSR "[knew] full well the current capacity of [Chinese] nuclear weapons."[26]

In fact, despite its rhetorical contradictions, the Chinese government's nuclear strategy in the late 1960s was a coherent one. As Lewis and Xue argue, the Chinese

> had chosen to create a force of high-yield, moderately accurate weapons that could with reasonable probability survive and retaliate if China suffered a nuclear blow of its own. Given Mao's well-known views about nuclear war, none would doubt that he had the will to order a second-strike retaliation, and it was this belief, coupled with several dozen survivable weapons, that led to Mao's prediction that the nuclear program would "boost our courage and scare others." De facto, Mao had embraced a form of minimum nuclear deterrence.[27]

In the context of the Ussuri River conflict, Chinese threats of boundless war in response to a possible Soviet strategic attack "meant limited nuclear retaliation at a time and against targets of Beijing's own choosing."[28]

Despite indications that the Soviets were considering a nuclear attack, such a move did not go beyond the contemplation stage. Aside from the possible activity at Siberian and Far Eastern air bases mentioned earlier, the Soviets do not appear to have taken any physical steps toward preparing to strike China. This may be because Soviet leaders, in signaling that a preventive strike on China might be in the offing, were seeking primarily to coerce the Chinese into settling the border dispute. As David Holloway argues, "There is no evidence to suggest that [the Soviets] were seriously contemplating a nuclear attack, that this was more than an attempt at intimidation."[29] The Chinese, for their part, never considered launching a nuclear first strike against the Soviets.

Although China seems to have possessed a reasonably effective nuclear retaliatory force and Mao no doubt would have responded to a Soviet attack with a second strike, China was in no position to initiate a nuclear conflict with the Soviet Union. Additionally, the first use of nuclear weapons would have violated the Chinese principle of avoiding nuclear "adventurism," behavior for which the Chinese bitterly criticized Khrushchev and the Soviet Union. In avoiding both "adventurism" and "capitulationism," the Chinese adhered to a policy of "tit for tat," by which they would respond to enemy actions in kind. This approach would justify a retaliatory strike but not the first use of nuclear weapons. As the Chinese government had argued in 1963, "in the hands of a socialist country, nuclear weapons must always be defensive weapons for resisting imperialist nuclear threats. A socialist country absolutely must not be the first to use nuclear weapons . . . "[30]

Conventional conflict between the Soviet Union and China in the Ussuri region thus never actually approached the brink of nuclear war. Nonetheless, nuclear confrontation was not completely beyond the realm of possibility and might have occurred if the situation had deteriorated further. Given the Soviets' deep concern over the border conflict, their contemplation of a nuclear strike on China during the crisis, and their general skepticism regarding the danger of Chinese retaliatory capabilities, Soviet leaders might well have decided to launch punitive nuclear attacks against Chinese military installations along the Sino-Soviet border had the Ussuri River fighting continued or expanded further. Doing so would have reminded the Chinese that they were dealing with an adversary far more powerful than themselves and that they risked catastrophe if they continued on their present course.[31]

The Chinese took this possibility quite seriously. According to Yang Kuisong, in the summer of 1969, a "war scare" gripped the Chinese leadership, as Mao became convinced that the "threat of a [Soviet] preemptive nuclear attack was very grave indeed." In August, the Chinese Communist Party (CCP) Central Committee and Central Military Commission ordered the establishment of the "Leading Group for People's Air Defence" and charged it with overseeing the evacuation of people and industry from large urban centers. Additionally, the CCP exhorted urban workers and residents to begin constructing air-raid shelters and storing daily necessities in preparation for a nuclear attack.[32] Even after Sino-Soviet tensions declined in the wake of the September Zhou-Kosygin meeting, the Chinese worried that the Soviet Union's softening stance was simply a ruse, and they continued to prepare for a Soviet strike. So great was their concern that in October Mao and other key Chinese leaders evacuated Beijing.[33] Had a Soviet nuclear attack occurred,

China would likely have responded in kind, given the high-yield, moderately accurate, and survivable nature of the Chinese arsenal, the Chinese strategy of tit for tat, and Mao's somewhat cavalier attitude toward nuclear weapons. Thus, it is not inconceivable that the 1969 Sino-Soviet border war could eventually have spiraled to the level of nuclear escalation.

Why would Chinese leaders have wished to provoke such a dangerous conflict with their large and powerful neighbor? As a U.S. State Department cable noted to Secretary of State Kissinger, the Chinese decision to attack the Soviets seemed "illogical."[34] Analysts have subsequently identified two main categories of possible motives for the Chinese aggression. First, the USSR's 1968 invasion of Czechoslovakia and promulgation of the Brezhnev Doctrine may have caused Chinese leaders to fear that China could become a target for Soviet intervention. By behaving aggressively to vindicate its stance on the Ussuri border, China demonstrated to the Soviets that it would not be another Czechoslovakia.[35] Second, Mao Zedong may have sought conflict with the Soviet Union to energize the Chinese people and boost the flagging Cultural Revolution. If this was the case, China's aggressive pursuit of its territorial goals in the Ussuri region was essentially a diversionary tactic related to Chinese domestic politics.[36]

Without attempting to discern the Chinese government's precise motive, or combination of motives, for its aggressive behavior at Zhenbao Island, it should be possible to determine whether the Ussuri River case fits the general framework that I have presented in this study. As noted, my argument expects that the acquisition of nuclear weapons may encourage conventionally weak, revisionist powers to engage in conventional aggression. China was the new nuclear state and the aggressor in the Ussuri River case. Does Chinese behavior in fact meet my argument's expectations? To answer this question, we must determine whether China occupied a weak, revisionist position in the Sino-Soviet conflict relationship. To decide whether this is the case, we must ascertain China's conventional military status relative to the Soviet Union as well as Chinese leaders' territorial preferences.

Let us turn first to the question of the conventional military balance between the Soviet Union and China during the Ussuri River conflict. There is little doubt that the overall Sino-Soviet conventional military balance in 1969 favored the Soviet Union. Soviet active-duty forces numbered approximately 3.3 million. The USSR fielded eighty-eight motorized rifle and forty-five tank divisions, with a total of over 32,000 medium and heavy tanks, and possessed nearly 10,000 combat aircraft. By contrast, the PRC's active-duty forces numbered approximately 2.8 million. The Chinese possessed only four armored and three cavalry divisions and 2,500 combat aircraft.[37]

Despite the Soviets' clear advantage in the overall conventional balance, there is some disagreement in the literature regarding Sino-Soviet conventional capabilities in the Ussuri region. The majority view holds that the Soviet Union enjoyed a substantial conventional advantage over China in the vicinity of the clashes. Indeed, according to one scholar, the balance of forces in the region was such that the "worst threat to Chinese security [in 1968–1969] existed in the North, from a former ally—the Soviet Union."[38] Goldstein, however, argues that in March 1969 regional force ratios favored China and gave it conventional superiority in the Ussuri region. He points out that China actually enjoyed an advantage in forces along the length of the Sino-Soviet border in 1969, where forty-seven Chinese divisions faced twenty-two Soviet divisions.[39]

Although the ratio of Chinese to Soviet forces in the Ussuri region is undoubtedly an important issue, comparing each side's number of divisions can paint a misleading picture of the balance of conventional power in the area. Divisional numbers alone would suggest that the Chinese enjoyed a regional manpower advantage over the Soviets of greater than 2:1.[40] However, several qualitative factors considerably mitigated the effects of Chinese local numerical superiority. First, the Soviets enjoyed a significant logistical advantage over the Chinese. The Soviet Union's Trans-Siberian Railroad essentially paralleled the length of the Sino-Soviet border, enabling the Soviets to move personnel and equipment rapidly to where it was needed.[41] Moreover, large Soviet Army and air bases were located along the railroad, further facilitating the rapid movement of men and materiel. The Chinese lacked an equivalent line of communication. Second, the Soviets benefited from the superiority of their equipment over that of the Chinese. While each side's precise quantity of armor, aircraft, and artillery in the region are unknown, the Soviets possessed greater numbers of these weapons overall and enjoyed significant qualitative advantages in each category of weaponry. And superior Soviet ground and air mobility enabled the Soviets to concentrate their equipment far faster than the Chinese, who still relied primarily on foot transport.[42] This enabled the Soviets to augment their forces and gain a local conventional advantage after the initial Sino-Soviet clashes.[43]

Third, in a protracted conflict, the Soviets could have shifted forces to the region from European and central and southern Russian bases, thereby compensating for any Chinese local numerical advantage.[44] Indeed, after 1969, the Soviet Union tripled its ground forces along the Sino-Soviet border.[45] Finally, domestic political events such as the Cultural Revolution had a deleterious impact on Chinese military effectiveness. The army's participation in the Cultural Revolution required extensive engagement in a broad range of nonmilitary pursuits, including the maintenance of domestic order, support for the Left, administrative and industrial supervision, and the spread of Mao Zedong thought. These activities dispersed Chinese forces thinly across the country, reduced their training opportunities, and significantly eroded the Chinese military's ability to deal with external threats.[46] Thus, weighing the numbers of Soviet and Chinese divisions does not capture the actual balance of conventional power in the Ussuri region, which was considerably more favorable to the Soviets than a numerical comparison would suggest.

Given this range of competing factors, Goldstein maintains that "no consensus emerges" in the literature "on whether the Soviets controlled the lower rungs of the escalation ladder in 1969."[47] However, even if we concede that the conventional picture in the Ussuri region in March 1969 is somewhat murky, it seems safe to conclude that despite any temporary local numerical advantages, China was the weaker party in the Sino-Soviet conflict relationship. The Chinese were far outclassed by Soviet logistics, qualitative equipment advantages, and overall numerical superiority, and they were hobbled by domestic politics. As one analyst put it, even as late as the mid-1970s, "net assessments . . . of the Sino-Soviet military balance including armor, close air support, naval forces, ground combat forces, and strategic forces will probably show that" the Chinese armed forces would have to improve "more than one thousand percent for the Chinese even to approach parity with the Soviet Union."[48]

Let us turn now to the question of Chinese preferences regarding territorial boundaries in the Ussuri region.[49] Did the Chinese wish to preserve the current territorial division in the region, or did they hope to alter existing boundaries? The evidence indicates that Chinese leaders were dissatisfied with territorial boundaries in the Ussuri region. As noted, the Treaty of Peking had formalized borders in the Ussuri region in 1860. For roughly the first ten years after the establishment of the PRC, China and the Soviet Union maintained these boundaries largely without controversy or incident. Sporadic border clashes began in 1959. The Chinese government then started openly challenging the legitimacy of the Ussuri River boundaries in 1963. According to the Chinese, borders in the region had resulted from a system of unequal treaties promulgated by the Russian tsarist regime and China's Ching Dynasty and therefore were open to reformulation.[50] As an editorial in the *Jen-min Jih-pao* put it, agreements such as the Treaty of Peking, which had established the Ussuri boundaries, were artifacts of "unbridled aggression against China," by which imperialist powers "annexed Chinese territory in the North, South,

East, and West." The People's Republic of China now had the right to re-examine these "treaties concluded by previous Chinese governments with foreign governments, these treaties . . . left over by history," and to "recognize, abrogate, revise or renegotiate them according to their respective contents."[51] Later that year, Mao stated, "About a hundred years ago, the area to the east of the Baikal became Russian territory, and since then Vladivostok, Khabarovsk, Kamchatka, and other areas have been Soviet territory. We have not yet presented our account for this list."[52]

These Chinese statements were of considerable concern to the Soviets, who took them as clear evidence of malign Chinese intentions and publicly charged China with harboring plans for Hitlerian expansionism in the region. In the midst of these recriminations, the two sides agreed to hold secret consultations in hopes of resolving the border issue. The meetings began in February 1964. During the talks, the Soviets agreed in principle to replace the old Sino-Russian treaties with a new comprehensive border treaty, provided that the new treaty would maintain the status quo by strengthening existing territorial boundaries. The Soviets also refused to terminate any existing treaties before they and the Chinese had consented to new ones. The Chinese, for their part, maintained that while they were willing to take the unequal treaties as the starting point for negotiation regarding alteration of territorial boundaries, all of the Sino-Russian border treaties signed prior to 1917 were in principle not valid. The Chinese insisted that the Soviets admit to the illegitimacy of these agreements before China consented to the formulation of any new treaties.[53]

Despite the clear differences between their positions, the Chinese and the Soviets held several important points in common. Both sides agreed that a new, comprehensive border treaty was needed, that existing treaties should remain operational until the new agreements were promulgated, and that the border controversy was confined primarily to a group of islands in the Ussuri River. Nonetheless, in the end, the Soviets were unwilling to invalidate existing treaties and admit to the illegitimacy of the territorial status quo prior to signing a new border treaty, whereas the Chinese insisted that they do so. Thus, the two sides were stuck at an impasse, and the talks broke off later in 1964. The Chinese and Soviet governments did not discuss the border issue again until October 1969, after the outbreak of the Ussuri River clashes.[54]

Does the argument that I have advanced in this study help to explain Chinese behavior in the Ussuri River case? Our discussion thus far makes clear that China was the conventionally weaker power in the Sino-Soviet conflict dyad and that the Chinese government had revisionist preferences regarding the territorial division of the Ussuri River region. Thus, the Ussuri River case is compatible with the argument in this book. But my argument would truly explain the case only if we could show that the acquisition of a nuclear weapons capacity directly encouraged the Chinese to initiate the Ussuri River conflict. Can we demonstrate that this actually occurred?

As we have seen, evidence does exist to support the view that nuclear weapons in fact played such a role in the outbreak of the conflict. The timing of China's initiation of the border dispute with the Soviet Union and of the Ussuri clashes is suggestive. In 1963, when it was on the brink of achieving a nuclear capability, China chose to raise a border issue publicly that had essentially been dormant since the nineteenth century. When the Soviets would not agree to Chinese terms, the Chinese then provoked a bloody and protracted series of clashes with Soviet forces. Despite contradictory public statements and writings and whatever their doubts regarding their nuclear capabilities, Chinese leaders believed that their nuclear weapons' deterrent effects were sufficiently robust to enable them to resist and even intimidate stronger adversaries. And they specifically hoped that their nuclear capacity would give them leverage in dealing with the Soviet government—as was evidenced by Chinese officials' leveling of nuclear threats against the Soviets during the Ussuri crisis. Given these facts, it is likely that Chinese leaders were at least somewhat emboldened to pursue an aggressive policy along the Sino-Soviet border by the belief that their nuclear weapons would help to insulate them against the danger of an all-out Soviet attack.

However, despite this circumstantial evidence, we have no direct proof that the acquisition of nuclear weapons drove Chinese behavior in this case. Given the information currently available, we simply do not know what was in Chinese leaders' minds when they decided to raise the Ussuri River border issue with the Soviets and to initiate the Ussuri clashes later. Although it is unlikely, it is possible that the timing of these Chinese actions was wholly a coincidence and that the Chinese raised the issue of their nuclear capabilities with the Soviets and third parties only as an afterthought. Therefore, we cannot definitively state that nuclear weapons directly encouraged a weak, revisionist China to initiate the Ussuri River clashes with the Soviet Union until more information becomes available as to the decision-making processes within the Chinese leadership. But we can conclude that the Ussuri case is broadly compatible with the expectations of my argument.

The North Korean Case

A potential proliferator about which the international community is gravely concerned is North Korea. International fears regarding North Korea stem primarily from two factors. First, the country is locked in a long-term security competition with a regional adversary. War between North and South Korea over the division of the Korean Peninsula erupted with the 1950 North Korean invasion of the South. Although the shooting ended in 1953, the two sides never signed a formal peace agreement, and the region has remained extremely tense and highly militarized. With their armed forces facing off along the demilitarized zone and their relationship characterized by bellicose rhetoric and sporadic confrontations, North and South Korea seem to be perpetually on the brink of major conflict.[55]

The second reason that the prospect of a nuclear North Korea has caused international alarm is that it is controlled by what many characterize as a "rogue" government. The North Korean regime is deeply illiberal and repressive in its domestic policies. It also has a record of involvement with international terrorist activities. The North Koreans have been implicated in the bombing of South Korean commercial aircraft, in a commando raid upon the residence of the South Korean president, and in the kidnapping of foreign nationals.[56] Some members of the international community fear that the acquisition of nuclear weapons could embolden a government such as North Korea's, encouraging it to engage in even more repugnant and dangerous behavior.[57] The North Koreans could also potentially transfer nuclear weapons or technology to terrorist groups, enabling these entities to launch devastating attacks without implicating the North Korean government.[58]

The status of the North Korean nuclear program is not entirely clear. The North Koreans began developing a nuclear weapons capacity in the 1960s with Soviet and subsequently Chinese assistance. By 1986, North Korea was able to begin operating a five-megawatt electric reactor at Yongbyon.[59] North Korea acceded to the Nuclear Non-Proliferation Treaty (NPT) in 1985 and in 1992 signed a "full scope safeguards agreement" with the International Atomic Energy Agency (IAEA). The safeguards agreement required the North Koreans to declare all of their nuclear materials and facilities, which were to be subject to IAEA inspections. However, when the IAEA determined that North Korea had not fully declared its plutonium production and requested access to certain nuclear waste facilities, Pyongyang refused. Instead, North Korea announced that it would withdraw from the NPT. These actions triggered the United Nations Security Council to pass Resolution 825, which "[called] upon the DPRK to reconsider" its withdrawal from the NPT, "to reaffirm its commitment to the Treaty," and "to honour its non-proliferation obligations under the Treaty and to comply with its safeguards agreement with the IAEA."[60]

To avert a looming crisis, the U.S. government opened bilateral nego-
tiations with North Korea in June 1993. The negotiations resulted in the
October 1994 Agreed Framework between the United States and the DPRK.
Under the framework, North Korea agreed to freeze its reactors and related facilities under IAEA supervision and ultimately to dismantle them. The North
Koreans also promised eventually to comply with the terms of their 1992
IAEA safeguards agreement. In return, the United States agreed that it would
organize an international consortium, which would supply light-water reactors to the DPRK. While the light-water reactor project was being completed, the consortium would provide North Korea with heavy oil for heating
and electricity production. Additionally, the two sides agreed to work toward
"peace and security on a non-nuclear Korean peninsula," which would include the United States formally assuring the DPRK against the threat or use
of nuclear weapons.[61]

The Agreed Framework provided only a temporary respite from the North
Korean nuclear problem. Before long, Pyongyang had devised a means of es-
caping the framework's strictures, secretly acquiring Pakistani gas-centrifuge
uranium enrichment technology between 1997 and 1998 in return for No
Dong intermediate-range ballistic missiles. When confronted with evidence
of its uranium enrichment efforts in October 2002, the North Koreans initially
admitted to the program, though they later claimed that the United States
lacked any evidence that North Korea had violated the Agreed Framework.[62]
The North Koreans subsequently offered to negotiate a bilateral settlement of
the nuclear issue with Washington, but the Bush administration refused to do
so, opting instead for a multilateral approach involving South Korea, Japan,
and China. In an effort to increase the pressure on North Korea, the Korean
Peninsula Energy Development Board (KEDO), the consortium created to
supply the DPRK with light-water reactors and fuel oil, announced in November 2002 that North Korea had to "visibly and quickly honor its commitment to give up its nuclear weapons program" and that KEDO would suspend
future fuel-oil shipments unless Pyongyang took "concrete and credible actions to dismantle its highly-enriched uranium program."[63] In response, the
North Koreans announced that they would restart their nuclear facilities, and
in late December 2002, they removed seals and surveillance equipment from
key sites and expelled IAEA inspectors from the country. Thus, by the end of
2002, the Agreed Framework was dead.[64]

North Korea's nuclear weapons capabilities at this point became the subject
of extensive speculation. The U.S. intelligence community estimated that the
North Koreans already possessed six to nine kilograms of weapons-grade plu-

tonium, enough for four or five medium–yield nuclear devices. Based on these approximations, the CIA believed that North Korea probably had one or two nuclear weapons. North Korea's future nuclear capabilities looked even more dangerous. Although not yet online, a fifty–megawatt reactor at Yongbyon and a 200–megawatt reactor at Taechon, operating at full capacity, could produce approximately 270 kilograms of plutonium each year. And the extent of North Korea's uranium enrichment program remained an open question. One analysis predicted that it would be able to produce between 40 and 100 kilograms of highly enriched uranium per year.[65]

In February 2005, North Korea attempted to end uncertainty regarding its nuclear weapons status, claiming for the first time that it in fact had developed nuclear weapons. "The U.S. disclosed its attempt to topple the political system in the DPRK at any cost, threatening it with a nuclear stick. This compels us to take a measure to bolster its nuclear weapons arena," the Korean Central News Agency (KCNA) announced. North Korea, the KCNA continued, had "manufactured nukes for self-defence to cope with the Bush administration's ever-more undisguised policy to isolate and stifle the DPRK."[66] The announcement was met with international reactions ranging from disappointment to alarm, though some U.S. officials pointed out that North Korea had offered no proof of its capability and speculated that Pyongyang could be bluffing. "They've indicated other things from time to time that haven't proved out," said Secretary of Defense Donald Rumsfeld.[67]

Despite apparent doubts on the part of some U.S. officials, it seems safe to assume that North Korea either does actually possess a small number of nuclear devices or is very close to obtaining them.[68] North Korea's archrival, South Korea, does not possess a nuclear weapons capacity. However, South Korea is closely allied with the United States, which has nearly 40,000 troops stationed in the South and has extended the protection of its nuclear umbrella to the South Koreans, reserving the right to employ nuclear weapons to defend the Republic of Korea (ROK) if necessary.[69] Thus, North Korea's adversary in any nuclear conflict would not be South Korea but rather would be the United States, extending nuclear deterrence to its South Korean ally.

Extended deterrence commitments are inherently less credible than deterrent threats designed to protect a state's homeland.[70] During the Cold War, the U.S. extended deterrent commitment to Western Europe became so unbelievable that the United States was forced to adopt a range of tactical and strategic measures to convince the Soviets that nuclear escalation was likely in the event of a European conflict. However, the American extended deterrence commitment to South Korea would be considerably more credible than this. The U.S.

commitment to Europe lacked believability because of the Soviets' capacity to inflict massive damage on the U.S. homeland in the event of an American nuclear attack. This Soviet capability was made possible by two factors: First, the Soviets had a sufficient quantity of weapons to destroy a large number of targets within the United States. Second, the Soviets possessed delivery vehicles capable of putting the weapons on their targets.

Neither of these factors holds in the case of North Korea. If the North Koreans have in fact managed to develop nuclear weapons, they actually possess a very small number of them, probably no more than a handful. Their arsenal is nowhere near the size of that of the former Soviet Union, which had a sufficient number of nuclear weapons to have destroyed the United States as a functioning society. Moreover, the North Koreans lack the ability to hit targets within the United States. Approximately 90 percent of the North Korean Air Force's (KPAF) combat aircraft are of Soviet or Chinese designs dating from the 1950s and 1960s. The North Koreans also suffer from a rudimentary command and control system as well as a shortage of fuel and spare parts. Thus, the KPAF "is primarily an air defense force, with limited offensive capability"[71] and does not possess the ability to deliver nuclear weapons against targets in the United States.

Given the limited capabilities of its air force, North Korea is likely to use ballistic missiles to deliver its nuclear weapons. The North Koreans have an extensive missile program. The DPRK possesses approximately 100 medium-range No Dong missiles, which, with a range of 1,350 kilometers and a payload of 1,200 kilograms, could threaten Japan and U.S. bases in Okinawa.[72] The North Koreans are also developing a long-range, multistage missile called the Taepodong, some versions of which could strike targets more than 10,000 kilometers away. Depending on their payload, these missiles could be able to reach Hawaii and the continental United States.

However, the Taepodongs are not yet fully operational. In a failed 1998 test intended to launch a satellite into orbit, a Taepodong 1 missile's third stage disintegrated.[73] The CIA estimated in 2003 that the Taepodong 2, with a range of over 6,000 kilometers, might be ready only for flight testing.[74] Moreover, the Taepodongs' ability to reach American targets would depend on their carrying relatively light payloads of no more than several hundred kilograms, sufficient only for chemical or biological weapons. Additionally, for the Taepodongs to operate effectively, the North Koreans would need to improve the missiles' guidance systems, devise more robust heat shields to prevent reentry burnup, and build larger booster engines, which would require materials and machining techniques currently unavailable to the DPRK.[75] Thus, the North Koreans currently lack missiles capable of reaching the U.S. homeland with nuclear weapons and are likely to do so for some time to come. As one analyst put it, the North Korean "ballistic missile threat to the United States [is] potentially real, but not immediate."[76]

For the foreseeable future, then, North Korea would be unable to use its nuclear weapons to inflict even limited damage on the U.S. homeland. Thus, the United States would not face the same constraints in escalating a Korean conventional conflict to the nuclear level that it faced when extending nuclear deterrence to Western Europe during the Cold War. Of course, significant disincentives to using nuclear weapons would still exist for the United States, including a desire not to violate the nuclear "taboo" that has existed since 1945[77] and the prospect of North Korean nuclear retaliation against South Korea or Japan. North Korea, for its part, would also face strong incentives to refrain from nuclear escalation in the event of conventional conflict. Despite their domestic repression and international thuggery, North Korean leaders have shown little evidence of being either irrational or suicidal. Indeed, as noted, the North Koreans have played a wily bargaining game with the international community over the disposition of their nuclear weapons program, securing significant concessions in return for promises to halt weapons development. Realizing that the use of nuclear weapons against South Korea would probably result in retaliation in kind, North Korean leaders would be unlikely to launch a nuclear attack and invite the destruction of their country and regime, except in the direst circumstances. Nonetheless, the fact remains that a major disincentive for American nuclear use in Cold War Europe would not exist in the Korean context. And while North Korean leaders would be unlikely to employ nuclear weapons carelessly or in a fit of "irrationality," they could resort to such extreme measures if the DPRK started to lose a conventional war badly in hopes of staving off catastrophic defeat and preserving their homeland.

What impact should the acquisition of nuclear weapons have on North Korean conventional military behavior? Should we expect it to embolden North Korea to behave aggressively at the conventional level, energizing its conflict with regional adversaries? Or should we expect that nuclear proliferation will not lead North Korea to engage in more aggressive conventional behavior? Knowing North Korea's territorial preferences and its conventional military capabilities relative to its adversaries can help us determine which outcome is most likely.[78]

Let us turn first to the question of the Korean conventional military balance. From a purely quantitative standpoint, North Korea appears to enjoy a significant military advantage over South Korean and American forces. In 2003, South Korean active-duty forces totaled 686,000. The Republic of Korea fielded over 2,300 main battle tanks, more than 2,500 armored personnel carriers and armored infantry fighting vehicles, and approximately 530 combat aircraft. These forces were augmented by approximately 37,000 American personnel, along with approximately 116 main battle tanks, more than 230 armored personnel carriers and armored infantry fighting vehicles, and over 80 combat aircraft.[79] Against these forces, North Korea had arrayed over 1 million active-duty personnel, approximately 3,500 main battle tanks, 2,500 armored personnel carriers, and more than 620 combat aircraft.[80]

A simple numerical comparison of North and South Korean forces would thus seem to reveal a significant DPRK advantage. However, this approach to assessing the conventional military balance in Korea overlooks several key factors. First, the quality of North Korean weaponry is poor relative to that of the United States and South Korea. In combat, American and South Korean tanks, aircraft, and munitions would considerably outperform North Korean weapons and equipment, much of which is of 1960s-era Soviet design.[81] Second, the geography of the Korean Peninsula puts North Korea at a military disadvantage. If the North Koreans wished to launch an offensive against the ROK, mountainous, obstacle-laden terrain would permit DPRK forces to travel South through only a handful of natural attack corridors. These corridors, ranging from four to fifteen kilometers in breadth, would slow the attackers' advance and channel them into some of the most heavily defended ground in the world.[82] U.S./ROK forces, by contrast, could conceivably attack North Korea without having to contend with these problems; their air mobility and amphibious capabilities could help them to avoid the peninsula's difficult terrain.[83] Third, American ground and air reinforcements would significantly augment South Korean defensive capabilities within weeks of the outbreak of conflict. Several months into a war, the U.S. heavy division capability would surpass that of either North or South Korea, and the United States would have three times as many fighter aircraft in theater as the number of ROK and DPRK aircraft combined.[84] Finally, North Korean demographic and economic indicators lag far behind those of South Korea. South Korean gross domestic product in 2003 was over $850 billion[85] compared to North Korea's approximately $30 billion.[86] The South Korean population of nearly 49 million was over twice that of North Korea's roughly 23 million.[87] And South Korean defense spending in 2001 was approximately $11 billion, as opposed to North Korea's roughly $2 billion defense budget.[88] Thus, despite the large size of its military, North Korea is clearly incapable of attacking and defeating the South; the DPRK is far and away the weaker party on the Korean Penin-sula.[89] As one analysis put it, in the event of war, "the ability of the [American and South Korean] allies can hardly be doubted, and the probability that they would lose substantial amounts of territory even temporarily is very low."[90]

Let us now turn to the issue of the North Korean government's territorial preferences. Is North Korea a status quo state, satisfied with regional territorial divisions? Or is it a revisionist power, anxious to alter the existing division of the Korean Peninsula? Unfortunately, it is difficult to answer this question de-finitively. Sufficient evidence exists to make a credible case for either possibility.

In the past, North Korean territorial revisionism has led it to engage in ag-gressive behavior. For example, DPRK leaders initiated the Korean War in 1950 in hopes of undoing the division of Korea and unifying the peninsula under the DPRK banner. Kim Il Sung had apparently become obsessed with the achieve-ment of this goal. As he told Soviet officials in an attempt to convince Stalin to approve a North Korean invasion of the South, "Lately I do not sleep at night, thinking about how to resolve the question of the unification of the whole country."[91] Some analysts believe that the North Korean regime has never abandoned its goal of reunification. For example, Nicholas Eberstadt argues that the DPRK is a state that has been designed specifically to achieve "three en-twined purposes: to conduct a war, to settle a historical grievance, and to fulfill a grand ideological vision. The vision is reunification of the Korean Peninsula under the 'independent, socialist' rule of the DPRK—i.e., unconditional an-nexation of present-day South Korea and liquidation of the Republic of Korea government." In this view, North Korean leaders see the Korean War as "an ongoing conflict—and North Korea's leadership is committed to an uncondi-tional victory, however long it might take and however much it might cost."[92]

Even if North Korean leaders do not currently hope to reunify the Korean Peninsula under the DPRK banner, they could still be deeply dissatisfied with a status quo in which growing military and economic weakness renders North Korea increasingly vulnerable to attack or collapse. Such dissatisfaction could lead to violent DPRK attempts to alter the existing politico-military environ-ment. Despite the danger of such behavior, the North Koreans could see it as preferable to doing nothing in the face of catastrophic decline. As Victor D. Cha argues, the DPRK could employ limited violence to "create small crises and then [negotiate] . . . to a bargaining outcome more to the North's ad-vantage than the status quo . . . At the worst-case end of the spectrum, through long-range artillery barrages, missile strikes, or chemical weapons attacks . . . the North could seek to hold Seoul hostage with the hope of renegotiating a new status quo."[93]

The physical evidence created by the regime's military preparations lends credence to these pessimistic views. As a recent analysis argues, North Korean forces are deployed so as to facilitate a potential invasion of the ROK. This aggressive force posture suggests that "The regime may even still harbor remote hopes of reunifying the peninsula under its rule; certainly its military doctrine appears to be based on such a plan. Its forces are generally not postured or prepared to fight defensively; its forward-deployed forces within 100 meters of the DMZ have increased from 40 percent to 70 percent of total troop strength over the past two decades."[94]

Despite these troubling possibilities, one can also make a powerful case that North Korea is probably a status quo rather than a revisionist state. In this view, there is little hard evidence to suggest that, at present, North Korean leaders seriously wish to alter the politico-military environment in the region. It is true that the Korean War was motivated by the North Korean government's desire to revise regional boundaries. And it is also the case that, in the absence of a peace treaty, the Korean War has never officially ended. Nonetheless, in more recent years, despite occasional instances of small-scale confrontation with ROK forces and sporadic terrorist activity, the North has scaled back its provocative behavior and made no serious attempt to take territory at the expense of South Korea.[95] Indeed, in the face of severe economic crises and food and energy shortages, as well as looming international threats, the North Korean regime's highest priority is probably not the revision of Korean territorial boundaries. Its primary goal may simply be to survive.

Proponents of this logic maintain that the DPRK's ongoing nuclear weapons and missile programs, as well as its robust conventional capacity, are not intended to facilitate North Korean aggression against South Korea or the United States. Rather, they are defensive in purpose, designed primarily to protect North Korea against the possibility of an American attack. As David C. Kang argues, North Korean military capabilities "are aimed at deterrence and defense." "North Korea does not threaten to take unprovoked military or terrorist actions. North Korea as a country fears the United States. Much of its behavior is designed to deter the U.S. from going after North Korea next, once the U.S. has finished with Iraq."[96]

In this vein, analysts also note that the DPRK faces severe domestic challenges. North Korea's economic and internal political situation is sufficiently dire that many observers are pessimistic as to the DPRK's ability to avoid collapse. "As time goes on," one analysis speculates, "North Korea will only grow economically poorer" and is "likely to implode."[97] Commentators also point out that Kim Jong Il's domestic position appears to be eroding. The combination of food shortages, growing access to information from the outside world, and government corruption has left Kim less revered by ordinary citizens and increasingly unable to rely on senior officials. These developments could seriously weaken the North Korean regime.[98] The DPRK has responded by increasing the penalties for criticizing the government or engaging in other "antistate" behaviors, clamping down on "antisocialist" activity in border regions, publicly executing citizens guilty of such "antirepublic" actions as unauthorized border crossing and dissemination of information, and banning the use of mobile telephones. The severity of the DPRK government's actions, far from ensuring the continuation of its absolute control over the North Korean population, underscores the seriousness of the emerging threats to its survival.[99] Regardless of these problems, some analysts remain sanguine as to the DPRK's longevity. According to this view, the North has made real, if limited, economic progress since the mid-1990s, which is likely to ensure the regime's continuation well into the future. Thus, one commentator argues, the United States should "accept the reality that North Korea is not on the verge of collapse." [100]

Despite this disagreement as to the depth of the DPRK's current predicament, the fact is that current debates over the future of the Korean Peninsula focus more on the longevity of the North Korean state than on the likelihood of major North Korean conventional aggression against the South. And whatever their differences, most observers agree that avoiding collapse or destruction is currently the North Korean government's primary goal. As one analyst put it, regardless of its provocative behavior, "Pyongyang regularly calls upon Seoul, Tokyo, Washington, and other international players to supply it with food and financial assistance. North Korea's policies have come to rely primarily on threats and blackmail. The name of their game is survival." [101] According to former U.S. ambassador to South Korea James R. Lilley, "North Korea is basically a failed state whose priority is survival. Its Achilles heel is its need for foreign economic assistance. It is surrounded by successful modern and powerful states (Japan, China, and South Korea) that have the assistance they need to survive." [102] North Korea's apparent willingness to consider renouncing its nuclear capability in return for economic aid, food and energy supplies, and a promise that the country will not be targeted for attack by the United States supports these claims. Such behavior again suggests that the DPRK's nuclear program is motivated by "economic and military insecurity" [103] and that Pyongyang is probably more interested in survival than revision of the status quo on the Korean Peninsula.

Given North Korea's considerable political and economic insecurity, it seems more likely that the DPRK should be classified as a status quo rather than a revisionist state. However, as noted, arguments in favor of the opposite view are plausible and cannot be wholly ruled out. This is especially true given the opaque nature of the DPRK regime, which makes it very difficult for observers accurately to discern North Korean intentions and preferences. Our purpose here is not to provide a definitive analysis of North Korean preferences or to adjudicate between the competing views that have been outlined. Rather, our object is to demonstrate how the analytic framework that I have developed in this study can help us to predict the conventional military behavior of new nuclear states. Therefore, I will briefly discuss the implications for future DPRK behavior of both arguments regarding North Korean territorial preferences. Readers can then draw their own conclusions regarding likely DPRK conventional behavior based on whether they believe the North Korean regime to be revisionist or status quo. The key point, from the standpoint of this study, is to note the importance of territorial preferences to our predictions regarding North Korea. How we expect a nuclear North Korea to act toward the South depends on our assessment of North Korean leaders' level of satisfaction with the status quo on the Korean Peninsula.

If the North Korean regime is seriously dissatisfied with the status quo and wishes to alter territorial boundaries in the region, then the DPRK is both weak and revisionist, as was Pakistan in the case of South Asia. In this scenario, North Korean and Pakistani behavioral incentives would be similar, and we should expect the DPRK's conventional actions to resemble those of Pakistan. North Korean leaders will be tempted to launch limited conventional challenges to the status quo while their new nuclear capability shields them from large-scale retaliation and attracts international attention. Such international attention could perhaps enable the North Koreans to achieve a territorial settlement preferable to the current division of the Korean Peninsula. It could also help Pyongyang to continue its strategy of extorting financial and energy assistance from the international community; the North Koreans could threaten to continue their risky conventional behavior unless outside states provide the support that the North Koreans demand.

On the other hand, if North Korean leaders do not wish to alter territorial boundaries in the region, our predictions regarding North Korean militarized behavior would be very different. In this case, North Korea would occupy a militarily weak, status quo position in the Korean conflict relationship. In such a scenario, North Korea's status quo territorial preferences would greatly reduce the probability that a newly nuclear Pyongyang would behave aggressively. Since the North Korean regime would be concerned primarily with ensuring its own survival rather than altering territorial divisions, it would be unlikely to attempt to undo existing regional boundaries from behind a nuclear shield. This is not to argue that such behavior would be impossible. As noted, a status quo state may behave aggressively if its leaders believe that doing so is essential to preserving its current position. The North Korean government could attempt to ensure its survival by blackmailing the international community, threatening to engage in conventional or nuclear aggression unless third parties provide it with financial assistance and security guarantees.

Although such aggression is possible, it is considerably less probable than it would be if North Korea had serious designs on South Korean territory. Thus, although the aforementioned dangers are real, the likelihood that nuclear weapons will encourage aggression by a status quo DPRK is relatively low. In this scenario, the greatest dangers resulting from North Korean nuclear proliferation are likely to be unrelated to DPRK conventional aggression. Instead, major risks would lie in the possibility that the financially strapped North Korean government could sell nuclear weapons or technology to third parties. North Korea's recent behavior suggests that such horizontal proliferation would be a very serious possibility. For example, as noted, the North Korean government and elements of the Pakistani nuclear weapons establishment[104] struck a deal by which the North Koreans acquired Pakistani uranium enrichment technology in exchange for No Dong missile plans. The DPRK may have reached a similar arrangement with Iran. The North Koreans have also sold missiles to Egypt, Iraq, Libya, Syria, and Yemen and have sought additional buyers.[105] Thus, according to one analysis, "The DPRK network of missile sales can be pictured as the hub and spokes of a wheel, with the DPRK at the center."[106] A nuclear North Korea could serve as the hub of a parallel proliferation ring—this time one that spreads nuclear weapons material and technology, rather than missiles, to the highest bidder. My findings neither indicate that such technology transfer is likely to happen nor offer any reassurance that it is unlikely; the question is beyond the scope of this study. However, given the dangers inherent in such a possibility, problems such as the further horizontal proliferation of nuclear technology should be at the forefront of our concerns—regardless of our views regarding Pyongyang's territorial preferences and the likelihood that acquisition of nuclear weapons will encourage North Korean conventional aggression.

The Middle East

The framework that I used to analyze the effects of nuclear weapons on India, Pakistan, China, and North Korea should be useful in other proliferation-prone areas around the globe. One such region is the Middle East, where many observers' greatest fear is that Iran could eventually acquire a nuclear weapons capacity. Iranian President Mahmoud Ahmadinejad is a "hardline religious conservative" [107] and has called for Israel to be "wiped off the map." [108] As one commentator put it, "the prospect of a nuclear bomb in the hands of a regime led by Ahmadinejad and the fundamentalist ayatollahs worries the entire international community." [109] Indeed, U.S. President George W. Bush has stated "we cannot allow" Iran to develop a uranium enrichment capability because such a capability could eventually enable Iran to produce nuclear weapons. "People know that an Iran with the capacity to manufacture a nuclear weapon is not in the world's interest. That's universally accepted." [110] Israeli opposition leader Benjamin Netanyahu has gone so far as to call for the destruction of Iranian nuclear facilities. According to Netanyahu, "Israel should not allow Iran to develop a nuclear threat against it." "The Iranian threat is a real one, a threat to the existence of Israel, from a state which has declared its intentions to destroy Israel." [111]

What type of behavior might we expect from a nuclear Iran? Would it attempt to undermine the regional status quo, perhaps through a strategy of low-intensity conflict or an increase in its support for international terrorism? [112] Or would a nuclear Iran simply seek to ensure its own security and avoid aggressive behavior?

An attempt to answer these questions would require us to take the same approach as we did in our earlier discussion of North Korea. Our expectations for a nuclear Iran would depend not on abstract theoretical arguments applicable to all nuclear-weapons states everywhere but rather would turn upon an assessment of Iran's specific territorial preferences and relative military capabilities. Our first task would be to determine the Iranian government's actual desires regarding the territorial status quo in the Persian Gulf and larger Middle East. Do the Iranians truly wish to alter territorial boundaries in the region? Or despite their frightening rhetoric and religious conservatism, are Iranian leaders in fact willing to accept existing territorial divisions? Second, we would need to ascertain the balance of conventional military capabilities between Iran and its potential enemies in the region, including Israel, Iraq, and the United States. How would Iran fare in a conflict against any one of these states or against a coalition involving two or more of them? Answering these questions will enable us to determine whether Iran is a weak, revisionist state. If Iran is not both weak and revisionist, international fears regarding a nuclear Iran may be exaggerated; the acquisition of nuclear weapons would be unlikely to encourage aggressive Iranian attempts to undo the territorial status quo. [113] If, by contrast, we determine that Iran is weak and that it is truly revisionist, a nuclear Iran's incentives for destabilizing behavior will be high.

These questions reach well beyond the scope of this book, and I make no attempt to answer them here. My point is simply that an assessment of nuclear weapons' likely effects on Iran would turn not on abstract principles that determine the behavior of all nuclear states but rather on political and military factors specific to the Iranian case. Just as in South Asia, Iranian territorial preferences and relative conventional capabilities will be crucial to determining nuclear proliferation's probable impact on Iran and on the larger Middle East.

Conclusion

In this chapter, I recapped the behavioral incentives for new nuclear powers that are likely to result from various combinations of territorial preferences, military capabilities, and strategic stability. I showed that the acquisition of nuclear weapons was likely to encourage aggressive conventional behavior only on the part of weak, revisionist states. No other combinations of territorial preferences and military capabilities were likely to encourage increased conventional aggression by new nuclear powers. I then applied these findings to the cases of the Sino-Soviet Ussuri River conflict and North Korea. In the Ussuri River case, I showed that while evidence is limited, Chinese behavior is compatible with my argument's expectation of limited conventional aggression by new nuclear powers that are conventionally weak and dissatisfied with the territorial status quo. In the case of North Korea, I argued that given the DPRK's conventional weakness relative to South Korean and American forces on the peninsula, the impact of nuclear proliferation on North Korea's behavior would hinge on its leaders' territorial preferences. If the North Koreans seriously desired to change the existing border on the Korean Peninsula, the acquisition of a nuclear weapons capability could embolden them to engage in conventionally aggressive behavior against the South. If, by contrast, North Korea was a status quo state concerned primarily with its own survival, the acquisition of nuclear weapons was unlikely to encourage North Korean conventional aggression. In this case, the North Koreans would be more likely to use nuclear weapons as a means of ensuring preservation of the territorial status quo. The primary danger of this scenario is that the North Koreans would use the sale of nuclear materials and technology as a means of earning hard currency from abroad. The chapter ended with a brief discussion of my argument's applicability to a newly nuclear Iran.

In the following chapter, I discuss the theoretical and policy implications of this study. I argue that my findings depart significantly not only from the optimist and pessimist strands of the nuclear proliferation literature but also from important aspects of general nuclear deterrence theory. My study shows that rather than impeding conventional conflict, as nuclear deterrence theory assumes, nuclear danger can actually encourage it. From a policy perspective, this means not only that nuclear weapons proliferation may fail to prevent conventional instability but that it may result in greater subnuclear violence. New nuclear states dissatisfied with the status quo may behave aggressively in hopes of changing territorial boundaries, while deterring retaliation by stronger adversaries and attracting international attention. This suggests that diplomacy to defuse ongoing territorial disputes will be an essential means of reducing the potential costs of future nuclear proliferation.

8

Dangerous Deterrent

In this study, I have sought to determine the effects that India's and Pakistan's acquisition of nuclear weapons has had on the South Asian security environment, focusing specifically on proliferation's impact on conventional military stability in the region. I first showed, through a quantitative analysis of the historical record, that a positive correlation exists between progressing nuclear proliferation and militarized disputes in the region. I explained this correlation between proliferation and conventional instability through case studies that closely examined Indo-Pakistani conventional military behavior during three periods of time during the proliferation process: a nonnuclear period from 1972 through 1989; a de facto nuclear period from 1990 through May 1998; and an overt nuclear period from June 1998 through 2002.

I argued that conventional conflict became more frequent and severe as proliferation progressed because of India's and Pakistan's territorial preferences and relative military capabilities. Pakistan's conventional military weakness vis-à-vis India and its revisionist preferences regarding the territorial division of Kashmir created strong incentives for conventional Pakistani aggression. This was the case for two reasons. First, nuclear weapons, by deterring all-out Indian conventional retaliation, enabled the Pakistanis physically to challenge territorial boundaries in Kashmir. Second, the danger of conventional hostilities escalating to the nuclear level drew international attention, potentially enabling Pakistan to secure outside mediation of the Kashmir dispute and to achieve a more favorable territorial settlement in Kashmir than it could have gotten by itself.

India's conventional strength and status quo preferences regarding the territorial division of Kashmir, by contrast, meant that the acquisition of nuclear weapons did not create direct incentives for India to become more conventionally aggressive or to alter its military behavior in any significant manner. This was the case because the Indian government was largely satisfied on the issue of Kashmir and did not seek to alter territorial boundaries in the region. Therefore, the Indians had little motivation to engage in cross-border aggression, with or without nuclear weapons. In addition, because India was conventionally stronger than Pakistan, the acquisition of nuclear weapons did not enable the Indians to undertake any aggression that they could not have launched earlier with purely conventional forces. Thus, we saw increasingly aggressive Pakistani behavior as proliferation progressed, while nuclear weapons did not have much direct impact on Indian behavior—though, by encouraging Pakistani adventurism, nuclear weapons did drive India to adopt increasingly forceful approaches to dealing with Pakistan.

In the case studies, I demonstrated this logic's impact on the Indo-Pakistani security relationship since 1972. Specifically, I showed that the first, nonnuclear time period from 1972 through 1989 was relatively peaceful, with 186 of 216 months completely free of militarized conflict. I argued that this was the case for two main reasons. First, the Indian government was satisfied with the territorial division of the subcontinent after its victory in the Bangladesh War and had no reason to undertake any aggression against Pakistan. Second, although Pakistani leaders were dissatisfied with the division of the subcontinent following the Bangladesh War, in its weakened state, Pakistan could not risk action to alter territorial boundaries and thus generally avoided confrontation with India.

I showed that the second, de facto nuclear time period was considerably more volatile than the nonnuclear period, with militarized disputes occurring over five times more frequently than they did from 1972 through 1989. I argued that this decreased stability resulted largely from Pakistan's support for the anti-Indian insurgency in Kashmir. This involvement in the insurgency was encouraged by Pakistan's de facto nuclear weapons capacity, which enabled Pakistan to pursue a low-intensity conflict strategy in Kashmir while insulated from all-out Indian conventional retaliation.

I showed that during the third, overt nuclear time period, the frequency of militarized Indo-Pakistani disputes increased nearly 14 percent beyond what it had been during the de facto nuclear period. Additionally, conflict during the overt period escalated above the hostility levels reached in either the nonnuclear or the de facto nuclear periods, crossing the threshold of outright war in 1999. I explained that the overt acquisition of nuclear weapons gave the Pakistan government even greater confidence in its ability to alter the territorial status quo in Kashmir through conventional aggression without fear of full-scale Indian retaliation. Furthermore, Pakistani leaders believed that conflict between two openly nuclear powers would attract international attention to and mediation of the Kashmir dispute, possibly resulting in a settlement superior to any that Pakistan could have secured on its own.

The case studies thus explained the positive correlation between progressing nuclear proliferation and increased conventional conflict identified in the first section of this study and made clear the importance of territorial preferences and military capabilities to determining nuclear proliferation's impact on the behavior of new nuclear states. In the sections that follow, I discuss the theoretical and policy implications of these findings.

Theoretical Implications

My study's findings have important implications for our theoretical understanding of nuclear proliferation's effects on international security. As noted, proliferation optimists argue that by threatening to raise the cost of war astronomically, nuclear weapons reduce the likelihood of conflict. My findings, however, indicate that this is not necessarily the case. Indeed, the study shows that the danger of nuclear weapons can in certain circumstances have the opposite effect. By potentially raising the costs of violence, nuclear weapons can make conflict *more* likely, encouraging a weak, revisionist state both to take territory while insulated from all-out conventional retaliation and to attempt to force third-party diplomatic intervention in ensuing crises. The high cost of nuclear war is precisely what promises to make such a strategy successful; nuclear danger deters adversaries and also attracts outside attention. If nuclear weapons were not so destructive, a weak, revisionist state would get neither of these benefits and would be less likely to engage in aggressive behavior. Thus, the high cost of nuclear war may not lead to lower level stability and can actually increase the likelihood of conflict.

This finding has important implications for the debate over nuclear proliferation's impact on South Asia, undercutting proliferation optimists' argument that the introduction of nuclear weapons has helped to stabilize the region. However, the finding's theoretical significance is considerably broader, transcending the debate over South Asian proliferation. Indeed, it goes to the heart of our understanding of nuclear deterrence itself.

A fundamental claim of nuclear deterrence theory is that an inverse relationship exists between nuclear risk and the probability of conventional conflict;

the likelihood of conventional conflict declines as the probability of conflict resulting in nuclear use increases. This relationship is captured in the concept of the stability/instability paradox. As noted, the stability/instability paradox holds that strategic stability reduces the danger of launching a conventional war but simultaneously makes the outbreak of lower level violence more likely. The paradox is not simply an arcane concept lurking in an obscure corner of the Cold War deterrence literature. Rather, it is the embodiment of a fundamental tenet of nuclear deterrence theory—namely, that nuclear danger makes conventional war less likely. Thus, when scholars claim that the stability/instability paradox explains ongoing violence in a nuclear South Asia, they are doing more than simply applying a convenient label to the regional security environment. They are reaffirming the relevance of traditional nuclear deterrence theory by claiming that its core logic applies to South Asia just as it applied to the United States and the Soviet Union during the Cold War.

However, as we have seen, close examination reveals that the stability/instability paradox does not in fact explain nuclear weapons' impact on the South Asian security environment. In Chapter 3, I showed that, from a deductive standpoint, the stability/instability paradox cannot account for increased violence in South Asia since the nuclearization of the region. This is the case because under the paradox, the possibility of conventional violence increases as the likelihood of nuclear conflict declines. However, the introduction of nuclear weapons to South Asia necessarily *increased* the likelihood of nuclear war in the region. Thus, according to stability/instability logic, South Asian proliferation should have made conventional conflict in the region *less* rather than more likely.

I also showed in Chapter 3 that the logic of the stability/instability paradox would facilitate aggressive behavior by conventionally strong powers but instill caution in conventionally weaker states. This is the case because reducing the likelihood of nuclear escalation would undermine the ability of a weak state's nuclear weapons to deter conventional attack. Such a reduction in deterrence would make conventional conflict more dangerous for a weak state and less so for a strong state. This was the problem that conventionally weak NATO faced as it tried to protect Western Europe from a Soviet invasion during the Cold War. Since it was very unlikely that conventional conflict in Europe would escalate to the strategic level, the Warsaw Pact could have been tempted to launch an attack against the West, emboldened by the belief that it could prevail over NATO in a purely conventional conflict. As a result, the United States took steps both at the tactical and strategic levels to increase the likelihood that a conventional war in Europe would escalate to the nuclear threshold.

This increased probability of nuclear escalation reduced the likelihood that the Warsaw Pact would be able to fight an exclusively conventional war in Europe and thus lowered the odds that the Pact would be willing to attack the West.

Similarly, in the South Asian security environment, stability/instability logic would embolden conventionally strong India to retaliate forcefully against provocations from its weaker adversary. If it were the case that a large conventional conflict was unlikely to escalate to the nuclear level, India would less likely be deterred from launching a full-scale response to Pakistani aggression in Kashmir; India could conventionally attack Pakistan secure in the knowledge that the ensuing conflict was unlikely to go nuclear. Such a highly stable strategic environment would have a cautionary effect on Pakistan because it would reduce Pakistani nuclear weapons' conventionally deterrent effects. This would leave Pakistan less protected from the full weight of India's conventional advantage and more vulnerable to catastrophic defeat in the event of a large-scale Indo-Pakistani conflict. Yet, as we have seen, Indian boldness and Pakistani caution is not the behavior that South Asia has actually witnessed. Rather, the South Asian security environment has been characterized by *Pakistani* boldness and *Indian* caution, with Pakistan or its proxies crossing de facto international boundaries to attack Indian territory, and India refusing to launch cross-border strikes in retaliation. Again, this is not the outcome that the stability/instability paradox would predict.

Pakistani aggression has relied not upon a high level of strategic stability, as per stability/instability logic, but rather upon the existence of a considerable measure of *instability* in the Indo-Pakistani strategic balance. Pakistani nuclear weapons could deter India from launching a full-scale conventional attack on Pakistan only if the escalation of conflict from the conventional to the nuclear level was a serious possibility. If the escalation of conflict to the nuclear level were highly unlikely, Pakistani nuclear weapons would lose their ability to deter Indian conventional retaliation, leaving Pakistan vulnerable to Indian conventional superiority. As we have seen, such an environment would encourage caution, rather than boldness, on the part of Pakistani leaders. This leads us once more to the conclusion that the stability/instability paradox does not explain ongoing conventional violence since India's and Pakistan's acquisition of nuclear weapons. Indeed, as I argued in Chapter 3, the phenomenon at work in South Asia would better be characterized as an "instability/instability paradox," under which instability in the strategic realm encourages instability at lower levels of conflict.

The foregoing analysis would seem to indicate that no strategic environment in South Asia is without conventional danger. Strategic instability encourages weaker Pakistan to engage in conventionally aggressive behavior, secure in the belief that its nuclear deterrent will insulate it from full-scale Indian retaliation. On the other hand, increased strategic stability, by reducing Pakistani nuclear weapons' conventionally deterrent effects, could encourage Indian conventional aggression. As we have seen, when the Indian government has believed the Indo-Pakistani strategic balance to be relatively stable, it has been willing to contemplate increasingly forceful behavior against Pakistan. Such policies as India's "limited war" doctrine and plans under Operation Parakram to engage Pakistan in protracted combat following the 2001 Parliament attack were a direct result of a growing conviction that conventional war on the subcontinent need not escalate to the nuclear level. In the future, if Indian leaders became convinced that escalation from the conventional to the nuclear threshold were very unlikely, the Indians could press their conventional advantage over Pakistan, engaging and perhaps critically damaging Pakistan without fear of nuclear confrontation. India could launch a conventional attack in direct response to a particular Pakistani provocation, or it could attack Pakistan preemptively or preventively, using force to deal with a looming problem before it grew too large. Thus, it would seem that no South Asian strategic relationship is entirely cost free; the perception of strategic instability has encouraged Pakistani conventional adventurism, while strategic stability would potentially embolden India at the conventional level.

Although it is true that strategic stability and strategic instability both create potential conventional costs in South Asia, it is not the case that the two environments are equally dangerous. Given India's territorial preferences in the region, strategic stability in fact is likely to make both the Indo-Pakistani nuclear and conventional relationship safer. Strategic stability could allow India to behave aggressively at the conventional level, but in the absence of serious provocation, India is unlikely to do so. This is the case because the Indian government has status quo preferences regarding the territorial division of the subcontinent and wishes to preserve existing boundaries rather than alter them. Thus, even if strategic stability could permit Indian conventional aggression, the Indians would be unlikely to take advantage of the situation and attack Pakistan. The Pakistan government, by contrast, seeks to change territorial divisions in Kashmir. Therefore, if strategic instability could potentially facilitate Pakistani conventional aggression, Pakistani leaders would be much more likely to take advantage of the opportunity, altering the territorial division of Kashmir in their favor. Therefore, while both strategic stability and strategic instability create potential costs at the conventional level, given the reality of India's and Pakistan's divergent territorial goals, strategic stability is in fact doubly preferable in South Asia; it should make both nuclear and conventional conflict considerably less likely.

The empirical record supports this argument. Their increased faith in strategic stability has led Indian policymakers to threaten only to retaliate against Pakistani adventurism in defense of the status quo. It has not caused them to attempt to attack Pakistan first or to alter territorial boundaries in India's favor. India's new approach has coincided with the emergence of more restrained Pakistani behavior and a decline in Indo-Pakistani tension.[1] This once again indicates that the inverse relationship between nuclear danger and conventional conflict envisioned by the stability/instability paradox does not apply in the South Asian case. A lowered likelihood of nuclear escalation makes conventional conflict less rather than more likely and renders the subcontinent more stable.

In demonstrating that the stability/instability paradox does not explain Indo-Pakistani military behavior in a nuclear South Asia, we have done much more than simply quibble over the appropriateness of a label. We have shown that the nuclear deterrence logic derived from the Cold War, which even proliferation pessimists have not fundamentally challenged, is not universally applicable. Nuclear danger does not necessarily discourage conventional violence. Indeed, depending on the territorial preferences and military capabilities of the states involved, nuclear danger may actually facilitate conventional conflict. New nuclear conflict relationships therefore may not repeat the Cold War experience of the United States and the Soviet Union.[2] As I argue in the next section, this will have important implications for the policies that we adopt in response to future cases of nuclear proliferation.

Beyond its ramifications for this core aspect of nuclear deterrence logic, what are the other theoretical implications of this study? First, my findings underscore the importance of unit-level variables, specifically territorial preferences and conventional military capabilities, to understanding nuclear proliferation's effects. As we have seen, although some scholars emphasize domestic and regional factors in assessing proliferation's effects on South Asia, other analysts view proliferating states more abstractly. This study, however, indicates that proliferating states' specific territorial preferences and conventional military capabilities create diverse behavioral incentives, which affect the policies that states adopt. The acquisition of nuclear weapons impacts the calculations of a weak, revisionist state such as Pakistan quite differently from those of a strong, status quo power like India and thus is likely to result in very different types of behavior between the two states. In assessing the probable effects of nuclear proliferation on South Asia, then, the specific preferences and capabilities of the states in question matter a great deal.

Second, this study shows that while the range of political, technological, and organizational problems typically emphasized by proliferation pessimists can make nuclear proliferation dangerous, proliferation can be destabilizing even without them. Some of these factors have undoubtedly contributed to conventional instability in South Asia. For example, in the Kargil case, the organizational biases of the Pakistan Army underlay key miscalculations that drove the decision to launch the incursions and could increase the likelihood of similar conflicts in the future. Other factors, such as small nuclear arsenals, technological shortcomings, and personnel problems, did not directly affect decision making during the crises discussed in this study but could make the ongoing Indo-Pakistani nuclear relationship particularly dangerous. As we have seen, however, the acquisition of nuclear weapons can also encourage conflict on the subcontinent due simply to the incentives that territorial preferences and relative military capabilities create for a new nuclear power; nuclear weapons give a weak, revisionist state like Pakistan strong military and diplomatic reasons to engage in conventional aggression. My findings thus highlight the dangers of nuclear proliferation quite apart from organizational biases, accidents, irrationality, terrorism, or windows of vulnerability.

My findings also differ from much of the proliferation pessimist literature in showing how nuclear weapons can contribute to the outbreak, rather than just to the escalation, of confrontations between nuclear powers. As noted, the pessimist literature focuses primarily on the possibility that nuclear weapons could be used in an ongoing crisis, with scholars arguing that political, technological, or organizational shortcomings could lead to deterrence failure in such a situation. However, these analyses pay relatively little attention to the question of whether nuclear weapons could encourage crises to occur in the first place. As we have seen, some South Asian security scholars do argue that nuclear weapons have contributed to general regional instability by encouraging Pakistan to support the Kashmir insurgency. And some maintain that nuclear weapons have helped to trigger specific regional crises such as Kargil by emboldening Pakistan to engage in cross-LoC aggression. However, these analyses do not offer any systematic argument to explain why nuclear weapons have encouraged general regional instability or the outbreak of specific crises in South Asia. Nor do they specify the general conditions under which this phenomenon is likely to happen. My findings, by contrast, explain that a weak, revisionist position in a conflict relationship creates incentives for new nuclear powers to engage in conventionally aggressive behavior, insulating them from conventional retaliation and attracting international attention. Thus, although this study shares proliferation pessimists' conviction as to nuclear weapons' deleterious effects, it differs from their analyses in fundamental respects, identifying proliferation dangers that the existing pessimist literature largely ignores.

Third, this study shows that, in a nuclear environment, states can seek to gain coercive leverage over their adversaries by manipulating the danger of conflict escalation not just within the nuclear sphere or between the conventional and nuclear levels but also within the conventional realm itself. As noted, during the Cold War, the United States sought to deter the Soviet Union from attacking Western Europe by implementing policies designed to generate the risk of conventional and limited nuclear conflict escalating to the level of general nuclear war. In the tactical realm, the United States stationed ground troops and battlefield nuclear weapons in Europe to ensure that these forces would be involved in any European war. Such a conflict could escalate from the conventional and tactical nuclear level to that of a strategic nuclear confrontation, even without a deliberate American decision to do so. At the strategic level, the United States threatened purposely to strike the Soviet Union with counterforce and limited nuclear options. Both of these policies created the risk that a European conflict would escalate to the level of strategic nuclear war.

The Indo-Pakistani case shows that a nuclear state can seek to deter an adversary from attacking by taking actions that create a risk of escalation not solely from the conventional to the nuclear level or within the nuclear realm but also within the conventional sphere itself. As noted, the Pakistanis have adopted a policy of limited conventional aggression against India, using both Pakistan Army forces and Pakistan-supported militants to attack targets and take territory in Indian Kashmir. In doing so, the Pakistanis implicitly threaten the Indians with escalation from limited to all-out conventional war in the event that India attempts a full-scale retaliation. The Indians have proven to be sensitive to this threat. The Indian government has repeatedly ruled out full-scale retaliation against Pakistan, largely out of recognition that such action would lead to all-out conventional conflict. Thus, we see India and Pakistan differentiating between various levels of conventional conflict and the Pakistani threat of escalation from limited to full-scale conventional war limiting Indian retaliation against Pakistani provocations.

Of course, India has been deterred by the danger of conventional escalation largely because of the possibility that full-scale conventional war could in turn trigger a nuclear conflict. India's desire to avoid all-out conventional conflict in responding to Pakistan's involvement in the Kashmir insurgency, its incursions at Kargil, and its implication in the Parliament attack turned on fear that India might cross the "red lines" marking Pakistan's nuclear threshold. Thus, Indian leaders have been willing to wage limited conventional war against Pakistan but have ruled out the possibility of retaliating against Pakistani provocations with full-scale conventional conflict. The conventional–nuclear connection therefore remains an important aspect of Indo-Pakistani calculations. Nonetheless, the South Asian case demonstrates the coercive leverage that nuclear states can generate by manipulating the risk of escalatory danger within the conventional realm itself and suggests that, in this respect, the conventional and nuclear spheres share important similarities; both consist of differing levels of conflict, and states can manipulate the risk of escalation between these conflict levels to deter their adversaries.

Finally, my findings show that the relationship between a state's conventional and nuclear capabilities can be symbiotic in nature, with each type of capability depending on the other for its own efficacy and relevance. As we have seen, Pakistan's nuclear arsenal is essential to making its conventional operations militarily effective, insulating them from full-scale Indian retaliation and the possibility of catastrophic defeat. Simultaneously, Pakistan's conventional military operations help to make its nuclear weapons politically relevant. By initiating conflict that could result in escalation to the nuclear level, Pakistan's conventional operations help its nuclear capacity to attract international attention to the Indo-Pakistani dispute and to increase the dangers of India's current Kashmir policy, thereby creating pressure for India to agree to a negotiated settlement of the conflict.

Policy Implications

If my argument is correct, the incentives will be high for weak, revisionist proliferants such as Pakistan to attempt to change the status quo by seizing territory and compelling third parties to intervene diplomatically in crises. How can we minimize the incentives for such behavior and thus reduce the likelihood of conventional and possibly nuclear war in South Asia and among new nuclear states generally?

The first way to minimize these incentives is to convince weak, revisionist states that their military efforts to alter the status quo will be unsuccessful. As noted in our discussion of the Kargil case, a key factor in Pakistan's decision to attack at Kargil was the Pakistanis' belief that India would be unable to dislodge Pakistani forces from the mountain heights. Had the Pakistanis known that the Indians were capable of ejecting them from Kargil, they might not have launched the incursion. Thus, strong powers need to realize that weak proliferants may challenge them conventionally, and strong states must make clear that they are prepared to prevail at the conventional level. Such deterrence by denial should significantly reduce revisionist states' incentives to attempt to take territory after acquiring nuclear weapons.

The second way to minimize weak, revisionist proliferants' incentives for aggression is to convince them that their efforts to enlist outside diplomatic support for their cause through conventional adventurism will be unsuccessful. Third parties must realize that weak states' risky behavior is calculated in large part to force outsiders to help resolve ongoing disputes in the weak states' favor. Therefore, third parties should signal clearly to weak, revisionist states that they will not assist diplomatically as long as these states are engaging in offensive behavior. This will help prevent weak states from miscalculating and reduce the likelihood that they will behave aggressively in the first place.[3]

The United States has a mixed record in this regard. As we have seen, intensive, high-level American intervention in the 1990 standoff probably played a role in defusing the crisis, but it also helped to convince the Pakistanis that American mediation would be forthcoming in future Indo-Pakistani militarized disputes. In the Kargil case, by contrast, President Clinton conditioned American assistance on improved Pakistani behavior, informing Nawaz Sharif that the United States could not help Pakistan as long as intruding forces remained on the Indian side of the Line of Control. During the 2001–2002 crisis, the United States used high-level emissaries to pressure the Pakistanis to curtail cross-border infiltration, while simultaneously reassuring the Indians and pressing them to scale down their mobilization—though without first securing promises from either party to cease offensive activities. Although all of these American interventions played constructive roles in defusing their respective crises, Clinton's policy during the Kargil conflict was probably the most effective of the American efforts from the standpoint of the third-party intervention problem. By expressly withholding American involvement until the Pakistanis restored the status quo, Clinton was able to force Pakistani withdrawal from the Line of Control without increasing diplomatic incentives for future Pakistani aggression.

Finally, both parties to new nuclearized conflicts need to recognize the increased danger of their situation. Pakistani leaders appear at one level to have understood the risk inherent in their policy. Indeed, the rationale for Pakistan's aggressive behavior turns on this risk; if such behavior did not create a potentially dangerous situation, the Indians would not be deterred, and outside parties like the United States would not feel compelled to get involved in the crisis. However, as we have seen, Pakistani decision makers may also view nuclear weapons as a trump card that in the end will insulate them from Indian retaliation and the outbreak of all-out war, regardless of their provocative behavior.

Indian leaders have historically proven sensitive to the dangers of conventional conflict between nuclear adversaries, refraining from large-scale retaliation against continued Pakistani provocations in Kashmir despite India's conventional military advantage. However, the Indians' confidence that they can fight a conventional war with Pakistan against a nuclear backdrop has been growing and resulting in increasingly forceful Indian responses to Pakistani adventurism. To some extent, the results of this increased Indian confidence appear to have been salutary. The perception of increased strategic stability on the subcontinent has coincided with a decline in provocative Pakistani behavior and a reduction in overall Indo-Pakistani tensions.

Nonetheless, the Indian government's faith in regional stability also has its dangers. Indian leaders may become overconfident that they can limit Indo-Pakistani conflict to the conventional level. Many Indian officials and security elites appear to believe that since nuclear escalation would be an irrational choice, it will never happen. As one senior scholar closely involved with the formulation of Indian nuclear policy said forcefully, "Regardless of what alarmist Western anti-proliferation *wallahs* would have you believe, both India and Pakistan are rational states; neither of us want nuclear war. Therefore, a nuclear conflict could happen only by accident, and there is no such thing as accidental war."[4] Indian leaders who do acknowledge the possibility of conventional conflict reaching the nuclear level downplay the likelihood of inadvertent, catastrophic escalation. Rather, they argue that the decision to escalate a war from the conventional to the nuclear level would be a deliberate, controllable process, "orchestrated with fine judgment," with the escalation ladder "carefully climbed in a carefully controlled ascent by both protagonists."[5]

At one level, these viewpoints are understandable. It is in India's interest to minimize the dangers of Pakistani brinkmanship, as this denies Pakistan important leverage over India and over third parties that the Pakistanis would like to draw into the dispute. In addition, many Indians deeply resented Western efforts to prevent them from acquiring nuclear weapons and to punish them once they had done so. They believed that this policy suggested that South Asians were incapable of handling nuclear weapons responsibly and was rooted in a highly discriminatory double standard on the part of existing nuclear states. Now to admit the possibility that a conventional conflict in South Asia could in fact escalate to the nuclear level might seem to validate Western anti-proliferation concerns.

Distasteful as it might be, however, Indian recognition of the danger of escalation is essential to handling the current situation safely and is in India's long-term interest. Failure to acknowledge the risks increases the likelihood that India will respond to continued Pakistani adventurism with more conventional force, confident that it can manage the escalation process and confine the conflict to the conventional level. Given the possibility of inadvertent escalation, such confidence could prove to be deadly. Indian leaders' overconfidence could also reduce the urgency with which they seek a viable diplomatic solution on Kashmir and thus lower the likelihood that the problem will ever be solved.

Ultimately, however, the achievement of nuclear safety in South Asia will depend largely on such diplomatic efforts. Until India and Pakistan arrive at an agreement on Kashmir that both sides view as acceptable, the fundamental incentive for aggressive behavior on the subcontinent will remain. Therefore, for India and Pakistan, and for new nuclear states in general, the resolution of ongoing territorial disputes will be crucial to reducing the potential costs of nuclear proliferation. In the absence of such political solutions, weak proliferants dissatisfied with the status quo are likely to attempt to alter territorial boundaries while insulated from retaliation by their stronger adversaries and while attracting international attention. Although this book is about the proliferation of nuclear weapons, its findings thus suggest that the best way to reduce proliferation's dangers may have more to do with diplomacy than with nuclear weapons themselves.

Reference Matter

Appendix

All figures are based on data from relevant years of International Institute for Strategic Studies, *The Military Balance*.

1971–1972

	India	Pakistan	Ratio India:Pak
Total Active Forces	980,000	392,000	2.5 : 1
Tanks	1,450	870	1.67 : 1
Combat Aircraft	672	285	2.36 : 1
Defense Spending	$1,656 million	$714 million	2.32 : 1
		Aggregate Ratio	2.21 : 1

1972–1973

	India	Pakistan	Ratio India:Pak
Total Active Forces	960,000	395,000	2.43 : 1
Tanks	1,490	660	2.26 : 1
Combat Aircraft	700	200	3.5 : 1
Defense Spending	$1,817 million	$405.5 million	4.48 : 1
		Aggregate Ratio	3.17 : 1

1973–1974

	India	Pakistan	Ratio India:Pak
Total Active Forces	948,000	402,000[a]	2.36:1
Tanks	1,990	1,060	1.88:1
Combat Aircraft	888	248	3.58:1
Defense Spending	$2,386 million	$433 million	5.51:1
		Aggregate Ratio	3.33:1

[a] Includes some 75,000 POWs.

1974–1975

	India	Pakistan	Ratio India:Pak
Total Active Forces	956,000	392,000	2.44:1
Tanks	1,930	1,160	1.66:1
Combat Aircraft	774	283	2.74:1
Defense Spending	$2,443 million	$575 million	4.25:1
		Aggregate Ratio	2.77:1

1975–1976

	India	Pakistan	Ratio India:Pak
Total Active Forces	956,000	392,000	2.44:1
Tanks	1,800	1,050	1.71:1
Combat Aircraft	776	278	2.79:1
Defense Spending	$2,660 million	$722 million	3.68:1
		Aggregate Ratio	2.66:1

1976–1977

	India	Pakistan	Ratio India:Pak
Total Active Forces	1,055,000	428,000	2.47:1
Tanks	2,030	1,050	1.93:1
Combat Aircraft	990	217	4.56:1
Defense Spending	$2,812 million	$807 million	3.49:1
		Aggregate Ratio	3.11:1

1977–1978

	India	Pakistan	Ratio India:Pak
Total Active Forces	1,096,000	428,000	2.56:1
Tanks	1,930	1,050	1.84:1
Combat Aircraft	716	247	2.9:1
Defense Spending	$3,720 million	$819 million	4.54:1
		Aggregate Ratio	2.96:1

1978–1979

	India	Pakistan	Ratio India:Pak
Total Active Forces	1,096,000	429,000	2.56 : 1
Tanks	1,850	1,065	1.74 : 1
Combat Aircraft	706	257	2.75 : 1
Defense Spending	$3.57 billion	$1.05 billion	3.4 : 1
		Aggregate Ratio	2.61 : 1

1979–1980

	India	Pakistan	Ratio India:Pak
Total Active Forces	1,096,000	429,000	2.56 : 1
Tanks	1,900	1,065	1.78 : 1
Combat Aircraft	665	256	2.6 : 1
Defense Spending	Info not available	$1.18 billion	
		Aggregate Ratio	2.31 : 1[b]

[b] Does not include Defense spending.

1980–1981

	India	Pakistan	Ratio India:Pak
Total Active Forces	1,104,000	438,600	2.52 : 1
Tanks	2,170	1,065	2.04 : 1
Combat Aircraft	680	256	2.66 : 1
Defense Spending	$4.4 billion	$1.54 billion	2.86 : 1
		Aggregate Ratio	2.52 : 1

1981–1982

	India	Pakistan	Ratio India:Pak
Total Active Forces	1,104,000	450,600	2.45 : 1
Tanks	2,120	1,350	1.57 : 1
Combat Aircraft	647	225	2.88 : 1
Defense Spending	$5.26 billion	$1.857 billion	2.83 : 1
		Aggregate Ratio	2.43 : 1

1982–1983

	India	Pakistan	Ratio India:Pak
Total Active Forces	1,104,000	478,600	2.31 : 1
Tanks	2,268	1,350	1.68 : 1
Combat Aircraft	670	222	3.02 : 1
Defense Spending	$5.556 billion	$1.829 billion	3.04 : 1
		Aggregate Ratio	2.51 : 1

1983–1984

	India	Pakistan	Ratio India:Pak
Total Active Forces	1,120,000	478,600	2.34 : 1
Tanks	2,100	1,321	1.59 : 1
Combat Aircraft	763	262	2.91 : 1
Defense Spending	$5.684 billion	$1.873 billion	3.04 : 1
		Aggregate Ratio	2.47 : 1

1984–1985

	India	Pakistan	Ratio India:Pak
Total Active Forces	1,120,000	478,600	2.34 : 1
Tanks	2,900	1,421	2.04 : 1
Combat Aircraft	957	317	3.02 : 1
Defense Spending	$6.907 billion	$1.957 billion	3.53 : 1
		Aggregate Ratio	2.73 : 1

1985–1986

	India	Pakistan	Ratio India:Pak
Total Active Forces	1,260,000	482,800	2.61 : 1
Tanks	2,650	1,506	1.76 : 1
Combat Aircraft	882	378	2.33 : 1
Defense Spending	$6.331 billion	$2.067 billion	3.06 : 1
		Aggregate Ratio	2.44 : 1

1986–1987

	India	Pakistan	Ratio India:Pak
Total Active Forces	1,260,000	480,600	2.62 : 1
Tanks	2,790	1,600	1.74 : 1
Combat Aircraft	753	376	2.00 : 1
Defense Spending	$7.97 billion	$2.27 billion	3.51 : 1
		Aggregate Ratio	2.47 : 1

1987–1988

	India	Pakistan	Ratio India:Pak
Total Active Forces	1,262,000	480,600	2.63 : 1
Tanks	2,750	1,600	1.72 : 1
Combat Aircraft	722	384	1.88 : 1
Defense Spending	$9.65 billion	$2.53 billion	3.81 : 1
		Aggregate Ratio	2.51 : 1

1988—1989

	India	Pakistan	Ratio India:Pak
Total Active Forces	1,362,000	480,600	2.83:1
Tanks	3,250	1,600	2.03:1
Combat Aircraft	742	341	2.18:1
Defense Spending	$9.59 billion	2.38 billion	4.03:1
		Aggregate Ratio	2.77:1

1989—1990

	India	Pakistan	Ratio India:Pak
Total Active Forces	1,260,000	520,000	2.42:1
Tanks	3,150	1,750	1.80:1
Combat Aircraft	867	455	1.91:1
Defense Spending	$8.94 billion	$2.58 billion	3.47:1
		Aggregate Ratio	2.40:1

1990—1991

	India	Pakistan	Ratio India:Pak
Total Active Forces	1,262,000	550,000	2.3:1
Tanks	3,250	1,850	1.76:1
Combat Aircraft	874	475	1.84:1
Defense Spending	$10.1 billion	$2.91 billion	3.47:1
		Aggregate Ratio	2.34:1

1991—1992

	India	Pakistan	Ratio India:Pak
Total Active Forces	1,265,000	565,000	2.24:1
Tanks	3,200	1,980	1.62:1
Combat Aircraft	676	333	2.03:1
Defense Spending	$8.07 billion	$3.23 billion	2.50:1
		Aggregate Ratio	2.10:1

1992—1993

	India	Pakistan	Ratio India:Pak
Total Active Forces	1,265,000	580,000	2.18:1
Tanks	3,900	1,980	1.97:1
Combat Aircraft	720	356	2.02:1
Defense Spending	$6.7 billion	$3.6 billion	1.86:1
		Aggregate Ratio	2.01:1

1993−1994

	India	Pakistan	Ratio India:Pak
Total Active Forces	1,265,000	577,000	2.19:1
Tanks	3,500	1,890	1.85:1
Combat Aircraft	771	397	1.94:1
Defense Spending	$7.14 billion	$3.3 billion	2.16:1
		Aggregate Ratio	2.04:1

1994−1995

	India	Pakistan	Ratio India:Pak
Total Active Forces	1,265,000	587,000	2.16:1
Tanks	3,400	1,950	1.74:1
Combat Aircraft	864	434	1.99:1
Defense Spending	$7.5 billion	$3.5 billion	2.14:1
		Aggregate Ratio	2.01:1

1995−1996

	India	Pakistan	Ratio India:Pak
Total Active Forces	1,145,000	587,000	1.95:1
Tanks	2,400	2,050	1.17:1
Combat Aircraft	912	434	2.10:1
Defense Spending	$10 billion	$3.6 billion	2.78:1
		Aggregate Ratio	2:1

1996−1997

	India	Pakistan	Ratio India:Pak
Total Active Forces	1,145,000	587,000	1.95:1
Tanks	3,500	2,050	1.71:1
Combat Aircraft	846	434	1.95:1
Defense Spending	$11.8 billion	$3.6 billion	3.28:1
		Aggregate Ratio	2.22:1

1997−1998

	India	Pakistan	Ratio India:Pak
Total Active Forces	1,145,000	587,000	1.95:1
Tanks	3,404	2,120	1.61:1
Combat Aircraft	845	436	1.94:1
Defense Spending	$12.8 billion	$3.9 billion	3.28:1
		Aggregate Ratio	2.20:1

1998–1999

	India	Pakistan	Ratio India:Pak
Total Active Forces	1,175,000	587,000	2.00:1
Tanks	3,504	2,120	1.65:1
Combat Aircraft	839	417	2.01:1
Defense Spending	$14.1 billion	$4 billion	3.53:1
		Aggregate Ratio	2.30:1

1999–2000

	India	Pakistan	Ratio India:Pak
Total Active Forces	1,173,000	587,000	2.00:1
Tanks	3,504	2,320	1.51:1
Combat Aircraft	853	396	2.15:1
Defense Spending	$14.2 billion	$3.5 billion	4.06:1
		Aggregate Ratio	2.43:1

2000–2001

	India	Pakistan	Ratio India:Pak
Total Active Forces	1,303,000	612,000	2.13:1
Tanks	3,504	2,285	1.53:1
Combat Aircraft	811	358	2.27:1
Defense Spending	$14.765 billion	$3.65 billion	4.05:1
		Aggregate Ratio	2.50:1

2001–2002

	India	Pakistan	Ratio India:Pak
Total Active Forces	1,263,000	620,000	2.04:1
Tanks	3,504	2,300	1.52:1
Combat Aircraft	775	358	2.17:1
Defense Spending	$13.967 billion	$2.414 billion	5.79:1
		Aggregate Ratio	2.88:1

2002–2003

	India	Pakistan	Ratio India:Pak
Total Active Forces	1,298,000	620,000	2.09:1
Tanks	3,898	2,357	1.65:1
Combat Aircraft	736	372	1.98:1
Defense Spending	$13.073 billion	$2.541 billion	5.15:1
		Aggregate Ratio	2.72:1

Notes

CHAPTER 1. *The Problem of Proliferation*

1. Michael Dobbs, "The World's Most Terrifying Danger, Then and Now," *Washington Post*, October 17, 2004, p. To5.

2. Mohamed ElBaradei, "Saving Ourselves from Self-Destruction," *New York Times*, February 12, 2004, p. A37.

3. Melvyn P. Leffler, *A Preponderance of Power: National Security, the Truman Administration, and the Cold War* (Stanford, CA: Stanford University Press, 1992), p. 326.

4. Ibid., pp. 326–27.

5. Nonnuclear states also agreed to submit to International Atomic Energy Agency safeguards designed to verify the fulfillment of their treaty obligations. The nuclear weapons powers, for their part, promised not to transfer nuclear weapons or nuclear explosive devices to any recipient or to assist nonnuclear weapons states in the manufacture of such weapons or devices. The nuclear powers also pledged to assist nonnuclear states in the development of nuclear energy for peaceful purposes and to work to end the global nuclear arms race and achieve eventual nuclear disarmament. See the text of Treaty on the Non-Proliferation of Nuclear Weapons at http://www.iaea.org/Publications/Documents/Infcircs/Others/infcirc140.pdf. The broader nonproliferation regime, of which the NPT is the foundation, consists of a range of bilateral and multilateral agreements designed to prevent the spread of nuclear weapons though such means as limiting the transfer of nuclear materials and technology, monitoring the use of nuclear materials, and preventing nuclear testing.

6. Brazil and Argentina, for example, initially refused to sign the Tlatelolco Treaty for the Prohibition of Nuclear Weapons in Latin America and launched nuclear weapons development programs during the 1970s. But the two countries subsequently abandoned their nuclear weapons programs, jointly committing themselves to employ nuclear energy for exclusively peaceful purposes in 1990 and ratifying the Tlatelolco Treaty in 1994. Argentina then acceded to the Nuclear Non-Proliferation Treaty in 1995, followed by Brazil in 1997. For detailed analysis of the Argentine-Brazilian case, see Mitchell Reiss, *Bridled Ambition:*

Why Countries Constrain Their Nuclear Capabilities (Washington, DC: Woodrow Wilson Center Press, 1995), pp. 45–88.

7. South Africa, for example, began a nuclear weapons development program in the 1970s and constructed six atomic bombs during the 1980s. South Africa ended its weapons program in 1989 and destroyed its nuclear weapons in 1991, signing the Nuclear Non-Proliferation Treaty that same year. And Ukraine, Kazakhstan, and Belarus, which at the time of their independence in 1991 had possessed large numbers of former Soviet nuclear weapons, ultimately decided to destroy or return the weapons to Russia and to sign the NPT. They acceded to the NPT in 1993 (Belarus) and 1994 (Ukraine and Kazakhstan). For analysis of the South African case, see Reiss, *Bridled Ambition*. On the former Soviet republics, see William C. Potter, "The Politics of Denuclearization: The Cases of Belarus, Kazakhstan, and Ukraine," Occasional Paper No. 22, Henry L. Stimson Center, April 1995. Why these states renounced their nuclear arsenals or their weapons development programs is the subject of debate. Three possible explanations include changed security environments; domestic political calculations; and international nonproliferation norms. For a discussion of these arguments, see Scott D. Sagan, "Why Do States Build Nuclear Weapons: Three Models in Search of a Bomb," *International Security*, 21, no. 3 (1996–1997), pp. 54–86.

8. The only other states that refused to sign the NPT were Cuba and Israel.

9. Patrick French, *Liberty and Death: India's Journey to Independence and Division* (London: HarperCollins, 1997), pp. 347–49.

10. Testimony of James Woolsey before the Senate Committee on Governmental Affairs, *Hearing on Proliferation Threats of the 1990s*, 103rd Cong., 1st Sess., February 24, 1993 (Washington, DC: U.S. Government Printing Office, 1993).

11. On these points and for a detailed analysis of the evolution of India's nuclear weapons program, see Šumit Ganguly, "India's Pathway to Pokhran II: The Prospects and Sources of New Delhi's Nuclear Weapons Program," *International Security*, 23, no. 4 (1999), pp. 148–77.

12. On these points and for a detailed analysis of the evolution of Pakistan's nuclear weapons program, see Samina Ahmed, "Pakistan's Nuclear Weapons Program: Turning Points and Nuclear Choices," *International Security*, 32, no. 4 (1999), pp. 178–204.

13. Jaswant Singh, "Against Nuclear Apartheid," *Foreign Affairs*, 77, no. 5 (1998), p. 43.

14. "Statement by Pakistan Ambassador Munir Akram to the Conference on Disarmament on the CTBT and Fissile Material Cut-off Treaty," July 30, 1998, available at http://www.clw.org/archive/coalition/pak0730.htm. Note that the Pakistan government believes that the nonproliferation regime discriminates not only against nonnuclear states generally but also against Pakistan specifically, with the international community repeatedly favoring India at Pakistan's expense. As Akram argues, "Despite the fact that every escalatory step on the nuclear proliferation ladder was initiated by India, it is Pakistan which has been consistently subjected to a series of discriminatory penalties, sanctions and restraints designed to prevent us from acquiring the capability to respond to the Indian escalation . . . [I]t is Pakistan and not India which is the real target of the non-proliferation crusade." "Statement by Ambassador Munir Akram in the Plenary Meeting of the Conference on Disarmament," May 14, 1998, available at http://www.acronym.org.uk/sppak.htm.

15. "Statement by Ambassador Munir Akram," May 14, 1998.

16. By "de facto," I mean that while India and Pakistan did not actually possess nuclear weapons, they could probably have assembled them in short order. The term *de facto* is of-

ten used in the nuclear proliferation literature to describe this state of affairs. See Hagerty, *The Consequences of Nuclear Proliferation*, pp. 124, 131, 132; Leonard Spector, *The Undeclared Bomb* (Cambridge: Ballinger, 1988). Scholars also use adjectives such as *incipient*, *opaque*, and *latent* when discussing Indo-Pakistani nuclear capabilities during this period. See, e.g., Ganguly, *Conflict Unending*; Hagerty, *The Consequences of Nuclear Proliferation*; Tellis, *India's Emerging Nuclear Posture*.

17. See, e.g., Lewis A. Dunn, *Controlling the Bomb: Nuclear Proliferation in the 1980s* (New Haven, CT: Yale University Press, 1982), pp. 44–48; Leonard Spector, *The Undeclared Bomb* (Cambridge, MA: Ballinger, 1988), pp. 69–70.

18. Spector, *The Undeclared Bomb*, p. 70.

19. Devin Hagerty, *The Consequences of Nuclear Proliferation: Lessons from South Asia* (Cambridge, MA: MIT Press, 1998), p. 188.

20. George Perkovich, *India's Nuclear Bomb: The Impact on Global Proliferation* (Berkeley: University of California Press, 1999), pp. 424–26.

21. Ibid., p. 433.

22. Note that despite international appeals for India and Pakistan to roll back their nuclear capabilities and join the global nonproliferation regime, there is virtually no chance that the two countries will do so. Pakistan will not renounce nuclear weapons as long as its conventionally superior archrival India retains them, and India will not relinquish its nuclear weapons as long as China remains a nuclear power. China, for its part, will not renounce its nuclear status while Russia and the United States retain their nuclear capacities. As Ashley Tellis argues, "Thanks to this long and extended chain of consequences, no movement toward denuclearization should be expected in the policy-relevant future." Tellis, *India's Emerging Nuclear Posture*, p. 22.

23. By "conventional military stability," I mean stability below the nuclear threshold, including both the level of interstate conflict and of guerrilla warfare. As will become clear, the quantitative section of this study analyzes Indo-Pakistani militarized dispute data only at the interstate level. However, the case studies offer extensive discussions of guerrilla and low-intensity warfare in Kashmir to explain its role as a link between nuclear weapons proliferation and Indo-Pakistani interstate conflict.

24. The cost of conventional conflict is not limited to war fighting. It includes the cost of preparing for war, which can inflict severe burdens on the economies of developing states like India and Pakistan. See Praful Bidwai, "India/Pakistan: Defense Spending Could Spiral Out of Control," *Asia Times*, March 4, 2000, available at http://www.atimes.com/ind-pak/BC04Df02.html.

25. Note that insecurity in South Asia undermines U.S. interests on a number of levels. First, the humanitarian effects of a major South Asian conflict would be devastating. In fact, U.S. intelligence analyses have estimated that a full-scale nuclear exchange between India and Pakistan would kill 12 million people outright and injure up to 7 million. Millions more would die in the following weeks and months from starvation and disease. See Tom Shanker, "12 Million Could Die at Once in an India-Pakistan Nuclear War," *New York Times*, May 27, 2002. Second, the recovery process on the subcontinent after a major war, and particularly after a nuclear exchange, would be extremely costly to the West and to the United States, which would probably bear much of the expense. A major war could also have a devastating effect on world markets. See Bill Nichols, "Nuclear Clash Would Batter World Financial Markets," *USA Today*, June 4, 2002. Third, Pakistan is a major ally in the U.S. war on terror, and American forces in that country could be at risk in a serious

Indo-Pakistani conflict. Additionally, the United States has an interest in maintaining stability in Pakistan so that it can systematically pursue terrorists in that country and in the
central Asian region. As assistant secretary of state for South Asian Affairs Christina Rocca
stated, "The continuing success of our alliance against terror . . . in South Asia depends on
productive and effective long-term relationships with each of the countries in the region,
combined with economic growth, stability, and the strengthening of democratic institutions." Christina Rocca, "Statement for the House International Relations Subcommittee,"
March 20, 2003. See also Anthony Spaeth, "Looking Down the Barrel," *Time Asia*, 159,
no. 1 (2002).

26. According to the U.S. Department of State, "An effective strategy for countering
WMD [weapons of mass destruction], including their use and proliferation, is an integral
component of the National Security Strategy of the United States of America." U.S. Department of State, *National Strategy to Combat Weapons of Mass Destruction*, December 23,
2002.

27. I measure conventional military stability according to the frequency and severity of militarized interstate disputes (MIDs) between South Asia's two leading powers, India and Pakistan. Militarized interstate disputes involve the threat, display, or use of
force, as well as war. By war I mean organized violence between the armed forces of
belligerent states that results in at least 1,000 battle deaths. See Melvin Small and J. David
Singer, *Resort to Arms: International and Civil Wars 1816–1929* (Los Angeles: Sage Publications, 1982).

28. Singh, "Against Nuclear Apartheid," p. 43.

29. Shamshad Ahmad, "The Nuclear Subcontinent: Bringing Stability to South Asia,"
Foreign Affairs, 78, no. 4 (1999), p. 123.

30. United Nations S/RES/1172 (1998), June 6, 1998.

31. See, e.g., John F. Burns, "India Sets Off 2 More Nuclear Blasts: U.S. and Japan
Impose Sanctions," *New York Times*, May 14, 1998; Tom Weiner, "After Anguished Plea
Fails, Clinton Penalizes the Pakistanis," *New York Times*, May 29, 1998.

32. Bill Richardson, "Statement on UN Security Council India-Pakistan Resolution,"
June 6, 1998.

33. William J. Clinton, Statement by the President, "Further Testing by Pakistan,"
May 30, 1998.

34. Charles Babington and Pamela Constable, "Kashmir Killings Mar Clinton Visit to
India," *Washington Post*, March 22, 2000, p. A1.

35. See generally Hagerty, *The Consequences of Nuclear Proliferation*. Scholars who believe
that nuclear weapons will have a pacifying effect on South Asia generally fall into the "optimist" camp in the broader debate over the impact of nuclear proliferation on international
security. Proliferation optimists maintain that nuclear weapons, by potentially making any
war catastrophically costly, induce extreme caution on the part of nuclear states and create stability between them. See, e.g., Waltz, *The Spread of Nuclear Weapons: More May Be
Better*, Adelphi Paper No. 171 (London: International Institute of Strategic Studies, 1981);
John J. Mearsheimer, "The Case for a Ukrainian Nuclear Deterrent," *Foreign Affairs*, 72,
no. 3 (1993), pp. 50–66; Bruce Bueno de Mesquita and William Riker, "An Assessment
of the Merits of Selective Nuclear Proliferation," *Journal of Conflict Resolution*, 26, no. 2
(1982), pp. 283–306. Scholars who believe that nuclear weapons will not produce such
stability in South Asia generally fall into the "pessimist" camp in the broader proliferation
debate. Proliferation pessimists believe that, despite nuclear weapons' ability to make war

extremely costly, they may fail to produce stability due to a range of political, technical, and organizational factors. Specific problems include risk-acceptant or irrational leaders, command-and-control difficulties, and preemption incentives for small arsenals. On these issues, see, e.g., Sagan, *The Limits of Safety: Organizations, Accidents, and Nuclear Weapons* (Princeton, NJ: Princeton University Press, 1993); Robert J. Art, "A Defensible Defense," in Sean M. Lynn-Jones and Steven E. Miller, eds., *America's Strategy in a Changing World* (Cambridge, MA: MIT Press, 1992), pp. 87–88; Lewis A. Dunn, *Controlling the Bomb: Nuclear Proliferation in the 1980s* (New Haven, CT: Yale University Press, 1982), pp. 69–94. This brief discussion does not purport to convey fully the arguments of scholars within the optimist and pessimist camps or to capture the often-nuanced differences between them; my aim here is not to analyze the proliferation debate but rather to locate basic scholarly disagreements regarding the effects of South Asian nuclear proliferation within a broader theoretical context. For detailed discussion and analysis of the proliferation literature, see Peter R. Lavoy, "The Strategic Consequences of Nuclear Proliferation," *Security Studies*, 4, no. 4 (1995), pp. 695–753; Jeffrey W. Knopf, "Recasting the Optimism–Pessimism Debate," *Security Studies*, 12, no. 1 (2002), pp. 41–96; David J. Karl, "Proliferation Pessimism and Emerging Nuclear Powers," *International Security*, 21, no. 3 (1996–1997), pp. 87–119.

36. Hagerty, *The Lessons of Nuclear Proliferation*, p. 184.

37. Ibid., p. 188.

38. Kenneth N. Waltz, "For Better: Nuclear Weapons Preserve an Imperfect Peace," in Scott D. Sagan and Kenneth N. Waltz, eds., *The Spread of Nuclear Weapons: A Debate Renewed* (New York: W. W. Norton, 2003), p. 117.

39. K. Subrahmanyam, "India and the International Nuclear Order," in D. R. SarDesai and Raju G. C. Thomas, eds., *Nuclear India in the Twenty-First Century* (New York: Palgrave-Macmillan, 2002) p. 83.

40. Shireen Mazari, "Kashmir: Looking for Viable Options," *Defence Journal*, 3, no. 6 (1999).

41. Sagan and Waltz, *The Spread of Nuclear Weapons*, pp. 106–7.

42. P. R. Chari, "Nuclear Restraint, Nuclear Risk Reduction, and the Security–Insecurity Paradox in South Asia," in Michael Krepon and Chris Gagné, eds., *The Stability–Instability Paradox: Nuclear Weapons and Brinkmanship in South Asia* (Washington, DC: Stimson Center, 2001), p. 16. See also Kanti Bajpai, "The Fallacy of an Indian Deterrent," in Amitabh Mattoo, ed., *India's Nuclear Deterrent: Pokhran II and Beyond* (New Delhi: HarAnand, 1999); Samina Ahmed, "Security Dilemmas of Nuclear-Armed Pakistan," *Third World Quarterly*, 21, no. 5 (2001), pp. 781–93; S. R. Valluri, "Lest We Forget: The Futility and Irrelevance of Nuclear Weapons for India," in Raju G. C. Thomas and Amit Gupta, eds., *India's Nuclear Security* (Boulder, CO: Lynne Rienner, 2000), pp. 263–73. It is worth noting that Sagan and other leading scholars in the proliferation "pessimist" camp accept the fundamental logic of deterrence theorists like Waltz and Hagerty. This strand of the pessimist literature does not deny the optimists' claim that by elevating the potential costs of war, nuclear weapons create disincentives to fight. Pessimists such as Sagan simply argue that particular pathologies undercut nuclear weapons' deterrent effects and make them dangerous despite the fundamental logic of deterrence. Viewed in this light, "the organizational and psychological arguments cited by pessimists need not . . . be seen as forming a complete alternative theory to the rational and systemic approaches favored by optimists . . . Rather they complement a rational actor theory, explaining some of the cases where that theory's predictions are incorrect." Jeffrey W. Knopf, "Recasting the

Proliferation Optimism–Pessimism Debate," *Security Studies*, 12, no. 1 (2002), pp. 54–55. Thus, even the supposed alternative to the deterrence theorists' position in fact shares their most fundamental assumptions—assumptions that this book challenges.

43. Ahmed, "Security Dilemmas," p. 791.

44. Jasjit Singh, "The Fourth War," in Jasjit Singh, ed., *Kargil 1999: Pakistan's Fourth War for Kashmir* (New Delhi: Knowledge World), pp. 128–29; Moti Dar, "Blundering Through," in *Guns and Yellow Roses: Essays on the Kargil War* (New Delhi: HarperCollins, 1999), pp. 73–76.

45. See Ganguly, *Conflict Unending*. On the problem of dysfunctional domestic politics, see also Ahmed, "Security Dilemmas of a Nuclear-Armed Pakistan," pp. 781–82; Valluri, "Lest We Forget," p. 269; Dunn, *Controlling the Bomb*, pp. 70, 75; Samina Ahmed and David Cortright, eds., *Pakistan and the Bomb: Public Opinion and Nuclear Options* (Notre Dame, IN: University of Notre Dame Press, 1998), p. 95.

46. Sagan points specifically to Pakistan's focus on the Kargil operation's tactical results rather than its broader strategic impact, its belief that nuclear weapons would enable it to take territory in Kashmir with impunity, and its failure to learn the appropriate political and military lessons from the Kargil conflict. See Sagan and Waltz, *The Spread of Nuclear Weapons*, pp. 96–98.

47. Ahmed and Cortright, *Pakistan and the Bomb*, p. 94; Chris Gagné, "Nuclear Risk Reduction in South Asia," in Michael Krepon and Chris Gagné, eds., *Nuclear Risk Reduction in South Asia* (New York: Palgrave Macmillan, 2004), p. 40; Dunn, *Controlling the Bomb*, pp. 72–73; Ahmed, "Security Dilemmas of a Nuclear-Armed Pakistan," p. 784; Quinlan, "How Robust Is India-Pakistan Deterrence?" p. 145; Sagan, "For the Worse," p. 103.

48. Ahmed, "Security Dilemmas of a Nuclear-Armed Pakistan," pp. 781, 784, 791; Quinlan, "How Robust Is India-Pakistan Deterrence?" p. 145; Dunn, *Controlling the Bomb*, pp. 69–70; Cortright and Ahmed, *Pakistan and the Bomb*, p. 63.

49. Ahmed, "Security Dilemmas of a Nuclear-Armed Pakistan," p. 782; Ahmed and Cortright, *Pakistan and the Bomb*, p. 71.

50. Quinlan, "How Robust Is India-Pakistan Deterrence?" p. 148.

51. Ahmed and Cortright, *Pakistan and the Bomb*, pp. 62, 94; Ahmed, "Security Dilemmas of a Nuclear-Armed Pakistan," p. 784; Quinlan, "How Robust Is India-Pakistan Deterrence?" pp. 148–49; Dunn, *Controlling the Bomb*, pp. 74–75.

52. Dunn, *Controlling the Bomb*, pp. 73–75; Sagan, "For the Worse," p. 105.

53. See Sagan and Waltz, *The Spread of Nuclear Weapons*, pp. 101–6.

54. By "revisionist" I mean that Pakistan is dissatisfied with current territorial boundaries in Kashmir and wishes to alter them. India, by contrast, is "status quo" regarding Kashmir's territorial division; it is satisfied with current territorial boundaries in Kashmir and wishes to maintain them. These definitions draw on Arnold Wolfers, "The Balance of Power in Theory and Practice," in Arnold Wolfers, ed., *Discord and Collaboration: Essays on International Politics* (Baltimore: Johns Hopkins University Press, 1962), pp. 125–26. According to Wolfers, status quo states "desire to preserve the established order," whereas the "ultimate national goal" of revisionist states is "a substantial change in the existing order." For an extensive discussions of revisionist versus status quo states, see also Randall L. Schweller, "Bandwagoning for Profit: Bringing the Revisionist State Back In," *International Security*, 19, no. 1 (1994), pp. 72–107; Charles L. Glaser, "Political Consequences of Military Strategy: Expanding and Refining the Spiral and Deterrence Models," *World Politics*, 44, no. 4 (1992), pp. 497–538. Note that "realists" are not the only group of international relations

scholars who define "revisionist" and "status quo" in this manner. "Constructivist" scholars use similar definitions. Alexander Wendt, for example, argues that a "status quo state is one that has no interest in conquering other states, redrawing boundaries, or changing the rules of the international system . . . Revisionist states, in turn, have the desire to conquer others, seize part of their territory, or change the rules of the game." Alexander Wendt, *Social Theory of International Politics* (Cambridge: Cambridge University Press, 1999), p. 124. On India's status quo preferences, see Ganguly, *Conflict Unending*, p. 128; Hagerty, *The Consequences of Nuclear Proliferation*, p. 135; Thomas Perry Thornton, "Pakistan: Fifty Years of Insecurity," in Selig S. Harrison, Paul H. Kreisberg, and Dennis Kux, eds., *India and Pakistan: The First Fifty Years* (Washington, DC: Cambridge University Press and the Woodrow Wilson Center, 1999), p. 184; Raja Menon, *A Nuclear Strategy for India* (New Delhi: Sage Publications, 2000), p. 195. On Pakistan's desire to alter the status quo in Kashmir, see Ashley J. Tellis, C. Christine Fair, and Jamison Jo Medby, *Limited Conflicts Under the Nuclear Umbrella: Indian and Pakistani Lessons from the Kargil Crisis* (Santa Monica, CA: RAND, 2001), p. 46; Hagerty, *The Consequences of Nuclear Proliferation*, p. 135.

55. By "limited" conventional conflict, I mean either conflict involving guerrilla or proxy forces or conflict involving states' regular militaries that does not cross official international borders on a scale sufficient to inflict catastrophic defeat on the loser. By "full-scale" conventional conflict, I mean conflict that involves states' regular militaries, that crosses official international boundaries, and that is of sufficient magnitude to threaten the loser with catastrophic defeat. Pakistan has undertaken or fomented limited conventional aggression against Indian targets in Kashmir since 1989. See John Lancaster and Kamran Khan, "Extremist Groups Renew Activity in Pakistan; Support of Kashmir Militants Is at Odds with War on Terrorism," *Washington Post*, February 8, 2003; Owen Bennett Jones, *Pakistan: Eye of the Storm* (New Haven, CT: Yale University Press, 2002), pp. 82–87; Robert G. Wirsing, *India, Pakistan, and the Kashmir Dispute: On Regional Conflict and Its Resolution* (New York: St. Martin's Press, 1994), pp. 118–22; Ganguly, *The Crisis in Kashmir: Portents of War, Hopes of Peace* (Cambridge: Cambridge University Press, 1997), p. 146; Samina Ahmed, "Pakistan: The Crisis Within," in Muthiah Alagappa, ed., *Asian Security Practice: Material and Ideational Influences* (Stanford, CA: Stanford University Press, 1998), p. 361. Existing work on proliferation in South Asia largely ignores nuclear weapons' potential for promoting this type of conflict, focusing instead on standard military-to-military confrontations. Hagerty, for example, examines proliferation's impact on conventional Indo-Pakistani military behavior during the "Brasstacks" exercise of 1987 and a militarized crisis in 1990 but does not explore proliferation's potential role in encouraging Pakistani support for the Kashmir insurgency—though he admits the possibility of such a nuclear-insurgency connection. See Hagerty, *The Consequences of Nuclear Proliferation*, p. 179.

56. Other scholars have argued that nuclear weapons create instability in South Asia by militarily and diplomatically emboldening Pakistan to engage in low-level violence against India and creating incentives for India to respond in a "tit-for-tat" fashion. See, e.g., Ashley J. Tellis, *Stability in South Asia* (Santa Monica, CA: RAND, 1997), pp. ix, 5, 43; Tellis, Fair, and Medby, *Limited Conflicts Under the Nuclear Umbrella*, pp. 48–49. See also K. Subrahmanyam, "India and the International Nuclear Order," in D. R. SarDesai and Raju G. C. Thomas, eds., *Nuclear India in the Twenty-First Century* (New York: Palgrave-Macmillan, 2002), pp. 74–76; Stephen P. Cohen, *The Pakistan Army* (Karachi: Oxford University Press, 1998), pp. 152–54. However, these scholars neither demonstrate nuclear weapons' long-term destabilizing effects on the region through systematic empirical analysis nor formulate

a theoretical explanation to account for this phenomenon that is applicable both to South Asia and to new nuclear states generally. This book undertakes both of these tasks.

57. This is not to deny that future conventional conflict in South Asia will ebb and flow due to nonnuclear factors, such as shifts in the larger international strategic environment or the vagaries of Indian and Pakistani domestic politics. However, as long as Pakistan remains dissatisfied with the territorial status quo, the propensity for Indo-Pakistani conflict in a nuclear South Asia will be significant.

58. My general theory was originally derived from my study of the 1999 Kargil War, which occurred during the book's last time period (June 1998 through 2002). Therefore, in the case of Kargil, I will test my theory against evidence from which the theory was derived. Is this methodologically acceptable? Prohibitions against testing theories with the same cases from which they were derived favor a blind-testing standard in the social sciences. However, imposing such a standard on social science is difficult because scholars are often familiar with their data before "testing" their theories, and thus, they can usually predict the outcome of their tests ahead of time—even if they exclude the specific cases from which their theories were derived. I therefore include the Kargil case in my test of my broader argument regarding the conventional effects of nuclear proliferation in South Asia. On the issue of blind testing in the social sciences, see Stephen Van Evera, *Guide to Methodology for Students of Political Science* (Cambridge, MA: MIT Defense and Arms Control Studies Program), pp. 21, 22.

59. Including this time period in the study is important for two reasons. First, it gives us a nonnuclear baseline, in the conventional military environment established after the dismemberment of Pakistan, against which to judge the conflict proneness of later de facto and overt nuclear periods. Second, determining why this nonnuclear period was peaceful can help us evaluate the strength of my causal argument as to why nuclear proliferation made the region more war prone later.

60. Of course, increased nuclearization was not the only difference between these three time periods. Other important processes and events, such as the increased Islamization of Pakistani society, the Soviet invasion of Afghanistan, and the emergence of an indigenous Kashmiri independence movement, also occurred during the years in question. I offer extended discussions of these issues and their effects on Indo-Pakistani security relations in the ensuing chapters.

61. The use of interview material can be problematic, as policymakers may have significant incentives to mislead authors and readers. However, good information on South Asian nuclear decision making is scarce, and if researchers are to offer a reasonably complete account of it, they must speak with the officials involved. One can try to assess the reliability of officials' claims in a number of ways. For example, one can ask how self-serving their arguments are. Self-serving information is not necessarily wrong, but it should raise more questions than information that casts the interviewee in a neutral or an unfavorable light. One can also check to see whether different interviewees' discussions of particular issues or events are consistent with each other and with information that we independently believe is true. I have included in the following chapters interview material that I believe is helpful to our understanding of the issues at stake in this study. Readers are of course free to assess it for themselves.

62. As Gary King, Robert O. Keohane, and Sidney Verba explain, "Observations are the fundamental components of social science research; we aggregate them to provide the evidence upon which we rely for evaluating our theories." One of the "main ways we can

find more observable instances of the process implied by our theory [is] . . . via variations across time." Gary King, Robert O. Keohane, and Sidney Verba, *Designing Social Inquiry: Scientific Inference in Qualitative Research* (Princeton, NJ: Princeton University Press, 1994), pp. 217, 219.

63. As Van Evera points out, such a "congruence procedure . . . can achieve strong controls by conducting the test against uniform background conditions." Van Evera, *Guide to Methodology for Students of Political Science*, p. 26.

CHAPTER 2. *Militarized Behavior During the South Asian Proliferation Process*

1. My analysis in this chapter is explicitly correlative, not causal; although it shows that nuclear proliferation has been associated with increased Indo-Pakistani conflict, it does not purport to explain this finding. I offer a causal explanation of the correlation between proliferation and conflict in Chapter 3 and in the case studies that follow.

2. Some scholars do emphasize domestic and regional factors in assessing proliferation's effects on South Asia. See, e.g., Hagerty, *The Consequences of Nuclear Proliferation*, p. 185; Ganguly, *Conflict Unending*, pp. 126–27; Perkovich, *India's Nuclear Bomb*; Chari, "Nuclear Restraint," in Krepon and Gagné, eds., *The Stability–Instability Paradox*; Tellis et al., *Limited Conflicts*; Ahmed, "Security Dilemmas," pp. 788–92.

3. Waltz, "For Better," in Sagan and Waltz, eds., *The Spread of Nuclear Weapons*, p. 117. Waltz and other optimists do believe that some characteristics specific to proliferating states, such as their ability to deploy survivable forces, to devise reliable command and control systems, and fully to grasp proliferation's strategic implications, have an important impact on nuclear weapons' deterrent effects. See Waltz, "More May Be Better," in Sagan and Waltz, eds., *The Spread of Nuclear Weapons*, p. 20; John Mearsheimer, "Back to the Future: Instability in Europe After the Cold War," *International Security*, 15, no. 1 (1990), pp. 37–40. Beyond this, however, state-specific considerations are relatively unimportant. As Waltz argues, "Whatever the identity of rulers, and whatever the characteristics of their states, the national behaviors they produce are strongly conditioned by the world outside." "In a nuclear world, any state—whether ruled by a Stalin, a Mao Zedong, a Saddam Hussein, or a Kim Jong Il—will be deterred by the knowledge that aggressive actions may lead to its own destruction." Waltz, "More May Be Better," in Sagan and Waltz, eds., *The Spread of Nuclear Weapons*, p. 117.

4. Sagan, "For the Worse," in Sagan and Waltz, eds., *The Spread of Nuclear Weapons*, p. 91. Sagan acknowledges that attributes specific to South Asia, such as small and relatively unsophisticated nuclear arsenals, close geographical proximity, disputed territory, and military control over Pakistani weapons, mean that India and Pakistan "will not make exactly the same mistakes as their superpower predecessors." Nonetheless, he argues that South Asia is likely essentially to follow the U.S.-Soviet model because there is "a crucially important similarity between the nuclear conditions that existed in [the] Cold War and those that exist in South Asia today. In both cases, the parochial interests and routine behaviors of the organizations that manage nuclear weapons limit the stability of nuclear deterrence." Ibid., p. 92.

5. Note that even scholars who downplay the theoretical importance of regional factors attempt to support their claims with empirical evidence from the region.

6. Some scholarship does analyze the Indo-Pakistani security relationship over time rather than focusing on particular incidents in isolation. However, such work tends to

explain the historical and political phenomena underlying the Indo-Pakistani conflict, or particular aspects of the conflict, without focusing specifically on the subject of nuclear weapons. Most work dealing specifically with South Asian proliferation traces the evolution of India's and Pakistan's nuclear programs, explaining how the programs developed and attempting to account for decisions made at various steps of the proliferation process. It tends not to offer a causal explanation of the impact that nuclear weapons have had on Indo-Pakistani military behavior. See, e.g., George Perkovich, *India's Nuclear Bomb: The Impact on Global Proliferation* (Berkeley and Los Angeles: University of California Press), 1999; Ganguly, "India's Pathway to Pokhran II"; Ahmed, "Pakistan's Nuclear Weapons Program."

7. Optimists also maintain that ongoing South Asian violence has not risen to a level sufficient to undermine their theories. For example, Kenneth Waltz, commenting on the fact that the 1999 Indo-Pakistani Kargil conflict erupted less than one year after the two countries' nuclear tests, argues that "if Kargil is called a war, then the definition of war requires revision." Waltz, "For Better," p. 115. In fact, the Kargil conflict, with more than 1,000 battle deaths, meets the standard social-science definition of war. Hagerty deals with the issue of Pakistan's proxy war in support of the Kashmir insurgency by apparently excluding cross-border guerrilla operations from his definition of war. Hagerty argues that South Asian proliferation demonstrates that nuclear states do not fight wars but also admits that proliferation will not stop cross-border guerrilla operations. Hagerty, *The Consequences of Nuclear Proliferation*, pp. 184, 191. The logical implication is that cross-border guerrilla operations do not constitute war. However, this definition does not rescue Hagerty from the problem of the Kargil War; as noted, the Kargil conflict was launched not by irregular jihadis but rather by soldiers of the Pakistan Army. This definition also excludes from Hagerty's analysis precisely the type of aggression that has given rise to militarized crises on the subcontinent in the past and that is most likely to lead to an all-out conflict in the future.

8. The 1948 Kashmir War resulted in approximately 2,000 battle deaths, the 1965 war in approximately 7,000 battle deaths, and the 1971 war in approximately 11,000 battle deaths. The Kargil conflict, by contrast, resulted in slightly under 1,300 battle deaths.

9. For optimistic arguments along these lines, see, e.g., Hagerty, *The Consequences of Nuclear Proliferation*, pp. 133–70; Waltz, *The Spread of Nuclear Weapons*, pp. 109–24; Ganguly, *Conflict Unending*, pp. 109–10; Subrahmanyam, "India and the International Nuclear Order," in SarDesai and Thomas, eds., *Nuclear India*, pp. 82–88; Menon, *A Nuclear Strategy for India*, pp. 197–98. For pessimistic arguments, see, e.g., Sagan, *The Spread of Nuclear Weapons*, pp. 90–108; Ahmed, "Security Dilemmas"; Chari, "Nuclear Restraint."

10. On this issue, see Lavoy, "The Strategic Consequences of Nuclear Proliferation," p. 698.

11. See Correlates of War 2 Project, The Pennsylvania State University, available at http://cow2.la.psu.edu.

12. Richard Sisson and Leo E. Rose, *War and Secession: Pakistan, India, and the Creation of Bangladesh* (Berkeley and Los Angeles: University of California Press, 1990), p. 224.

13. Shahid Amin, *Pakistan's Foreign Policy: A Reappraisal* (Karachi: Oxford University Press, 2002), p. 70.

14. As Robert Gilpin explains, large power imbalances can stabilize international systems, making clear to potentially revisionist states that they have no hope of winning any conflict with the leading state and thereby deterring potential challengers from engaging in aggressive behavior. See generally Robert Gilpin, *War and Change in World Politics* (Cambridge: Cambridge University Press, 1981).

15. Note that these data do not include the Kashmir insurgency. The insurgency is not just an internal conflict between separatist insurgents and the Indian government but is also a low-intensity war being waged between India and Pakistan. However, since Pakistani actions are covert and deeply intertwined with indigenous efforts, this conflict is difficult to code. I discuss the insurgency in considerable detail in the chapters that follow. However, I leave it out of my quantitative analysis due to the thorniness of the coding issue and because doing so actually stacks the empirical evidence against my argument by undercounting Indo-Pakistani conflict after 1990.

16. In the Brasstacks crisis, a large-scale Indian military exercise triggered a spiral of force deployments and a major Indo-Pakistani standoff. For details, see Chapter 4.

17. I code dispute 1111 as Indian initiated because the Brasstacks crisis was sparked by an Indian military exercise. However, I label neither India nor Pakistan as revisionist, as it appears that neither state sought to achieve territorial change through the dispute. I code MID 1111's hostility level as "display of force" because it involved only mobilization and did not result in combat.

18. I retain for MID 1112 the COW coding of Pakistani initiation and revisionism from MID 4007. I code MID 1112's hostility level as "war" and MID 4007's hostility level as "use of force." I do so because the Kargil conflict broke the standard 1,000 battle-death threshold for war, while the conflict captured in MID 4007 did not.

19. I retain the COW coding of Indian initiation and Pakistani revisionism from MID 4277. I also retain MID 4277's hostility coding of "use of force," since a clash occurred from December 23–31, after MID 1113 began.

20. I use months rather than years as my unit of analysis because doing so allows me to capture more information. For example, if years were my unit of analysis, a calendar year that included six months of peace and six months of dispute would be counted simply as one dispute year. Using months as my unit of analysis, by contrast, allows me to capture the fact that the year was evenly divided between peace and dispute. Also, using months rather than years enables me to include more observations in my analysis, making my findings more robust.

21. Some scholars analyzing the relationship between conflict and other variables such as democracy count just the unit of time in which a dispute broke out as an observation of conflict; they do not count all the units of time through which the conflict continued. Thus, a war that lasted three years would count as just one conflict observation. See, e.g., Henry S. Farber and Joanne Gowa, "Polities and Peace," *International Security*, 20, no. 2 (1995), pp. 123–46. Scholars employ this approach because they are assessing only democracies' propensity to start conflicts, not their likelihood of continuing a conflict once it has begun. By contrast, I am assessing nuclear weapons' effects on India's and Pakistan's overall willingness to engage in conflict. This includes not just starting militarized disputes but also continuing them. If nuclear weapons have made India and Pakistan more militarily cautious, the two countries should be less likely to start disputes and more likely to end them quickly. Therefore, I am not interested only in the start of disputes. I am also interested in their duration. Thus, I include in my analysis each month in which a militarized dispute occurred. It is worth noting that a state's choice to continue a dispute is not entirely different from its decision to start one. For each unit of time, a state involved in an ongoing dispute must decide whether or not to engage in hostile action. Thus, each additional unit of time in which a dispute continues essentially represents another decision to engage in hostile activities.

22. According to deterrence logic, nuclear weapons discourage outright conventional war between nuclear-armed adversaries because such confrontation could escalate to the

nuclear level. Nuclear states refrain from waging outright war against each other, then, to avoid escalatory danger. But escalatory danger does not apply exclusively to outright war. Smaller scale confrontation between nuclear powers could escalate to the level of war, which could then threaten to spiral into a nuclear confrontation. And thus the same danger that discourages nuclear states from waging outright war against each other should also make them less willing to engage in lower level confrontations. Admittedly, nuclear states may behave somewhat less cautiously at the lower rungs of the escalation ladder and be more willing to engage in low-level provocations against each other than they are to engage in higher level violence. Still, nuclear-armed states should be more hesitant to engage even in lower level confrontation than they would be in the absence of nuclear weapons; in a nuclear environment, nuclear escalation—even from low-level disputes—is always a possibility, whereas such an outcome is not possible in a nonnuclear environment.

23. Escalatory danger can exist regardless of whether a militarized dispute results in significant numbers of fatalities. For example, a crisis involving large-scale force deployments and heated cross-border rhetoric may not directly kill anyone, but it does threaten to trigger a bloody confrontation. And there is no guarantee that such violence, if it occurred, would stop at the conventional level. Thus, even militarized disputes involving few or no battle deaths are potentially serious events and worthy of our attention.

24. I borrow these categories from the Correlates of War MID data set. The data set specifies five hostility levels: No militarized action, Threat to use force, Display of force, Use of force, and War. See Faten Ghosn and Glenn Palmer, "Codebook for the Militarized Dispute Data," Version 3.0, April 14, 2003, Correlates of War 2 Project, available at http://cow2.la.psu.edu. MIDs are categorized according to the highest level of hostility that they reach. Note that my data do not include any disputes classified as "Threat to use force." In addition to hostility levels, the COW data set provides MID fatality numbers. However, I generally do not use these figures in measuring dispute severity. I avoid the fatality numbers for several reasons. First, fatalities are not always a good measure of dispute severity; a major militarized crisis resulting in no fatalities could be much more dangerous and destabilizing than a minor confrontation that killed a modest number of people. Also, the COW fatality numbers are problematic. Figures are missing for some disputes. Where the data exist, they provide ranges of possible fatalities. And the data set does not specify the temporal distribution of fatalities across a given MID. Thus, if a dispute spans two nuclear periods, it is not clear in which period the fatalities occurred. The COW hostility levels are blunt measures of dispute severity, but they avoid these problems. The hostility level that I assign to one case, the Kargil conflict, does turn on the number of fatalities that occurred during that dispute; I code Kargil as a war, rather than a use of force, because it crossed the threshold of 1,000 battle deaths. However, this fatality level was far above the number of losses in any of the other disputes in question, occurred during a narrow window of time, and is documented by multiple sources independent of the COW data set. For details on Kargil, see Chapter 6.

25. In theory, it is also possible that increasing Pakistani conventional capabilities could have led Indian leaders to behave aggressively in an effort to damage Pakistan before India's relative conventional decline made doing so impossible. As we will see, however, Pakistan initiated most of the militarized disputes during the time period in question.

26. For an in-depth discussion of preventive-war or "window" logic, see Stephen Van Evera, *Causes of War: Power and the Roots of Conflict* (Ithaca, NY: Cornell University Press, 1999), pp. 73–104.

27. The numbers that I use are based on data drawn from relevant years of the International Institute for Strategic Studies' *The Military Balance*. Note that in some cases spending figures are based on defense budgets rather than actual expenditures.

28. I do not incorporate differences between the quality of Indian and Pakistani forces into my analysis. Although such factors could in theory be important, I have found no evidence to suggest that major shifts in relative quality occurred between Indian and Pakistani forces over the time period in question. As T. V. Paul puts it, "Since 1971, India has maintained the 'slight edge' in . . . qualitative defense areas." See T. V. Paul, "Causes of the India-Pakistan Enduring Rivalry," in T. V. Paul, ed., *The India-Pakistan Conflict: An Enduring Rivalry* (Cambridge: Cambridge University Press, 2005), p. 13.

29. India's conventional advantage over Pakistan is reduced by its need to defend both the Indo-Pakistani and the Sino-Indian borders. For a discussion of this point, see p. 213. Note, however, that India's two-front defense problem is a constant throughout the time period in question and could not have caused any fluctuation in the balance of Indo-Pakistani conventional capabilities.

30. See the Appendix.

31. RAND published a highly detailed assessment of the Indo-Pakistani conventional balance in 1997, essentially at the lowest level of Indian conventional superiority during the time span in question. The study argued that while India could not win quickly, it could nonetheless achieve decisive victory in a protracted Indo-Pakistani conventional conflict. See Ashley J. Tellis, *Stability in South Asia* (Santa Monica, CA: RAND, 1997), pp. vii, 23.

32. I also cross-tabulated the data as they originally appeared in the COW data set without the modifications that I list on pp. 18–19. The results were similar, yielding 190 months of peace (84.1 percent of months) in a nonnuclear South Asia versus 36 months of peace (15.9 percent of months) in a nuclear environment; 26 months of dispute when the subcontinent was nonnuclear (19.4 percent of months) versus 108 months of dispute after nuclearization (80.6 percent of months); and a chi-square p-value of < .001.

33. I ran this as a one-tailed test using the Kendall's tau-b correlation coefficient. Running it as a two-tailed test and substituting Spearman's rho and Pearson coefficients yielded very similar results.

34. I also ran the correlative test on the data as they originally appeared in the COW data set without the modifications that I list on pp. 18–19. The results of this test were slightly stronger, yielding a .609 correlation between nuclearization and hostility, again with a significance of < .001.

35. As I explain in Chapter 3, a strong, status quo state may use force to thwart a weak, revisionist adversary's attempts to alter the status quo. This strong-state behavior could include preemptive or preventive military action. Thus, even though nuclear weapons do not directly create incentives for strong, status quo state aggression, forceful behavior initiated by such states could increase in a nuclear environment in response to growing provocations by weak, revisionist challengers. As the case studies make clear, this logic accounts for increasingly forceful Indian behavior as the proliferation process continued.

CHAPTER 3.   *Territorial Preferences and Military Capabilities*

1. Although one could imagine other plausible definitions of strategic stability, I adhere to this definition throughout this study; for my purposes, strategic stability refers to the probability that conventional conflict will escalate to the nuclear level. This is the mean-

ing of strategic stability originally embedded in the stability/instability paradox, and in my view, it is the one that we must employ if we are to analyze the paradox rather than some other phenomenon. Note that the probability of conventional conflict escalating to the nuclear level is not an objective fact but rather is a function of decision makers' perceptions, which may change over time.

2. Charles L. Glaser, *Analyzing Strategic Nuclear Policy* (Princeton, NJ: Princeton University Press, 1990), p. 46. See also Robert Jervis, *The Meaning of the Nuclear Revolution: Statecraft and the Prospect of Armageddon* (Ithaca, NY: Cornell University Press, 1989), p. 20. For the original discussion of the stability/instability paradox, see Glenn H. Snyder, "The Balance of Power and the Balance of Terror," in Paul Seabury, ed., *The Balance of Power* (San Francisco: Chandler, 1965), pp. 198–99.

3. Text of the Lahore Declaration, United States Institute of Peace, Peace Agreements Digital Collection, available at http://www.usip.org/library/pa/ip/ip_lahore19990221 .html.

4. "AFP Asia-Pacific News Summary," *Agence France Presse*, February 17, 2004.

5. Author interview of senior Indian Ministry of External Affairs official, New Delhi, India, April 2004; author interview of Pakistan Ministry of Foreign Affairs Director General for South Asia, Jalil Jilani, Islamabad, Pakistan, April 2004. See also Pakistani High Commissioner to the United Kingdom Maleeha Lodhi, advocating the implementation of a South Asian "strategic restraint regime . . . to prevent the use of nuclear weapons by accident, miscalculation, or design" as well as policies "to promote [conventional] regional stability," such as "conventional arms control," and the adoption of "measures to eliminate the threat of surprise or preemptive [conventional] strikes by either country." Maleeha Lodhi, "Security Challenges in South Asia," *The Nonproliferation Review*, 8, no. 2, pp. 121, 122.

6. Clearly, the Cold War case differs from the current South Asian security environment in a number of significant respects. For example, neither India nor Pakistan seeks to extend nuclear deterrence to a third party; Indo-Pakistani strategic behavior is subject to far more international pressure than American and Soviet nuclear policy was during the Cold War, and this pressure may act as a check on conflict escalation in South Asia; and India and Pakistan maintain small nuclear arsenals, lacking the large array of tactical and strategic forces that the superpowers deployed during the Cold War. Nonetheless, many scholars and policymakers believe that the same basic logics that governed superpower nuclear behavior during the Cold War should hold for new nuclear states such as India and Pakistan. See, e.g., Waltz, "For Better," in Sagan and Waltz, eds., *The Spread of Nuclear Weapons*, p. 117; Mearsheimer, "Back to the Future," pp. 37–40; Sagan, "For the Worse," in Sagan and Waltz, eds., *The Spread of Nuclear Weapons*, p. 91; Jaswant Singh, "Against Nuclear Apartheid," p. 43.

7. Ganguly, *Conflict Unending*, pp. 122–23. For earlier arguments as to the stability/instability paradox's effects on the subcontinent, see Šumit Ganguly, "Conflict and Crisis in South and Southwest Asia," in Michael E. Brown, ed., *The International Dimensions of Internal Conflict* (Cambridge, MA: MIT Press, 1996), p. 170; Šumit Ganguly, "Indo-Pakistani Nuclear Issues and the Stability/Instability Paradox," *Studies in Conflict and Terrorism*, 18, no. 4 (1995), pp. 325–34.

8. Waltz, "For Better," in Sagan and Waltz, *The Spread of Nuclear Weapons*, p. 122.

9. David J. Karl, "Lessons for Proliferation Scholarship in South Asia: The Buddha Smiles Again," *Asian Survey*, 41, no. 6 (2001), p. 1020. India and Pakistan fought for approximately eight weeks in the Kargil sector of the Line of Control. For more discussion of the Kargil conflict, see below.

10. Feroz Hasan Khan, "Challenges to Nuclear Stability in South Asia," *The Nonproliferation Review*, 10, no. 1 (2003), p. 64.

11. Knopf, "Recasting the Optimism–Pessimism Debate," p. 52.

12. Lowell Dittmer, "South Asia's Security Dilemma," *Asian Survey*, 41, no. 6 (2001), p. 903.

13. Ganguly, *Conflict Unending*, pp. 122–23.

14. Dittmer, "South Asia's Security Dilemma," p. 903.

15. Waltz, "For Better," in Sagan and Waltz, eds., *The Spread of Nuclear Weapons*, p. 122.

16. Feroz Hasan Khan, "Challenges to Nuclear Stability in South Asia," *The Nonproliferation Review*, 10, no. 1 (2003), p. 64.

17. Sagan, "For the Worse," in Sagan and Waltz, eds., *The Spread of Nuclear Weapons*, p. 97. Other scholars who mention lack of escalatory potential in their discussions of the paradox include Khan, "Challenges to Nuclear Stability in South Asia," p. 64.

18. Knopf, "Recasting the Optimism–Pessimism Debate," p. 52.

19. Chari, "Nuclear Restraint, Nuclear Risk Reduction, and the Stability–Instability Paradox," in Krepon and Gagné, eds., *The Stability–Instability Paradox*, pp. 20–21. I do not claim that these authors offer fully developed arguments or comprise three entirely coherent schools of thought on the workings of the stability/instability paradox in South Asia. My point, rather, is that the literature contains three broad categories of discussion on this issue, one of which emphasizes the danger of nuclear escalation, another of which emphasizes the lack of such danger, and a third of which refers generally to "nuclear deterrence."

20. I offer this brief overview for illustrative purposes only and do not purport to provide a comprehensive discussion of American strategic nuclear policy during the Cold War.

21. George H. Quester, *Nuclear Diplomacy: The First Twenty-Five Years* (New York: Dunellen, 1970), p. 96.

22. Richard Smoke, *National Security and the Nuclear Dilemma: An Introduction to the American Experience in the Cold War* (New York: McGraw-Hill, 1993), p. 51.

23. Ibid., p. 84; Bernard Brodie, *Escalation and the Nuclear Option* (Princeton, NJ: Princeton University Press, 1966), p. 28; John Lewis Gaddis, *Strategies of Containment: A Critical Appraisal of Postwar American National Security Policy* (New York: Oxford University Press, 1982), pp. 165–66.

24. In 1955, NATO had fewer than twenty-five effective fighting divisions, against approximately twenty-eight to thirty Soviet divisions in Eastern Europe and an additional sixty to seventy Soviet divisions in the western USSR. See Stephen J. Flanagan, *NATO's Conventional Defenses* (Cambridge, MA: Ballinger, 1988), p. 14. Note that such a comparison does not precisely reflect the European conventional balance, as it does not capture qualitative and quantitative differences between each side's divisions. See Mearsheimer, "Why the Soviets Can't Win Quickly in Central Europe," pp. 6–8. Nonetheless, analysts broadly agreed that the Soviets enjoyed a substantial conventional advantage over NATO during this period. See, e.g., Flanagan, *NATO's Conventional Defenses*, pp. 9–14; Smoke, *National Security and the Nuclear Dilemma*, pp. 66, 85; Gaddis, *Strategies of Containment*, p. 168; Brodie, *Escalation and the Nuclear Option*, p. 124; Ronald E. Powaski, *The Cold War: The United States and the Soviet Union, 1917–1991* (Oxford: Oxford University Press, 1998), pp. 102–3. The U.S. government, for its part, estimated that in the event of conflict during this period, the Soviets would be able to capture most of Western Europe quickly. As NSC-68 argued, "Should a major war occur in 1950 the Soviet Union and its satellites are considered by the

Joint Chiefs of Staff to be in a sufficiently advanced state of preparation immediately to . . .
overrun Western Europe, with the possible exception of the Iberian and Scandinavian Pen-
insulas." See the text of NSC-68, available at http://www.fas.org/irp/offdocs/nsc-hst/nsc-
68.htm. Note that this view of the European conventional balance was subsequently called
into serious question, with scholars arguing that Soviet conventional superiority had been
substantially exaggerated and that even numerically inferior NATO defenses probably could
have prevented a quick Warsaw Pact victory in Europe. See, e.g., Barry R. Posen, "Measuring the European Conventional Balance: Coping with Complexity in Threat Assessment,
International Security, 9, no. 3 (1984–1985), pp. 47–88; Barry R. Posen, "Is NATO Decisively
Outnumbered?" *International Security*, 12, no. 4 (1988), pp. 186–202; Mearsheimer, "Why
the Soviets Can't Win Quickly in Central Europe," pp. 3–39; Matthew Evangelista, "Stalin's Postwar Army Reappraised," *International Security*, 7, no. 3 (1982–1983), pp. 110–38.

25. Nikita Khrushchev explicitly used this argument to threaten the United States with
Soviet action against Berlin between 1958 and 1962. Khrushchev stated that growing Soviet nuclear capabilities "meant that the ultimate American sanction behind its deterrence
policy in Berlin, the threat of a strategic strike, was effectively voided." If this were the
case, "nothing prevented the Soviets from employing their overwhelming superiority in
local conventional forces in any Berlin crisis." Alexander L. George and Richard Smoke,
Deterrence in American Foreign Policy: Theory and Practice (New York and London: Columbia
University Press, 1974), pp. 395–96.

26. Robert Jervis, *The Illogic of American Nuclear Strategy* (Ithaca, NY: Cornell University
Press, 1984), pp. 66, 67. See also Gaddis, *We Now Know*, p.137; Quester, *Nuclear Diplomacy*,
p. 94.

27. Not all analysts believed that the stability/instability paradox significantly undermined U.S. nuclear deterrence in Europe. Some "minimum deterrence" theorists argued
that since nuclear escalation would be so costly, even a slight threat of such an outcome
would be sufficient to deter conventional war. As Jervis put it, "Because the specter of dev-
astation is present in any superpower confrontation, the fear of all-out war can deter many
adventures even though starting such a war would be irrational. The stability–instability
paradox then is not as stark as it is often portrayed." Jervis, *The Meaning of the Nuclear
Revolution*, p. 22. See also Bernard Brodie, "The Development of Nuclear Strategy," in
Bernard Brodie, Michael D. Intriligator, and Roman Kolkowicz, eds., *National Security
and International Stability* (Cambridge: Oelgeschlager, Gunn & Haith, 1983), pp. 15–17;
MacGeorge Bundy, *Danger and Survival: Choices About the Bomb in the First Fifty Years* (New
York: Random House, 1988), pp. 598–601. Although this is an important argument, it
does not deny the basic logic of the stability/instability paradox. This is the case because
the minimum deterrence theorists assume that nuclear escalation is at least possible; if the
likelihood of nuclear escalation were zero, nuclear weapons would be unable to deter conventional conflict. Thus, in moving from nuclear conflict being impossible to being possible, we have moved from no deterrence to deterrence. This means that as the likelihood
of nuclear escalation increased, the likelihood of conventional conflict decreased—which,
of course, is the core logic of the stability/instability paradox. Thus, while minimum deterrence theorists did not believe that the stability/instability paradox would significantly
erode nuclear weapons' ability to deter conventional conflict in Europe, their arguments
did not deny the paradox's fundamental logic.

28. As Bernard Brodie put it, in an environment in which one cannot "seriously and
convincingly . . . use for political ends threats of strategic nuclear attack . . . one *can*

threaten . . . lesser actions that *could* start events moving in that direction." Such a threat "is a deterrent as good or better than any threat of general war, especially since it is far less subject to being doubted." Brodie, *Escalation and the Nuclear Option*, pp. 30, 101.

29. See Thomas C. Schelling, *Arms and Influence* (New Haven, CT: Yale University Press, 1966), pp. 43–44.

30. This denial capacity was an important component of American strategy. Under the concept of "flexible response," the United States sought the capability to meet and deter Soviet aggression at every step of the escalation ladder. At the tactical level, a U.S./NATO ability to mount a robust battlefield defense of Western Europe could make aggression prohibitively costly for the Soviet Union. Thus, even if the Soviets were confident that a conventional war in Europe would not escalate to the nuclear level, the fact that they could not prevail easily on the battlefield could dissuade them from launching a conventional attack. Although, like risk creation, this strategy relied on the deployment of conventional forces and tactical nuclear weapons, the logic underlying it was different in that it sought to fight and win at lower levels rather than simply to create the risk of escalation to the level of a strategic exchange. See Smoke, *National Security and the Nuclear Dilemma*, pp. 87–89.

31. Schelling, *Arms and Influence*, p. 47.

32. Powaski, *The Cold War*, p. 103. See also Walter LaFeber, *America, Russia, and the Cold War 1945–1992* (New York: McGraw-Hill, 1993), pp. 125–26; Quester, *Nuclear Diplomacy*, p. 95; Marc Trachtenberg, *History and Strategy* (Princeton, NJ: Princeton University Press, 1991), p. 217; Gaddis, *Strategies of Containment*, p. 168.

33. Quester, *Nuclear Diplomacy*, p. 221.

34. The threat to use these weapons was deemed sufficiently credible, despite the fact that such use could lead to a strategic exchange, because of the weapons' vulnerability in the midst of any European conflict and because of their smaller size, which meant that the choice to use them was not as devastating as a decision to use strategic weapons—even if such a choice ultimately resulted in a strategic conflict. See Jervis, *The Illogic of American Nuclear Strategy*, pp. 93–94. For a discussion of likely escalatory pressures on tactical nuclear forces during a European conflict, see Desmond Ball et al., *Crisis Stability and Nuclear War* (Ithaca, NY: Cornel University Peace Studies Program, 1987), pp. 66–70.

35. Jervis, *The Illogic of American Nuclear Strategy*, p. 92. See also Gaddis, *We Now Know*, p. 137; Quester, "The Continuing Debate on Minimal Deterrence," in T. V. Paul, Richard J. Harknett, and James J. Wirtz, eds., *The Absolute Weapon Revisited: Nuclear Arms and the Emerging International Order* (Ann Arbor: University of Michigan Press, 1998), p. 169. This logic holds for both tactical and intermediate-range nuclear forces, leading Jervis to question the need for the deployment of INF to Europe as a generator of risk. See Jervis, *The Illogic of American Nuclear Strategy*, pp. 90–95.

36. Glaser, *Analyzing Strategic Nuclear Policy*, pp. 216–17. See also Schelling, *Arms and Influence*, pp. 190–92, 202–3.

37. As Glaser points out, however, counterforce was probably not necessary to enhance limited nuclear options. By choosing to strike only a restricted set of nonnuclear targets with countervalue weapons, the United States could launch a limited nuclear attack on the Soviet Union without targeting Soviet nuclear weapons. See Glaser, *Analyzing Strategic Nuclear Policy*, pp. 216–22.

38. Jervis, *The Illogic of American Nuclear Policy*, p. 70; Glaser, *Analyzing Strategic Nuclear Policy*, p. 224; Schelling, *Arms and Influence*, pp. 193–94. Note that many analysts doubted

that counterforce could actually provide the United States with any meaningful damage-limitation capability in an environment of mutually assured destruction. See, e.g., Glaser, *Analyzing Strategic Nuclear Policy*, pp. 32–35; Jervis, *The Illogic of American Nuclear Policy*, pp. 54–55. For an opposing view, see Colin Gray and Keith Payne, "Victory Is Possible," *Foreign Policy*, no. 39 (1980), p. 25.

39. Schelling, *Arms and Influence* p. 191.

40. See Robert Powell, "The Theoretical Foundations of Strategic Nuclear Deterrence," *Political Science Quarterly*, 100, no. 1 (1985) pp. 75–76. Powell characterizes the first approach as predicated upon a "spectrum of risk" and the second as predicated upon a "spectrum of violence." See Ibid., pp. 91–92.

41. This is the case because the presence of nuclear weapons necessarily creates at least the theoretical possibility of their use. While under certain circumstances that possibility might be very small, the likelihood of nuclear use would have to be greater in a nuclear environment than it would be if nuclear weapons were not present.

42. My purpose here is not to make definitive claims about actual Soviet intentions regarding Western Europe. My point, rather, is that the principal Cold War danger as perceived by the United States and NATO was that the Warsaw Pact would attempt to seize territory in Western Europe. As the literature cited makes clear, the Western alliance's primary goal during the Cold War therefore was to confine the Pact to Eastern Europe and prevent this from happening.

43. Note that relative Soviet weakness would have been unlikely to encourage NATO aggression because the alliance's goal was to contain Soviet power and defend Western Europe rather than to seize territory in the East. Thus, NATO would probably have used conventional superiority to maintain the status quo rather than to alter it.

44. This is not to claim that the stability/instability paradox rules out the possibility of subnuclear aggression when a substantial likelihood of nuclear escalation exists; a state highly motivated to alter the status quo could opt for aggressive behavior despite a substantial likelihood of triggering nuclear conflict. Under the stability/instability paradox, however, such a high likelihood of nuclear escalation is an impediment to lower level violence, and increasing the probability of nuclear escalation therefore makes lower level violence less likely. In contemporary South Asia, by contrast, increasing the likelihood of nuclear escalation—up to a point—facilitates lower level aggression. In fact, in this environment, the outbreak of lower level violence actually *requires* a significant degree of strategic instability.

45. Of course, an *extremely* high level of strategic instability would discourage subnuclear violence in South Asia. If the Indo-Pakistani strategic balance were so unstable that even limited conventional aggression was likely to result in immediate nuclear escalation, limited aggression would be excessively risky and thus unlikely. As noted, however, this is not an accurate description of the South Asian strategic environment; limited conventional aggression on the subcontinent is unlikely to escalate to the nuclear level immediately.

46. Although status quo preferences greatly reduce a state's incentives for aggression, they do not rule aggression out completely; a status quo state could behave aggressively if it believes that doing so is necessary to preserve its current position. As Charles Glaser argues, "a status-quo state may in fact be unwilling to accept the status quo—it is satisfied with existing international borders and thus uninterested in expansion, *except* if necessary to protect its security in the status quo." Therefore, under certain circumstances, "status-

quo powers may be willing to launch wars." Glaser, "Political Consequences of Military Strategy: Expanding and Refining the Spiral and Deterrence Models," *World Politics* 44, no. 4 (1992), 501.

47. Barry Posen, *Inadvertent Escalation* (Ithaca, NY: Cornell University Press, 1991), pp. 2–4.

48. Muhammad Irshad, "Crises of Nuclear Neighbors," *Defence Journal*, 6, no. 2 (2002), pp. 120–25.

49. V. R. Raghavan, "Limited War and Nuclear Escalation in South Asia," *Nonproliferation Review* (Fall–Winter 2001), p. 16.

50. See Ganguly, *Conflict Unending*, pp. 45, 46, 69, 73.

51. Aga Shahi, Zulfikar Ali Khan, and Abdul Sattar, "Securing Nuclear Peace," *News International*, October 5, 1999, in *Strategic Digest*, 30, no. 1 (2000), p. 16.

52. Stephen P. Cohen identifies the use of war to internationalize ongoing disputes as a main component of Pakistan's "strategic style." Stephen P. Cohen, *The Pakistan Army* (Karachi: Oxford University Press, 1998), p. 145.

53. Thomas Schelling, *Arms and Influence*, p. 103.

54. Ibid., p. 97.

55. Ibid., p. 109.

56. By deterrence, I mean the use of conditional threats to convince an adversary not to take certain actions that it might otherwise have taken. By compellance, I mean the use of conditional threats to convince an adversary to change its behavior, either ceasing to take a certain proscribed action or beginning a certain prescribed action. For an extensive discussion of the relationship between deterrence and compellance, see Schelling, *Arms and Influence*, pp. 69–91.

57. Ian Talbot, *Pakistan: A Modern History* (New Delhi: Oxford University Press, 1999), p. 113. For a detailed treatment of the first war for Kashmir, see C. Dasgupta, *War and Diplomacy in Kashmir 1947–48* (New Delhi: Sage Publications, 2002).

58. For an overview of the Indo-Pakistani conflict over Kashmir, see generally Robert G. Wirsing, *India, Pakistan, and the Kashmir Dispute: On Regional Conflict and Its Resolution* (New York: St. Martin's Press, 1998).

59. Alastair Lamb, *Kashmir: A Disputed Legacy 1846–1990* (Karachi: Oxford University Press, 1993), p. 2. Despite these facts, "Kashmir's strategic and diplomatic importance has waxed and waned. While it was the central objective of the first two India-Pakistan wars," from 1966 to 1989 "it was not an issue of high priority for either state." Since 1989, Kashmir has come to dominate Indo-Pakistani relations once more, with the dispute promoting regional instability and nuclear proliferation and bogging down in "a bloody stalemate." Stephen P. Cohen, *India: Emerging Power* (Washington, DC: Brookings Institution Press, 2001), pp. 217, 220.

60. Indian Prime Minister Jawaharlal Nehru promised in 1947 to hold a plebiscite in Kashmir to ratify the territory's accession to India, but the vote was deferred until normal conditions could be reestablished in the territory. India has yet to hold the plebiscite. See Ganguly, *The Crisis in Kashmir*, p. 10.

61. "Excerpts from Pakistani President Pervez Musharraf's Address to the Nation," May 27, 2002, BBC Monitoring, available at http://news.bbc.co.uk/1/hi/world/monitoring/media_reports/2011509.stm.

62. K. J. M. Varma, "Pak Not Ready to Sideline Kashmir: Musharraf," *Press Trust of India*, June 17, 2003.

63. Cohen, *India*, pp. 212–13; Talbot, *Pakistan*, p. 114; Lamb, *Kashmir*, p. 148; Singh, "The Kashmir Issue," in Singh, ed., *Kargil 1999*, pp. 2–3.

64. The Indian state of Jammu and Kashmir is approximately 64 percent Muslim and 32 percent Hindu. Kashmir Valley, the heart of J&K state, is approximately 95 percent Muslim. See Wirsing, *India, Pakistan, and the Kashmir Dispute*, p. 125.

65. On these points, see Ganguly, *The Crisis in Kashmir: Portents of War, Hopes of Peace* (New York: The Woodrow Wilson Center and Cambridge University Press, 1997); Cohen, *India*, p. 215; Lamb, *Kashmir*, pp. 149–50; Talbot, *Pakistan*, p. 114.

66. Cohen, *India*, p. 219. The cease-fire line (CFL) dividing Kashmir between India and Pakistan after the 1948 war was redrawn and renamed the Line of Control in the Simla Agreement, which ended the 1971 Bangladesh War. For a detailed discussion, see Wirsing, *India, Pakistan, and the Kashmir Dispute*, pp. 61–83.

67. Wirsing, *India, Pakistan, and the Kashmir Dispute*, pp. 219–20. Officially, Indian policy calls not merely for the solidification of the Line of Control but also for Pakistan's complete withdrawal from Kashmir. In truth, however, the Indian government would be willing to settle for the division of Kashmir along the LoC. As Tellis et al. point out, despite their official stance, Indian leaders seek "the conversion of the LoC (perhaps with some modifications) into a de jure international border, a fact privately admitted in interviews at the highest levels of the Indian government. Such a concession, if offered in the context of a lasting agreement with Pakistan, would ipso facto involve India's renunciation of its present claims over 'Pakistan occupied Kashmir' and the Northern Territories." See Tellis et al., *Limited Conflicts*, p. 69.

68. Tellis et al., *Limited Conflicts*, p. 46. On the issue of Pakistani revisionism and Indian satisfaction with the status quo, see also Raja Menon, *A Nuclear Strategy for India* (New Delhi: Sage Publications, 2000), 195; Thomas Perry Thornton, "Pakistan: Fifty Years of Insecurity," in Selig S. Harrison, Paul H. Kreisberg, and Dennis Kux eds., *India and Pakistan: The First Fifty Years* (New York: Cambridge University Press and the Woodrow Wilson Center, 1999), p. 184; Ganguly, *Conflict Unending*, p. 128; Hagerty, *The Consequences of Nuclear Proliferation*, p. 135.

69. See, e.g., Ganguly, *The Crisis in Kashmir*; Sumantra Bose, *Kashmir: Roots of Conflict, Paths to Peace* (Cambridge, MA: Harvard University Press, 2003); Victoria Schofield, *Kashmir in Conflict: India, Pakistan, and the Unending War* (London: I. B. Tauris, 2003).

70. See generally V. R. Raghavan, *Siachen: Conflict Without End* (New Delhi: Viking Press, 2002); Wirsing, *India, Pakistan, and the Kashmir Dispute*, pp. 75–83.

71. For a concise discussion of these conflicts, see Ganguly, *Conflict Unending*.

72. J. N. Dixit, *India-Pakistan in War and Peace* (New Delhi: Books Today, 2002), p. 212.

73. International Institute for Strategic Studies, *The Military Balance 2001–2002* (Oxford: Oxford University Press, 2001), pp. 162, 167.

74. R. K. Jasbir Singh, ed., *Indian Defence Yearbook 2002* (Dehra Dun: Natraj Publishers, 2002), pp. 311, 317.

75. *The Military Balance 2002–2003*, pp. 129–30, 133–34. For a full breakdown of Indian and Pakistani forces, see Ibid., pp. 129–31, 133–35. In addition to this numerical advantage, Indian forces enjoy a qualitative edge over Pakistan. India has "a much larger defense industrial base, can manufacture and assemble more advanced arms, and gets most of its arms from Russia—an advanced supplier. Pakistan imports most of its arms from China and Eastern Europe and they are notably less advanced than those imported by India." Anthony

H. Cordesman, *The India-Pakistan Military Balance* (Washington, DC: Center for Strategic and International Studies, 2002), p. 4.

76. *The Military Balance 2001–2002*, pp. 162, 167.

77. Cordesman, *The India-Pakistan Military Balance*, p. 3.

78. India must disperse its forces to protect long borders and face two potential adversaries in the region: Pakistan and China. Pakistan, by contrast, has shorter borders and can concentrate most of its military capabilities against India. See Dixit, *India-Pakistan*, p. 341.

79. Tellis, *Stability in South Asia*, pp. 20–21. See also V. K. Sood and Pravin Sawhney, *Operation Parakaram: The War Unfinished* (New Delhi: Sage Publications, 2003), pp. 145–52; Kanwar Sandhu, "Can India's War Machine Deliver the Killer Punch?" *Hindustan Times*, January 10, 2002, p. 11.

80. Cohen, *The Pakistan Army*, p. 145.

81. Ayaz Ahmed Khan, "Armed Forces War Gaming," *Defence Journal*, 6, no. 1 (2002), available at http://www.defencejournal.com/2002/august/gaming.htm. See also Tellis, *Stability in South Asia* (Santa Monica, CA: RAND, 1997), pp. 17–18; Cohen, *The Pakistan Army*, p. 145.

82. Beg, "Deterrence, Defence, and Development," p. 5.

83. Author interview of President Pervez Musharraf, Rawalpindi, Pakistan, April 2004. See also Ayaz Ahmed Kahn, "Armed Forces War Gaming"; Tellis, *Stability in South Asia*, pp. 17–18; Kanwar Sandhu, "Pak Strategy Will Be to Sever Link with J&K," *Hindustan Times*, January 11, 2002, p. 11.

84. Sandhu, "Pak Strategy Will Be to Sever Link with J&K."

85. Tellis, *Stability in South Asia*, 23, p. viii.

86. See John J. Mearsheimer, *Conventional Deterrence* (Ithaca, NY: Cornell University Press, 1983).

87. Quoted in Ganguly, *Conflict Unending*, p. 38.

88. See Cloughley, *A History of the Pakistan Army*, pp. 79–92. Ganguly, *Conflict Unending*, pp. 33, 43–46, 48; Jones, *Pakistan*, p. 78.

89. Tellis, *Stability in South Asia*, pp. 21, 23. Although devoting large numbers of forces to a conflict with Pakistan could in theory leave India vulnerable to Chinese aggression, there are good reasons to believe that this is not a serious problem. First, despite past territorial disputes, both India and China now have status quo preferences regarding contested regions. In addition, relations between India and China substantially improved during the 1990s. Second, unlike in the past, the Sino-Indian military balance currently favors India. The highly defense-dominant tactical environment along the Sino-Indian border compounds this Indian advantage; Himalayan terrain makes any successful offensive military action in the area extremely difficult. Finally, India possesses nuclear weapons, which should deter major Chinese aggression apart from Chinese territorial preferences and Indian conventional capabilities. Thus, it is unlikely that China would attempt to take advantage of a crisis in which India temporarily shifted the bulk of its forces to deal with Pakistan. See Tellis, *India's Emerging Nuclear Posture*, pp. 136, 137, 275–76; Talbot, *Pakistan*, p. 22; George Perkovich, *India's Nuclear Bomb*, p. 440; Rodney Jones, "Debating New Delhi's Nuclear Decision," *International Security*, 24, no. 4 (2000) pp. 182–83.

90. Tellis, *Stability in South Asia*, pp. 15–16, 23.

91. Tellis, *India's Emerging Nuclear Posture*, p. 133.

92. This is not to argue that Pakistan's status as a weak, revisionist proliferator was the only variable underlying aggressive Pakistani behavior. Indeed, such factors as military rule,

Islamization, and deep territorial dissatisfaction may have made Pakistan particularly aggression prone even apart from nuclear weapons. My claim here is simply that, in addition to these factors, Pakistan's status as a weak, revisionist proliferator created significant further incentives for belligerent behavior. Indeed, nuclear weapons were essential to making aggressive behavior possible by ensuring that it would not result in catastrophic Pakistani defeat.

93. See P. R. Chari and Pervaiz Iqbal Cheema, *The Simla Agreement 1972: Its Wasted Promise* (New Delhi: Manohar, 2001), pp. 140–41, 158–59.

94. Ganguly, *Crisis Unending*, pp. 72, 79.

95. "Statement of Nawaz Sharif in ATC-1," *Dawn*, March 9, 2000.

96. "Excerpts from Pakistani Prime Minister Mohammad Nawaz Sharif's Address to Nation Broadcast on National TV," *World Media Watch*, July 12, 1999.

97. Ibid.

98. For example, imperfect information, generated by dysfunctional military or intelligence organizations, could lead decision makers who wish to avoid nuclear danger to adopt policies that actually increase the risk of nuclear conflict.

99. Though it does not deny the destabilizing effect these factors could have on newly nuclear states.

100. A. F. K. Organski and Jacek Kugler, *The War Ledger* (Chicago and London: University of Chicago Press, 1980), p. 19.

101. Ibid., p. 28.

102. Ibid., p. 19.

103. Gilpin, *War and Change in World Politics*, p. 198. Note that, unlike in Organski and Kugler's model, in Gilpin's theory the weak state is not necessarily more likely to start the war. According to Gilpin, hegemonic war theory "does not necessarily concern itself with whether the declining or rising state is responsible for the war. In fact, the identification of the initiator of a particular war is frequently impossible to attain and authorities seldom agree." See Robert Gilpin, "The Theory of Hegemonic War," in Robert I. Rotberg and Theodore K. Rabb, eds., *The Origin and Prevention of Major Wars* (Cambridge: Cambridge University Press, 1988), p. 26.

104. Ibid., p. 203.

105. See T. V. Paul, *Asymmetric Conflicts: War Initiation by Weaker Powers* (Cambridge: Cambridge University Press, 1994).

106. Ibid., pp. 26–27.

107. Ibid., p. 13.

108. Ibid., p. 217 (italics in original).

109. Gilpin, *War and Change*, p. 214.

110. Ibid., p. 217.

111. Ibid., p. 218.

112. Paul, *Asymmetric Conflicts*, pp. 175–76.

113. My discussion here assumes symmetric acquisition of nuclear weapons.

114. The Pakistani economy has recently managed to avoid catastrophic stagnation, increasing its gross domestic product (GDP) growth rate from 1.9 percent in 2001 to 5.1 percent in 2003 and 8.4 percent in 2005. It is forecast to grow 6.5 and 7.3 percent in fiscal years 2006 and 2007. However, the Indian economy grew 5.8 percent in 2001, 8.5 percent in 2003, and 8.1 percent in 2005, and is forecast to grow 7.6 and 7.8 percent in fiscal years 2006 and 2007. See Asian Development Bank, "Key Indicators of Developing Asian and Pacific

Countries 2005, Pakistan," available at http://www.adb.org/Documents/Books/Key_Indicators/2005/pdf/PAK.pdf; "Key Indicators of Developing Asian and Pacific Countries 2005, India," available at http://www.adb.org/Documents/Books/Key_Indicators/2005/pdf/IND.pdf; "South Asia's Growth to Moderate but Remain Strong in 2006-2007, Says ADB," available at http://www.adb.org/Media/Articles/2006/9635-South-Asia-Asian-Development-Outlook-2006/; "Asian Development Bank Outlook 2006: Pakistan," available at http://www.adb.org/Documents/Books/ADO/2006/documents/pak.pdf; and "Asian Development Outlook 2006: India," available at http://www.adb.org/Documents/Books/ADO/2006/documents/ind.pdf.

115. Paul discusses the role that outside powers may play in encouraging weak-state aggression, but he does so in the context of alliances, or at least preexisting diplomatic relationships. According to Paul, a weak power is more likely to attack a stronger adversary if the weak state believes that it can count on politico-military support for its venture from powerful friends. See Paul, *Asymmetric Conflicts*, pp. 31–33. My argument, by contrast, shows that nuclear weapons can encourage weak aggressors by promising to secure third-party diplomatic intervention in ongoing disputes, and they do so regardless of preexisting alliances or relationships. The danger of nuclear confrontation alone drives third parties to seek to defuse crises created by weak nuclear-state aggression.

116. This is not to argue that Paul does not address nuclear weapons' implications for his theory. Paul does address this issue, as I explain later. My point is that the theory itself turns on the emboldening effects of a conventional limited aims strategy and thus does not explain how the acquisition of nuclear weapons would encourage a weak state to behave aggressively toward a stronger adversary.

CHAPTER 4. *The Nonnuclear Period*

1. See, e.g., Cohen, *India*, p. 217.

2. Despite basic Indian satisfaction with the Kashmiri status quo, India did seize Siachen Glacier in Northern Kashmir in 1984. On this issue, see pp. 82–83 of this book.

3. For a detailed discussion of these events, see Sisson and Rose, *War and Secession*.

4. The most help that Pakistan received was a feint toward the Bay of Bengal by a U.S. aircraft carrier task force. The move infuriated Indian leaders but had no bearing on the Bangladesh conflict.

5. For a concise discussion of these military operations, see Ganguly, *Conflict Unending*.

6. The Hamoodur Rehman Commission of Inquiry into the 1971 War, Report as Declassified by the Government of Pakistan, Part 4, "Military Aspect" (Lahore, Pakistan: Vanguard Books, 2000), p. 281.

7. Amin, *Pakistan's Foreign Policy*, p. 43.

8. As noted, although Pakistan had not won decisive victories in its previous conflicts with India, it had at least been able to achieve stalemates and thus could cling to the notion that a Muslim army could not lose to Hindus.

9. Ganguly, *Conflict Unending*, pp. 71–72. See also S. M. Burke and Lawrence Ziring, *Pakistan's Foreign Policy: An Historical Analysis* (Karachi: Oxford University Press, 1990), pp. 420–21.

10. Amin, *Pakistan's Foreign Policy*, p. 72.

11. See Ganguly, *Conflict Unending*, p. 70; Rafi Haza, *Zulfikar Ali Bhutto and Pakistan: 1967–1977* (Karachi: Oxford University Press, 1997), pp. 206–16.

12. Text of Simla Agreement, in P. R. Chari and Pervaiz Iqbal Cheema, *The Simla Agreement 1972: Its Wasted Promise* (New Delhi: Manohar, 2001), pp. 204–6.

13. Chari, "The Simla Agreement: An Indian Appraisal," in Ibid., p. 61.

14. Text of Simla Agreement, in Ibid., p. 205.

15. Pervaiz Iqbal Cheema, "The Simla Agreement: Current Relevance?" in Ibid., p. 135.

16. Zulfikar Ali Bhutto, *If I Am Assassinated* (New Delhi: Vikas Publishing House, 1979), p. 130. See also Stanley A. Wolpert, *Zulfi Bhutto of Pakistan: His Life and Times* (New York: Oxford University Press, 1993), p. 194.

17. Author interview of former Pakistani Prime Minister Benazir Bhutto, August 2004.

18. Text of Simla Agreement, in Chari and Cheema, eds., *The Simla Agreement 1972*, p. 206.

19. Zulfikar Ali Bhutto, "The Simla Accord," *Pakistan Horizon*, 25, no. 3 (1972), pp. 7–9.

20. Author interview of Benazir Bhutto, August 2004.

21. Cheema, "The Simla Agreement," p. 159.

22. Lawrence Ziring, *Pakistan: At the Crosscurrent of History* (Oxford: Oneworld Oxford Publications, 2003), pp. 131–32.

23. Ziring, *Pakistan*, p. 138; Mubashir Hasan, *The Mirage of Power: An Inquiry into the Bhutto Years 1971–1977* (Karachi: Oxford University Press, 2000), pp. 153–54.

24. Quoted in Wolpert, *Zulfi Bhutto*, pp. 194, 195; see also pp. 191–92; Mehrunnisa Ali, "The Simla and Tashkent Agreements," in Mehrunnisa Ali, ed., *Readings in Pakistan Foreign Policy* (Karachi: Oxford University Press, 2001), p. 87.

25. See Ziring, *Pakistan*, pp. 138–39; Amin, *Pakistan's Foreign Policy*, pp. 76–78; Raza, *Zulfikar Ali Bhutto*, pp. 227–36; Burke and Ziring, *Pakistan's Foreign Policy*, pp. 422–24.

26. Ziring, *Pakistan*, p. 136; Burke and Ziring, *Pakistan's Foreign Policy*, pp. 416–17.

27. Cohen, *The Pakistan Army*, pp. 73, 109, 139; Bhutto, *If I Am Assassinated*, pp. 116–17; Ziring, *Pakistan*, pp. 135–36.

28. Ahmed, "Pakistan's Nuclear Weapons Program," p. 183.

29. Ganguly, *Conflict Unending*, p. 101; George Perkovich, *India's Nuclear Bomb: The Impact on Global Proliferation* (Berkeley and Los Angeles: University of California Press, 1999), p. 186.

30. For a statement to this effect from the Indian Defense Minister, Jagjivan Ram, see "Indian Rules Out Atomic Arms' Use," *New York Times*, May 23, 1974.

31. Ashley Tellis, *India's Emerging Nuclear Doctrine: Between Recessed Deterrent and Ready Arsenal* (Santa Monica, CA: RAND, 2001), pp. 196–97.

32. Perkovich, *India's Nuclear Bomb*, p. 177; see also pp. 181–83.

33. Ganguly, "India's Pathway to Pokhran II," pp. 159–60.

34. Perkovich, *India's Nuclear Bomb*, p. 186.

35. Ziring, *Pakistan*, p. 152.

36. Ibid.

37. Ibid.; Cohen, *The Pakistan Army*, p. 157.

38. Cohen, *The Pakistan Army*, p. 89.

39. Bhutto's PPP, which had been expected to win only a narrow victory, achieved a solid majority in the 1977 elections. Charges of election rigging and widespread demonstrations followed, forcing the government to declare a state of emergency. See Craig Baxter, "Restructuring the Pakistan Political System," in Shahid Javed Burki and Craig

Baxter, eds., *Pakistan Under the Military: Eleven Years of Zia ul-Haq* (Boulder, CO: Westview Press, 1991), pp. 29–30.

40. See Ziring, *Pakistan*, pp. 153, 157–60; Talbot, *Pakistan*, pp. 222, 245–50; Burki, "Zia's Eleven Years," in Burki and Baxter, eds., *Pakistan Under the Military*, pp. 5–8.

41. Note that the Islamization process had actually begun under Bhutto in the aftermath of the 1977 elections. To insulate himself from criticism by conservative Islamic groups, Bhutto banned alcohol and gambling and announced introduction of Shariat law within six months. See Baxter, "Restructuring the Pakistan Political System," in Burki and Baxter, eds., *Pakistan Under the Military*, pp. 29–30.

42. Ziring, *Pakistan*, pp. 164–65; Shaid Javed Burki, *Pakistan: Fifty Years of Nationhood*, 3rd ed. (Boulder, CO: Westview Press, 1999), pp. 51–52.

43. Talbot, *Pakistan*, p. 270.

44. Ziring, *Pakistan*, pp. 171, 183, 184–85; Talbot, *Pakistan*, pp. 270–83; Burki, *Pakistan*, pp. 52–53; Mir Zohair Hussain, "Islam in Pakistan Under Bhutto and Zia-ul-Haq," in Hussin Mutalib and Taj ul-Islam Hashmi, eds., *Islam, Muslims, and the Modern State* (New York: St. Martin's Press, 2004), pp. 60–68.

45. Cohen, *The Pakistan Army*, pp. 88–89.

46. Ibid., pp. 63–65; Brian Cloughley, *A History of the Pakistan Army: Wars and Insurrections* (Karachi: Oxford University Press, 1999), pp. 34–39.

47. Cohen, *The Pakistan Army*, p. 89.

48. Ibid., pp. 95–96; See also Cloughley, *A History of the Pakistan Army*, pp. 272, 277–279.

49. Ziring, *Pakistan*, pp. 175–76.

50. Ibid., pp. 180–82, 186, 196–97. On the Afghan War, see generally Steve Coll, *Ghost Wars: The Secret History of the CIA, Afghanistan, and Bin Laden, from the Soviet Invasion to September 10, 2001* (New York: Penguin Press, 2004).

51. See Ahmed, "Pakistan's Nuclear Weapons Program," pp. 184–85.

52. Ibid., p. 187.

53. Paul Wallace, "Political Violence and Terrorism in India: The Crisis of Identity," in Martha Crenshaw, ed., *Terrorism in Context* (University Park, PA: Pennsylvania State University Press, 1995), pp. 401–3; Ganguly, *Conflict Unending*, p. 85; Stephen Philip Cohen, *The Idea of Pakistan* (New Delhi: Oxford University Press, 2004), pp. 108–9; C. Christine Fair, *Urban Battlefields of South Asia: Lessons Learned from Sri Lanka, India, and Pakistan* (Santa Monica, CA: RAND, 2004), p. 81; K. P. S. Gill, "Endgame in Punjab: 1988–1993," *Faultlines*, 1 (1999), available at http://www.satp.org/satporgtp/publication/faultlines/volume1/Fault1-kpstext.htm. For an in-depth discussion of the Sikh insurgency, see Wallace, "Political Violence," in Crenshaw, ed., *Terrorism in Context*, pp. 352–409.

54. I offer a detailed discussion of the Brasstacks crisis later in this chapter.

55. Wallace, "Political Violence," in Crenshaw, ed., *Terrorism in Context*, p. 354.

56. Fair, *Urban Battlefields*, p. 81.

57. Cohen, *The Idea of Pakistan*, pp. 108–9.

58. Bajpai et al., *Brasstacks and Beyond*, pp. 127, 166.

59. For a detailed discussion of the Kargil operation, see Chapter 6.

60. Author discussion with C. Christine Fair. According to Fair, the basic differences between Pakistani involvement in the Sikh uprising and in the Kashmir insurgency were that Pakistani involvement in the Punjab was (1) of shorter duration and (2) of lower intensity.

61. Wallace, "Political Violence," in Crenshaw, ed., *Terrorism in Context*, p. 403.

62. Text of Simla Agreement, in Chari and Cheema, *The Simla Agreement 1972*, pp. 204–6.

63. Cohen, *India*, p. 219; Katherine Frank, *Indira: The Life of Indira Gandhi Nehru* (New York: Houghton Mifflin, 2002), pp. 346–47; Surjit Mansingh, *India's Search for Power: Indira Gandhi's Foreign Policy 1966–1982* (New Delhi: Sage Publications, 1984), p. 229.

64. P. N. Dhar, "Kashmir: The Simla Solution," *Times of India*, April 4, 1995, quoted in Chari and Cheema, *The Simla Agreement*, p. 57.

65. Chari and Cheema, *The Simla Agreement*, pp. 57–59.

66. Bhutto, *If I Am Assassinated*, p. 130. See also Wolpert, *Zulfi Bhutto*, p. 191.

67. Cohen, *India*, p. 219.

68. Cheema, "Current Relevance," in Chari and Cheema, *The Simla Agreement*, 144–46.

69. Ibid., pp. 146–47. See also Talbot, *Pakistan*, pp. 235–37.

70. Cohen, *India*, pp. 58–59.

71. Text of Karachi Agreement, available at http://safdic.southasiafoundation.org/saf/doc/india_pak/pak_04.htm.

72. For a detailed discussion of the Siachen issue, see Raghavan, *Siachen*.

73. Robert G. Wirsing, *India, Pakistan, and the Kashmir Dispute: On Regional Conflict and Its Resolution* (New York: St. Martin's Press, 1998), pp. 81–83. See also Tellis et al., *Limited Conflicts Under the Nuclear Umbrella*, p. 44.

74. India's seizure of Siachen is not reflected in the COW data set. I do not add it to the data because the Indian operation took unoccupied, undemarcated territory. In any case, adding one dispute month to the data set to reflect the Siachen operation would not significantly affect my quantitative findings.

75. Perkovich, *India's Nuclear Bomb*, pp. 6–7, 457–59.

76. Ganguly, "India's Pathway to Pokhran II," p. 173.

77. Scott D. Sagan, "Why Do States Build Nuclear Weapons?" pp. 65–69.

78. Baldev Raj Nayar and T. V. Paul, *India in the World Order: Searching for Major-Power Status* (Cambridge: Cambridge University Press, 2003), pp. 2–3; see also pp. 171–75.

79. Ziring, *Pakistan*, p. 133.

80. Note that the Brasstacks crisis did not have a direct nuclear element. It does appear that, during the standoff, Pakistani scientist A. Q. Khan told an Indian journalist that Pakistan was capable of assembling a nuclear weapon. However, the report of Khan's claim did not surface until after the Brasstacks episode was over. Thus, even if Khan's statement was accurate, it did not inject a nuclear factor into the crisis. See Hagerty, *The Consequences of Nuclear Proliferation*, pp. 102–3, 110–12.

81. Sagan, "For the Worse," in Sagan and Waltz, eds., *The Spread of Nuclear Weapons*, p. 94.

82. P. N. Hoon, *Unmasking Secrets of Turbulence* (New Delhi: Manas Publications, 2000), p. 102, quoted in Sagan, "For the Worse," in Sagan and Waltz, eds., *The Spread of Nuclear Weapons*, p. 94.

83. Sagan, "For the Worse," in Sagan and Waltz, eds., *The Spread of Nuclear Weapons*, p. 95.

84. Hagerty, *The Consequences of Nuclear Proliferation*, pp. 106–7.

85. Ibid., p. 107.

86. Ganguly, *Conflict Unending*, p. 85.

87. Ibid.

88. Kanti P. Bajpai, P. R. Chari, Pervaiz Iqbal Cheema, Stephen P. Cohen, and Šumit Ganguly, *Brasstacks and Beyond: Perception and Management of Crisis in South Asia* (New Delhi: Manohar, 1995), pp. 23–25, 27, 28, 37–38, 81.

89. Ibid., p. 41.

90. See Perkovich, *India's Nuclear Bomb*, p. 13.

91. The possibility remains that despite the preemptive nature of the contemplated Indian attack, the Brasstacks exercises were nonetheless part of a larger preventive strategy, engineered by Sundarji to provoke a conflict and destroy burgeoning Pakistani nuclear capabilities before they could become a serious threat. However, as noted, the evidence in support of a preventive-war interpretation is limited—particularly if we classify India's potential January 1987 attack as preemptive—and is outweighed by information suggesting that the Brasstacks crisis in fact resulted largely from a spiral of miscommunication and misperception.

CHAPTER 5. *The De Facto Nuclear Period*

1. As noted, Brasstacks, the most serious crisis of the nonnuclear period, reached only the level of "display of force." Also, the crisis resulted not from deliberate provocation by either party but rather from a spiral of Indo-Pakistani miscommunication and misperception.

2. This is not to argue that nuclear weapons were the only factor underlying Pakistani support for the Kashmir insurgency. As we will see, variables such as the Islamization of Pakistani society, the Afghan War, and Kashmiris' spiraling disaffection with Indian rule were also important determinants of Pakistani policy. Beyond these factors, however, nuclear proliferation played a critical permissive role in the formulation of Pakistani policy in Kashmir; Pakistani leaders believed that nuclear weapons' deterrent effects and potential to attract outside attention enabled them safely to pursue an aggressive approach in the region.

3. Bose, *Kashmir*, p. 51. Šumit Ganguly, "Explaining the Kashmir Insurgency: Political Mobilization and Institutional Decay," *International Security*, 21, no. 2 (1996), p. 80.

4. For detailed accounts of these events, see Prem Shankar Jha, *Kashmir 1947: Rival Versions of History* (Delhi: Oxford University Press, 1996); H. V. Hodson, *The Great Divide: Britain-India-Pakistan* (Karachi: Oxford University Press, 1985); Wirsing, *India, Pakistan, and the Kashmir Dispute*.

5. Bose, *Kashmir*, p. 41. For a concise discussion of the first Kashmir War, see Ganguly, *Conflict Unending*, pp. 15–30.

6. United Nations Security Council, S/726, April 21, 1948.

7. Bose, *Kashmir*, p. 40.

8. United Nations Security Council, S/726, April 21, 1948.

9. For opposing scholarly treatments of these issues, see Jha, *Kashmir 1947*; Lamb, *Kashmir: A Disputed Legacy*.

10. The Union List contains subjects that fall under the purview of the federal government, and the Concurrent List contains subjects over which the federal government shares jurisdiction with the states. See Bose, *Kashmir*, p. 273. Indian Constitution, Article 370, available at http://www.constitution.org/cons/india/p21370.html.

11. Bose, *Kashmir*, p. 59; Iffatt Malik, *Kashmir: Ethnic Conflict International Dispute* (Oxford: Oxford University Press, 2002), pp. 95–96.

12. Ganguly, "Explaining the Kashmir Insurgency," pp. 82–83.

13. The rioting was precipitated by the Hazbatral affair, in which a relic, believed to be a piece of the Prophet Muhammad's hair, was stolen from a mosque in Srinagar. See Malik, *Kashmir*, pp. 113–14, 121. The Pakistanis were also emboldened by what they perceived as a weak Indian response to Pakistan's limited probe at the Rann of Kutch earlier that year and a favorable international environment, characterized by improved relations with Russia and China and a close relationship with the United States. See Ganguly, *Conflict Unending*, pp. 40–43; Malik, *Kashmir*, p. 120.

14. Dixit, *India-Pakistan in War and Peace*, p. 146; Ganguly, *The Crisis in Kashmir*, p. 57; Malik, *Kashmir*, p. 122. Even after this abject failure of their plan's first phase, the Pakistanis proceeded with its second element, Operation Grand Slam, launching a conventional military invasion of Kashmir and setting off the 1965 Indo-Pakistani War.

15. The All Jammu and Kashmir National Conference was Kashmir's leading political party. Originally founded in 1932 under Sheikh Mohammed Abdullah, the Conference allied itself closely with the Indian National Congress and espoused a progressive agenda, including the implementation of land reform, universal adult franchise, and guaranteed civil liberties. Despite its ostensibly liberal roots, the Conference operated in a highly authoritarian manner, concentrating power in Abdullah and preventing the emergence of any political opposition in Kashmir. See Ganguly, *The Crisis in Kashmir*, pp. 27–29.

16. Ganguly, "Explaining the Kashmir Insurgency," p. 99. See also Malik, *Kashmir*, pp. 164, 167–68.

17. Text of Kashmir Accord, available at http://www.jammu-kashmir.com/documents/kashmiraccord.html.

18. Schofield, *Kashmir in Conflict*, p. 123. Sheikh Abdullah agreed to the Accord but claims to have done so in the hope that it would bolster Kashmiri autonomy and to have been disappointed to discover otherwise. "I agreed to co-operate with the Congress," he wrote, "but soon regretted my decision." Sheikh Mohammed Abdullah, *Flames of the Chinar* (New Delhi: Viking Press, 1993), p. 164, cited in Schofield, *Kashmir in Conflict*, p. 122. Malik suggests that Abdullah's agreement was part of a quid pro quo with the State Congress Party, which enabled Abdullah to be elected chief minister of Kashmir. See Malik, *Kashmir*, p. 144.

19. On these points, see Ganguly, *The Crisis in Kashmir*, pp. 65–73; Malik, *Kashmir*, pp. 143–45, 147, 170; Bose, *Kashmir*, pp. 97–101.

20. Sayeed's daughter was returned after the Indian government released five militants from custody.

21. On these points, see Ganguly, *The Crisis in Kashmir*, pp. 65–73; Wirsing, *India, Pakistan, and the Kashmir Dispute*, pp. 113–18; Schofield, *Kashmir in Conflict*, pp. 137, 138; Bose, *Kashmir*, pp. 107–35; Malik, *Kashmir*, pp. 158–60, 283.

22. Ganguly, "Explaining the Kashmir Insurgency," pp. 84–85.

23. Wirsing, *India, Pakistan, and the Kashmir Dispute*, p. 115.

24. Bose, *Kashmir*, p. 126; Author interview of E. N. Rammohan, former director-general of Indian Border Security Force (BSF), New Delhi, India, April 2004.

25. Wirsing, *India, Pakistan, and the Kashmir Dispute*, p. 121.

26. See John Lancaster and Kamran Khan, "Extremist Groups Renew Activity in Pakistan; Support of Kashmir Militants Is at Odds with War on Terrorism," *Washington Post*, February 8, 2003; Wirsing, *India, Pakistan, and the Kashmir Dispute*, p. 121.

27. See, e.g., Press Trust of India, "Musharraf Accuses Vajpayee of 'Brinksmanship,'" February 5, 2002; Agence France Presse, "Pakistan Willing to Adopt Every Means of Defusing Tension: FM," May 22, 2002.

28. Thus, as Wirsing argues, the infiltration of militants across the Line of Control into Indian Kashmir "has been *necessarily* a Pakistan-directed operation." See Wirsing, *India, Pakistan, and the Kashmir Dispute*, p. 121.

29. See Lancaster and Khan, "Extremist Groups Renew Activity in Pakistan"; Malik, *Kashmir*, pp. 295–98.

30. Wirsing, *India, Pakistan, and the Kashmir Dispute*, p. 134.

31. Malik, *Kashmir*, pp. 229, 300–301; K. Santhanam, Sreedhar, Sudhir Saxena, and Manish, *Jihadis in Jammu and Kashmir* (New Delhi: Sage Publications, 2003), pp. 23–25, 168. See also Paula R. Newberg, *Double Betrayal: Repression and Insurgency in Kashmir* (Washington, DC: Carnegie Endowment for International Peace, 1995), pp. 31–35.

32. Bose, *Kashmir*, p. 131. See also Malik, *Kashmir*, p. 299.

33. Bose, *Kashmir*, pp. 135–36.

34. Hagerty, *The Consequences of Nuclear Proliferation*, pp. 184, 191.

35. Waltz, "For Better," in Sagan and Waltz, eds., *The Spread of Nuclear Weapons*, p. 122.

36. I rely largely upon Indian Home Ministry and Army statistics in this section. Using these numbers is not without its problems; the methodology employed in compiling the figures is not clear, and the Indian government could have an incentive to misrepresent them. However, no other organization provides as much detailed information as the Indian government regarding the events in question. Also, the likely nature of Indian misrepresentation is not obvious. Would the Indians exaggerate the number of violent events in Kashmir to make the insurgency seem worse than it is and justify an extremely heavy-handed approach to defeating it? Or would the Indians be likely to undercount violent events to minimize the appearance of a serious ongoing conflict in Kashmir and to create the impression that Indian counterinsurgency efforts are effectively dealing with rebellion? The answer is not evident. Thus, in the absence of better sources and a clear Indian government bias, I use the Home Ministry and Army numbers. Where possible, I have checked official figures against those available from independent organizations and noted any discrepancies between them.

37. Government of India, Ministry Home Affairs, cited in Wirsing, *India, Pakistan, and the Kashmir Dispute*, p. 138.

38. Government of India, Ministry of Home Affairs, *Annual Report 2003–2004*, p. 12. The independent South Asia Terrorism Portal (SATP) estimates the number of civilian deaths during this time period as 3,328. See http://www.satp.org/satporgtp/countries/india/states/jandk/data_sheets/annual_casualties.htm.

39. Indian Army civilian casualty statistics available at http://www.armyinkashmir.org/v2/human_rights/cc_actual_data.shtml.

40. Government of India, Ministry of Home Affairs, cited in Wirsing, *India, Pakistan, and the Kashmir Dispute*, p. 128.

41. Government of India, Ministry of Home Affairs, *Annual Report 2003–2004*, p. 12. SATP puts the number of terrorist incidents during 1990 and 1993 at 3,905 and 4,457, respectively. See http://www.satp.org/satporgtp/countries/india/states/jandk/data_sheets/annual_casualties.htm.

42. Wirsing, *India, Pakistan, and the Kashmir Dispute*, pp. 143–46. Not all of these deployments resulted from the insurgency. Some of these forces would have been stationed in Kashmir even in the absence of rebellion.

43. See Bose, *Kashmir*, pp. 119–24; Malik, *Kashmir*, pp. 290–92, 318–21.

44. Human Rights Watch, *India's Secret Army in Kashmir: New Patterns of Abuse Emerge in the Conflict*, 8, no. 4 (1996). See also Wirsing, *India, Pakistan, and the Kashmir Dispute*, pp. 154–62; Schofield, *Kashmir in Conflict*, pp. 168–72; Ganguly, *The Crisis in Kashmir*, p. 3; Malik, *Kashmir*, pp. 287–88, 307–13.

45. See Schofield, *Kashmir in Conflict*, p. 169; Newberg, *Double Betrayal*, pp. 2–4, 25–30; author interview of former Director-General of BSF, E. N. Rammohan, April 2004.

46. In the 1948 Kashmir War, 1,000 Indians died; 3,261 Indians died in the 1965 war, and 8,000 in the Bangladesh War. See Correlates of War Project, Interstate War Data.

47. *Newsline*, May 1990, p. 17, quoted in Schofield, *Kashmir in Conflict*, p. 149.

48. Author interview of Benazir Bhutto, August 2004.

49. Ibid. See also Ahmed Rashid, *Taliban: Militant Islam, Oil, and Fundamentalism in Central Asia* (New Haven, CT: Yale University Press, 2000), pp. 137, 186.

50. Author interview of Benazir Bhutto, August 2004.

51. Schofield, *Kashmir in Conflict*, p. 142. See also "Op Topac," a semifictional account of Pakistan's low-intensity strategy in Kashmir, in *Indian Defence Review* (July 1989), pp. 35–48. "Op Topac" began as an Indian Army study focused primarily on operational security issues but evolved into a speculative analysis of Pakistani involvement with the Kashmir insurgency. Author interview of Major General (retired) Afsir Karim, author of "Op Topac," Noida, India, March 2004.

52. Author interview of Benazir Bhutto, August 2004. Note that Indian leaders dispute the notion that an Indo-Pakistani nuclear exchange would result in mutual suicide. They argue that, given India's large population and physical size, a Pakistani nuclear attack would be damaging but would fail to destroy India as a functioning society. An Indian nuclear attack on far smaller Pakistan, however, would result in the annihilation of that country. On these points, see Chapter 6. Both India and Pakistan maintain relatively small arsenals; Pakistan is believed to possess approximately twenty-four to forty-eight nuclear weapons, whereas India is believed to possess approximately thirty to fifty-five. See Robert S. Norris, Hans M. Kristensen, and Joshua Handler, "NRDC: Nuclear Notebook, Pakistan's Nuclear Forces, 2001," *Bulletin of the Atomic Scientists*, 58, no. 1 (2002), pp. 70–71; Robert S. Norris, William Arkin, Hans M. Kristensen, and Joshua Handler, "NRDC: Nuclear Notebook, India's Nuclear Forces, 2002," *Bulletin of the Atomic Scientists*, 58, no. 2 (2002), pp. 70–72.

53. "The Rediff Interview/Benazir Bhutto," March 12, 2004, available at http://www.rediff.com/news/2004/mar/12inter.htm.

54. Ethnic divisions pose one of the most serious challenges to the Pakistani state, especially in the restive province of Sindh. See generally Veena Kukreja, *Contemporary Pakistan: Political Processes, Conflicts and Crises* (New Delhi: Sage Publications, 2003), pp. 112–53; Jones, *Pakistan*, pp. 109–45. The Pakistanis have often accused India of encouraging ethnic tensions in Sindh. See Hagerty, *The Consequences of Nuclear Proliferation in South Asia*, pp. 93–94. However, there is no evidence that Indian interference in the region has been anywhere near the level of Pakistani involvement in Kashmir.

55. Author interview of Benazir Bhutto, August 2004.

56. Ibid. On this point, see also Samina Ahmed, arguing that as Pakistan attained de facto nuclear status under the Zia regime, it began to employ "nuclear diplomacy" in its "strategy of undermining Indian security through a proxy war in Indian-administered Kashmir" and by 1990 was "implicitly threatening to use nuclear weapons if India intervened militarily

across the Line of Control"; Ganguly, maintaining that nuclear proliferation was one of the "compelling reasons" that "emboldened the Pakistani military to aid the insurgency in Kashmir despite the possibility of Indian military escalation." "[T]hey believed that their incipient nuclear capabilities had effectively neutralized whatever conventional military advantages India possessed"; and Pervez Hoodbhoy, arguing that Pakistani leaders' confidence that Pakistan's nuclear weapons shielded it from Indian retaliation encouraged its policy of supporting the Kashmir insurgency and underlay the 1990 militarized Indo-Pakistani crisis over Kashmir. Samina Ahmed, "Pakistan's Nuclear Weapons Program," *International Security*, 32, no. 4 (1999), pp. 189–90; Ganguly, *Crisis Unending*, p. 92; Pervez Hoodbhoy, "Pakistan's Nuclear Future," in Ahmed and Cortright, eds., *Pakistan and the Bomb*, p. 71.

57. Author interview of Benazir Bhutto, August 2004. Shireen Mazari lays out the logic of Pakistan's strategy even more bluntly: "With nuclear deterrence making an all-out war between Pakistan and India a receding reality, the opportunity for limited warfare in Kashmir becomes a viable option. At the very least, more material assistance can be given to the Kashmiri freedom fighters while Pakistan waits for the Indians to eventually come to the table for talks on Kashmir . . . [T]he freedom fighters do not have to defeat India militarily. As long as the Indian military cannot put down the struggle, they are the losers." Shireen Mazari, "Kashmir: Looking for Viable Options," *Defence Journal*, 3, no. 2 (1999), available at http://defencejournal.com/feb-mar99/kashmir-viable.htm. A retired senior Indian diplomat recalls that the Pakistanis openly communicated this message in meetings with their Indian counterparts. "You can't keep up a low-intensity conflict in Kashmir indefinitely," Pakistani officials told former Indian High Commissioner to Pakistan G. Parthasarathy, "and you won't escalate against us for fear of nuclear weapons." Author interview of former Indian High Commissioner to Pakistan G. Parthasarathy, New Delhi, India, August 2004. See also Samina Ahmed, "Pakistan's Nuclear Weapons Program," p. 6; Pervez Hoodbhoy, "Pakistan's Nuclear Future," in Ahmed and Cortright, eds., *Pakistan and the Bomb*, p. 71; Ganguly, *Crisis Unending*, p. 92; Raghavan, "Limited War and Nuclear Escalation in South Asia," p. 4.

58. As one U.S. congressional study put it, the Pakistani nuclear capacity served not as "merely a trip-wire of last resort in the event of a major invasion of Pakistan. Instead, nuclear weapons now became a key to Islamabad's assertive strategy in Kashmir under a nuclear umbrella." Report of the Task Force on Terrorism and Unconventional Warfare, House Republican Research Committee, House of Representatives, Washington, DC, August 24, 1994.

59. See P. R. Chari, Pervaiz Iqbal Cheema, and Stephen Philip Cohen, *Perception, Politics and Security in South Asia: The Compound Crisis of 1990* (London: RoutledgeCurzon, 2003), pp. 2–4.

60. Ibid., p. 138.

61. This summary draws upon detailed accounts of the 1990 crisis in Hagerty, *The Consequences of Nuclear Proliferation*, and Chari, Cheema, and Cohen, *Perception, Politics and Security in South Asia*.

62. Mark Fineman, "Attacks Spark War Fears Between India, Pakistan," *Toronto Star*, 15 April 1990, p. A24.

63. See Hagerty, *The Consequences of Nuclear Proliferation*, pp. 147–48.

64. See Ibid., pp. 150–52; Chari, Cheema, and Cohen, *Perception, Politics, and Security in South Asia*, pp. 104–14.

65. Chari, Cheema, and Cohen, *Perception, Politics, and Security in South Asia*, p. 111.

66. Ganguly, *Conflict Unending*, p. 94.

67. Hagerty, *The Consequences of Nuclear Proliferation*, p. 166.

68. Alexander L. George and Richard Smoke, *Deterrence in American Foreign Policy: Theory and Practice* (New York: Columbia University Press, 1974), pp. 59, 62. See also Elli Lieberman, "The Rational Deterrence Theory Debate: Is the Dependent Variable Elusive?" *Security Studies*, 3, no. 3 (1994), pp. 384–427.

69. Hagerty acknowledges this point. See Hagerty, *The Consequences of Nuclear Proliferation*, p. 166.

70. Ibid., pp. 164, 166, 163.

71. Thus, as Chari, Cheema, and Cohen put it, "while remaining concerned with the possibility of a nuclear dimension intruding, neither side appears to have believed at that juncture there was a serious likelihood of this occurring." Chari, Cheema, and Cohen, *Perception, Politics, and Security in South Asia*, p. 139.

72. Author correspondence with former Indian Foreign Secretary S. K. Singh, January 2005.

73. See Chapter 6. It is also worth noting that Pakistani leaders such as Benazir Bhutto, who would have an incentive to argue that Pakistan's nuclear capacity had deterred an Indian attack in 1990, make no such claim. On this point, see below.

74. Hagerty, *The Consequences of Nuclear Proliferation*, pp. 148–49.

75. Author interview of retired Indian general, New Delhi, India, August 2004.

76. Author interview of former Indian Army Chief of Staff Satish Nambiar, New Delhi, India, August 2004.

77. Chari, Cheema, and Cohen, *Perception, Politics, and Security in South Asia*, pp. 90–91.

78. Author correspondence with S. K. Singh, January 2005.

79. Author interview of Benazir Bhutto, August 2004.

80. Chari, Cheema, and Cohen, *Perception, Politics, and Security in South Asia*, p. 8. See also George Perkovich, arguing that "There is no evidence to date . . . that leaders wanted anything but to avoid a war." Perkovich, *India's Nuclear Bomb: The Impact on Global Proliferation* (Berkeley and Los Angeles: University of California Press, 1999), p. 311.

CHAPTER 6.   *The Overt Nuclear Period*

1. The Pakistan government still officially maintains that its forces did not initiate the Kargil conflict. Thus, Pakistani leaders have not publicly explained the Kargil operation's planning process or their decision to undertake the incursions. Pakistani President Pervez Musharraf has admitted that Pakistan Army forces participated in the conflict but claimed that they became involved only after the fighting was already underway. "Kargil was a decision taken by the mujahideen," he said, "and we got involved because of the action by Indian troops." "Troops Were in Kargil, General Doesn't Rule Out Repeat," *Indian Express*, June 14, 2003. Any discussion of the Pakistani decision to launch Kargil must therefore rely to some extent on conjecture. The following points are based on my analysis of Pakistani, Indian, and foreign sources on this issue as well as my own interviews of Pakistani and Indian scholars, analysts, and government officials.

2. Author interview of Benazir Bhutto, August 2004. Other Pakistani leaders who reportedly were presented with and rejected plans for Kargil-like incursions include Foreign Minister Sahibzada Yakub Khan and Chief of Army Staff (COAS) General Jehangir

Karamat. According to Altaf Gauhar, General Zia ul-Haq personally authorized the preparation of a plan for incursions at Kargil in 1987 but was dissuaded from executing the
plan by Sahibzada Yaqub Khan. There has been some speculation that Karamat's later
rejection of the plan played a role in his replacement as COAS in 1998. Karamat, for his
part, denies ever having been briefed on the Kargil operation. Altaf Gauhar, "Four Wars,
One Assumption," *Nation*, September 5, 1999; Y. M. Bammi, *Kargil 1999: The Impregnable Conquered* (India: Gorkha Publishers, 2002), pp. 470–80; Robert Wirsing, *Kashmir
in the Shadow of War: Regional Rivalries in a Nuclear Age* (Armonk, NY: M. E. Sharpe,
2003), p. 42; author interview of Ejaz Haider, news editor, *Friday Times*, Lahore, Pakistan,
April 2004; Kargil Review Committee, *From Surprise to Reckoning*, p. 91; Pravin Sawhney,
The Defence Makeover: 10 Myths That Shape India's Image (New Delhi: Sage Publications,
2002), p. 307.

3. Author interview of Benazir Bhutto, August 2004.

4. Ibid.

5. This group consisted of 10 Corps Commander Lieutenant General Mahmud Ahmed,
Chief of General Staff Lieutenant General Mohammed Aziz, and General Officer Com-
manding Frontier Constabulary of the Northern Areas Major General Javed Hassan.

6. Shaukat Qadir, "An Analysis of the Kargil Conflict 1999," *Royal United Service Institution Journal* (April 2003), pp. 25–26. Note that Qadir did not participate in the Kargil
operation's planning or execution. Rather, his analysis is based on his "considerable knowledge of the course of events (pieced together from private discussions with friends and
colleagues in positions of authority, who played a role)" as well as his "(not inconsiderable)
personal knowledge of: the terrain around Kargil; the character of the principal actors in
the Pakistan army; the decision making process in the Pakistan army . . . ; and the collective
character of the Pakistan army." Ibid., 24.

7. Kargil Review Committee, *From Surprise to Reckoning*, pp. 91–95.

8. Jones, *Pakistan*, pp. 101–2.

9. An NLI soldier who died prior to mid-October 1998 was later honored by the
Pakistan government for his service in the Kargil campaign. Thus, the operation appears to
have begun as early as autumn 1998. See Ibid., p. 92. See also Brian Cloughley, *A History
of the Pakistan Army: Wars and Insurrections* (Karachi: Oxford University Press, 2000), p. 376.

10. See Rafaqat Ali, "Hundreds of Soldiers Fell in Kargil: Army Kept Government in
Dark: Nawaz," *Dawn*, June 13, 2000. "Nawaz Vows to Expose Kargil 'Debacle,'" *Dawn*,
June 14, 2000.

11. Jones, *Pakistan*, p. 101.

12. Bruce Riedel, "American Diplomacy and the 1999 Kargil Summit at Blair House,"
Center for Advanced Study of India, University of Pennsylvania (2002) p. 11. Riedel was
special assistant to the president and senior director for Near East and South Asia affairs at
the National Security Council during the Kargil conflict.

13. Author interview of former Pakistani Prime Minister Mohammed Nawaz Sharif,
London, United Kingdom, June 2006.

14. See "Q&A: Tense Words, Tough Talk; Pakistan's Gen. Pervez Musharraf," *Wash-
ington Post*, March 12, 2000; A. Rashid, "Responsibility for Kargil," *Dawn*, July 22, 2000;
"Kargil and Nawaz," *Dawn*, June 14, 2000; Mirza Aslam Beg, "Kargil Withdrawal and
'Rogue Army' Image," *Defence Journal*, 3, no. 8 (1999), pp. 8–11; Shireen M. Mazari,
"Re-examining Kargil," *Defence Journal*, 3, no. 11 (2000), pp. 44–46; "Who Really Runs
Pakistan?" *Economist*, June 26, 1999.

15. Author interview of Benazir Bhutto, August 2004.

16. See Kargil Review Committee, *From Surprise to Reckoning*, p. 95.

17. Jones, *Pakistan*, p. 103.

18. Author interview of Mohammed Nawaz Sharif, June 2006. According to Sharif, the officers involved were Lieutenant Generals Mahmood Ahmed and Mohammed Aziz and Major General Javed Hassan.

19. I do not purport to give a complete account of the Kargil conflict here. For detailed histories, see Kargil Review Committee, *From Surprise to Reckoning*; Amarinder Singh, *A Ridge Too Far: War in the Kargil Heights 1999* (New Delhi: Motibagh Palace Patiala, 2001); Bammi, *Kargil*; Ashok Krishna, "The Kargil War," in Ashok Krishna and P. R. Chari, eds., *Kargil: The Tables Turned* (New Delhi: Manohar Publishers, 2001), pp. 77–138.

20. Qadir, "An Analysis of the Kargil Conflict 1999," p. 26.

21. The composition of the Pakistani force has been the subject of some disagreement. Indian intelligence estimates ranged from a force of virtually all regular army personnel, to a regular/irregular ratio of 60:40, to a ratio of 70:30. The Kargil Review Committee report argues that the "regular/irregular ratio may well have been in the range of 70:30, if the overall numbers are taken into account." See Kargil Review Committee, *From Surprise to Reckoning*, p. 97. Note that other analysts have classified Pakistan's Northern Light Infantry as a "paramilitary" rather than a "regular" force. See, e.g., International Institute for Strategic Studies, *The Military Balance 2002–2003* (Oxford: Oxford University Press, 2002), pp. 134–35. See also Cloughley, *A History of the Pakistan Army*, p. 376.

22. The Kargil sector, which extends 168 kilometers along the Line of Control from Kaobal Gali to Chorbat La, is "extremely inhospitable." "It is characterised by forbiddingly precipitous mountains," whose peaks average 5,000 meters in height, "extreme cold, glaciated valleys and the absence of roads and tracks." The area is snowbound from November to April or May. "Therefore, local conditions impose severe limitations on the conduct of any sustained large size operations." Kargil Review Committee, *From Surprise to Reckoning*, p. 83. In fact, due to the harshness of the terrain and climate, Indian forces habitually did not occupy the sector's defensive positions year-round, abandoning many of them in the winter and reoccupying them in the spring. "[I]t was felt that the terrain . . . of the area would be a natural preventive factor against any extensive Pakistani military intrusion" during winter. However, "Pakistani forces took advantage of this situation," infiltrating the area in early spring 1999 before the Indians had reoccupied their positions. J. N. Dixit, "A Defining Moment," in Sankarshan Thakur, ed., *Guns and Yellow Roses: Essays on the Kargil War* (New Delhi: HarperCollins, 1999), p. 188. For details of India's winter posture in the region, see Kargil Review Committee, *From Surprise to Reckoning*, pp. 84–85.

23. In February 1999, Prime Ministers Vajpayee and Sharif had presided over the commencement of a bus service between the Indian city of Amritsar and the Pakistani city of Lahore. This "bus diplomacy" had culminated in an agreement signed at Lahore affirming several earlier agreements and calling for both countries to take steps to reduce the likelihood of accidental or unauthorized use of nuclear weapons as well as for the development of nuclear and conventional confidence-building measures. According to Ganguly, many in the Indian government believed that this "Lahore Process" signaled a major turning point in Indo-Pakistani relations. "As a consequence, the routine gathering of intelligence on [Pakistan] . . . was slackened. Moreover, many senior officials became . . . unwilling to

countenance the prospect of Pakistani malfeasance in Jammu and Kashmir." See Ganguly, *Conflict Unending*, pp. 115, 123. On bus-diplomacy "euphoria," see also Moti Dar, "Blundering Through," in Thakur, ed., *Guns and Yellow Roses*, pp. 171–72.

24. For a discussion of Indian surprise at the Kargil incursions, see Kargil Review Committee, *From Surprise to Reckoning*, pp. 146–60.

25. Gurmeet Kanwal, "Pakistan's Military Defeat," in Jasjit Singh, ed., *Kargil 1999: Pakistan's Fourth War for Kashmir* (New Delhi: Institute for Defence Analysis, 1999), p. 153.

26. For a discussion of Indian Air Force operations during the Kargil conflict, see D. N. Ganesh, "Indian Air Force in Action," in Ibid.

27. See Singh, "Pakistan's Military Defeat," in Ibid., p. 154.

28. For a critique of this subordination of military logic to larger political goals, see Dar, "Blundering Through," in Thakur, ed., *Guns and Yellow Roses*, pp. 173–77.

29. Ganguly, *Conflict Unending*, p. 120; D. Subha Chandran, "Role of the United States: Mediator or Mere Facilitator?" in Krishna and Chari, eds., *Kargil*, pp. 213–14.

30. See Tellis et al., *War Under the Nuclear Umbrella*, pp. 38–39; Shireen M. Mazari, "Kargil: Misguided Perceptions," *Pakistan Institute for Air Defence Studies Home Page* (2003), available at http://www.piads.com.pk/users/piads/mazari1.html.

31. The Pakistanis maintained that intruding forces were indigenous Kashmiri militants and not members of the Pakistan Army. Riedel, "American Diplomacy and the 1999 Kargil Summit at Blair House," p. 3; Zahid Hussain, "On the Brink," *Newsline*, June 1999.

32. See Ganguly, *Conflict Unending*, pp. 118–19; Hussain, "On the Brink."

33. Author interview of Mohammed Nawaz Sharif, June 2006.

34. Ibid. Sharif claimed that the Pakistan military did not attempt to prevent him from traveling to Washington because "Musharraf was keen that I resolve the matter." "And then," he continued, "they rewarded me by staging a coup against me." Ibid.

35. Riedel, "American Diplomacy and the 1999 Kargil Summit at Blair House," pp. 10–13.

36. Ibid.

37. In his address, Sharif referred to "mojahedin" rather than regular Pakistani forces, thus maintaining the official position that the Pakistan Army was not involved in the Kargil incursions. See "Excerpts from Pakistani Prime Minister Mohammad Nawaz Sharif's Address to Nation Broadcast on National TV," *World Media Watch*, July 12, 1999; Ganguly, *Conflict Unending*, p. 120.

38. Singh, *A Ridge Too Far*, pp. 101–3. For other estimates putting the number of battle deaths over 1,000, see Bose, "Kashmir," p. 150; K. Alan Kronstadt, "Nuclear Weapons and Ballistic Missile Proliferation in India and Pakistan: Issues for Congress," Congressional Research Service, Report RL30623, July 31, 2000, p. 5; Ghosn and Palmer, "Associated Document for the Militarized International Dispute Data, Version 3.0," p. 3. Nawaz Sharif claimed that Pakistan alone lost more than 4,000 soldiers at Kargil. See "Over 4,000 Pakistanis Killed During Kargil Conflict: Nawaz Sharif," *Press Trust of India*, August 16, 2003. Benazir Bhutto claims that approximately 3,000 Pakistani personnel were killed at Kargil. According to Bhutto, most perished following Nawaz Sharif's call for withdrawal, falling victim to hunger, thirst, exposure, and Indian artillery barrages as the Pakistanis attempted a disorderly retreat from the mountain peaks. Bhutto claims that the Pakistan government covered up the large number of losses, secretly storing the bodies and releasing them to their villages in small numbers, to avoid media scrutiny and a public outcry. Author interview of Benazir Bhutto, August 2004.

39. "Excerpts from Pakistani Prime Minister Mohammad Nawaz Sharif's Address to Nation Broadcast on National TV." See also Kargil Review Committee, *From Surprise to Reckoning*, p. 89; D. Suba Chandran, "Why Kargil? Pakistan's Objective and Motivation," in Krishna and Chari, eds., *Kargil*, pp. 23–38; Tellis et al., *Limited Conflicts Under the Nuclear Umbrella*, p. 38; Beg, "Kargil Withdrawal and 'Rogue Army' Image"; Husain, "Kargil: The Morning After," *Dawn*, April 29, 2000; Rashid, "Responsibility for Kargil"; Hussain, "On the Brink," p. 30. As noted, the use of war to internationalize ongoing disputes has long been a characteristic of Pakistani strategic behavior. While the Pakistan government has consistently sought to attract international mediation of the Kashmir conflict, Indian leaders have rejected any third-party involvement, maintaining that the two countries must resolve their disagreements on a purely bilateral basis. See Cohen, *India*, p. 219; Jones, *Pakistan*, pp. 80, 107.

40. Author interview of President Pervez Musharraf, Rawalpindi, Pakistan, April 2004.

41. Ibid.

42. Author interview of Pakistan Ministry of Foreign Affairs Director General for South Asia, Jalil Jilani, Islamabad, Pakistan, April 2004. See also Kargil Review Committee, *From Surprise to Reckoning*, p. 89; Singh, "The Fourth War," in Singh, ed., pp. 123, 132–33; author interviews with retired senior Indian Army officers, New Delhi, May 2002; Mazari, "Re-examining Kargil." Other Pakistani goals at Kargil probably included undermining the legitimacy of the Line of Control and bolstering the anti-Indian insurgency in Kashmir, which in recent years had been flagging. See Kargil Review Committee, *From Surprise to Reckoning*, pp. 89–90; Dixit, "A Defining Moment," in Thakur, ed., *Guns and Yellow Roses*, pp. 188–91; Lodi, "Kargil: Its Aftermath," *Defence Journal*, 3, no. 6 (1999), pp. 7–8; Nasim Zehra, "Anatomy of Islamabad's Kargil Policy," *Defence Journal*, 3, no. 7 (1999), pp. 2–4; Ganguly, *Conflict Unending*, pp. 121–22; Dixit, "A Defining Moment," in Thakur, ed., *Guns and Yellow Roses*, p. 189; Tellis et al., *Limited Conflicts Under the Nuclear Umbrella*, p. 38; Husain, "Kargil: The Morning After"; Ayaz Amir, "What Is the Political Leadership Up To?" *Dawn*, July 2, 1999; Hussain, "On the Brink," p. 24; Qadir, "An Analysis of the Kargil Conflict 1999," p. 3.

43. M. S. Qazi, "High Temperatures at High Mountains," *Pakistan Institute for Air Defence Studies Home Page*, available at http://www.piads.com.pk/users/piads/qazi1.html. See also Lodi, "India's Kargil Operations: An Analysis," *Defence Journal*, 3, no. 10 (1999), pp. 2–3; Mazari, "Re-examining Kargil," p. 1.

44. Javed Nasir, "Calling the Indian Army Chief's Bluff," *Defence Journal*, 3, no. 2 (1999), p. 25 (capitalization in original). See also Kargil Review Committee, *From Surprise to Reckoning*, p. 91; Beg, "Kargil Withdrawal and 'Rogue' Army Image"; Ayaz Ahmed Khan, "Indian Offensive in the Kargil Sector," *Defence Journal*, 3, no. 5 (1999), pp. 7–8; Qadir, "An Analysis of the Kargil Conflict 1999," pp. 2–3. Author interviews of retired senior Indian Army officers, New Delhi, May 2002.

45. Kargil Review Committee, *From Surprise to Reckoning*, p. 90; Ganguly, *Conflict Unending*, p. 122; Tellis et al., *Limited Conflicts*, p. 38; Mazari, "Kargil: Misguided Perceptions"; Zehra, "Anatomy of Islamabad's Kargil Policy"; Beg, "Deterrence, Defence, and Development," *Defence Journal*, 3, no. 6 (1999), pp. 4–6. As several analysts have noted, Pakistani leaders' expectation of international support was based on scant evidence. According to Ganguly, in launching Kargil, "the Pakistani leadership simply assumed that the United States and other major states would step in to prevent an escalation of the crisis . . . [F]alse

optimism was at work—there is little or no evidence that the leadership had any tangible basis for their belief in international support." Ganguly, *Conflict Unending*, p. 122. As Tellis et al. put it, "Pakistan made unrealistic assumptions about the range of possible outcomes. Fundamentally, Pakistan did not anticipate the intolerance that the international community . . . would demonstrate for its attempts to alter the status quo even if the community was otherwise sympathetic to its dilemmas in the face of India's nuclear tests." Tellis et al., *Limited Conflicts*, pp. 38–39. Ejaz Haider maintains that Pakistani leaders' unfounded optimism extended beyond Kargil to the larger Indo-Pakistani conflict over Kashmir. According to Haider, the Pakistanis believed not only that the international community would seek to mediate Kargil but that (1) international involvement in Kargil would likely lead to outside pressure to settle the Kashmir dispute and (2) the international community would press for a solution of Kashmir according to United Nations resolutions calling for a plebiscite in the territory. Haider argues that the Pakistani leadership had no empirical or logical basis for their beliefs. They were based simply on faith that the international community would see the justice of the Pakistani position on Kashmir. Author interview of Ejaz Haider, April 2004.

46. Aga Shahi, Zulfikar Ali Khan, and Abdul Sattar, "Securing Nuclear Peace," *News International*, October 5, 1999, in *Strategic Digest*, 30, no. 1 (2000), p. 16. According to the authors, these occasions were in the mid-1980s, when India was contemplating an attack on Pakistani nuclear facilities at Kahuta, during the crisis precipitated by India's "Brasstacks" war games in 1986–1987, and during the 1990 militarized Indo-Pakistani dispute over Kashmir. Shahi and Sattar were former Pakistani foreign ministers, and Khan a former Air Chief Marshal.

47. Author interview of Jalil Jilani, Islamabad, Pakistan, April 2004.

48. As Ganguly puts it, the Pakistanis had developed a "sense of false optimism. Pakistani decision-makers had convinced themselves that their achievement of rough nuclear parity with India now enabled them to probe along the LoC with impunity. In their view, the Indian leadership . . . would decline to use overwhelming force and would also avoid a dramatic escalation or expansion of the conflict." Ganguly, *Conflict Unending*, p. 122. According to Samina Ahmed, "During the course of the Kargil episode . . . Pakistan's authoritative decisionmakers had decided to conduct a large-scale military operation across the LoC in the belief that the presence of nuclear weapons would prevent conventional war with India." Samina Ahmed, "Pakistan's Nuclear Weapons: Moving Forward or Tactical Retreat?" Joan B. Kroc Institute for International Peace Studies, February 2000, p. 18. See also Ahmed, "Security Dilemmas of Nuclear-Armed Pakistan," p. 788. Zahid Hussain reports that Pakistani leaders believed that "the induction of nuclear weapons has totally changed" the security situation in South Asia. As one senior official said, "The Indians cannot afford to extend the war to other areas in Kashmir, leave aside launching an attack across international boundaries," in large part because of the "risk of nuclear conflagration." Hussain, "On the Brink," pp. 24–25. See also V. R. Raghavan, "Limited War," pp. 1–18.

49. "Excerpts from Pakistani Prime Minister Mohammad Nawaz Sharif's Address to Nation Broadcast on National TV." See also A. Rashid, arguing that because of Kargil, "The explosive nature of the Kashmir problem has been highlighted in an unprecedented manner. In fact, during the entire Kargil operation, the whole world remained on tenterhooks owing to fear of a nuclear exchange between the two upstart atomic powers." Rashid, "Responsibility for Kargil."

50. Author interview of Mohammed Nawaz Sharif, June 2006.

51. Tellis et al., *Limited Conflicts*, p. 48. See also P. R. Chari, arguing that "the tit-for-tat nuclear tests conducted by India and Pakistan in May 1998 probably succeeded in making the Kargil conflict possible . . . The availability of the nuclear deterrent to Pakistan encouraged its undertaking the Kargil intrusions . . . " Chari, "Nuclear Restraint," in Krepon and Gagné, eds., *The Stability–Instability Paradox*, p. 21.

52. *Indian Express*, "Troops Were in Kargil." See also Tellis et al., arguing that in the view of Pakistani elites, Kargil reinforced the notion that "Pakistan's nuclear capabilities have become the key to . . . its political strategies at multiple levels. Nuclear weapons not only enable Islamabad to pursue 'strategic diversion' and immunize the country from a violent Indian counter-response, they also serve to catalyze the attention . . . of the international community. Consequently, they have acquired centrality in Pakistan's national strategy." Tellis et al., *Limited Conflicts*, pp. 30, 49.

53. In the immediate aftermath of the Indian nuclear tests, some Indian leaders did engage in bellicose rhetoric. For example, Home Minister L. K. Advani announced that India's acquisition of an overt nuclear capacity had resulted in a "change in the geostrategic situation in the region and world" and "brought about a qualitatively new stage in Indo-Pakistan relations." Advani suggested that Indian forces might now engage in "hot pursuit" of militants across the Line of Control into Pakistani Kashmir. See Steve Coll, "South Asian Nightmare," *Washington Post*, May 22, 1998, p. A25; John F. Burns, "Nuclear Anxiety: The Overview; Leaders in India and Pakistan Tone Down Crisis," *New York Times*, May 30, 1998, p. A1. It is difficult to know whether Advani actually believed his own statements or whether he was simply attempting to score domestic political points in the heady posttest atmosphere. In private conversations, some Indian officials have argued that Advani's statements were part of an Indian strategy of goading the Pakistanis into conducting their own nuclear tests, which would trigger an avalanche of international opprobrium and sanctions against Pakistan, resulting in serious damage to the weak Pakistani economy. In any case, Advani's rhetoric did not translate into aggressive Indian military behavior in the wake of the nuclear tests.

54. Mazari, "Kashmir: Looking for Viable Options," *Defence Journal*, 3, no. 2 (1999), p. 64; Mazari, "Low-Intensity Conflicts: The New War in South Asia," *Defence Journal*, 3, no. 6 (1999), p. 41.

55. The Kargil Committee Report downplays the notion that overt nuclearization contributed to Pakistan's sense of invulnerability and appetite for adventurism beyond what its de facto nuclear capability had already given it. See Kargil Review Committee, *From Surprise to Reckoning*, pp. 183–213. However, as Cohen argues, this view "reflects a profound misunderstanding of Pakistani strategic thinking, which was not that dissimilar from that of . . . military experts anywhere in the world: there is an important difference (at least in the minds of the Pakistanis) between a theoretical nuclear capability and a proven capability," with a proven capability far more likely to create a sense of invulnerability and to encourage aggressive behavior than a merely theoretical one. See Cohen, *India*, p. 186.

56. Nawaz Sharif, "Statement of Nawaz Sharif in ATC-1," *Dawn*, March 9, 2000.

57. Author interview of Jalil Jilani, Islamabad, Pakistan, April 2004.

58. Author interview of former Indian Army Chief of Staff, V. P. Malik, New Delhi, India, April 2004. As numerous analysts have pointed out, India was highly successful in its battle for international opinion, and this proved to be one of its major accomplishments

during the Kargil conflict. See, e.g., Lodhi, "Anatomy of a Debacle"; Tellis et al., *War Under the Nuclear Umbrella*, pp. 21–28; Husain, "Kargil: The Morning After."

59. Author interview of former Indian High Commissioner to Pakistan G. Parthasarathy, August 2004.

60. Author interview of former Indian National Security Advisor Brajesh Mishra, New Delhi, India, June 2006.

61. Author interview of Brajesh Mishra, New Delhi, India, May 2005.

62. Author interview of V. P. Malik, April 2004.

63. Ibid. Note that while Malik's account could be seen as self-serving, it would be just as beneficial to the Indian position for Malik to argue that the Indian government had never actually considered horizontal escalation at Kargil. Doing so would undercut the claim that India had been deterred by Pakistani nuclear weapons and would also reinforce the reputation for restraint that India clearly prizes. Also, Malik's argument that Pakistani nuclear deterrence did not play a critical role at Kargil rests in large part on his claim of Indian conventional weakness and miscalculation at the outset of the crisis; as noted, Malik maintains that one important reason for Indian restraint at Kargil was the Indian military's initial failure to recognize and respond to the Pakistani incursions. This is not a flattering admission for an army chief to make, and Malik would seem to be unlikely to have done so if it were not in fact true. Below, former Defense Minister George Fernandes makes an argument similar to Malik's, identifying the Indian military's lack of readiness during the initial stages of the Kargil conflict as one important factor in India's failure to expand the fighting across the Line of Control.

64. Author interview of Brajesh Mishra, May 2005.

65. Author interview of G. Parthasarathy, August 2004.

66. Ibid.

67. Author interview of former Indian Defense Minister George Fernandes, New Delhi, India, August 2004.

68. George Fernandes, "Opening Address," in Jasjit Singh, ed., *Asia's New Dawn: The Challenges to Peace and Security* (New Delhi: Knowledge World, 2000), p. xvii, quoted in Chari, "Nuclear Restraint," p. 19.

69. Author interview of former Indian Prime Minister Atal Bihari Vajpayee, New Delhi, India, June 2006.

70. See Sagan, "For the Worse," pp. 97, 197.

71. Author interview of Mohammed Nawaz Sharif, June 2006. Riedel describes Sharif, during the prime minister's meeting with Clinton, as "a man possessed with fear of war." Riedel, "American Diplomacy and the Summit at Blair House," p. 11.

72. By "full-scale," I mean a war designed to achieve catastrophic Pakistani defeat, as described on p. 52.

73. Author interview of V. P. Malik, April 2004.

74. See Tellis et al., *Limited Conflicts Under the Nuclear Umbrella*, pp. x, 41, 55; Husain, "On the Brink"; Jones, *Pakistan*, p. 104; Irfan Husain, "The Cost of Kargil," *Dawn*, August 14, 1999; Husain, "Kargil: The Morning After"; Shireen M. Mazari, "Kargil: Misguided Perceptions," Pakistan Institute for Air Defence Studies, available at http://www.piads.com.pk/users/piads/mazari1.html; Ahmed, "Pakistan's Nuclear Weapons Program," p. 16; "Statement of Nawaz Sharif in ATC-1," *Dawn*, March 9, 2000.

75. See Sayantan Chakravarty, "The Plot Unravels," *India Today*, December 31, 2001, pp. 6–8.

76. See Rana Lakshmi, "Indians Blame Attacks on Pakistan-Based Group; Fears of Re-newed Tension Increase," *Washington Post*, December 15, 2001, p. A23; Ewan MacAskill, "India Says It Has Evidence Linking Pakistan with Raid," *Guardian*, December 17, 2001, p. 13; Chakravarty, "The Plot Unravels." For detailed discussions of these and other militant groups in Kashmir, see K. Santhanam, Sreedhar, Sudhir Saxena, and Manish, *Jihadis in Jammu and Kashmir: A Portrait Gallery* (New Delhi: Sage Publications, 2003).

77. Sood and Sawhney, *Operation Parakram*, pp. 147–48.

78. Author interview of senior Indian scholar and nuclear policy advisor closely in-volved with the formulation of Indian nuclear doctrine, New Delhi, April 2004.

79. Author interview of senior serving Indian Army officer, New Delhi, India, April 2004.

80. Author interview of George Fernandes, August 2004.

81. See Gaurav Kampani, "India's Compellance Strategy: Calling Pakistan's Nuclear Bluff Over Kashmir," Monterey Institute of International Studies, p. 3, available at http://www.cns.miis.edu/pubs/week/020610.htm.

82. Author interview of V. P. Malik, April 2004. Significantly, in such a "similar" op-eration, India's "Strategy adopted for Kargil, including the Line of Control constraints, may not be applicable." Address by V. P. Malik at "National Seminar on The Challenge of Limited War: Parameters and Options," Institute for Defence Studies and Analysis, New Delhi, January 6, 2000. Discussions with senior serving army and Ministry of External Af-fairs personnel evinced a similar viewpoint.

83. Kampani, "India's Compellence Strategy," p. 11; Karl, "Lessons for Proliferation Scholarship in South Asia," p. 1021. See also Khan, "Challenges to Nuclear Stability in South Asia," pp. 64–65. On the conceptual roots of this policy, see C. Raja Mohan, "Fernandes Unveils 'Limited War' Doctrine," *The Hindu*, January 24, 2000.

84. Sood and Sawhney, *Operation Parakram*, p. 10.

85. See Praveen Swami, "Beating the Retreat," *Frontline*, 26 (2002).

86. Author interview of George Fernandes, August 2004.

87. Sood and Sawhney, *Operation Parakram*, p. 73.

88. See President Pervez Musharraf's Address to the Nation, January 12, 2002, available at http://www.jang-group.com/thenews/spedition/speech_of_musharraf/index.html.

89. Alan Sipress and Rajiv Chandrasekaran, "Powell 'Encouraged' by India Visit," *Washington Post*, January 19, 2002, p. A19; Robert Marquand, "Powell Tiptoes Indo-Pak Divide," *Christian Science Monitor*, January 18, 2002, p. 6; "India-Pakistan Standoff Easing, Powell Says," *Boston Globe*, January 18, 2002, p. A3.

90. Author interview of Brajesh Mishra; Sood and Sawhney, *Operation Parakram*, p. 80.

91. See Raj Chengappa and Shishir Gupta, "The Mood to Hit Back," *India Today*, May 27, 2002, pp. 27–30. On May 27, 2002, President Musharraf announced in an ad-dress to the nation that "we feel sad" about this attack on civilians and vowed that "Paki-stani soil would not be allowed to be used for terrorism against anybody." However, Musharraf simultaneously maintained, "A liberation movement is going on in Occupied Kashmir and Pakistan cannot be held responsible for any action against the Indian tyranny and repression." Text of speech available at http://www.embassyofpakistan.com/address_27_05_02.htm.

92. Rahul Bedi and Anton La Guardia, "India Ready for 'Decisive Battle,'" *Daily Tele-graph*, May 23, 2002, p. 1.

93. Sood and Sawhney, *Operation Parakram*, pp. 80–83. In an interview with the author, Brajesh Mishra declined to discuss the details of Indian military plans during the 2001–2002 crisis. However, Mishra argued that there was little substantive difference between Indian strategy in January and May 2002. Given the seriousness of the Parliament attack, the size of the Indian deployment, and Fernandes's statement that India was prepared to launch a conventional war against Pakistan in January, it seems doubtful that India's actual January plans were significantly less extensive than those that Sood and Sawhney describe. Thus, if Mishra's claim is correct, Sood and Sawhney either overstate Indian plans in May, or understate them in January. In either case, though, the fundamental point remains: During the 2001–2002 crisis, Indian leaders planned to launch a major conventional attack against Pakistan if Pakistan did not comply with Indian demands. Author interview of Brajesh Mishra, June 2006.

94. Author interview of former Indian Vice Chief of Army Staff V. K. Sood, New Delhi, India, August 2004.

95. Fahran Bokhari and Edward Luce, "Western Pressure Brings Easing of Kashmir Tension," *Financial Times*, June 8, 2002, p. 7; C. Raja Mohan, "Musharraf Vows to Stop Infiltration: Armitage," *The Hindu*, June 7, 2002; Sood and Sawhney, *Operation Parakram*, pp. 95, 98–99. Indian Defence Minster George Fernandes claimed in November 2002 that crossborder infiltration during the first ten months of that year was down to 53 percent of what it had been during the same period in 2001. See "India: Fernandes Says Forward Mobilization of Troops Achieved Objectives," *World News Connection*, November 21, 2002; "Government Carrying Out Strategic Relocation of Army," *Press Trust of India*, November 20, 2002.

96. Author interview of Brajesh Mishra, May 2005.

97. During this time frame, the United States also put diplomatic and economic pressure on India to de-escalate through the issuance of a State Department travel advisory, which warned Americans against visiting that country during the crisis. An advisory against travel to Pakistan had already been issued in March 2002, following the bombing of a church in Islamabad. See Thom Shanker and Elisabeth Bumiller, "Citing Tension, U.S. Advises Americans in India to Leave," *New York Times*, May 31, 2002, p. A1.

98. Author interview of George Fernandes, August 2004.

99. Author interview of Brajesh Mishra, May 2005.

100. Author interview of Atal Bihari Vajpayee, June 2006.

101. Sood and Sawhney, *Operation Parakram*, pp. 80, 82, 87; V. Sudarshan and Ajith Pillai, "Game of Patience," *Outlook*, May 27, 2002; author interview of retired Indian generals, New Delhi, August 2004.

102. Sudarshan and Pillai, "Game of Patience"; Shishir Gupta, "Keeping the Heat On," *India Today*, May 20, 2002, pp. 40–41; "The General's Broken Promise," *Washington Post*, May 15, 2002, p. A26. According to the Indian Ministry of Home Affairs, a total of 4,038 terrorist incidents occurred in Jammu and Kashmir during 2002, an overall decline of approximately 11 percent from 4,522 total incidents in 2001. See Government of India Ministry of Home Affairs, *2003–2004 Annual Report*, p. 12. According to the Indian Army, total of 1,063 non-Kashmiri terrorists were killed in 2002 by security forces in Jammu and Kashmir compared to 1,198 killed in 2001, an overall decline of roughly the same percentage. Indian Army statistics available at http://www.armyinkashmir.org/v2/statistical_facts/ft_actual_data.shtml.

103. Author interview of V. K Sood, August 2004.

104. Author interview of former Indian Army Chief of Staff Shankar Roychoudhry, New Delhi, India, August 2004.

105. Swami, "Beating the Retreat."

106. Sood and Sawhney, *Operation Parakram*, p. 11.

107. Author interview with V. P. Malik, April 2004.

108. See Sujit Chatterjee, "Pak Has Taken Steps to Put Down Cross-Border Terror: Fernandes," *Press Trust of India*, February 11, 2004; Vasantha Arora, "India Might Reconsider Stand on Troops for Iraq: Natwar," *Indo-Asian News Service*, June 11, 2004; Chidanand Rajghatta, "India, U.S. Pledge Stronger Ties," *Times of India*, June 12, 2004; "Natwar, Powell Discuss Bilateral, Regional Issues," *Press Trust of India*, June 11, 2004.

109. See Center for Strategic and International Studies, *South Asia Monitor*, no. 67 (2004), p. 1; Ahmed Rashid, "My Own Soldiers Tried to Kill Me, Says Musharraf," *Daily Telegraph*, May 28, 2004, p. 17; "Musharraf Announces New Crackdown on Terrorism, Seeks to End Divisions Within Pakistan," *Associated Press*, May 2, 2002; "U.S.: Pakistani Efforts Go Beyond Words," *United Press International*, June 4, 2002.

110. Author interview of Brajesh Mishra, May 2005.

111. Author interview of Atal Bihari Vajpayee, June 2006.

112. Author interview of V. K. Sood, August 2004.

CHAPTER 7. *Beyond South Asia*

1. Though, as noted, strong-state aggressive behavior could increase in the wake of nuclear proliferation in response to growing weak-proliferator provocation.

2. Neville Maxwell describes Zhenbao as "lozenge-shaped . . . about 2–2.5 kilometres in length, and about half a kilometer in breadth. It has thin timber around the edges, but most of the surface is marsh, and at high-water it is regularly submerged . . . [T]he Soviet shore is about 400 metres from the island, while the river arm which separates it from the Chinese bank is about 100 metres across." Neville Maxwell, "The Chinese Account of the 1969 Fighting at Chenpao," *The China Quarterly*, no. 56 (1973), p. 731.

3. Federation of American Scientists, Military Analysis Network, "Sino-Soviet Border Clashes," available at http://www.fas.org/man/dod-101/ops/war/prc-soviet.htm; U.S. Department of State, *Intelligence Note*, George C. Denney Jr. to Secretary of State, "USSR/ China: Soviet and Chinese Forces Clash on the Ussuri River," March 4, 1969, p. 1; Peter Jones and Siân Kevill, *China and the Soviet Union 1949–84* (New York: Longman, 1985), pp. 87–90.

4. Lyle J. Goldstein, "Return to Zhenbao Island: Who Started Shooting and Why It Matters," *China Quarterly*, no. 168 (2001), p. 987.

5. The dispute over the Ussuri River boundaries occurred in the context of a much broader deterioration in Sino-Soviet relations, which emerged in the mid-1950s with Chinese concern over Soviet de-Stalinization efforts, intensified with the withdrawal of Soviet technical support for China's nuclear weapons program, and continued through the Cultural Revolution. Thomas W. Robinson, "The Sino-Soviet Border Dispute: Background, Development, and the March 1969 Clashes," *American Political Science Review*, 66, no. 4 (1972), p. 1176. For a discussion of the roots of the decline in Sino-Soviet relations, see also Jonathan D. Spence, *The Search for Modern China* (New York: W. W. Norton, 1990), pp. 583–90.

6. U.S. Department of State, *Intelligence Note*, Denney to Secretary of State, March 4, 1969; Central Intelligence Agency, *Weekly Review*, March 21, 1969, p. 12; U.S. Department

of State, *Intelligence Note*, Thomas L. Hughes to Secretary of State, "Peking's Tactics and Intentions Along the Border," June 13, 1969, p. 1.

7. Maxwell, "The Chinese Account of the Fighting at Chenpao," pp. 734–36. Other analysts blaming Soviet forces for instigating the Zhenbao clashes include Henry Kissinger, *Diplomacy* (New York: Simon & Schuster, 1994), p. 722; and Barbara Barnouin and Yu Changgen, *Chinese Foreign Policy During the Cultural Revolution* (London: Kegan Paul International, 1998), pp. 87–88.

8. Shulsky, *Deterrence Theory and Chinese Behavior* (Santa Monica, CA: RAND, 2000), pp. 75, 76. See also Goldstein, "Return to Zhenbao Island," pp. 988–89; Alfred D. Low, *The Sino-Soviet Dispute: An Analysis of the Polemics* (Rutherford, NJ: Fairleigh Dickinson University Press, 1976), p. 277.

9. Lyle Goldstein, "Do Nascent WMD Arsenals Deter? The Sino-Soviet Crisis of 1969," *Political Science Quarterly*, 118, no. 1 (2003), p. 59. See also Yang Kuisong, arguing that even "propagandistic" official Chinese accounts suggest that "the Zhenbao Island Incident was indeed initiated by the Chinese side." Yang Kuisong, "The Sino-Soviet Border Clash of 1969: From Zhenbao Island to Sino-American *Rapprochement*," *Cold War History*, 1, no. 1 (2000), p. 27.

10. Goldstein, "Do Nascent WMD Arsenals Deter?" p. 59.

11. U.S. State Department Memorandum of Conversation, "U.S. Reaction to Soviet Destruction of CPR Nuclear Capability; Significance of Latest Sino-Soviet Border Clash; Internal Opposition." August 18, 1969, pp. 1–3. See also Shulsky, *Deterrence Theory*, pp. 13–14.

12. Henry Kissinger, *The White House Years* (Boston: Little, Brown, 1979), pp. 183–84; Wich, *Sino-Soviet Crisis Politics*, p. 190, cited in Goldstein, "Do Nascent WMD Arsenals Deter?" pp. 60–61; Yang, "The Sino-Soviet Border Clash of 1969," p. 34.

13. Goldstein, "Do Nascent WMD Arsenals Deter?" p. 61.

14. Author interview of David Holloway, Stanford, California, March 2005.

15. See Goldstein, "Do Nascent WMD Arsenals Deter?" pp. 67–70.

16. Author interview of David Holloway, March 2005.

17. "Conversation Between Mao Zedong and E. F. Hill" in *"All Under Heaven Is Great Chaos"—Beijing, the Sino-Soviet Border Clashes, and the Turn Toward Sino-American Rapprochement, 1968–69*, cited in Goldstein, "Do Nascent WMD Arsenals Deter?" pp. 69–71.

18. Quoted in Sergei N. Goncharov, John W. Lewis, and Xue Litai, *Uncertain Partners: Stalin, Mao, and the Korean War* (Stanford, CA: Stanford University Press, 1993), p. 297 n. 28.

19. Stuart R. Schram, *The Political Thought of Mao Tse-tung* (New York: Praeger, 1963), p. 279.

20. "A Magnificent Victory for Mao Tse-tung's Thought," *Liberation Army Daily*, June 1967, p. 18, in *Foreign Broadcast Information Service*, Daily Report no. 118, June 19, 1967, *Communist China*, ccc4.

21. "China Successfully Tests 1st Hydrogen Bomb," *Peking NCNA International Service in English*, June 17, 1967, in *Foreign Broadcast Information Service*, Daily Report no. 118, June 19, 1967, ccc2.

22. Quoted in John Wilson Lewis and Xue Litai, *China Builds the Bomb* (Stanford, CA: Stanford University Press, 1988), p. 211.

23. "Outstanding Members of PLA," *Peking International News Service in English*, June 20, 1967, in *Foreign Broadcast Information Service*, Daily Report no. 119, June 20, 1967, *Communist China*, ccc13.

24. "H-Bomb Tests Continue to Draw Acclamation," Peking NCNA International Service in English, June 19, 1967, in *Foreign Broadcast Information Service*, Daily Report no. 119, June 20, 1967, *Communist China*, 20 cccio.

25. State Department cable 130100 to U.S. Embassy, Taipei, "Nur Khan's Meeting with Chou En-lai," August 5, 1969, p. 2.

26. Ministry of Foreign Affairs of the People's Republic of China, "Meeting between Zhou Enlai and Kosygin at the Beijing Airport," available at http://www.fmprc .gov.cn/eng/ziliao/3602/3604/t18005.htm. At least one Russian source claims that Zhou's threat was not to launch a nuclear strike but rather to wage a protracted nonnuclear conflict against the Soviet Union. See Goldstein, "Do Nascent WMD Arsenals Deter?" p. 71.

27. Lewis and Xue, *China Builds the Bomb*, pp. 215–16.

28. Ibid., p. 216.

29. David Holloway, *The Soviet Union and the Arms Race* (New Haven, CT: Yale University Press, 1983), p. 86.

30. Editorial Departments of *People's Daily* and *Red Flag*, "Two Different Lines on the Question of War and Peace: Fifth Comment on the Open Letter of the Central Committee of the CPSU," in *The Polemic of the General Line of the International Communist Movement* (Beijing: Foreign Languages Press, 1965), pp. 246, 249–50.

31. Author interview of David Holloway, March 2005.

32. Yang, "The Sino-Soviet Border Clash of 1969," pp. 36–37.

33. Ibid., pp. 39–42, 49.

34. U.S. Department of State, *Intelligence Note*, Hughes to Secretary of State, June 13, 1969, p. 1.

35. Ibid., p. 3; Shulsky, *Deterrence Theory*, p. 76; Melvin Gurtov and Byong-Moo Hwang, *China Under Threat: The Politics of Strategy and Diplomacy* (Baltimore: Johns Hopkins University Press, 1980), pp. 191, 216–21; U.S. Department of State, *Intelligence Note*, Hughes to Secretary of State, June 13, 1969, p. 3. For an argument that China was responding to Soviet action against Czechoslovakia but not out of fear of actual Soviet intervention in China, see Richard Wich, *Sino-Soviet Crisis Politics: A Study of Political Change and Communication* (London: Council on East Asian Studies—Harvard University, 1980). For an argument that China was not primarily responding to Soviet aggression in Czechoslovakia, see Goldstein, "Return to Zhenbao Island," pp. 990–94.

36. Goldstein, "Return to Zhenbao Island," pp. 994–95, 997; U.S. Department of State, *Intelligence Note*, Hughes to Secretary of State, June 13, 1969, p. 4; Yang, "The Sino-Soviet Border Clash of 1969," pp. 22, 48; Thomas Robinson, "China Confronts the Soviet Union: Warfare and Diplomacy on China's Inner Asian Frontiers," in Roderick MacFarquhar and John K. Fairbank, eds., *The Cambridge History of China, Volume 15, The People's Republic, Part 2: Revolutions Within the Chinese Revolution, 1966–1982* (Cambridge: Cambridge University Press, 1991), p. 50. See also Chen Jian, *Mao's China and the Cold War* (Chapel Hill: University of North Carolina Press, 2001), pp. 238–49. As Yang notes, one important result of the Sino-Soviet confrontation was an improvement in China's relationship with the United States. However, there is no evidence that improving Sino-American ties was part of Chinese leaders' original plan in launching the Ussuri conflict. See Yang, "The Sino-Soviet Border Clash of 1969," pp. 21–22, 48.

37. Institutes for Strategic Studies, *The Military Balance 1968–1969* (London: Institute for Strategic Studies, 1968), pp. 6–8, 10–11.

38. Jian, *Mao's China*, pp. 239–41. See also Shulsky, *Deterrence Theory*, pp. 12, 55; U.S. Department of State, *Intelligence Note*, Hughes to Secretary of State, June 13, 1969, pp. 1–3; U.S. Department of State, Bureau of East Asian and Pacific Affairs, Office of Asian Communist Affairs, "Implications of Sino-Soviet Developments: Meeting of June 21," June 23, 1969, pp. 1–2; Robinson, "China Confronts the Soviet Union," in MacFarquhar and Fairbank, eds., *The Cambridge History of China*, p. 257.

39. Goldstein, "Do Nascent WMD Arsenals Deter?" pp. 75–76.

40. Earlier estimates put the Chinese manpower advantage over the Soviets in the Ussuri region closer to 3:5, with China fielding approximately thirty-five to forty division equivalents and the Soviet Union fielding approximately twenty to twenty-four division equivalents. See Robinson, "The Sino-Soviet Border Dispute," p. 1184.

41. Though, as Goldstein points out, the Soviet railroad would have been vulnerable to Chinese attack. See Goldstein, "Do Nascent WMD Arsenals Deter?" p. 75.

42. Ibid.

43. Goldstein, "Return to Zhenbao Island," pp. 991–95.

44. Robinson, "The Sino-Soviet Border Dispute," p. 1185.

45. Michael P. Pillsbury, "Future Sino-American Security Ties: The View from Tokyo, Moscow, and Peking," *International Security*, 1, no. 4 (1977), p. 130.

46. See Gurtov and Hwang, *China Under Threat*, pp. 187, 195.

47. Goldstein, "Do Nascent WMD Arsenals Deter?" p. 77.

48. Pillsbury, "Future Sino-American Security Ties," p. 136.

49. China's dissatisfaction with the Ussuri boundaries did not, however, reach Pakistan's current level of dissatisfaction with the border in Kashmir. As noted, the territory of Kashmir engages a host of strategic and symbolic issues critical to both India and Pakistan. The territory of Zhenbao Island and the Ussuri region, by contrast, was not in itself valuable to China; the border conflict was symptomatic of larger, unrelated strategic and domestic political issues. See Low, *The Sino-Soviet Dispute*, p. 278; Goldstein, "Return to Zhenbao Island," pp. 994–95, 997.

50. Robinson, "The Sino-Soviet Border Dispute," p. 1178.

51. "A Comment on the Statement of the Communist Party of the USA," *Jen-min Jih-pao*, March 8, 1963, available at http://www.etext.org/Politics/MIM/classics/mao/polemics/CPUSA.html.

52. Quoted in Robinson, "The Sino-Soviet Border Dispute," p. 1178.

53. See Ibid., pp. 1178–80.

54. See Ibid., pp. 1180–81. Note that during their September 11, 1969, meeting, Zhou reportedly told Kosygin that a settlement of the border disputes did not require the abrogation of the unequal treaties. See Yang, "The Sino-Soviet Border Clash of 1969," p. 38.

55. Selig S. Harrison, "Time to Leave North Korea?" *Foreign Affairs*, 80, no. 2 (2001), pp. 62, 69.

56. Don Oberdorrer, *The Two Koreas: A Contemporary History* (Reading, MA: Addison-Wesley, 1997), pp. 11, 183–86, 348–49; Michael O'Hanlon and Mike Mochizuki, *Crisis on the Korean Peninsula: How to Deal with a Nuclear North Korea* (Washington, DC: Brookings, 2003), pp. 24–25.

57. See, e.g., President George W. Bush, "State of the Union Address," January 29, 2002, available at http://www.whitehouse.gov/news/releases/2002/01/20020129-11.html.

58. See James Brooke, "U.S. Envoy to Japan Assails North Korea's Arms Program," *New York Times*, February 17, 2005, p. A3.

59. Robert S. Norris, Hans M. Kristensen, and Joshua Handler, "North Korea's Nuclear Program, 2003," *Bulletin of the Atomic Scientists*, 59, no. 2 (2003), pp. 74–75.

60. S/RES/825, May 11, 1993. See also Gary Samore, "The Korean Nuclear Crisis," *Survival*, 45, no. 1 (2003), pp. 8–9.

61. See text of Agreed Framework Between the United States of America and the Democratic People's Republic of Korea, available at http://www.kedo.org/pdfs/AgreedFramework.pdf.

62. See Samore, "The Korean Nuclear Crisis," pp. 10–12.

63. The Executive Board of the Korean Peninsula Energy Development Organization (KEDO), "Promoting Peace and Stability on the Korean Peninsula and Beyond," available at http://www.kedo.org/news_detail.asp?NewsID=23.

64. See generally Samore, "The Korean Nuclear Crisis," pp. 13–16.

65. Norris, Kristensen, and Handler, "North Korea's Nuclear Program, 2003," p. 75.

66. See "DPRK FM on Its Stand to Suspend Its Participation in Six-Party Talks for Indefinite Period," Korean Central News Agency, available at http://www.kcna.co.jp/index-e.htm.

67. Mure Dickie, Guy Dinmore, Daniel Dombey, Anna Fifield, Mariko Sanchanta, and Peter Spiegel, "N. Korea Tells World It Has Built N-Weapons," *Financial Times*, February 11, 2005, Asia-Pacific, p. 9.

68. O'Hanlon and Mochizuki, *Crisis on the Korean Peninsula*, p. 15.

69. Oberdorfer, *The Two Koreas*, pp. 256–60; Selig Harrison, "The Missiles of North Korea," *World Policy Journal*, 13, no. 3 (2000), p. 14.

70. As we have seen, this is the case because states are less likely to incur costs and risks to protect an ally than they are to ensure their own security.

71. Joseph S. Bermudez Jr., *Shield of the Great Leader: The Armed Forces of North Korea* (Sydney, Australia: Allen & Unwin, 2001), pp. 6, 123. The North Korean Air Force (KPAF) possesses a total of nearly 1,700 aircraft.

72. Ibid., pp. 276–77; Norris, Kristensen, and Handler, "North Korea's Nuclear Program," p. 76.

73. Bermudez, *Shield of the Great Leader*, pp. 275–76; Norris, Kristensen, and Handler, "North Korea's Nuclear Program," p. 76.

74. Central Intelligence Agency, "Unclassified Report to Congress on the Acquisition of Technology Relating to Weapons of Mass Destruction and Advanced Conventional Munitions, 1 January Through 30 June 2003," available at http://www.odci.gov/cia/reports/721_reports/jan_jun2003.htm.

75. Selig Harrison, "The Missiles of North Korea," pp. 19–21.

76. Scott Snyder, "Pyongyang's Pressure," *The Washington Quarterly*, 23, no. 3 (2000), p. 167.

77. See Nina Tannenwald, "The Nuclear Taboo: The United States and the Normative Basis of Nuclear Non-Use," *International Organization*, 53, no. 3 (1999), pp. 433–68.

78. I offer this discussion only as an illustration of how my framework can help us predict the likely behavior of new nuclear states. It does not purport to be an in-depth study of North Korea or to offer definitive codings of the DPRK's military capabilities and territorial preferences.

79. International Institute for Strategic Studies, *The Military Balance: 2002–2003* (Oxford: Oxford University Press, 2002), pp. 25, 154–55.

80. Ibid., pp. 153–54.

81. U.S. and South Korean weaponry could be as much as two to four times more effective than that of the DPRK. Taik-young Hamm, *Arming the Two Koreas: State, Capital and Military Power* (London: Routledge, 1999), pp. 45–48; Michael O'Hanlon, "Stopping a North Korean Invasion: Why Defending South Korea Is Easier Than the Pentagon Thinks," *International Security*, 22, no. 4 (1998), p. 142.

82. Nick Beldecos and Eric Heginbotham, "The Conventional Balance in North Korea," *Breakthroughs*, 4, no. 1 (1995), pp. 2–3; O'Hanlon, "Stopping a North Korean Invasion," pp. 140, 149, 158.

83. O'Hanlon, "Stopping a North Korean Invasion," p. 140.

84. Ibid., pp. 145–47.

85. The World Factbook, "Korea, South," available at http://www.cia.gov/cia/ publications/factbook/geos/ks.html.

86. The World Factbook, "Korea, North," available at http://www.cia.gov/cia/ publications/factbook/geos/kn.html.

87. Ibid.; The World Factbook, "Korea, South," available at http://www.cia.gov/ cia/publications/factbook/geos/ks.html.

88. International Institute for Strategic Studies, *The Military Balance 2002–2003*, p. 334.

89. Note, however, that in the event of hostilities, North Korean artillery could inflict considerable damage on Seoul, which is located a mere forty-one kilometers from the demilitarized zone. At least 250 of the DPRK's approximately 10,000 artillery tubes are located within range of the South Korean capital and could probably hit Seoul with several thousand rounds during a conflict. This capability would not enable the DPRK to prevail over South Korea in the event of conflict, but it would significantly escalate the costs of war for the ROK, potentially resulting in tens of thousands of civilian deaths and tens of billions of dollars in damage. See O'Hanlon, "Stopping a North Korean Invasion," p. 148.

90. O'Hanlon, "Stopping a North Korean Invasion," p. 148. Former U.S. Ambassador to South Korea James R. Lilley summarized North Korea's military situation as follows: "North Korea's conventional military is decaying. It has not yet pulled off a successful sabotage or paramilitary operation in the 21st century. It has not tested a nuclear weapon and it has not fired the multistage Taepodong since 1998." James R. Lilley, Testimony Before the House Committee on International Relations, March 3, 2005, available at http:// www.aei.org/publications/pubID.22096,filter.all/pub_detail.asp.

91. See Oberdorfer, *The Two Koreas*, pp. 8–9.

92. Nicholas Eberstadt, "What Surprise? The Nuclear Core of North Korea's Strategy," *Washington Post*, March 1, 2005, p. A15.

93. Victor D. Cha, "Weak but Still Threatening," in Victor D. Cha and David C. Kang, eds., *Nuclear North Korea: A Debate on Engagement Strategies* (New York: Columbia University Press, 2003), p. 24.

94. O'Hanlon and Mochizuki, *Crisis on the Korean Peninsula*, p. 65.

95. See Ibid., pp. 29–30.

96. David C. Kang, "Threatening, but Deterrence Works," in Cha and Kang, eds., *Nuclear North Korea*, pp. 43, 67.

97. Nicholas Eberstadt, "Hastening Korean Reunification," *Foreign Affairs*, 76, no. 2 (1997), p. 79.

98. Young Howard, "The Real Threat to Kim," *International Herald Tribune*, February 25, 2005.

99. Jong-Heon Lee, "North Korea Launches Harsh Crackdown," *United Press International*, March 11, 2005.

100. Selig Harrison, "Time to Leave Korea?" p. 76.

101. Hong Soon-Young, "Thawing Korea's Cold War," *Foreign Affairs*, 78, no. 3 (1999), p. 9.

102. James R. Lilley, Testimony Before the House Committee on Foreign Relations, March 3, 2005, available at http://www.aei.org/publications/pubID.22096,filter.all/pub_detail.asp.

103. Selig Harrison, "Did North Korea Cheat?" *Foreign Affairs*, 84, no. 1 (2005), p. 109.

104. The Pakistan government denies that it played any role in spreading nuclear designs or equipment to third parties. It maintains steadfastly that Pakistani scientist A. Q. Khan, director of Khan Research Laboratories, along with a group of colleagues, did so without government authorization. See Edward Luce, "Pakistan in Nuclear 'Cover-up' Row," *Financial Times*, February 14, 2004, p. 1.

105. Chaim Braun and Christopher F. Chyba, "Proliferation Rings: New Challenges to the Nuclear Nonproliferation Regime," *International Security*, 29, no. 2 (2004), pp. 11–14, 20–21.

106. Ibid., p. 21.

107. "Victory for a Religious Hardliner in Iran," *Economist*, June 27, 2005.

108. "Is the New President Truly an Exterminator?" *Economist*, November 3, 2005.

109. Leslie Susser, "Israel Weighs Options on Iran," *Canadian Business News*, November 17, 2005, p. 9.

110. "Press Conference of the President," December 19, 2005, available at http://www.whitehouse.gov/news/releases/2005/12/20051219-2.html.

111. Susser, "Israel Weighs Options."

112. The U.S. Department of State's 2003 "Patterns of Global Terrorism" report argues that Iran is the world's "most active state sponsor of terrorism." See U.S. Department of State, "Patterns of Global Terrorism" (2003), p. 88, available at http://www.state.gov/documents/organization/31944.pdf.

113. Of course, this would not mean that Iranian acquisition of nuclear weapons would be completely free of danger; horizontal proliferation of nuclear materials and technologies from Iran to other countries, as well as the possibility of nuclear theft or accident, would still be important causes for concern. However, unless Iran were both militarily weak and dissatisfied with existing territorial boundaries, the acquisition of nuclear weapons would be unlikely to encourage aggressive Iranian behavior in the Middle Eastern region.

CHAPTER 8. *Dangerous Deterrent*

1. This may suggest that the early stages of an adversarial nuclear relationship will be especially dangerous; over time, status quo nuclear states can devise conventional military strategies to thwart the ambitions of their revisionist nuclear opponents. Despite recently improved Indo-Pakistani relations, however, the basic incentives for aggressive Pakistani behavior have not changed, and levels of violence in Kashmir and infiltration into the region remain significant. See "Rebels Stepping Up Violence to Sabotage Peace, Say J-K Leaders," *Hindustan Times*, November 16, 2003; "Devastating Quake Fails to Affect Infiltration Bids," *Press Trust of India*, November 6, 2005. Indo-Pakistani tension could easily increase once

again if the Pakistan government decides that the domestic costs of a moderate policy with regard to India are too high or if the Pakistani leadership changes altogether.

2. Though like the United States and Soviet Union, nuclear India and Pakistan have thus far managed to avoid an all-out conventional war.

3. Given outside powers' enormous incentives to avert possible nuclear confrontations, it will be difficult for them to claim credibly that they will remain uninvolved in such crises. However, President Clinton's refusal during Kargil to assist Pakistan until its forces had withdrawn from Indian territory demonstrates that outside states may in fact prove unwilling to intervene and could lend their warnings to this effect some credibility.

4. Interview with senior Indian scholar and nuclear policy advisor closely involved with the formulation of India's Draft Nuclear Doctrine, New Delhi, May 2002.

5. V. P. Malik, "Closing Address," National Seminar on the Challenge of Limited War: Parameters and Options, Institute for Defence Studies and Analysis, New Delhi, January 6, 2000.

Bibliography

BOOKS AND MONOGRAPHS:

Amin, Shahid. *Pakistan's Foreign Policy: A Reappraisal* (Karachi: Oxford University Press, 2002).

Bajpai, Kanti P., P. R. Chari, Pervaiz Iqbal Cheema, Stephen P. Cohen, and Sumit Ganguly. *Brasstacks and Beyond: Perception and Management of Crisis in South Asia* (New Delhi: Manohar, 1995).

Ball, Desmond, et al. *Crisis Stability and Nuclear War* (Ithaca, NY: Cornell University Peace Studies Program, 1987).

Barnouin, Barbara, and Yu Changgen. *Chinese Foreign Policy During the Cultural Revolution* (London: Kegan Paul International, 1998).

Bermudez, Joseph S. Jr. *Shield of the Great Leader: The Armed Forces of North Korea* (Sydney, Australia: Allen & Unwin, 2001).

Bhutto, Zulfikar Ali. *If I Am Assassinated* (New Delhi: Vikas Publishing House, 1979).

Bose, Sumantra. *Kashmir: Roots of Conflict, Paths to Peace* (Cambridge, MA: Harvard University Press, 2003).

Brodie, Bernard. *Escalation and the Nuclear Option* (Princeton, NJ: Princeton University Press, 1966).

Bundy, McGeorge. *Danger and Survival: Choices About the Bomb in the First Fifty Years* (New York: Random House, 1988).

Burki, Shahid Javed. *Pakistan: Fifty Years of Nationhood*, 3rd ed. (Boulder, CO: Westview Press, 1999).

Cha, Victor, and David C. Kang. *Nuclear North Korea: A Debate on Engagement Strategies* (New York: Columbia University Press, 2003).

Chari, P. R., and Pervaiz Iqbal Cheema. *The Simla Agreement 1972: Its Wasted Promise* (New Delhi: Manohar, 2001).

Chari, P. R., Pervaiz Iqbal Cheema, and Stephen Philip Cohen. *Perception, Politics and Security in South Asia: The Compound Crisis of 1990* (London: RoutledgeCurzon, 2003).

Chen, Jian. *Mao's China and the Cold War* (Chapel Hill: University of North Carolina Press, 2001).

Cloughley, Brian. *A History of the Pakistan Army: Wars and Insurrections* (Karachi, Pakistan: Oxford University Press, 2000).

Cohen, Stephen P. *The Pakistan Army* (Karachi: Oxford University Press, 1998).

———. *India: Emerging Power* (Washington, DC: Brookings, 2001).

———. *The Idea of Pakistan* (New Delhi: Oxford University Press, 2004).

Coll, Steve. *Ghost Wars: The Secret History of the CIA, Afghanistan, and Bin Laden, from the Soviet Invasion to September 10, 2001* (New York: Penguin Press, 2004).

Cordesman, Anthony H. *The India-Pakistan Military Balance* (Washington, DC: Center for Strategic and International Studies, 2002).

Dasgupta, C. *War and Diplomacy in Kashmir 1947–48* (New Delhi: Sage Publications, 2002).

Dixit, J. N. *India-Pakistan in War and Peace* (New Delhi: Books Today, 2002).

Dunn, Lewis A. *Controlling the Bomb: Nuclear Proliferation in the 1980s* (New Haven, CT: Yale University Press, 1982).

Fair, C. Christine. *Urban Battle Fields of South Asia: Lessons Learned from Sri Lanka, India, and Pakistan* (Santa Monica, CA: RAND, 2004).

Flanagan, Stephen J. *NATO's Conventional Defenses* (Cambridge, MA: Ballinger, 1988).

French, Patrick. *Liberty and Death: India's Journey to Independence and Division* (London: HarperCollins, 1997).

Gaddis, John Lewis. *Strategies of Containment: A Critical Appraisal of Postwar American National Security Policy* (New York: Oxford University Press, 1982).

———. *We Now Know: Rethinking Cold War History* (Oxford: Oxford University Press, 1997).

Ganguly, Šumit. *The Crisis in Kashmir: Portents of War, Hopes of Peace* (Cambridge: Cambridge University Press, 1997).

———. *Conflict Unending: India-Pakistan Tensions Since 1947* (New Delhi: Oxford University Press, 2002).

George, Alexander L., and Richard Smoke. *Deterrence in American Foreign Policy: Theory and Practice* (New York and London: Columbia University Press, 1974).

Gilpin, Robert. *War and Change in World Politics* (Cambridge: Cambridge University Press, 1981).

Glaser, Charles. *Analyzing Strategic Nuclear Policy* (Princeton, NJ: Princeton University Press, 1990).

Gurtov, Melvin, and Byong-Moo Hwang. *China Under Threat: The Politics of Strategy and Diplomacy* (Baltimore: Johns Hopkins University Press, 1980).

Hagerty, Devin. *The Consequences of Nuclear Proliferation: Lessons from South Asia* (Cambridge, MA: MIT Press, 1998).

Hamm, Taik-young. *Arming the Two Koreas: State, Capital and Military Power* (London: Routledge, 1999).

Hasan, Mubashir. *The Mirage of Power: An Inquiry into the Bhutto Years 1971–1977* (Karachi: Oxford University Press, 2000).

Haza, Rafi. *Zulfikar Ali Bhutto and Pakistan: 1967–1977* (Karachi: Oxford University Press, 1997).

Hodson, H. V. *The Great Divide: Britain-India-Pakistan* (Karachi: Oxford University Press, 1985).

Holloway, David. *The Soviet Union and the Arms Race* (New Haven, CT: Yale University Press, 1983).

Human Rights Watch. *India's Secret Army in Kashmir: New Patterns of Abuse Emerge in the Conflict*, 8, no. 4 (May 1996).

Institute for Strategic Studies. *The Military Balance 1968–1969* (London: Institute for Strategic Studies, 1968).

International Institute for Strategic Studies. *The Military Balance 1971–1972 Through 2001–2002* (Oxford: Oxford University Press, 1972–2001).

Jervis, Robert. *The Illogic of American Nuclear Strategy* (Ithaca, NY: Cornell University Press, 1984).

———. *The Meaning of the Nuclear Revolution: Statecraft and the Prospect of Armageddon* (Ithaca, NY: Cornell University Press, 1989).

Jha, Prem Shankar. *Kashmir 1947: Rival Versions of History* (New Delhi: Oxford University Press).

Jones, Owen Bennett. *Pakistan: Eye of the Storm* (New Haven, CT: Yale University Press, 2002).

Jones, Peter, and Siân Kevill. *China and the Soviet Union 1949–84* (New York: Longman, 1985).

King, Gary, Robert O. Keohane, and Sidney Verba. *Designing Social Inquiry: Scientific Inference in Qualitative Research* (Princeton, NJ: Princeton University Press, 1994).

Kukreja, Veena. *Contemporary Pakistan: Political Processes, Conflicts and Crises* (New Delhi: Sage Publications, 2003).

LaFeber, Walter. *America, Russia, and the Cold War 1945–1992* (New York: McGraw-Hill, 1993).

Lamb, Alastair. *Kashmir: A Disputed Legacy 1846–1990* (Karachi: Oxford University Press, 1993).

Leffler, Melvyn P. *A Preponderance of Power: National Security, the Truman Administration, and the Cold War* (Stanford, CA: Stanford University Press, 1992).

Lewis, John Wilson, and Xue Litai. *China Builds the Bomb* (Stanford, CA: Stanford University Press, 1988).

Low, Alfred D. *The Sino-Soviet Dispute: An Analysis of the Polemics* (Rutherford, NJ: Fairleigh Dickinson University Press, 1976).

Malik, Iffatt. *Kashmir: Ethnic Conflict International Dispute* (Oxford: Oxford University Press, 2002).

Mansingh, Surjit. *India's Search for Power: Indira Gandhi's Foreign Policy 1966–1982* (New Delhi: Sage Publications, 1984).

Mearsheimer, John J. *Conventional Deterrence* (Ithaca, NY: Cornell University Press, 1983).

Menon, Raja. *A Nuclear Strategy for India* (New Delhi: Sage Publications, 2000).

Newberg, Paula R. *Double Betrayal: Repression and Insurgency in Kashmir* (Washington, DC: Carnegie Endowment for International Peace, 1995).

Oberdorfer, Don. *The Two Koreas: A Contemporary History* (Reading, MA: Addison-Wesley, 1997).

O'Hanlon, Michael, and Mike Mochizuki. *Crisis on the Korean Peninsula: How to Deal with a Nuclear North Korea* (New York: McGraw-Hill, 2003).

Organski, A. F. K., and Jacek Kugler. *The War Ledger* (Chicago and London: University of Chicago Press, 1980).

Paul, T. V. *Asymmetric Conflicts: War Initiation by Weaker Powers* (Cambridge: Cambridge University Press, 1994).

Perkovich, George. *India's Nuclear Bomb: The Impact on Global Proliferation* (Berkeley: University of California Press, 1999).

Posen, Barry. *Inadvertent Escalation* (Ithaca, NY: Cornell University Press, 1991).

Powaski, Ronald E. *The Cold War: The United States and the Soviet Union, 1917–1991* (Oxford: Oxford University Press, 1998).

Quester, George H. *Nuclear Diplomacy: The First Twenty-Five Years* (New York: Dunellen, 1970).

Raghavan, V. R. *Siachen: Conflict Without End* (New Delhi: Viking Press, 2002).

Sagan, Scott D. *The Limits of Safety: Organizations, Accidents, and Nuclear Weapons* (Princeton, NJ: Princeton University Press, 1993).

Sagan, Scott D., and Kenneth N. Waltz. *The Spread of Nuclear Weapons: A Debate Renewed* (New York: W. W. Norton, 2003).

Santhanam, K., Sreedhar, Sudhir Saxena, and Manish. *Jihadis in Jammu and Kashmir* (New Delhi: Sage Publications, 2003).

Sawhney, Pravin. *The Defence Makeover: 10 Myths That Shape India's Image* (New Delhi: Sage Publications, 2002).

Schelling, Thomas C. *Arms and Influence* (New Haven, CT: Yale University Press, 1966).

Schofield, Victoria. *Kashmir in Conflict: India, Pakistan, and the Unending War* (London: I. B. Tauris, 2003).

Schram, Stuart R. *The Political Thought of Mao Tse-tung* (New York: Praeger, 1963).

Singh, R. K. Jasbir, ed. *Indian Defence Yearbook 2002* (Dehra Dun: Natraj Publishers, 2002).

Sisson, Richard, and Leo E. Rose. *War and Secession: Pakistan, India, and the Creation of Bangladesh* (Berkeley and Los Angeles: University of California Press, 1990).

Small, Melvin, and J. David Singer. *Resort to Arms: International and Civil Wars 1816–1929* (Los Angeles: Sage Publications, 1982).

Smoke, Richard. *National Security and the Nuclear Dilemma: An Introduction to the American Experience in the Cold War* (New York: McGraw-Hill, 1993).

Sood, V. K., and Pravin Sawhney. *Operation Parakaram: The War Unfinished* (New Delhi: Sage Publications, 2003).

Spector, Leonard. *The Undeclared Bomb* (Cambridge, MA: Ballinger, 1988).

Spence, Jonathan D. *The Search for Modern China* (New York: W. W. Norton, 1990).

Talbot, Ian. *Pakistan: A Modern History* (New Delhi: Oxford University Press, 1999).

Tellis, Ashley J. *Stability in South Asia* (Santa Monica, CA: RAND, 1997).

Tellis, Ashley J., C. Christine Fair, and Jamison Jo Medby. *Limited Conflicts Under the Nuclear Umbrella: Indian and Pakistani Lessons from the Kargil Crisis* (Santa Monica, CA: RAND, 2001).

Trachtenberg, Marc. *History and Strategy* (Princeton, NJ: Princeton University Press, 1991).

Van Evera, Stephen. *Guide to Methodology for Students of Political Science* (Cambridge, MA: MIT Defense and Arms Control Studies Program, 1997).

————. *Causes of War: Power and the Roots of Conflict* (Ithaca, NY: Cornell University Press, 1999).

Wendt, Alexander. *Social Theory of International Politics* (Cambridge: Cambridge University Press, 1999).

Wirsing, Robert G. *India, Pakistan, and the Kashmir Dispute: On Regional Conflict and Its Resolution* (New York: St. Martin's Press, 1994).

————. *Kashmir in the Shadow of War: Regional Rivalries in a Nuclear Age* (Armonk, NY: M. E. Sharpe, 2003).

Wolpert, Stanley A. *Zulfi Bhutto of Pakistan: His Life and Times* (New York: Oxford University Press, 1993).

Ziring, Lawrence. *Pakistan: At the Crosscurrent of History* (Oxford: Oneworld Oxford Publications, 2003).

JOURNAL ARTICLES AND BOOK CHAPTERS

Ahmad, Shamshad. "The Nuclear Subcontinent: Bringing Stability to South Asia," *Foreign Affairs*, 78, no. 4 (1999).

Ahmed, Samina. "Pakistan: The Crisis Within," in Muthiah Alagappa, ed., *Asian Security Practice: Material and Ideational Influences* (Stanford, CA: Stanford University Press, 1998).

———. "Pakistan's Nuclear Weapons Program: Turning Points and Nuclear Choices," *International Security*, 32, no. 4 (1999).

———. "Pakistan's Nuclear Weapons: Moving Forward or Tactical Retreat?" Joan B. Kroc Institute for International Peace Studies, February 2000.

———. "Security Dilemmas of Nuclear-Armed Pakistan," *Third World Quarterly*, 21, no. 5 (2000).

Ali, Mehrunnisa. "The Simla and Tashkent Agreements," in Mehrunnisa Ali, ed., *Readings in Pakistan Foreign Policy* (Karachi: Oxford University Press, 2001).

Art, Robert J. "A Defensible Defense," in Sean M. Lynn-Jones and Steven E. Miller, eds., *America's Strategy in a Changing World* (Cambridge, MA: MIT Press, 1992).

Bajpai, Kanti. "The Fallacy of an Indian Deterrent," in Amitabh Mattoo, ed., *India's Nuclear Deterrent: Pokhran II and Beyond* (New Delhi: HarAnand, 1999).

Beg, Mirza Aslam. "Deterrence, Defence, and Development," *Defence Journal*, 3, no. 6 (1999).

———. "Kargil Withdrawal and 'Rogue Army' Image," *Defence Journal*, 3, no. 8 (1999).

Beldecos, Nick, and Eric Heginbotham. "The Conventional Balance in North Korea," *Breakthroughs*, 4, no. 1 (1995).

Bhutto, Zulfikar Ali. "The Simla Accord," *Pakistan Horizon*, 25, no. 3 (1972).

Braun, Chaim, and Christopher F. Chyba. "Proliferation Rings: New Challenges to the Nuclear Nonproliferation Regime," *International Security*, 29, no. 2 (2004).

Brodie, Bernard. "The Development of Nuclear Strategy," in Bernard Brodie, Michael Intriligator, and Roman Kolkowicz, eds., *National Security and International Stability* (Cambridge: Oelgeschlager, Gunn & Hain, 1983).

Bueno de Mesquita, Bruce, and William Riker. "An Assessment of the Merits of Selective Nuclear Proliferation," *Journal of Conflict Resolution*, 26, no. 2 (1982).

Center for Strategic and International Studies, *South Asia Monitor*, no. 67 (2004).

Chandran, D. Subha. "Role of the United States: Mediator or Mere Facilitator?" in P. R. Chari and Ashok Krishna, eds., *Kargil: The Tables Turned* (New Delhi: Manohar, 2001).

Chari, P. R. "Nuclear Restraint, Nuclear Risk Reduction, and the Security-Insecurity Paradox in South Asia," in Michael Krepon and Chris Gagné, eds., *The Stability–Instability Paradox: Nuclear Weapons and Brinksmanship in South Asia* (Washington, DC: Stimson Center, 2001).

Dar, Moti. "Blundering Through," in Sankarshan Thakur, ed., *Guns and Yellow Roses: Essays on the Kargil War* (New Delhi: HarperCollins, 1999).

Dittmer, Lowell. "South Asia's Security Dilemma," *Asian Survey*, 41, no. 6 (2001).

Dixit, J. N. "A Defining Moment," in Sankarshan Thakur, ed., *Guns and Yellow Roses: Essays on the Kargil War* (New Delhi: HarperCollins, 1999).

Eberstadt, Nicholas. "Hastening Korean Reunification," *Foreign Affairs*, 76, no. 2 (1997).

Evangelista, Matthew. "Stalin's Postwar Army Reappraised," *International Security*, 7, no. 3 (1982–1983).

Farber, Henry S., and Joanne Gowa. "Polities and Peace," *International Security*, 20, no. 2 (1995).

Federation of American Scientists, Military Analysis Network. "Sino-Soviet Border Clashes," available at http://www.fas.org/man/dod-101/ops/war/prc-soviet.htm.

Ganguly, Šumit. "Indo-Pakistani Nuclear Issues and the Stability/Instability Paradox," *Studies in Conflict and Terrorism*, 18, no. 4 (1995).

———. "Conflict and Crisis in South and Southwest Asia," in Michael E. Brown, ed., *The International Dimensions of Internal Conflict* (Cambridge, MA: MIT Press, 1996).

———. "Explaining the Kashmir Insurgency: Political Mobilization and Institutional Decay," *International Security*, 21, no. 2 (1996).

———. "India's Pathway to Pokhran II: The Prospects and Sources of New Delhi's Nuclear Weapons Program," *International Security*, 32, no. 4 (1999).

Glaser, Charles. "Political Consequences of Military Strategy: Expanding and Refining the Spiral and Deterrence Models," *World Politics*, 44, no. 4 (1992).

Goldstein, Lyle J. "Return to Zhenbao Island: Who Started Shooting and Why It Matters," *China Quarterly*, 168 (2001).

———. "Do Nascent WMD Arsenals Deter? The Sino-Soviet Crisis of 1969," *Political Science Quarterly*, 118, no. 1 (2003).

Gray, Colin, and Keith Payne. "Victory Is Possible," *Foreign Policy*, no. 39 (1980).

Harrison, Selig S. "The Missiles of North Korea," *World Policy Journal*, 13, no. 3 (2000).

———. "Time to Leave North Korea?" *Foreign Affairs*, 80, no. 2 (2001).

———. "Did North Korea Cheat?" *Foreign Affairs*, 84, no. 1 (2005).

Harrison, Selig S., Paul H. Kreisberg, and Dennis Kux, eds. *India and Pakistan: The First Fifty Years* (Washington, DC: Cambridge University Press and the Woodrow Wilson Center, 1999).

Hong Soon-Young. "Thawing Korea's Cold War," *Foreign Affairs*, 78, no. 3 (1999).

Hoodbhoy, Pervez. "Pakistan's Nuclear Future," in Samina Ahmed and David Cortright, eds., *Pakistan and the Bomb: Public Opinion and Nuclear Options* (South Bend, IN: University of Notre Dame Press, 1998).

Hussain, Mir Zohair. "Islam in Pakistan Under Bhutto and Zia-ul-Haq," in Hussin Mutalib and Taj ul-Islam Hashmi, eds., *Islam, Muslims, and the Modern State: Case-Studies of Muslims in Thirteen Countries* (New York: St. Martin's Press, 1994).

Irshad, Muhammad. "Crises of Nuclear Neighbors," *Defence Journal*, 6, no. 2 (2002).

Jones, Rodney. "Debating New Delhi's Nuclear Decision," *International Security*, 24, no. 4 (2000).

Kampani, Gaurav. "India's Compellance Strategy: Calling Pakistan's Nuclear Bluff Over Kashmir," Monterey Institute of International Studies, available at http://www.cns.miis.edu/pubs/week/020610.htm.

Kanwal, Gurmeet. "Pakistan's Military Defeat," in Jasjit Singh, ed., *Kargil 1999: Pakistan's Fourth War for Kashmir* (New Delhi: Institute for Defence Analysis, 1999).

Kapur, S. Paul. "Nuclear Weapons, the Kargil Conflict, and South Asian Security," *Security Studies*, 13, no. 1 (2003).

Karl, David J. "Proliferation Pessimism and Emerging Nuclear Powers," *International Security*, 21, no. 3 (1996–1997).

————. "Lessons for Proliferation Scholarship in South Asia: The Buddha Smiles Again," *Asian Survey*, 41, no. 6 (2001).

Khan, Ayaz Ahmed. "Indian Offensive in the Kargil Sector," *Defence Journal*, 3, no. 5 (1999).

————. "Armed Forces Wargaming," *Defence Journal*, 6, no. 1 (2002).

Khan, Feroz Hasan. "Challenges to Nuclear Stability in South Asia," *The Nonproliferation Review*, 10, no. 1 (2003).

Knopf, Jeffrey W. "Recasting the Optimism–Pessimism Debate," *Security Studies*, 12, no. 1 (2002).

Lavoy, Peter R. "The Strategic Consequences of Nuclear Proliferation," *Security Studies*, 4, no. 4 (1995).

Lodhi, Maleeha. "Security Challenges in South Asia," *The Nonproliferation Review*, 8, no. 2 (2002).

Lodi, F. S. "Kargil: Its Aftermath," *Defence Journal*, 3, no. 6 (1999).

————. "India's Kargil Operations: An Analysis," *Defence Journal*, 3, no. 10 (1999).

Maxwell, Neville. "The Chinese Account of the 1969 Fighting at Chenpao," *The China Quarterly*, no. 56 (1973).

Mazari, Shireen. "Kashmir: Looking for Viable Options," *Defence Journal*, 3, no. 6 (1999).

————. "Kargil: Misguided Perceptions," *Pakistan Institute for Air Defence Studies Home Page*, available at http://www.piads.com.pk/users/piads/mazari1.html.

————. "Low-Intensity Conflicts: The New War in South Asia," *Defence Journal*, 3, no. 6 (1999).

————. "Re-examining Kargil," *Defence Journal*, 3, no. 11 (2000).

Mearsheimer, John J. "Why the Soviets Can't Win Quickly in Central Europe," *International Security*, 7, no. 1 (1982).

————. "Back to the Future: Instability in Europe After the Cold War," *International Security*, 15, no. 1 (1990).

————. "The Case for a Ukrainian Nuclear Deterrent," *Foreign Affairs*, 72, no. 3 (1993).

Nasir, Javed. "Calling the Indian Army Chief's Bluff," *Defence Journal*, 3, no. 2 (1999).

Norris, Robert S., Hans M. Kristensen, and Joshua Handler. "North Korea's Nuclear Program, 2003," *Bulletin of the Atomic Scientists*, 59, no. 2 (2003).

O'Hanlon, Michael. "Stopping a North Korean Invasion: Why Defending South Korea Is Easier Than the Pentagon Thinks," *International Security*, 22, no. 4 (1998).

"Op Topac," *Indian Defence Review* (1989).

Pillsbury, Michael P. "Future Sino-American Security Ties: The View from Tokyo, Moscow, and Peking," *International Security*, 1, no. 4 (1977).

Posen, Barry R. "Measuring the European Conventional Balance: Coping with Complexity in Threat Assessment," *International Security*, 9, no. 3 (1984–1985).

————. "Is NATO Decisively Outnumbered?" *International Security*, 12, no. 4 (1988).

Powell, Robert. "The Theoretical Foundations of Strategic Nuclear Deterrence," *Political Science Quarterly*, 100, no. 1 (1985).

Qadir, Shaukat. "An Analysis of the Kargil Conflict 1999," *Royal United Service Institution Journal* (April 2003).

Qazi, M. S. "High Temperatures at High Mountains," *Pakistan Institute for Air Defence Studies Home Page*, available at http://www.piads.com.pk/users/piads/qazi1.html.

Quester, George. "The Continuing Debate on Minimal Deterrence," in T. V. Paul, Richard J. Harknett, and James J. Wirtz, eds., *The Absolute Weapon Revisited: Nuclear Arms and the Emerging International Order* (Ann Arbor: University of Michigan Press, 1998).

Raghavan, V. R. "Limited War and Nuclear Escalation in South Asia," *The Nonproliferation Review*, 8, no. 3 (2001).

Riedel, Bruce. "American Diplomacy and the 1999 Kargil Summit at Blair House," Center for the Advanced Study of India, University of Pennsylvania (2002).

Robinson, Thomas W. "The Sino-Soviet Border Dispute: Background, Development, and the March 1969 Clashes," *American Political Science Review*, 66, no. 4 (1972).

Sagan, Scott D. "Why Do States Build Nuclear Weapons: Three Models in Search of a Bomb," *International Security*, 21, no. 3 (1996–1997).

Samore, Gary. "The Korean Nuclear Crisis," *Survival*, 45, no. 1 (2003).

Schweller, Randall L. "Bandwagoning for Profit: Bringing the Revisionist State Back In," *International Security*, 19, no. 1 (1994).

Shahi, Aga, Zulfikar Ali Khan, and Abdul Sattar. "Securing Nuclear Peace," *News International*, October 5, 1999, in *Strategic Digest*, 30, no. 1 (2000).

Singh, Jasjit. "The Fourth War," in Jasjit Singh, ed., *Kargil 1999: Pakistan's Fourth War for Kashmir* (New Delhi: Knowledge World).

Singh, Jaswant. "Against Nuclear Apartheid," *Foreign Affairs*, 77, no. 5 (1998).

Snyder, Glenn H. "The Balance of Power and the Balance of Terror," in Paul Seabury, ed., *The Balance of Power* (San Francisco: Chandler, 1965).

Snyder, Scott. "Pyongyang's Pressure," *The Washington Quarterly*, 23, no. 3 (2000).

Subrahmanyam, K. "India and the International Nuclear Order," in D. R. SarDesai and Raju G. C. Thomas, eds., *Nuclear India in the Twenty-First Century* (New York: Palgrave-Macmillan, 2002).

Tannenwald, Nina. "The Nuclear Taboo: The United States and the Normative Basis of Nuclear Non-Use," *International Organization*, 53, no. 3 (1999).

Thornton, Thomas Perry. "Pakistan: Fifty Years of Insecurity," in Selig S. Harrison, Paul H. Kreisberg, and Dennis Kux, eds., *India and Pakistan: The First Fifty Years* (Washington, DC: Cambridge University Press and the Woodrow Wilson Center, 1999).

Valluri, S. R. "Lest We Forget: The Futility and Irrelevance of Nuclear Weapons for India," in Raju G. C. Thomas and Amit Gupta, eds., *India's Nuclear Security* (Boulder, CO: Lynne Rienner, 2000).

Wallace, Paul. "Political Violence and Terrorism in India: The Crisis of Identity," in Martha Crenshaw, ed., *Terrorism in Context* (University Park, PA: Pennsylvania State University Press, 1995).

Waltz, Kenneth. *The Spread of Nuclear Weapons: More May Be Better*, Adelphi Paper No. 171 (London: International Institute of Strategic Studies, 1981).

Wolfers, Arnold. "The Balance of Power in Theory and Practice," in Arnold Wolfers, ed., *Discord and Collaboration: Essays on International Politics* (Baltimore: Johns Hopkins University Press, 1962).

Yang, Kuisong. "The Sino-Soviet Border Clash of 1969: From Zhenbao Island to Sino-American Rapprochement," *Cold War History*, 1, Issue 1 (2000).

Zehra, Nasim. "Anatomy of Islamabad's Kargil Policy," *Defence Journal*, 3, no. 7 (1999).

DOCUMENTS

"A Comment on the Statement of the Communist Party of the USA," *Jen-min Jih-pao*, March 8, 1963, available at http://www.etext.org/Politics/MIM/classics/mao/polemics/CPUSA.html.

Central Intelligence Agency, *Weekly Review*, March 21, 1969.

Central Intelligence Agency, "Unclassified Report to Congress on the Acquisition of Technology Relating to Weapons of Mass Destruction and Advanced Conventional Munitions, 1 January Through 30 June 2003," available at http://www.odci.gov/cia/reports/721_reports/jan_jun2003.htm.

Foreign Broadcast Information Service, Daily Report No. 118, June 19, 1967.

Foreign Broadcast Information Service, Daily Report No. 119, June 20, 1967.

Government of India, Ministry of Home Affairs, *Annual Report 2003–2004*.

Hamoodur Rehman Commission of Inquiry into the 1971 War, Report as Declassified by the Government of Pakistan, Part 4, "Military Aspect," (Lahore, Pakistan: Vanguard Books, 2000).

Indian Constitution, Article 370, available at http://www.constitution.org/cons/india/p21370.html.

Kargil Review Committee, *From Surprise to Reckoning: The Kargil Review Committee Report* (New Delhi: Sage Publications, 1999).

Kronstadt, K. Alan. "Nuclear Weapons and Ballistic Missile Proliferation in India and Pakistan: Issues for Congress," Congressional Research Service, Report RL30623, July 31, 2000.

Lilley, James R. Testimony Before the House Committee on International Relations, March 3, 2005, available at http://www.aei.org/publications/pubID.22096,filter.all/pub_detail.asp.

Ministry of Foreign Affairs of the People's Republic of China, "Meeting Between Zhou Enlai and Kosygin at the Beijing Airport," available at http://www.fmprc.gov.cn/eng/ziliao/3602/3604/t18005.htm.

Musharraf, Pervez. Address to the Nation, January 12, 2002, available at http://www.jang-group.com/thenews/spedition/speech_of_musharraf/index.html.

———. Address to the Nation, May 27, 2002, available at http://www.embassyofpakistan.com/address_27_05_02.htm.

President George W. Bush, "State of the Union Address," January 29, 2002, available at http://www.whitehouse.gov/news/releases/2002/01/20020129-11.html.

Rocca, Christina. "Statement for the House International Relations Subcommittee," March 20, 2003.

State Department Cable 130100 to U.S. Embassy, Taipei, "Nur Khan's Meeting with Chou En-lai," August 5, 1969.

"Statement by Ambassador Munir Akram in the Plenary Meeting of the Conference on Disarmament," May 14, 1998, available at http://www.acronym.org.uk/sppak.htm.

"Statement by Pakistan Ambassador Munir Akram to the Conference on Disarmament on the CTBT and Fissile Material Cut-off Treaty," July 30, 1998, available at http://www.clw.org/archive/coalition/pak0730.htm.

Testimony of James Woolsey Before the Senate Committee on Governmental Affairs, *Hearing on Proliferation Threats of the 1990s*, 103rd Cong., 1st Sess., February 24, 1993 (Washington, DC: U.S. Government Printing Office, 1993).

Text of Agreed Framework Between the United States of America and the Democratic People's Republic of Korea, available at http://www.kedo.org/pdfs/Agreed Framework.pdf.

Text of Karachi Agreement, available at http://safdic.southasiafoundation.org/saf/doc/india_pak/pak_04.htm.

Text of Kashmir Accord, available at http://www.jammu-kashmir.com/documents/kashmiraccord.html.

Text of Lahore Declaration, United States Institute of Peace, Peace Agreements Digital Collection, http://www.usip.org/library/pa/ip/ip_lahore19990221.html.

Text of Simla Agreement, in P. R. Chari and Pervaiz Iqbal Cheema, *The Simla Agreement 1972: Its Wasted Promise* (New Delhi: Manohar, 2001).

United Nations Security Council, S/726, April 21, 1948.

United Nations S/RES/825 (1993) May 11, 1993.

United Nations S/RES/1172 (1998), June 6, 1998.

U.S. Department of State, *Intelligence Note*, George C. Denney Jr. to Secretary of State, "USSR/China: Soviet and Chinese Forces Clash on the Ussuri River," March 4, 1969.

U.S. Department of State, *Intelligence Note*, Thomas L. Hughes to Secretary of State, "Peking's Tactics and Intentions Along the Border," June 13, 1969.

U.S. Department of State, Bureau of East Asian and Pacific Affairs, Office of Asian Communist Affairs, "Implications of Sino-Soviet Developments: Meeting of June 21," June 23, 1969.

U.S. Department of State, *National Strategy to Combat Weapons of Mass Destruction*, December 23, 2002.

U.S. State Department Memorandum of Conversation, "U.S. Reaction to Soviet Destruction of CPR Nuclear Capability; Significance of Latest Sino-Soviet Border Clash; Internal Opposition." August 18, 1969.

Index

Note: Locators in italic indicate tables; *n* refers to endnotes.

Studies in Asian Security

A SERIES SPONSORED BY THE EAST–WEST CENTER

Muthiah Alagappa, Chief Editor
Director, East-West Center Washington